Effective Environmental Regulation in China

Though recently improved, Chinese legislation on environmental permits is still weak and urgent measures are needed to help the country in moving towards an effective permitting system. This book examines this legislation gap and presents a contribution to solving China's pollution problems.

By analysing the deficiencies of current Chinese provisions on permitting in light of EU legislation, and its Italian application, the book determines which permitting legislative structure and approach China should embrace in practice in order to build more comprehensive legislation on emission permitting. It is argued that a set of *ad hoc* legislative measures should be implemented so as to strengthen China's environmental protection and efficiently tackle pollution.

The book will be a valuable resource for researchers, academics and policy-makers working in the areas of international environmental law and comparative law.

Federico Pasini is Head of the Program Management Office – Sino-Italian Cooperation Program for Environmental Protection, Beijing, China.

The Rule of Law in China and Comparative Perspectives

Series Editors:
Yuwen Li, Erasmus University Rotterdam, The Netherlands and Fu Hualing, University of Hong Kong, Hong Kong

There is no doctrine more effective than the rule of law in portraying the complex transformation of Chinese society from the rule of men towards the rule of law – a process inaugurated in post-Mao China which is continuing to advance legal reforms to the present day. In other parts of the world, striving for the rule of law is also evident: countries in transition face a similar mission, while the developed democratic countries are forced to tackle new challenges in retaining the high benchmark of the rule of law that has been established.

Research on the legal system in China and in comparison with other countries in the framework of the rule of law covers broad topics of public and private law, substantive law and procedural law, citizens' rights and law enforcement by courts. Based on this broad understanding of the rule of law, the series presents international scholarly work on modern Chinese law including: comparative perspectives, interdisciplinary, and empirical studies.

Other titles in this series:

National Security Review of Foreign Investment
A Comparative Legal Analysis of China, the United States and the European Union
Cheng Bian

Law and Social Solidarity in Contemporary China
A Durkheimian Analysis
Han Peng

The Making of Chinese Criminal Law
The Preventive Shift in the Context of the Eighth Amendment
Ying Ji

Effective Environmental Regulation in China
Reflections on the Experience of European Union Legislation on Environmental Permits
Federico Pasini

Effective Environmental Regulation in China

Reflections on the Experience of European Union Legislation on Environmental Permits

Federico Pasini

Routledge
Taylor & Francis Group
LONDON AND NEW YORK

First published 2021
by Routledge
2 Park Square, Milton Park, Abingdon, Oxon OX14 4RN

and by Routledge
605 Third Avenue, New York, NY 10158

Routledge is an imprint of the Taylor & Francis Group, an informa business

British Library Cataloguing-in-Publication Data
A catalogue record for this book is available from the British Library

Library of Congress Cataloging-in-Publication Data
Names: Lupo-Pasini, Federico, author.
Title: Effective environmental regulation in China : reflections on the experience of European Union legislation on environmental permits / Federico Pasini.
Description: Milton Park, Abingdon, Oxon ; New York, NY : Routledge, 2021. | Series: The rule of law in china and comparative perspectives | Includes bibliographical references and index.
Identifiers: LCCN 2020055518 (print) | LCCN 2020055519 (ebook) | ISBN 9780367655525 (hardback) | ISBN 9781003130062 (ebook)
Subjects: LCSH: Environmental permits--China. | Environmental permits--European Union countries.
Classification: LCC KNQ3128 .L87 2021 (print) | LCC KNQ3128 (ebook) | DDC 344.5104/6--dc23
LC record available at https://lccn.loc.gov/2020055518
LC ebook record available at https://lccn.loc.gov/2020055519

ISBN: 978-0-367-65552-5 (hbk)
ISBN: 978-0-367-65553-2 (pbk)
ISBN: 978-1-003-13006-2 (ebk)

Typeset in Galliard
by Taylor & Francis Books

To Lucio, Maura, Francesco and Valeria

Contents

Foreword

It is with pleasure that I write a foreword to this book, an in-depth and timely legal analysis of China and European Union's legislations on environmental permits.

China's recently approved 14th Five Year Plan shows an unprecedented attention to environment and sustainable development issues and, lately, Chinese authorities have started to undertake the first step related to a new legislative framework on permits. Environmental permitting system is at the frontier of China's environmental law and, for this reason, the Chinese government is currently aiming to fully re-shape and reform it.

In this view, the publication of Federico Pasini's important work comes at an auspicious time. Perhaps never in the evolution of international environmental law the concept of sustainable development received the actual worldwide attention. Also, despite the growing interest in the study of environmental law in China, the available literature on Chinese environmental permits' regulation is still limited and fragmented, so much so that it is possible to consider this as the first ever comprehensive study on the topic. In this respect, the book provides, at a critical stage, a valuable reference for China's forthcoming legislation on environmental permits.

A main objective of academic writing should be to identify and portray patterns and relations in a body of legal rules so as to make it feasible and operational. The present work succeeds in doing this to a significant degree.

Dr. Pasini's book touches on a key issue: what is the current status of Chinese permitting regulation, why does it need to be improved and what measures can be taken to enable effective environmental regulation in China? This is the open question that this book is seeking to answer and that, I believe, is of substantial interest to environmental law and regulatory readers.

The author's statement that "enhancing effectiveness in the development of China's legislation on environmental permits is possible and the way to follow is the integrated approach" is, on one hand, the result of the analysis of the strengths and weaknesses of the current Chinese regulations on permitting vis-à-vis EU legislation and, on the other hand, the premise to a set of recommendations that, if applied by the Chinese legislator, may ensure an efficient emission permits system.

A perusal of this book will readily reveal to the reader that the pursuit of effectiveness in (environmental) law is very challenging and this is why the present study provides thorough legal analysis as well as empirical evidence so as to ultimately set a standard at which effectiveness should be evaluated. Many international environmental law books today tend not to delve that deeply into primary legal material, relying only on commentaries or grey literatures to support their academic arguments. The present analysis instead is very detailed in places and allows the reader to understand the law from each of the jurisdictions taken into consideration.

The author begins with the definition, function and key features of environmental permits (Chapter 1), thereby laying a strong foundation for the exhaustive examination of the EU legislation on integrated permits that follows (in Chapter 2). The careful scrutiny of the application of the IPPC Directive and IED (carried out in Chapter 3) allows a step forward to be made in the identification of the fundamental characteristics and implications of the integrated pollution prevention and control legislative model, particularly towards the achievement of sustainable development. The analysis in detail of the current status of Chinese legislation on environmental permits (in Chapter 4) amply demonstrates what needs to be further developed or reformed, and why, thus establishing – and here I borrow Federico's words – that "the introduction of modern regulatory principles, in line with the actual environmental challenges China is facing, proves to be a necessary but insufficient condition to secure the implementation of permits, the enforcement of which strongly depends on the capacity of the institutions to put the permitting regulations into practice". The author brings his analysis full circle by drawing a set of illuminating recommendations (in Chapter 5) that, if applied, may lead to the realization of an effective environmental regulation.

Yet one result of this study is to make an important step towards rationalisation, for it does, by its very able and incisive exposition, enable one to see the complexity of the problem, both from the viewpoint of EU and China's legislation, and to get some sort of conspectus of the existing Chinese legislation related to environmental permits. Not least, the book demonstrates that it is no longer possible adequately to develop a tailored legislation without taking cognisance of the structure and means regulating the same issue elsewhere, and this is even more relevant at this stage of China's legislative development.

Dr. Pasini, who for many years has lived and studied both in EU and China and worked vis-à-vis the European and Chinese environmental institutions at the highest level, is especially positioned, and passionately committed to, international environmental issues. As a result, this is a book that masterfully ties together theory and practice, ending up in being of great interest for both academicians and policy makers.

Mingde CAO
Professor of Environmental Law at
China University of Political Science and Law;
Vice President of China Society of Environmental
and Natural Resources Law (CSERL)

Acknowledgements

In conducting this research over the last three and a half years, I have accumulated debts to many people and institutions. The drafting of this book would have never been possible without all their support.

For the enlightening discussions and suggestions since our very first meeting, my heartfelt thanks go to Professor Cao Mingde – a leading China environmental scholar, environmental law professor at China University of Political Science and Law (CUPL), and many other things. His insightful comments have inspired me throughout the whole study and have been fundamental for the ultimate completion of the present work.

My sincere gratitude goes also to my friend and colleague, Ms. Ren Yanming. Knowing her has been a breakthrough in my 'Chinese' life; she is responsible for having encouraged me to embark on this long journey and I hope she still feels a bit guilty for it.

Further thanks are due to Dr. Dilini Pathirana, Senior Lecturer at the University of Colombo, and Dr. Mao Tao, Director at the Centre for International Economic and Technological Cooperation of the Ministry of Industry and Information Technology of China, for their incredible generosity, precious advice and indispensable contribution.

I am truly fortunate to have had the invaluable assistance of the whole Routledge team. In particular, my profound appreciation goes to Alison Kirk, Senior Commissioning Editor, Cathryn Henderson, Production Editor, Emily Summers, Editorial Assistant, and Alison Jones, Copy Editor, for their patience and outstanding skill. It goes without saying that I am solely responsible for any error and oversight.

Finally, I am immensely grateful to my family and brother for their endless support and I especially owe to my parents for giving me the freedom to follow my dreams and spend the last ten years in China, far away from them.

I dedicate this book to them and to my wife Valeria, who stands me every day and who welcomed this crazy idea with her beautiful smile.

List of abbreviations

ARPA	Regional Environmental Protection Agency
BAT	Best Available Technique
BAT-AEL	Emission Level Associated with the Best Available Techniques
BATNEEC	Best Available Technology Not Entailing Excessive Cost
BEE	Bureau of Ecology and Environment
BPEO	Best Practicable Environmental Option
BREFs	BAT Reference Documents
EIA	Environmental Impact Assessment
ELVs	Emission Limit Values
EMAS	Eco-Management and Audit Scheme
EPA	Environmental Protection Act
EPB	Environment Protection Bureau
EPL	Environment Protection Law
ERA	Environmental Risk Assessment
EU	European Union
HMIP	Her Majesty's Inspectorate of Pollution
IED	Industrial Emission Directive
IPC	Integrated Pollution Control
IPPC	Integrated Pollution Prevention and Control
ISPRA	Institute for Environmental Protection and Research
MEE	Ministry of Ecology and Environment
MEP	Ministry of Environmental Protection
NPC	China National People's Congress
OECD	Organisation for Economic Co-operation and Development
SEA	Strategic Environmental Assessment
SEPA	State Environmental Protection Administration
SPC	Supreme People's Court of China
TEC	Total Emission Control
TFEU/TEU	Treaty on Functioning of the European Union – Lisbon Treaty
TUA	Testo Unico dell'Ambiente – Consolidated Law on Environment
UK	United Kingdom
UN	United Nations

Introduction

Following the UN Declaration on the Human Environment of 1972, and the increased scientific knowledge of environmental processes during the succeeding decades, environmental permits gradually became one of the key tools of pollution prevention and control for lowering the impact of industrial emissions. Permits regulate all kinds of planning, development, construction and discharge activities possibly harming the environment, and they are now recognised as the key pillar of environmental protection and pollution prevention laws worldwide.

During the same period, at the international level, environmental concerns gained an ever-growing importance particularly in the EU, where environmental protection was included among the fundamental objectives first of the European Community, and later of the European Union. In particular, under the EU legislative framework, Italy developed a comprehensive legislation on regulating permits which gave rise to enhanced environmental governance and reduced environmental impact.

Environmental permits were first launched in China in the late 1980s in the field of water pollution control. Progressively, different provisions regulating permits have been introduced in numerous laws, administrative guidelines and regulations. That said, during almost three decades permits worked mainly as a complementary measure of emission reporting rather than as a pollution management policy. More recently, however, China's policy makers have recognized the critical role played by environmental permits for decreasing industry's polluting discharges and emissions, so much so that – especially since 2014 – all the newly issued Chinese environmental laws and regulations contain permit-related elements and means aimed at fostering pollution prevention and control.

Yet, China is still lacking comprehensive and solid legislation on permitting. Hence, it is critical for the country's policy makers to acknowledge the lessons learnt from international legislation – and its practical application at the national level – so as to be able ultimately to put forward consistent regulation on pollution prevention and control.

Against this background, the study intends to identify which permitting legislative framework and tools China should put into practice so as to increase environmental protection and effectively tackle pollution.

Through the scrutiny of both the shortcomings and limitations of existing Chinese provisions on environmental permits vis-à-vis the EU legislation – and its Italian application – this work aims to determine the key legislative measures that China's legislator should urgently espouse for building a comprehensive legislation in support of an efficient emission permitting system. The results of this study may constitute a useful reference for Chinese policy makers as well as for scholars willing to progress this research further.

Analysing Chinese provisions on environmental permits vis-à-vis the structure and means regulating the same issue in an international system and a country (i.e. the EU and Italy) is not only almost compulsory in doctrinal legal research, but also extremely relevant specifically at this stage of China's (legislative) development. The country's existing need to find a balance between economic growth and environmental sustainability gives momentum to the necessity of scrutinising what Chinese policy makers are currently planning to do, compared with what other legislators have already done elsewhere, in light of international environmental law.

The case of Italy is particularly relevant to China because, in spite of the differences in size, stage of development and population, Italy shares with China some fundamental characteristics: it is a civil law country; it has developed – in the twentieth century – a strong and heavily polluting industry (which led it to becoming the second largest manufacturing country in EU)[1]; and it faced, and partly still faces, numerous environmental challenges deriving from such fast pace industrialization. Moreover, the definition provided by the Italian legislation of *sustainable development* is much closer to the modern Chinese conceptualization of *ecological civilization* than the vaguer definitions of the same concept present in international legislation (e.g. the UN Stockholm and Rio Declarations, Brundtland Commission, EU legislation).

Certain key features and requirements of EU and Italian law may be fully replicated into the Chinese permitting system, others may need only to be adjusted, and still others may be ignored. The present study verifies this hypothesis so as to ultimately provide a fundamental reference for China's forthcoming legislation on environmental permits.

In order to test this hypothesis, the book expects to answer three main research questions. Firstly, what characteristics should an effective environmental regulation have in order to guarantee environmental protection and efficiently tackle pollution? Secondly, what is the origin and current status of Chinese permitting regulation and why does it need to be improved? Thirdly, in light of international environmental legislation, what recommendations can be made to enable comprehensive Chinese legislation on environmental permitting?

1 Eurostat, Statistical Classification of Economic Activities in the European Community – NACE Rev. 2 – Manufacturing Statistics, March 2020, 5–6; available at https://ec.europa.eu/eurostat/statistics-explained/pdfscache/10086.pdf. Eurostat, Industrial Production Statistics, December 2020; available at https://ec.europa.eu/eurostat/statistics-explained/index.php/Industrial_production_statistics#Industrial_production_by_country

In order to answer these questions, this study carried out qualitative research based on the following structure and methods.

Chapters 1 and 2 provide the definition, function and key features of permits as well as the legislative framework in which they are implemented at the EU level. Therefore, such chapters put forward the introduction to, and the contextual and conceptual background for, the analytical chapters that follow. The methodology primarily employed to develop these two chapters is the traditional legal research method, such as the review of international legislation and literature and examination of EU Directives as well as other applicable international pieces of legislation and agreement relevant to this study.

Chapter 3 analyses the Italian environmental legislation on permits by focusing on the application and implications deriving from the implementation of the EU legislation as well as the permits' releases and management procedures, ultimately identifying the key legal principles of permitting in Italy. The doctrinal analysis method is employed in the third chapter as it expects to examine and demonstrate how the Italian law on permits has been developed and applied.

Chapter 4 scrutinises the current status of Chinese legislation related to environmental permits and ascertains what needs to be further developed or modified, and why. In this chapter the comparative method is employed to assess the case of China vis-à-vis that of the EU and Italy and to develop a reference for China's future legal reform in the field of environmental permits.

Finally, Chapter 5 makes suggestions and recommendations to China for the development of comprehensive legislation on environmental permitting. Both descriptive and comparative methods are utilized for identifying – in light of the lessons learnt from EU and Italian legislation on environmental permits – those *ad hoc* legislative measures that could ensure the effectiveness of China's emission permitting system in the coming years.

The discussion on EU and Italian legislation on environmental permits aims to identify the key characteristics/elements and ways forward for China's effective environmental regulation, ultimately providing the first ever comprehensive study on this topic. The Chinese Ministry of Ecology and Environment has recently started to make its first steps in building a new legislative framework on permits. In this respect, the present book seizes the moment and aims to become even more valuable. Indeed, this study may not only contribute to advancing the scholarship in the field of international environmental law by highlighting – from a legal perspective – the challenges and potentials of the Chinese permitting system; it may also provide recommendations which ultimately aim to be helpful for China's policy makers for improving future legislation on environmental permits.

The discussion on international legislation related to environmental permits contributes to the existing literature on the topic by providing an objective scrutiny on the strengths and weaknesses of the EU regulatory framework for pollution prevention and control.

The legal analysis on EU, Italian and Chinese permitting legislations is the most inventive aspect of this research which eventually allows identification of the shortcomings in the existing Chinese emission permitting system and their root causes as well as providing recommendations on how to overcome them. Also, such legal analysis puts forward an absolutely new intellectual and pragmatic contribution by determining – with regard to international environmental law – which permitting legislative structure and means China should embrace in practice in order to reinforce environmental protection, efficiently tackle pollution and ultimately achieve sustainable development.

1 Fundamentals of environmental permitting

From a traditional to integrated regulatory approach

1.1 Defining environmental permits: a premise

It is difficult, if not impossible, to reach an unanimously accepted legal definition of *environment* and this is the reason why, also at the juridical level, different approaches to such a concept have been adopted according to its divergent understandings. As a consequence, the regulatory measures conceived for tackling the phenomenon of pollution have often been numerous and diverse too.

It is possible to argue that all legal interpretations of the environmental concept fall under two main approaches: the *traditional approach*, which conceives the environment as the sum of diverse components put together with one another; and the *integrated approach*, which understands the environment as a unique and organic entity.[1]

This chapter will describe and discuss the key features of these two approaches, eventually highlighting how different types of environmental legal tools and permits derive from each of them. However, prior to this, it is necessary to define the concept of environmental permitting.

Environmental permitting is one of the fundamental tools in the hands of regulatory authorities to abate pollution and reduce (industry's) environmental impacts, facilitate its compliance with environmental requirements and foster technological innovation. The main objective of permits is to protect the environment and human health by defining – in a transparent and accountable manner – legally binding requirements for major sources of pollution.[2] Hence, the permitting system regulates all kinds of planning, development, construction and discharge activities possibly affecting the environment and, particularly since the 1970s, it is broadly recognised as the key pillar of environmental protection and pollution prevention laws worldwide.[3]

1 OECD, "Integrated Environmental Permitting Guidelines for EECCA Countries," (2005): 12–13.
2 OECD, "Guiding Principles of Effective Environmental Permitting Systems," (2007): 3 and 8.
3 Id. 4.

Given this definition of environmental permitting, it is now necessary to make a step backward and define the characteristics of the traditional and integrated approaches.

A closer look at each of those approaches is necessary to better identify what elements need to be taken into consideration when tackling environmental problems, and eventually to understand whether it is possible to establish, if not a unanimously accepted legal definition of the environment, at least one that is consistent and useful. Finally, because the role of environmental permits – and their required functions – varies according to the overall context of the environmental regulatory system in which they operate, understanding what would be the preferable approach will also lead us to select the kind of permits more suitable to abate pollution effectively.

1.2 The traditional regulatory approach

Since the late 1960s, when dramatic events[4] pushed countries to consider the problem of pollution in all its perilousness, the dominant approach consisted of separately regulating each damaged environmental sector on a case-by-case basis. Having to deal with particularly serious cases of pollution, the normal and most logical response by authorities was to tackle the problem by finding a direct solution to it: indeed, rather than looking at the broad picture, decision makers tended to address pollution cases by focusing on the immediate identification of an effective solution, thus adopting specific legislative measures aimed to solve the problem. Environmental crises generally affect a single environmental medium, hence the links between media were unknown or voluntarily ignored.[5]

It followed that the environment was such a heterogeneous element, characterized by frequent interrelations among its components, that it was practically impossible or too costly to properly assess and establish suitable intervention measures for facing its overall pollution problems. As a result, pollution started to be understood as the sum of many single problems, factors and episodes that had to be considered separately, one at a time, according to when and how they took place. For this reason, up until the beginning of the 1980s, each regulation that

4 See the environmental impact of marine pollution generated by the numerous shipwrecks of oil tankers that occurred in the late 1960s. For example, it is possible to recall – inter alia – the case of the Korean oil tanker *Sea Star* which dumped around 115,000 tonnes of crude oil in the Gulf of Oman as well as the case of the oil tanker *Othello* which sank on 20 March 1970 off the coast of Sweden. Finally, it is important to recall the Italian industrial accident of 10 July 1976, known as the Seveso chemical spill, in which a chemical manufacturing plant in the north west of Italy caused the highest known dioxin exposure in residential populations. The accident not only gave rise to several scientific studies, but it also led the EU to standardize industrial safety regulations – described later in this chapter – known as the Seveso Directive. Dagmar Schmidt Etkin, "Historical Overview of Oil Spills from All Sources (1960–1998)" (International Oil Spill Conference Proceedings, March 1999, Vol. 1999, No. 1, 1097–1102).

5 Nicola Lugaresi, *Diritto dell'Ambiente* (Vicenza: Wolters Kluwer, 2015), 75–76.

was put in place at the international and EU levels focused only on a single environmental medium.[6]

This traditional approach deals with pollution abatement through the adoption of three main sets of sectorial regulations, well mirrored by the Directives introduced by the European Economic Community (later European Union)[7] in the mid-1970s and early 1980s.

First, it focuses on the type of environmental medium affected, namely air, soil or water. A good example is Council Directive 76/464/EEC of 4 May 1976 on Pollution Caused by Certain Dangerous Substances Discharged into the Aquatic Environment of the Community. This Directive applies to inland surface water, territorial waters, internal coastal waters and groundwater.[8] EU Member States are required to take the appropriate steps to eliminate pollution of the above-mentioned waters by certain dangerous substances (a list of the families and groups of such substances is provided in the Annexes to the Directive).[9] Another example is Council Directive 84/360/EEC on the Combating of Air Pollution from Industrial Plants which, as mentioned in its title, lays down measures and procedures designed to prevent or reduce as far as possible air pollution from industrial plants within the Community. For the purposes of these provisions, "plant" shall mean any establishment or other stationary plant used for industrial or public utility purposes which is likely to cause air pollution.[10] According to Article 4 of the Directive, authorization may be issued only when the competent national authority has verified that: 1) all appropriate preventive measures against pollution have been adopted; 2) the use of plant will not cause significant air pollution, particularly from the emission of the indicated polluting substances; 3) none of the emission limit values applicable will be exceeded; and 4) all the air quality limit values applicable will be taken into consideration.[11]

The second method in which the traditional (or fragmented) approach deals with pollution reduction and control is by tackling specific polluting substances. Among the many pieces of legislation adopted at the EU level between the late 1970s and early 1980s, it is worth mentioning Council Directive 80/779/EEC of 15 July 1980 on Air Quality Limit Values and Guide Values for Sulphur Dioxide and Suspended Particulates. This Directive establishes limit and guide values for sulphur dioxide and suspended particulates in the atmosphere and the conditions for their application in order to increase the protection of human health and the environment. In the areas in which a given Member State deems it necessary to reduce or prevent a foreseeable

6 At the national level, only a few countries (France and UK in particular) started to move away from the traditional approach during 1980s; in those years, neither China nor Italy made any step in this respect. Joseph Di Mento, *The Global Environment and International Law* (Austin, TX: University of Texas Press, 2003), 2–6.

7 The European Economic Community, created with the Treaty of Rome of 1957, was dissolved into the European Union by the Lisbon Treaty in 2009. https://europa.eu/european-union/about-eu/history_en.

8 Council Directive 76/464/EEC, Official Journal L 129, Article 1.

9 Id. Article 2.

10 Council Directive 84/360/EEC, Official Journal L 188, Article 2.

11 Id. Article 4.

increase in pollution by sulphur dioxide and suspended particulates in the wake of development, in particular urban or industrial development, such Member State shall fix values which must be lower than the limit values foreseen by the Directive.[12] Another example in this respect is provided by Council Directive 84/491/EEC of 9 October 1984 on Limit Values and Quality Objectives for Discharges of Hexachlorocyclohexane (HCH), which lays down limit values and quality objectives for discharges of a specific toxic and polluting chemical substance. The limit values shall normally apply at the point where wastewaters containing HCH leave the industrial plant. The Member States concerned shall be accountable for monitoring the aquatic environment affected by industrial discharges. This Directive applies to the waters referred to in Article 1 of the aforementioned Directive 76/464/EEC with the exception of groundwater.[13]

The third way in which the traditional approach faces the challenge of pollution is by legally regulating the different subjects or activities affected by the polluting substances. An example of such regulations is Council Directive 70/157/EEC on the Approximation of the Laws of the Member States Relating to the Permissible Sound Level and the Exhaust System of Motor Vehicles.[14] This Directive sets limits for the noise level of the mechanical parts and exhaust systems of the vehicles concerned. For the purposes of these provisions, *vehicle*

> means any motor vehicle intended for use on the road, with or without bodywork, having at least four wheels and a maximum design speed exceeding 25 kilometres per hour, with the exception of vehicles which run on rails, agricultural tractors and machinery and public works vehicles.[15]

1.2.1 Pragmatic incrementalism

Hence, the decision-making model of the traditional approach applies an incremental and progressive logic in which the priority is to adopt more and more tailored (and effective) abatement and control measures against pollution rather than comprehensively tackling environmental problems with laws and regulations capable of reflecting the complexity of such challenges. To define this modus operandi, some scholars argue about a "pragmatic incrementalism" or "step-by-step approach", others define it a "trial-and-error approach" or "a way of muddling through", meaning a way to deal with the problem and somehow work it out.[16]

12 Council Directive 80/779/EEC, Official Journal L 229.

13 Id. Article 1; Council Directive 84/491/EEC, Official Journal L 274, see the 7 Articles and 4 Annexes.

14 Council Directive 70/157/EEC, Official Journal L 42.

15 Directive 84/360/EEC, Official Journal L 188, Article 1 and Annexes I.2 and I.3.

16 Lakshman Guruswamy, "Integrating Thoughtways: Re-opening of the Environmental Mind?," *Wisconsin Law Review* 463 (1989): 483; James Krier and Mark Brownstein, "On Integrated Pollution Control," *Environmental Law* 22 (1) (1992): 123; Charles E. Lindblom, "The Science of 'Muddling Through'," *Public Administration Review* 19 (2) (1959): 79–88.

In other words, "single-medium permitting – the traditional regulatory approach – derives from the way that environmental regulation developed as specific environmental problems needed to be addressed".[17] In this respect, for instance, as soon as the importance of a clean water supply was acknowledged, the legislation for protecting aquatic resources was introduced and the needed authorities created. Analogously, separate arrangements were created to protect air quality, manage solid wastes and deal with different environmental issues. Over the years, the list of permits required for the operation of a single major installation was translated into a very high number of documents, issued and controlled by a variety of separate authorities that did not necessarily function in a coordinated or cooperative manner.[18] As will be discussed in Chapter 4, China only started to face these issues from the mid-1980s when permits were first introduced in the field of water pollution control.

Still, in the first couple of decades since its first application in the 1970s, the traditional approach did achieve some progress and provided some benefit in terms of environmental protection. However, as time went by, the development of knowledge (in terms of natural phenomena, environmental processes, connection among environmental elements etc.) revealed its worrying limitations and ineffectiveness.

1.2.2 The limits of the traditional approach

As mentioned above, the traditional approach showed, throughout time, several limitations. First of all, it does not take into consideration the role played by the so-called *inputs*; namely, the raw material and its characteristics, that eventually generate the noxious residues. This strict link between the use of a given raw material and the production of pollutants is particularly evident in the field of electricity generation. A coal-fired power plant, for instance, produces sulphur dioxide (SO_2), nitrogen oxides (NOx), particulate matter as well as other pollutants. The quantity of SO_2 produced by the power plant inherently depends on the quantity of sulphur present within the coal, which is the main *input* of the energy production process. This is why an improvement in the environmental performance of such a plant, in terms of SO_2 emission reduction, depends also on the quality and characteristics of the raw material used.[19]

Moreover, the traditional approach does not take into account that certain characteristics of the end product may ultimately be the cause of the release of pollutants. Put another way, if the production of an object with a given characteristic is very polluting, the exclusion of such a characteristic is not even considered as an option. This is also the reason why laws and regulations on pollution have always focused on the removal of already formed contaminants from a stream

17 OECD, "Integrated Environmental Permitting Guidelines for EECCA Countries," (2005): 12.

18 Ibid.

19 Bruce Ackerman, "Beyond the New Deal: Coal and the Clean Air Act," *Faculty Scholarship Series* 155 (1980): 1470–1472.

of air, water, waste and products in general; that is, only at the end of the production cycle. Indeed, such end-of-line or end-of-pipe methods do not consider either the inputs or the final products to be part of the problem.

Also, the lack of consideration of such factors turned the traditional approach to the environment into an ineffective and often counterproductive method for pollution abatement, in particular with regard to the so-called ***media-shifting*** phenomenon. This definition refers to the now well-known capacity of pollutants, once they have been disposed of or released into the environment, to move within each environmental medium and migrate from one medium to the other, in fact shifting and sometimes mutating.[20]

According to two different types of factors, this shifting or transformation of the pollutants may be direct or indirect. On one hand, the shifting or transformation is caused by the very same measures adopted to tackle pollution, which – though reducing or depleting polluting substances from a specific medium – may channel them into another medium. This has been the case, for instance, in the wide deployment of sulphur dioxide scrubbers (namely, flue gas desulphurization systems) made by China in the last decades to reduce SO_2. Indeed, this air pollution mitigation measure has led to soil pollution, resulting in sludges rich in pollutants – which in turn need to be disposed of.[21] A similar problem regarding sludge disposal derives from the application of filters for water pollution monitoring. As argued by Krier and Brownstein, "water pollution control measures regularly result in sludges, which in turn have to be burned (contributing to air pollution) or buried (contributing to land pollution, and perhaps to water pollution again as the sludges leach out of their graves)".[22] In both such cases a direct shifting of pollution from one medium to another takes place.

On the other hand, the shifting or transformation may be caused by atmospheric agents (e.g. wind, rain) or the mutation of the chemical structure of the pollutants due to their interaction with the environment, for instance in presence of solar radiation or biological organisms. In this case the shifting of pollution among media is indirect, involuntary and therefore uncontrollable, but just as devastating. A good example of this is the long-standing problem of acid rain, particularly in cities. This dangerous precipitation (containing high levels of nitric and sulphuric acids) was a very relevant problem in Europe during the 1970s and 1980s and it is unfortunately a serious problem in China nowadays. In both cases, acid rain has a strong negative impact on the ecological balance, particularly on aquatic environments (i.e. lakes, streams, wetlands etc.). By making waters acidic, it causes the absorption of pollutants that make their way from soil into lakes and streams, damaging both aquatic environments and animals and, ultimately, via the

20 Lakshman Guruswamy, "Integrating Thoughtways": 473.

21 Yana Jin, Henrik Andersson and Shiqiu Zhang, "Air Pollution Control Policies in China: A Retrospective and Prospects," *International Journal of Environmental Research and Public Health* 13 (12) (2016): 1–2; Yuan Xu, "Improvements in the Operation of SO_2 Scrubbers in China's Coal Power Plants," *Environmental Science and Technology* 45 (2) (2011): 380–385.

22 James Krier and Mark Brownstein, "On Integrated Pollution Control": 122.

food chain, non-aquatic species such as birds. Moreover, acid rain also damages forests by depriving soil of its fundamental nutrients, affecting the trees' capacity to reproduce and take up water and making plants less able to cope with cold temperatures, insects and diseases.[23]

Interestingly, as stressed by Rabe and Zimmerman:

> the majority of this cross-media contamination does not stem from illegal dumping of wastes or failure to enforce various permit standards. Instead, much of the problem may stem from pollution control and waste disposal strategies deemed perfectly legal under single-medium based legislation.[24]

Returning to the example of a coal-fired power plant, by not focusing on the source of the pollution, the traditional approach with its fragmented control gives no indication of the necessity for planning the plant with respect to such sources or to the consequent paths followed by the pollutants and their shifting between different media. Indeed, since the planning phase, the final destination of the emissions or discharges may be steered to allow an effective distribution of pollution among the different environmental media, capable of exploiting the self-regenerating capacities of the environment. A pollution control method capable of making an optimum use of the environment and its possible assimilative capacities would therefore be to divide the wastes into three media categories, namely air, water and soil. Such a method to control pollution, recently applied by China – as we will see in Chapter 4 – proves to be more efficient and cost-effective if compared with the one implemented by the traditional approach.[25]

Hence, the end-of-line pollution control methods – foreseen by the traditional approach – do not make full use of the opportunity to reduce pollution. Also, they avoid the adoption of measures which take into account the possible interactions among different environmental components and different types of pollution, possibly produced by a single plant. As a consequence, such pollution control methods are economically inefficient, which translates into higher costs to be borne by the public administration. Indeed, as described above, the phenomenon of media-shifting is a key limitation: the first pollution remediation measures to contain the noxious residues within a specific environmental medium need to be followed by other measures to tackle the same pollution that has in the meantime shifted into another medium. Inevitably, more monitoring and controls coincide with higher costs for pollution abatement.

For all these reasons, in the 1970s a new approach to the environment took its first steps on the basis of the greater awareness that all environmental elements are

23 Thorjørn Larssen et al., "Acid Deposition and its Effects in China: An Overview" *Environmental Science & Policy* 2 (1) (1999): 9–12.

24 Barry Rabe and Janet Zimmerman, "Cross-Media Environmental Integration in the Great Lakes Basin," *Environmental Law* 22 (1) (1992): 259.

25 Lakshman Guruswamy, "Integrating Thoughtways": 475–476.

all closely interlinked, so much so that environmental pollution cannot (only) be tackled in a compartmentalized way.

It is possible to argue that this new awareness had its roots in the declaration of principles coming out from the United Nations Conference on the Human Environment held in Stockholm in June 1972. The Stockholm Declaration, albeit non-binding in nature, undeniably represents a major milestone in the evolution of international environmental law and it is generally regarded as the foundation of modern international environmental law. The Stockholm Declaration is key in bringing out a greater focus on the environment and its axiomatic relationship with development (see Principle 8); it establishes a State's sovereign right to "exploit" its natural resources, but at the same time a State's responsibility to guarantee that its activities do not cause damage to the environment of other States (see Principle 21); and it affirms human-centric and instrumentalist logic towards the environment (see Principles 1, 2 and 5) confirmed by the Chairman of the delegation from the People's Republic of China to the conference, Mr. Tang Ke, when claiming: "We hold that of all things in the world, people are the most precious".[26]

Besides its political and moral commitments, the Declaration evinces a strong holistic approach postulating that all environmental elements interact with each other within the same system, hence interdependently. In this respect, Principle 2 stipulates that: "The natural resources of the earth, [...] and especially representative samples of natural eco-systems, must be safeguarded for the benefit of present and future generations through careful planning or management, as appropriate".[27] In the same vein, Principle 6 states that:

> The discharge of toxic substances or of other substances and the release of heat, in such quantities or concentrations as to exceed the capacity of the environment to render them harmless, must be halted in order to ensure that serious or irreversible damage is not inflicted upon ecosystems ... .[28]

Hence, both Principles conceive the environment as a system, or eco-system, which needs to be considered and protected as a whole. This new awareness became the basis for a new way to address environmental problems, namely the ***integrated approach***, which seeks to address the limitations and problems deriving from the fragmentation of the traditional approach through a so-called "integration".

Therefore, it is no coincidence that the first steps towards a new understanding and approach to the environment and pollution – also under the regulatory point of view – took place within a specific and limited period, namely in the mid-1970s, right after the Stockholm international conference of 1972.

26 UN General Assembly, "United Nations Conference on the Human Environment", 15 December 1972; UNEP, "Integrating Environment and Development 1972–2002," (2002): 2.
27 UN General Assembly, "United Nations Conference on the Human Environment": Principle 2.
28 Id. Principle 6.

1.3 The integrated approach

In general terms, the word "integration" indicates the act of putting together, of merging two or more elements. Nevertheless, in environmental terms, integration has two different and separate meanings. One is "external integration", referring to the integration of exogenous elements with respect to the environmental topic; the other is "internal integration", which vice versa integrates endogenous elements of the environmental dimension.[29]

There are different definitions of external integration: some scholars define it as "the incorporation of environmental considerations into non-environmental sectors such as manufacturing, energy, agriculture, and transportation"; others as "the integration of environmental issues into other non-environmental policy areas such as economic and social policy"; and again others as "the influence of the environmental policy on other policy areas".[30] In other words, external integration focuses on the relationship between the environmental policy and the other policies related to different sectors, by ensuring that every decision taken with regard to the latter will take into account – and therefore integrate – the environmental needs considered by the former.

Conversely, internal integration focuses exclusively on the environmental realm and it deals with the decisions concerning the instruments, measures and solutions to tackle pollution and protect the environment. Put another way, internal integration indicates the application of an integrated approach to environment and pollution, more commonly known as *integrated pollution control.*

Though different from one another, these two kinds of integration occur simultaneously and inevitably influence each other. They share the basic idea that the environment needs to be considered as a whole and they are instrumental to each other, since the achievement of internal integration allows the incorporation of environmental issues into other (non-environmental) sectors. Indeed, it is easier to integrate an organic environmental policy rather than a patchy set of fragmented measures.[31]

Going back to internal integration, Rodgers defines the integrated approach as "an approach which seeks to avoid the mistakes of the past which treated the environment as easily separable into discrete media".[32] Though correct, such an explanation is not sufficient. A more comprehensive definition is provided by the Organisation for Economic Co-operation and Development (OECD) Council Recommendation in Integrated Pollution Prevention and Control of 1991, which states that the integrated approach takes into account:

29 Philippe Sands, *Principles of International Environmental Law* (Manchester: Manchester University Press, 1995), 205.

30 Ibid.

31 Frances Irwin, "An Integrated Framework for Preventing Pollution and Protecting the Environment," *Environmental Law* 22 (1), in *Integrated Pollution Control: A Symposium* (1992): 17 and 23.

32 William Rodgers, *Environmental Law* (Eagan, MN: West Publishing Company, 1994), 59.

> the effects of activities and substances on the environment as a whole and the whole commercial and environmental life cycle of substances when assessing the risks they pose and when developing and implementing controls to limit their release.[33]

Such a statement highlights the key characteristics of the new and integrated approach, and those elements that differ from the traditional, fragmented one. First, the reference to the effects of activities and polluting substances, as well as to their life cycles, identifies *media-shifting* as the main problem to get to grips with; second, the definition of the objective pursued, namely "implementing controls to limit their release", abandons the general approach to environmental protection through the mere treatment of emissions, paving the way towards reducing the delivery of polluting and hazardous substances into the environment, i.e. prevention. Third, the expression "the environment as a whole" affirms both the ecological and the holistic perspective of the integrated approach.

The ecological perspective conceives *environment* as the ecological balance of the biosphere or of the single eco-systems of reference; therefore, *environmental protection* is to be understood as the protection of the biosphere's ecological balance or the ecological balance of eco-systems.[34]

The holistic perspective triggers a transition from the above-mentioned pragmatic incrementalism of policy making to what is defined as the "comprehensive rationality" of decision-making processes, which supports the pursuit of integration. The fundamental characteristic of this systemic concept, which is at the heart of ecology, is the *comprehensive* nature of the analysis behind the decisions, so that every important factor is taken into account.[35] Also, different from the incremental model, comprehensive rationality does not simply try to meet a specific environmental need; its purpose is to adopt the optimal solution to environmental problems. Recalling Simon's definition of "satisficing" – namely, "the tendency to aim for satisfactory rather than optimal achievements of goals" – Diver describes the change made by comprehensive rationality on decision-makers' behaviour as follows: "they may not merely 'satisfice'; they must – at least within the limits of their cognitive capacity – optimize".[36]

Therefore, the ecological and holistic perspectives are the conceptual foundations of the integrated approach which, in order to work properly, needs to take into account the great complexity of its assumptions. Indeed, to move from theory to practice, the integrated approach has to develop new tools for data collection and analysis.

New and better data on environmental conditions and on pollution sources are an extremely important integrating tool because they provide indispensable

33 OECD, "Council Recommendation on Integrated Pollution Prevention and Control," (1991): par. I (a).
34 Lakshman Guruswamy, "Integrating Thoughtways": 536; Colin Diver, "Policymaking Paradigms in Administrative Law," *Harvard Law Review* 95 (2) (1981): 394–395.
35 Charles E. Lindblom, "The Science of 'Muddling Through'": 81.
36 Colin Diver, "Policymaking Paradigms in Administrative Law": 418.

information for comparing the effectiveness of different control efforts, set cross-programme risk-based priorities and multimedia enforcement, and eventually build properly constructed integrated approaches.[37]

The shift toward new data integration capabilities and integrated environmental management may also be accelerated by the refinement of a variety of methodological tools that, compared with the past, facilitate taking into account cross-media and cross-jurisdictional pollution transfers. Many of these tools fall under the category of mass balance approaches.

> Under such approaches, the quantity of contaminants that enter an eco-system or sub-system less the quantities stored, transformed, or degraded within the system must be equal to the quantity leaving the system. If the quantities do not balance, either there are sources that have not been identified and quantified, or the measurement of the quantities entering or leaving is not accurate.[38]

Hence, appropriate tools are critical to fill what was an important gap in the traditional approach: the lack of sufficient and reliable data, which prevented pragmatic incrementalism to adopt a holistic perspective to environmental problems.

In this light, the special focus of integrated pollution control on the media-shifting problem and the consequent identification of *prevention* can be better understood as the crucial objective of the integrated approach. Indeed, the latter does not simply aim to overcome the limits and flaws highlighted by the fragmented or traditional approach when dealing with pollutants already disposed of or delivered by a plant or a production process; it also aims to abate the total amount of noxious residues and waste by "questioning" the relevance of the different industrial products and processes through prevention.

In this respect, prevention has a twofold meaning: first, it is an objective of environmental policy, understood as the willingness to reduce pollution and protect the environment; second, it is one implementing modality to reach such environmental protection. A closer look at the definition and characteristics of prevention further helps to pinpoint the nature of this second meaning: preventing pollution, as opposed to treating or containing pollution after it has been produced, is intrinsically multimedia per se, so as well as being an environmental policy goal, pollution prevention emerges as a major vehicle for trying to diminish overall pollution releases and cross-media shifting.[39]

So, prevention helps to solve the media-shifting problem. In other terms, one of the main reasons for promoting prevention efforts is that these efforts prevent pollution from being transferred from one environmental medium to another. The more pollution prevention approaches are implemented, the more integrated the control system will be. Moreover, the growing evidence of cross-media pollution

37 Clarence Davies, "Some Thoughts on Implementing Integration," *Environmental Law* 22 (1), in *Integrated Pollution Control: A Symposium* (1992): 143.

38 Barry Rabe and Janet Zimmerman, "Cross-Media Environmental Integration": 271.

39 Id. 268; Clarence Davies, "Some Thoughts on Implementing Integration": 142.

transfer – together with the discovery that many alleged control strategies may, in fact, become involuntary transfer methods – has given progressively more appeal to increasingly preventive approaches that allow a reducing or elimination of the volumes of pollution being generated.[40]

In sum, the integrated approach is fully concerned with the source of the pollutant, focusing on where and how it is generated and where it ends up, adopting measures to reduce the pollutant's quantity and streamlining its distribution in the environment. Hence, the integrated approach deals with the life cycle of polluting substances, which translates into a greater focus on polluting emission sources through the application, inter alia, of the (EU) principle that environmental damage should as a priority be rectified at source.[41] Such a principle, analysed in more detail in Section 1.4.3, provides that action should be taken as soon as the environmental damage is caused, so as to prevent the latter becoming the source of further pollution. Hence, what was not taken into account by the traditional approach – that is, the role played both by raw materials (inputs) and final products (outputs) – has now moved centre stage. But there is more. The integrated approach analyses the ways in which products are developed and produced, and also their influence on the polluting capacity of the productive facility itself. As stated by Irwin, "the second shift to the source that is particularly significant for pollution is the focus on the facility or the technology and its associated products".[42]

This particular aspect is a determining factor in the application of the integrated approach and the principles connected with it because it allows for the identification of good reasons – among which are *economic* reasons – in favour of integrated pollution control. Indeed, the economic dimension of environmental protection policies is a key booster for their evolution and consolidation within the principles of environmental law. This will be further evident in the next chapter, when it comes to the EU context and legislation. Indeed, the demand for increasingly more clean and eco-efficient technologies is conducive to the spawning of new markets with high innovation rates. In turn, such added value helps countries to achieve economic development and social progress, which are the basis of the EU policies.

Finally, the integrated approach also takes into consideration the "realms" (or reference eco-systems) into which, once produced, polluting substances are disposed of or delivered to. To do so, it is necessary to carefully consider the context, including the role played by physical elements such as wind and water courses, of pollutant transfer. This is why performing monitoring and control at the local level is – at this stage – very important for ensuring a proper identification of the sources and assessment of the effects.

40 Ibid.

41 See Treaty establishing the European Community, Article 130r(2), now – after amendment – Article 174(1) EC.

42 Frances Irwin, "An Integrated Framework": 36–37.

1.3.1 The first signs of an integrated approach in EU national legislations

In the previous sections, I have highlighted the peculiar characteristics of the two approaches to environment and pollution: the traditional approach and the integrated approach. In particular, from the mid-1970s, the latter took its first steps at the national and international level; however, it was firmly enshrined at the EU level only in 1996 with the first Integrated Pollution Prevention and Control (IPPC) Directive.[43]

Before proceeding with the analysis of the IPPC Directive in Chapter 2, it is necessary to outline the first examples of the application of integrated pollution control within national legislations. Though partial, these first steps show the concrete presence of those elements and characteristics that give the integrated approach its specificity and distinguish it from the traditional and fragmented approach.

From a legal and regulatory point of view, the integrated approach generally manifests itself through different policy instruments. As argued by Irwin:

> An integrated framework means asking questions and making decisions that take the entire environment into account [...] It does mean making decisions using [...] policy instruments, such as multimedia permitting and enforcement, that are integrated across media.[44]

All such policy instruments serve three broad areas. First of all, the organizational area, which foresees the presence of a single authority responsible for putting in place all environment protection measures and regulations, as opposed to numerous authorities focused on single environmental sectors or media.

Secondly, the formal or procedural area, under which the integration of methods and instruments allows all subjects involved in the permitting process (e.g. local administrations, public authorities, agencies etc.) to coordinate with each other. Procedural integration can take various forms. Its highest expression is the so-called *multi-media permit*, specifically a permit covering all types of pollution caused by a single plant or industrial facility which replaces the numerous permits that are focused on single environmental media. However, procedural integration can have a lighter form, such as a simple coordination of the separate procedures for issuing permits by setting, for instance, a common date for the renewal of different permits which have already been issued.

The third and most important area is the substantive one, which foresees the environmental compatibility assessment of the pollutant caused by a given facility. As already mentioned, in this case integration consists of cross-media and holistic assessments. On the one hand, these assessments are cross-cutting and are therefore not differentiated according to the type of environmental media (air, water, soil). Hence, they are capable of weighing and balancing both the positive and negative aspects of the environmental picture being considered. On the other hand, they are

43 Council Directive 96/61/EC, Official Journal L 257, Concerning Integrated Pollution Prevention and Control (IPPC).

44 Id. 18.

comprehensive and synergic in that they involve all the, possibly interlinked, factors that generate polluting emissions at all stages of the process or production.[45]

Starting from the mid-1970s, two European countries – the United Kingdom (UK) and France – began to introduce into their legislation some instruments and mechanisms related to integrated pollution control.[46]

In particular, in 1976 the UK Royal Commission on Environmental Pollution recommended establishing an integrated pollution control system through the creation of a joint inspectorate. However, because of the difficulties in amending the national environmental legislation, such a recommendation was not acted upon until the 1980s, when the European Commission adopted two Directives – in 1984 and 1988 – respectively focused on Combating of Air Pollution from Industrial Plants and on the Limitation of Emissions of Certain Pollutants into the Air from Large Combustion Plants.[47] Although, as mentioned in Section 1.2 with regard to the 1984 Directive, these two Directives did not force Member States to implement any kind of integration, their compulsory transposition into the national legislation nevertheless provided the UK government with the opportunity to reform its entire environmental regulation on industrial pollution. In other words, the EU Directives did not support the creation of an integrated pollution control system; however, they pushed the UK government to implement changes to existing structure and practices.[48] In 1987, 10 years after the recommendation by the Royal Commission, Her Majesty's Inspectorate of Pollution (HMIP) was established by placing together in one single regulatory body the several inspectorates focused on air, water, waste and radioactive material. A few years later, HMIP was also responsible for the implementation of the Integrated Pollution Control (IPC), established in April 1991 following the entry into force of the Environmental Protection Act (EPA) of 1990.[49]

The mechanism established by the IPC was based on the requirement to obtain a permit to start any kind of production process laid down in the regulation, and it was characterised by two key elements: (1) the use of the Best Available Technology Not Entailing Excessive Cost (BATNEEC)[50] – for preventing, reducing

45 Nicola Lugaresi, *Diritto dell'Ambiente*, 87–91.

46 The only other example of a pioneering country in this realm is the USA. See Richard Andrews, "The EPA at 40: An Historical Perspective" (paper presented at the Duke Environmental Law and Policy Forum Symposium, January 24, 2011).

47 See Council Directive 84/360/EEC on the Combating of Air Pollution from Industrial Plants and Council Directive 88/609/EEC on the Limitation of Emissions of Certain Pollutants into the Air from Large Combustion Plants.

48 Andrew Jordan, "Integrated Pollution Control and the Evolving Style and Structure of Environmental Regulation in the UK," *Environmental Politics* 2 (3) (1993): 405–409.

49 Susan Owens, "Integrated Pollution-Control in the United Kingdom: Prospects and Problems," *Environment and Planning C: Government and Policy* 7 (1) (1989): 81–91.

50 In fact, BATNEEC can be considered the predecessor of the concept of Best Available Technology (BAT) contained in Council Directive 96/61/EC, Official Journal L 257, Concerning Integrated Pollution Prevention and Control (IPPC).

and rendering harmless the emission of pollutants while maintaining established environmental quality standards; and (2) the adoption of the so-called Best Practicable Environmental Option (BPEO) – for the identification of the BATNEEC to be implemented when the polluting activity applying for the permit releases substances in more than one environmental medium. Indeed, by requiring companies to seek out the best practicable solution, the BPEO aims to minimize the impact on the environment, taking into consideration all emissions caused by a production process as well as all their environmental consequences.[51]

Through the EPA and IPC, the UK environmental legislation was capable of influencing and somehow anticipating the EU legislation, eventually "exporting" many of its solutions into the IPPC. Still, the UK's IPC was not comprehensive. Although it was targeted at air, water and soil, in practice the production of waste was expressly not included and waste management and disposal remained under the control of the Waste Regulation Authorities. Moreover, the integrated control foreseen by the IPC ended up focusing almost entirely on air emissions, neglecting the prevention of chemical seepage into the soil and emissions to water – which continued to be the subject of existent discharge permits.[52] Finally, all emissions and waste outside of the production process, such as the supply of raw materials or energy, were not taken into consideration. For these reasons, though the IPC indeed was an important step towards an integrated pollution control system, it was not really an integrated approach able to embrace the whole life cycle of substances as required by the OECD definition.[53]

The French regulatory system also played a pioneering role in the development of a new approach for tackling pollution, in particular with regard to the control of environmental polluting activities.

The relevant legislation for those installations that carry out activities which impose a risk to the environment (*Installations Classées pour la Protection de l'Environnement* – ICPE), was initially set out by the Law of 19 July 1976 – later supplemented by the related implementing Decree n. 1133 of 1977. The law provided for a prior checking of these activities and installations and eventually oversaw the issuing of a permit by the prefecture of the territory in which such activities were located. The permit ensured the environmental compatibility of a given installation and laid down limitations able to prevent environmental hazards and incidents, thanks to the adoption of feasible measures specified by the prefecture in the permit.

An innovative aspect of the *Installations Classées* was the obligation to submit, together with the application for the permit, an impact assessment (*obligation*

51 EPA, "An In-depth Look at the United Kingdom Integrated Permitting System," US Environmental Protection Agency, National Center for Environmental Innovation (NCEI) (2008): 9.

52 John Gray, Tim James and John Dickson, "Integrated Regulation. Experiences of IPPC in England and Wales," *Water and Environment Journal* 21 (1) (2007): 70.

53 Neil Emmott and Nigel Haigh, "Integrated Pollution Prevention and Control: UK and EC Approaches and Possible Next Steps," *Journal of Environmental Law* 8 (2) (1996): 304.

d'étude d'impact, Art. 3, Par. 4) containing an initial review of the site and analysis of the surrounding environment in terms of natural resources, agricultural, forest and maritime areas along with material assets and cultural heritage affected by the plant as well as the analysis of the direct and indirect (and temporary or permanent) effects of the activity or installation on landscapes, flora and fauna, ecological balance and health of neighbouring communities. Moreover, this impact assessment had to specify: the nature and severity of the foreseen pollution in the air, water and soil; the volume and type of waste pollution; the acoustic and vibration level of the machineries to be used; and the conditions and methods of water supply and use.[54]

Hence, such an impact assessment analysis set out very ambitious targets, revealing a strong ecological concern, particularly for the environment, something that is even more important if one considers it was only the late 1970s. And what is more, it reflects the new perception and understanding of pollution, which refers to all environmental media: air, water and soil. Therefore, it is possible to argue that the French legislation here represents an early example of a multi-media and integrated approach, particularly if we look at the significance given to the conditions and methods of water supply and use, which can be seen as a sign of attention to both the implementation of the production process and its impact on the environment (in the water sector).

Conceived in these terms, an impact assessment analysis is a highly innovative instrument that is able to increase the level of integration. Indeed, this concept would be at the basis of one EU Directive introducing the integrated approach at the European level – the EIA Directive (85/337/EEC) that came into force in 1985. Unlike the EIA Directive, however, in the French regulatory legislation the 'integration' takes place almost exclusively in procedural terms , with only the prefect able to authorize, with a single permit, the carrying out of the polluting activity and the environmental compatibility measures.[55]

1.3.2 A new understanding of environment and development

In the light of what has been argued above, it is now possible to stress how in the EU, as far back as the mid-1970s, some very important steps had been made at the national level towards a new understanding of (approaching) environment and, consequently, towards new ways to deal with the phenomenon of pollution. In response to the increased knowledge of natural phenomena, environmental processes, interconnections among environmental elements and as a legacy of the Stockholm Conference, both the UK and France were able to put in place a set of new (and similar) measures reflecting a more comprehensive approach to the environment and pollution.

54 Christian Gabolde, *Les Installations Classées pour la Protection de l'Environnement* (Paris: Sirey, 1978), 97.

55 See Council Directive 85/337/EEC on the Assessment of the Effects of Certain Public and Private Projects on the Environment, Official Journal L 175.

Though an excellent starting point, these pioneering integration initiatives did not succeed in building organic systems able to establish all the key elements and instruments that make the integrated approach a holistic and comprehensive one. True, the creation of an inspectorate of pollution (HMIP) in the UK and the French provision assigning to the prefect the task of issuing a permit to carry out polluting activities, well illustrate what was classified above as the first type of integration – i.e. organizational integration. Also, procedural integration was ensured by the creation of single permits for several environmental media, both in France and the UK. Nevertheless, neither initiative was able to meet the substantive scope of integration: cross-media assessments (analysing all environmental media within a single picture) and holistic assessments (taking into account at all stages the interactions possibly polluting the environment) were not performed.

Indeed, it is in the supranational dimension – that is at the EU level – that the integrated approach to the environment and pollution will make a qualitative leap forward, eventually triggering decisive impacts on the national legislations of Member States, including Italy.

1.4 Integrated pollution control: fundamental principles of environmental protection regulation

Before analysing in depth the EU legislation on integrated permitting, it is now worth defining the fundamental principles and objectives which developed at the international level and which the EU environmental policy used as its basis for the achievement of effective environmental regulation.

As argued above, the United Nations Conference on the Human Environment held in Stockholm in June 1972 pushed the topic of the environment up the agenda at the global level. However, it is important to highlight that, on the international stage, it is primarily in the EU context that environmental concerns gained momentum, so much so that environmental protection became one of the key objectives first of the European Community, and later of the European Union. Put another way, since the 1970s the environment has become a consolidated topic within the EU political agenda, with positive implications on the level of innovation included in its environmental legislation – through directives, regulations, decisions and acts.[56]

The principles and objectives that progressively inspired and gave direction to the emergence of an European legislative framework on integrated pollution prevention and control are included in the Title XX – Environment (Climate Change) of the Lisbon Treaty. In particular, Article 191, Paragraph 2, stipulates that:

> [The European] Union policy on the environment shall aim at a high level of protection taking into account the diversity of situations in the various regions of the Union. It shall be based on the precautionary principle and on the

56 Lisbon Treaty, Title XX, Article 191 – ex Article 174 of the Treaty Establishing the European Community (TEC). See also Articles 192 and 193 of Lisbon Treaty.

principles that preventive action should be taken, that environmental damage should as a priority be rectified at source and that the polluter should pay … .[57]

As well as these four principles, it is also necessary to take into consideration the principle of sustainable development and the principle of integration, both established by Article 11 of the Treaty on the Functioning of the European Union (TFEU-Lisbon Treaty). This Article sets out a comprehensive legal duty to integrate environmental protection requirements in the policies and activities of the European Union.

Analysing such principles of environmental regulation will not only allow for a better understanding of the foundations of the regulatory system on which integrated pollution control is built on but it will also be helpful in establishing a definition of *environment* in legal terms.

1.4.1 Principle of sustainable development and principle of integration

Sustainable development is a commonly used concept, the meaning of which evolved first at the international level, throughout non-binding declarations, and then – at different stages – within multinational and national contexts.[58] It was initially introduced at the global level in 1987 within the Report of the World Commission on Environment and Development (the so-called Brundtland Commission), which defined it as "a development that meets the needs of the present without compromising the ability of future generations to meet their own needs".[59] A few years later, the United Nations Conference on Environment and Development, held in Rio de Janeiro in 1992, further developed the concept. Indeed, the Rio Conference applied the notion of sustainable development to some of the principles previously stated by the 1972 UN Stockholm Conference on the Human Environment. In this respect, by providing that "States have … the sovereign right to exploit their own resources pursuant to their own environmental and developmental policies …", Principle 2 of the Rio Declaration represents, as it stands, an improved version of Principle 21 of the Stockholm Declaration, according to which "States have […] the sovereign right to exploit their own resources pursuant to their own environmental policies […]".[60] In the same respect,

57 Lisbon Treaty, Title XX, Article 191, Paragraph 2.

58 For the evolution of the concept in the EU and Italy, see the present Section. In China, this concept is linked to that of ecological civilization, first coined in 1987 by the agricultural economist Ye Qianji. Such a concept did not have a widespread use until 2007, and in 2012 it was inserted among the five key objectives in the country's overall development plan at the 18th National Congress of the Communist Party of China, when President Xi Jinping was elected General Secretary of the CPC Central Committee. For more information on sustainable development and ecological civilization see Chapter 4 of the present study.

59 Report of the *World Commission on Environment and Development: Our Common Future* (Oxford: Oxford University Press, 1987), 41.

60 UN General Assembly, "United Nations Conference on Sustainable Development", Principle 2.; UN General Assembly, "United Nations Conference on the Human Environment", Principle 21.

the Rio Declaration brought together two topics under the concept of sustainable development – socio-economic development and environmental protection – which the Stockholm Declaration, as highlighted above, had considered to be separate.

At EU level, it is the 1993 Maastricht Treaty which first introduces the concept of sustainable development when it states that the EU shall "promote *economic* and *social progress* which is *balanced* and *sustainable*".[61] Subsequently, it is with the 1997 Treaty of Amsterdam that such a concept (i.e. sustainable development) starts to be recognised as one of the General Principles of the EU law/policies. Indeed, Article 11 of TFEU-Lisbon Treaty (ex art. 6 of the Treaty establishing the European Community – TEC) stipulates that: "environmental protection requirements must be integrated into the definition and implementation of the Union policies and activities, in particular with a view to promoting sustainable development".[62] Despite the provision clearly expressing the need to converge all EU policies and activities towards the goal of sustainable development, it does not provide a definition of it.

As already discussed, the formula for *sustainable development* certainly combines a focus on socio-economic development, on one hand, and environmental protection on the other. However, as often observed by scholars and experts, in practice the two components are not always equally relevant, and the former usually prevails over the latter. In other words, development tends to be the real subject, and defining it as "sustainable" denotes a passive and instrumental role to the environment.

In light of the UN declarations following the Rio Conference, it is then possible to argue that sustainable development is not simply made of an even balance between economic development and environmental protection. The Declaration of the World Summit on Sustainable Development, held in Johannesburg in 2002, expands the concept of sustainable development, breaking away from the dichotomy of economic development / environmental protection in favour of three interdependent pillars. Indeed, Article 5 of the Declaration affirms the need to strengthen sustainable development, defining it as the combination of economic development, environmental protection as well as "social development". Moreover, Article 11 stipulates that the key objectives and the essential prerequisites for sustainable development are "poverty eradication, changing consumption and production patterns and protecting and managing the natural resource base for economic and social development ...".[63] Therefore, over time, the sustainable development concept has broadened to include issues such as health, education, technology transfer, trade, fight against hunger and poverty, in addition to environmental protection.

Given all these points concerning the evolution of sustainable development, it is useful to acknowledge that: 1) in spite of the fact that this concept is often

61 Resolution of the Council of the European Communities and of the Representatives of the Governments of the Member States, Treaty on European Union, Official Journal C 326.

62 Lisbon Treaty, Article 11.

63 UN Documents, "Gathering a Body of Global Agreements: Johannesburg Declaration on Sustainable Development," (2002): Articles 5 and 11, http://www.un-documents.net/jburgdec.htm.

perceived mainly as the pursuing of economic development, it also *equally* includes environmental protection; 2) this notion includes topics which goes beyond the economic development / environmental protection dichotomy; 3) the integrated approach to environment and pollution is not only crucial for environmental protection but it also serves other important goals.

In other words, without such premises it is not possible to fully understand the real impact of the integrated environmental regulation as an instrument for both tackling pollution and addressing goals which, though not directly attributable to environmental protection, are indeed part of the broad concept of sustainable development, such as: the promotion of a rational management of raw materials (including energy), the development of a technology market and the research for technological innovation.

Besides the principle of sustainable development, Article 11 of TFEU encompasses the aforementioned principle of external integration by affirming that all economic and social policies or commitments undertaken at the EU level need to integrate environmental considerations as an element of sustainable development.[64] Hence, as in the case of sustainable development, the goal of external integration is wide; indeed, according to Article 11, environmental protection should not only be a subject of concern for environmental decision-makers but it should also be an important consideration when other policies are drafted and implemented.[65] In this respect, the principle of integration becomes essential for attaining sustainable development, since the latter requires a certain level of integration among different actions for achieving the above-mentioned balance between economic activities and the other goals involved. This is also confirmed by the conclusions of several European Councils,[66] in which the relationship between sustainable development and integration is expressed as follows: "The Union's Sustainable Development Strategy is based on the principle that the economic, social and environmental effects of all policies should be examined in a coordinated way and taken into account in decision-making".[67]

As a matter of fact, the Italian environmental protection legislation (see Law 152 of 3rd April 2006 – also known as TUA, Article 3-quater, Paragraph 3), provides a well-defined definition of sustainable development, stipulating the need to ensure a balance between environmental protection and economic development needs, and avoiding a prominent role of the latter. This particular attention to environmental protection is even more evident in Paragraph 4 of the same Article, which states that the resolution of questions regarding environmental issues needs to be addressed guaranteeing sustainable development, hence ensuring the proper functioning and evolution of natural eco-systems and preventing the risk of

64 Philippe Sands, *Principles of International Environmental Law*, 205.
65 Michael Faure, "The Harmonization, Codification and Integration of Environmental Law: A Search for Definitions," *European Environmental Law Review* 9 (2000): 178.
66 See, for instance, the European Councils of Cardiff (June 1998), Vienna (December 1998), Cologne (June 1999), Helsinki (December 1999).
67 See Presidency Conclusions of Goteborg European Council, June 15–16, 2001, page 4, https://www.consilium.europa.eu/media/20983/00200-r1en1.pdf.

negative impacts possibly caused by human activity. In this context, the objective of sustainable development is not merely to integrate the environmental demands into the economic dynamics; rather, it is to safeguard the integrity of the ecosystem from harmful human activity.[68]

Finally, Paragraph 2 goes even further by introducing the duty of public authorities to "primarily take into consideration" the environmental protection issues when public and private interests are at stake. This leads to a twofold outcome: on one hand, it establishes a hierarchy among the involved interests; on the other, it provides a practical action rule which makes the set-out principle ready to be implemented.

As regards China's environmental protection legislation, the concept of sustainable development appears explicitly in Article 1 of the Environmental Protection Law of 2014. Nevertheless, although mentioning the need for "facilitating economic and social sustainable development", such provision does not go further or specify how sustainable development should be facilitated and what should be the balance between its economic and social meaning. Moreover, still in Article 1, the concept of sustainable development is linked to, and to a certain extent overcome by, the concept of *ecological civilization*, the improvement of which should be promoted.[69] Compared with sustainable development, ecological civilization is a more sociological concept and it focuses on the achievement of a harmonious relationship between man and nature. Such a concept, first coined in 1987 by the agricultural economist Ye Qianji, did not have a widespread use until 2007, when it was inserted among the five key objectives in the country's overall development plan, as confirmed five years later by the 18th National Congress of the Communist Party of China when President Xi Jinping was elected General Secretary of the CPC Central Committee.[70]

1.4.2 The precautionary principle and principle of preventive action

The precautionary principle and the principle of preventive action (here also referred to as "prevention") are closely interlinked and are often regarded as two sides of the same coin.

Despite its introduction in European law long before the precautionary principle, it is still difficult to provide a unique definition of the principle of preventive action and its content. As discussed in Section 1.3, it is indeed a key aspect of the integrated approach to environment and pollution. The logic behind it is that, as often argued in the field of health, "prevention is better than cure". In fact, environmental damage caused by human activity often cannot be remediated and

68 Italian Law 152 of 3rd April 2006 (known as TUA, Testo Unico dell'Ambiente – i.e. Consolidated Law on Environment), Article 3-quater, Paragraphs 3 and 4.

69 Environmental Protection Law of the People's Republic of China 2014: Article 1.

70 Zhilin Mu, Shuchun Bu and Bing Xue, "Environmental Legislation in China: Achievements, Challenges and Trends," *Sustainability* 6 (2014): 8976–8977.

this makes it preferable to deal with environmental and pollution problems by adopting an ex-ante approach rather than an ex-post one.

The precautionary principle was first introduced by the Maastricht Treaty and its content and impact are expressed in the texts of several international declarations. The provision that defines it is Principle 15 of the 1992 Rio Declaration which expresses that "Where there are threats of serious or irreversible damage, lack of full scientific certainty shall not be used as a reason for postponing cost-effective measures to prevent environmental degradation".[71] Given this definition, it is possible to argue that in one respect the precautionary principle is a decision-making criterion for establishing whether to adopt measures to prevent environmental degradation and, yet, it is based on peculiar conditions such as scientific uncertainty and risk assessment.

At the juridical level, both prevention and precaution turn into control measures which, with different intensity levels, are implemented before negative consequences for the environment may occur.

The principle of preventive action encourages an environmental compatibility assessment to limit, from the very first stage, the environmental degradation caused by given processes or activities with a significant impact on the environment.[72] In other words, this principle gives rise to the legal instrument known as an Environmental Impact Assessment (EIA), the implementation of which is a key element in most environmental protection regulations including, as discussed in the following chapters, those of China and Italy. Also, the principle of preventive action plays an important role when regulating the issuing of permits related to the discharge of polluting substances in air, water and soil. As has already been mentioned, this has been the case, for instance, of European environmental legislation since the mid-1970s. Either way, the prevention modifies, where necessary, the standards or parameters that a given facility needs to comply with to be considered environmentally sustainable. Having said that, as it will be shown later in this book, a case in which a permit might not be issued simply on the basis of the principle of preventive action is very unlikely.

As well as the principle of preventive action, the precautionary principle also allows for an assessment of negative effects on the environment, but – differently from the former – the latter focuses on the *potential* negative impacts, which may or may not occur. Among the applicable measures, the principle enables putting environmental security over environmental risk, and this is the reason why such a principle is often depicted as requiring the regulator to ban an activity or technology, despite the fact that this is not spelled out in any declaration in such absolute terms.[73] Put another way, in cases where the impact of a certain activity may harm the ecological balance, the precautionary principle may impose its ban prior to the implementation of prevention measures. Though bans may be enforced in some cases, still the implementation of precautionary principle may

71 UN General Assembly, "United Nations Conference on Environment and Development," 14 June 1992: Principle 15.
72 Nicola Lugaresi, *Diritto dell'Ambiente*, 95.
73 John Applegate, "The Taming of the Precautionary Principle," *William and Mary Environmental Law and Policy Review* 13 (2002): 19.

mean process controls, field or pre-release testing, limited periods of approval, identification of alternatives or further research.[74] The principle gives rise to the legal instrument known as an Environmental Risk Assessment (ERA), the implementation of which is quite recent in the European law, particularly in the pharmaceutical field.[75] Hence, because it is able to enforce a more advanced and higher level of environmental protection, the precautionary principle can be considered an improved version of the principle of preventive action in terms of impact.

In turn, by requiring human activity to abate or eliminate all negative environmental impacts, the principle of preventive action is critical in ensuring sustainable development and environmental compatibility. Principle 8 of the Rio Declaration seems to refer to this very causal link when stating: "To achieve sustainable development and a higher quality of life for all people, States should reduce and eliminate unsustainable patterns of production and consumption ...".[76] Furthermore, the prevention principle is strictly linked with external integration: by putting forward the need of environmental protection, it integrates the latter with the implementation of non-environmental policies. This prevents the exclusion of environmental protection issues from other (non-environmental) policies as well as the need to adopt environmental protection measures only at a later stage through either remedial measures (i.e. rectifying environmental damage at source) or compensatory measures (i.e. polluter-pays). Both these topics will be the subject of the next section.

In this respect, by requiring all operators to reduce the environmental impact of their activities, *prevention* becomes complementary to internalization. Hence, from the 1980s, the principle of preventive action is at the heart of the all EU environmental regulations, including the IPPC Directive, which will maximize its potential implications.

1.4.3 The principles of polluter-pays and rectifying environmental damage at source

The polluter-pays principle has a strong economic connotation and it is mainly related to environmental protection and, particularly, to environmental pollution. Indeed, the environment holds an economic value which allows for the definition of environmental costs; that is, the costs involved in undertaking a certain activity which, rather than being borne by the party carrying out the activity, are at the expense of the community or third party to whom the natural resource belongs.

74 Id. 29.

75 See, for example, Council Directive 91/414/EEC Concerning the Placing of Plant Protection Products on the Market, Articles 1.3, 11 and 14; Council Directive 2001/79/EC Fixing Guidelines for the Assessment of Additives in Animal Nutrition, Section IV: 18-21; Council Directive 2001/83/EC Related to Medicinal Products for Human Use, Article 8.

76 UN General Assembly, "United Nations Conference on Environment and Development," 14 June 1992: Principle 8.

This is what in environmental terms is defined as the problem of *negative externalities*. Its solution is the so-called "internalization" of third-party costs, for example, by requiring a polluter to remedy to the damage caused to the environment. This prevents citizens from having to bear the social costs deriving from the pollution caused by economic activities.[77]

In economic terms, the correction, or internalization of externalities has a repercussion on the allocation of resources. Indeed, the polluting company is selling products at a price which does not take into account the social cost linked to pollution. This generates a distortion of consumers' economic behaviour and a consequent misallocation of total wealth. On one hand, there is an over-production due to the use of apparently free resources, on the other, the over-use of environmental resources leads to their over-consumption. Both elements reflect what has already been argued with respect to sustainable development.[78]

The first definition of this issue at international level is included in the OECD Recommendation of the Council of 26 May 1972 on Guiding Principles Concerning International Economic Aspects of Environmental Policies, which in 1974 was further defined by the OECD Declaration on Environmental Policy and the Recommendation on the Implementation of the Polluter-Pays Principle. It stipulates that: "The principle to be used for allocating costs of pollution prevention and control measures to encourage rational use of scarce environmental resources and to avoid distortions of international trade and investment is the so-called 'Polluter-Pays Principle'".[79] Years later, the Rio Declaration reaffirmed the same need in its Principle 16, under which:

> National authorities should endeavour to promote the internalization of environmental costs and the use of economic instruments, taking into account the approach that the polluter should, in principle, bear the cost of pollution with regard to the public interest and without distorting international trade and investments.[80]

In this light, it is possible to argue that the internalization of environmental costs and the polluter-pays principle overlap with each other, so much so that the latter can be considered the instrument for satisfying the former's need.

Hence, the polluter-pays principle establishes that, rather than being paid by the community, environmental costs should be borne by the party carrying out the environmental polluting activities. In this way the principle also works as a preventive measure of environmental protection. In fact, the internalization of environmental costs can take place through the implementation of three kinds of legal

77 Nicolas De Sadeleer, *Essential Concepts of Global Environmental Governance* (New York, Routledge: 2015), 152–156; Nicola Lugaresi, *Diritto dell'Ambiente*, 97–99.
78 Ibid.
79 OECD, "Recommendation of the Council on Guiding Principles Concerning International Economic Aspects of Environmental Policies," (1972).
80 UN General Assembly, "United Nations Conference on Environment and Development," 14 June 1992: Principle 16.

measures: the definition of standards, with provisions establishing the pollution thresholds that have to be met by the operator; the imposition of tax measures, which require the payment of pollution-based fees (i.e. the more one pollutes the more one pays); and the establishment of civil liabilities for environmental and pollution damage.

Both the definition of standards and the imposition of tax measures are instruments of preventive action, as in each case the operator has an incentive to reduce their emissions or discharges and to develop less polluting products and technologies. In the first case, in order to meet the standards set out in law, the polluter has to bear an environmental cost which consists of the expenses for acquiring the appropriate equipment to abate or eliminate pollution. In the second case, the tax or fee the polluter needs to pay is directly proportional to the pollution they cause: in this respect, the preventive effect is even more intuitive since the operator will try to reduce the quantity of discharged pollutants as much as possible in order to pay less.[81]

Hence, the polluter-pays principle promotes environmental protection through preventive measures and fulfils the need to encourage a well-functioning and efficient market. Given this economic feature, it can be argued that such a principle is perfectly in line with that of sustainable development. Indeed, that being the case, it became a major reference for all environmental regulations and strongly influenced international, EU as well as national environmental regulations. In fact, it is the legal basis of several public measures targeted towards economic activities, for eventually promoting environmental protection, such as the issuing or not of permits for activities responsible for environmental damage and the definition of standards related to quality of environment, products and technologies.

These environmental regulation measures can be adopted in combination with each other and, as described in the next chapter with respect to IPPC Directive, integrated permits give a solid and advanced demonstration of how effective such a combination can be. Put another way, integrated permits dictate emission limit values set out on the basis of a specific technological standard, that is the "best available technology".

Finally, it is worth highlighting that, by setting the apportioning of civil liability in the environmental field, the polluter-pays principle is often perceived *only* as a remedial or as a compensatory measure[82]; namely, an environmental protection measure to be used only once pollution has been caused. This misperception needs to be taken into account when applying the polluter-pays principle.

In addition to the polluter-pays principle, the remaining fundamental principle of integrated environmental regulation is that of rectifying environmental damage at source. Such a principle is complementary to the principle of preventive action

81 Nicolas De Sadeleer, *Essential Concepts of Global Environmental Governance*, 155–156.

82 *Remedial measure* refers to the establishment of the aforementioned civil liabilities for environmental and pollution damage caused by the single operator; *compensatory measure* refers to the above-mentioned imposition of the payment of pollution-based fees.

and it specifies a rule of action and behaviour. Unlike the polluter-pays principle, it requires the offending parties to rectify the environmental damage rather than compensate it. In other words, as argued above, the polluter-pays principle is based on a remedial and compensatory logic, which states that the parties that caused the environmental damage are responsible for the costs to adopt measures for pollution abatement; the principle of rectifying environmental damage at source, on the other hand, aims to re-establish the status quo which existed before the damage or, in cases where this is impossible, at least to prevent further harmful effects on the environment .[83]

This is exactly what the polluter-pays principle does not aim to do. Indeed, it does not expect to limit pollution or environmental damages caused by a given production facility and this objective is only indirectly pursued on the basis that operators would be persuaded to abate pollution emissions in order to reduce environmental costs imposed through taxes or other forms of regulation. That said, this does not prevent operators from continuing to pollute, deliberately accepting to bear the costs deriving from their environmental damage liability or from environmental taxes. This is also why, in some cases, operators perceive the polluter-pays principle as the principle of "whoever pays can pollute".

In comparison, the principle of rectifying environmental damage at source aims not only to ensure the depletion of adverse environmental effects, but also to consider environmental damage as a priority to be addressed at source. Hence it recommends direct action as soon as the damage has occurred, limiting the spreading of harmful consequences. In this respect it confirms its strong link and complementarity with the principle of preventive action.[84]

1.5 The implementation of the principles through environmental legislation

In the previous sections it has been verified that European environmental policy is based on some fundamental principles that work in close connection with each other, resulting in a robust system that meets multiple needs related to the environment: from protection to resource management through the construction of a single market. All these requirements are however expressed so as not to constitute an obstacle or a brake to the economic development of the European Union. The environmental policy outlined in this way by the principles of the Lisbon Treaty (TFEU or TEU) is then further clarified and concretized in the various Action Plans in which the Union identifies the specific objectives to be pursued and the various steps that must lead to their realization. Hence, the lines of development of the European legislation can be traced through regulations and directives, as well as the set of individual specific interventions. That said, it should be noted that already in the Treaty of Lisbon there is the presence of what have

83 Nicolas De Sadeleer, *Essential Concepts of Global Environmental Governance*, 153.
84 Ibid.

been variously defined as "criteria" or "parameters" which the Union must take into account in the preparation of its policies.

Indeed, Article 114 of the Lisbon Treaty, Paragraph 3, provides that "the Commission, in its proposals envisaged in paragraph 1 concerning health, safety, environmental protection and consumer protection, will take as a base a high level of protection, taking account in particular of any new development based on scientific facts ...",[85] whereas Article 191, Paragraph 3, affirms that

> in preparing its policy on the environment, the Union shall take account of: available scientific and technical data, environmental conditions in the various regions of the Union, the potential benefits and costs of action or lack of action, the economic and social development of the Union as a whole and the balanced development of its regions.[86]

From the two mentioned Articles, it is possible to derive at least three guiding criteria that the Treaty wished to make explicit, and that play an important role in determining the ways in which an environmental policy must be concretely promoted.

The first of these criteria concerns "*scientific and technological development*", which Paragraph 3 of Article 114 puts in direct connection with the pursuit of a "high level of protection" in environmental protection policies and that Paragraph 3 of Article 191 recalls by imposing that the "available scientific and technical data" are taken into consideration. Research and technological development also find space in the Title XIX of the Lisbon Treaty that precedes the one dedicated to the environment. In particular, Article 179, Paragraph 1, states that

> The Union shall have the objective of strengthening its scientific and technological bases by achieving a European research area in which researchers, scientific knowledge and technology circulate freely, and encouraging it to become more competitive, including in its industry, while promoting all the research activities deemed necessary by virtue of other Chapters of the Treaties.[87]

The joint reading of these provisions makes it possible to highlight the Treaty's focus on a strong link between technological innovation and environmental protection on the one hand, and between technological innovation and markets, on the other. The link between technological innovation and environmental protection is explicitly stated, as mentioned above, by Article 191, Paragraph 3.

This relationship between technological change and environmental policy has been the subject of increasing attention in recent years, in part for the reason that the environmental impact of human activities is significantly influenced by

85 Lisbon Treaty, Title VII, Article 114, Paragraph 3.
86 Lisbon Treaty, Title XX, Article 191, Paragraph 3.
87 Lisbon Treaty, Title XIX, Article 179, Paragraph 1.

technological progress, and in part due to the fact that environmental policies themselves can create limitations and incentives that condition the technological development process.

This relationship between technology and innovation in the environmental field, however, is not reflected in the text of the Treaty, but it is explicitly mentioned in previous international documents, respectively in Principle 20 of the Stockholm Declaration and Principle 9 of the Rio Declaration. Indeed, the first provides that

> Scientific research and development in the context of environmental problems, both national and multinational, must be promoted in all countries, especially the developing countries. In this connection, the free flow of up-to-date scientific information and transfer of experience must be supported and assisted, to facilitate the solution of environmental problems;

the second affirms that "States should co-operate to strengthen endogenous capacity-building for sustainable development by improving scientific understanding through exchanges of scientific and technological knowledge, and by enhancing the development, adaptation, diffusion and transfer of technologies, including new and innovative technologies".[88]

As regards the relationship between technological innovation and the market, it should be noted that Paragraph 3 of Article 114 explicitly operates on the basis of Paragraph 1, which guarantees the establishment and functioning of the internal market:

> The European Parliament and the Council shall … adopt the measures for the approximation of the provisions laid down by law, regulation or administrative action in Member States which have as their object the establishment and functioning of the internal market.[89]

From this systematic reading we can argue that the development of scientific knowledge, and its implications in terms of technological innovation in the environmental field, is a way to follow for achieving the primary objective of the (unique) market and its development. The environmental legislation is conceived as a real instrument of economic development: the measures concretely adopted in view of the pursuit of environmental principles are considered an opportunity to promote the economic growth of the European system. This aspect is so accepted and inherent in the EU structure that it is present and described in the so-called Fourth Environmental Action Programme of 1987, where it is claimed that "where higher environmental standards are more and more being required, the

88 UN General Assembly, "United Nations Conference on the Human Environment", 15 December 1972: Principle 20; UN General Assembly, "United Nations Conference on Environment and Development," 14 June 1992: Principle 9.

89 Lisbon Treaty, Title VII, Article 114, Paragraph 3.

achievement of such standards must increasingly be seen as an essential element in the future economic success of the Community".[90]

Moreover, as is clear from the communications relating to the Environmental Policy Review that are transmitted each year by the Commission to the Parliament and the European Council, this conviction is constantly at the heart of European environmental policy. For example, in the Communication concerning the 2004 Review, the Commission highlighted that the implementation of an Action Plan for Compatible Technologies, which favours the integration of environmental costs and the adoption of resource and waste management strategies, could only benefit the competitiveness of European markets. More recently, in the 2009 Communication, the European Commission – referring to the economic crisis at the time – affirmed that a stronger environmental policy could serve to boost economic recovery and a lasting competitiveness of the EU.[91]

To get a better idea of how much the development of the environmental technologies market, or at least of everything related to environmental protection and management, has relevance for the economy, it is sufficient to mention the data provided in the same Communication, which showed how the turnover of the so-called 'eco-industry' in Europe was equal to 2.5 per cent of the entire gross domestic product (i.e. more than 300 billion euro a year) and how, compared with the average, the productivity of the sector had grown more quickly than the manufacturing industry. This had a positive impact also on the employment rate: indeed, "according to a recent study, in 2008 around 5.6 million people were directly employed in jobs related to the environment, and 3.4 million people (i.e. 1.5% of total employed) were directly employed in the EU eco-industry".[92]

Technological development in environmental matters therefore plays a decisive role in achieving the main objectives of both economic and environmental policy; technological innovation in fact satisfies both the needs of sustainable development and prevention. As argued by Kneese and Schultze: "The effects of environmental policies on the development and spread of new technologies may, in the long run, be among the most important determinants of success or failure of environmental protection efforts".[93] As it will be highlighted later, with particular reference to the IPPC Directive, the most recent EU environmental legislation has been characterised by the adoption of methods and measures based, inter alia, on the imposition of technological standards, which have the ability not only to

90 Council Resolution of 19 October 1987 on the Continuation and Implementation of a European Community Policy and Action Programme on the Environment (1987–1992), 7. http://eur-lex.europa.eu/legal-content/EN/TXT/PDF/?uri=CELEX:41987X1207&from=IT

91 2009 Environment Policy Review, Staff Working Paper SEC (2010) 975 final, 77.

92 Ibid.

93 Adam Jaffe et al., "Technological Change and the Environment," in *Handbook of Environmental Economics*, Vol. 1, edited by K.G. Maler and J.R. Vincent (Amsterdam and Boston, MA: Elsevier Science, 2003), 468. Original quote in Kneese, A. and C. Schultze, *Pollution, Prices, and Public Policy* (Washington, D.C.: Brookings Institution, 1975.)

guarantee the achievement of a high level of environmental protection (without burdening the operators too much in terms of costs) but also to trigger the phenomena of growth and economic progress. The imposition of standards and high levels of environmental quality compel companies to invest economic resources in research and technological development in order to make their production compatible with the requirements imposed at the regulatory level by the environmental disciplines in the various sectors. In fact, as stated by Jaffe et al., "Performance and technology standards can be explicitly designed to be 'technology forcing' mandating performance levels that are not currently viewed as technologically feasible or mandating technologies that are not fully developed".[94]

A second guiding criterion for the adoption of an environmental policy is that deriving from the reference to "*environmental conditions in the various regions of the Union*". In terms of the European treaty, this provision refers to macro areas within the territory of the Union, with the aim of allowing such areas, within individual Member States or parts of them, to differentiate or otherwise adapt the individual policies to the different environmental conditions that may be present. This is the expression of a principle considered to be of a general nature, namely that of differentiation. Such differentiation is the possibility, foreseen by the EU, that individual Member States, or certain territorial entities that have normative capacity in the single national laws, will/may face specific issues/problems related to the territories of the same States introducing integrations, exceptions, improvements or even possible worsening of the level of environmental protection expected in Europe.

Such a possibility, expressly recognized to local legislators to differentiate (their own) environmental legislation in order to better adapt the individual systems according to the different conditions of the environmental context, shows the root of a more operative intervention criterion for any public decision-maker. Indeed, the environment poses global issues, which must be tackled according to a supranational perspective of cooperation between states (and requires specific answers calibrated on the concrete situation in which one wants to intervene). In other words, if it is true, as it will be (more broadly) argued later, that the environment must no longer be dealt with exclusively at sectorial and autonomous levels – but on the contrary in an integrated and unitary manner by the various subjects involved – it is also true that the concrete protection activities cannot ignore the correct evaluation of individual concrete situations. Using a metaphor, it would be inappropriate to think of treating all the "patients" of the environment with the same medicine (or with its equal dosage).

That said, this diversified approach is one of the most important aspects of the IPPC Directive: in that context, the specific state of environmental conditions becomes one of the most relevant parameters within the assessment through which the environmental regulator shapes and issues the permit to carry out a given polluting activity.[95]

94 Id. 469.
95 Philippe Sands, *Principles of International Environmental Law*, 207.

Finally, the last criterion of reference that can be drawn from Paragraph 3 of Article 191 is that concerning the necessary evaluation of the "*the potential benefits and costs of action or lack of action*". Such a criterion expresses the general need to perform cost-benefit analysis before taking any decision regarding the environmental sector. This specific forecast is linked to the environmental accounting matrix, which, in turn, refers to the idea of a meeting of different skills and disciplines (law, economics, ecology, sociology). Environmental accounting would have the function of measuring the consistency of natural resources, their flows and changes, and the effects of human actions on the environment. In other words, it would measure the sustainability of development over time and over the course of its life cycle.

The cost-benefit analysis, as a decision-making tool to guide choices in the presence of risk situations, has been elaborated on and established – as it is known – from its origins in US neoclassical economics. It implies that, based on the information available for calculating the expected value of costs and benefits, the best choice is the one in which the net benefits expected are higher than the costs entailed. From this point of view such a criterion is opposed to the precautionary principle which, in its stronger formulations, foresees the impossibility of carrying on a certain activity if there is uncertainty about its environmental hazard.[96]

Therefore, it is possible to argue that this criterion based on the comparison of advantages and burdens should not be considered as overlapping, as far as its scope is concerned, with that of precaution. In its strongest form the precautionary principle can determine the ban of an activity or technology by the regulator, as a measure to prevent environmental degradation. Indeed, the principle allows putting environmental security over environmental risk. While in its weak form it is essentially an informal analysis of cost-benefits aimed at maximizing the benefit of those who are averse to risk. However, independently of how one may consider the precautionary principle, expressed in Paragraph 2 of Article 191 of the Lisbon Treaty, the criterion of advantages and burdens set out in Paragraph 3 must be interpreted as responding to a different role and meaning, the value of which is not limited to choices under risk conditions, but it is more extensive, recalling a different dimension of sustainability, understood as the economic sustainability of the decisions taken. Thus, this refers to a criterion of decision that is very concrete and leaves no room for further interpretations, but confirms once again how the economic factor represents a preponderant element in the process of elaboration of all European policies, including the environmental one.[97]

In conclusion, the three criteria we have just considered represent interrelated and interdependent elements; i.e. they are able to influence each other, in addition to the variables that come into play at the time of adopting a specific measure in the field of environmental protection. From these brief considerations it is still difficult to fully understand how the various elements are able to affect the implementation of an environmental policy and, to this end, focus needs to be directed on the examination

96 Lakshman Guruswamy, "Integrating Thoughtways": 480–85; James Krier and Mark Brownstein, "On Integrated Pollution Control": 125–27.

97 Charles E. Lindblom, "The Science of 'Muddling Through'," *Public Administration Review* 19 (2) (1959): 79–88.

of a specific regulation, such as that introduced by the IPPC Directive. That said, it is from now on possible to observe how technology, specific environmental context and costs are determinant and competing factors in modulating a tangible answer to the environmental protection needs that one wants to satisfy. For example, compliance with a specific emission limit or an environmental quality standard cannot always be achieved with the same methods or operating solutions. A specific environmental context will require different technologies and a specific technology will entail different costs depending on the actual location of the plant to which it will be applied.

In this way the strongly "relative" nature of the environmental protection activity is highlighted, capable of modifying itself and of behaving differently according to the diverse conditions in which it is called on to intervene. As will be discussed later, this characteristic of the 'relativity' of environmental protection will also need to be considered in relation to time and its effect on interventions. Environmental protection, implemented through instruments of administrative regulation, is mainly realized in the preparation of mechanisms of authorization of temporary validity. This aspect will be addressed later in this study as a characteristic element of so-called *reflexive regulation*, of which the IPPC Directive is a concrete manifestation.

1.5.1 The first steps towards the IPPC Directive

The process of progressive growth that has characterized integrated pollution control has developed not only, as mentioned, at the national level, finding space in the jurisdictions of different countries, but also in a supranational dimension, first in the framework of the so-called European programmes of environmental action, then in real directives. Since the early 1970s the European Communities have prepared a series of programmes which have set out in detail the objectives and policies to be implemented by the Commission and the Member States in order to ensure greater environmental protection in compliance with the fundamental principles expressed in the texts of the founding treaties.

From the analysis of these multi-year programmes, it is clear how the issue of internal integration, and more precisely of an integrated approach to pollution control, only appeared on the Community landscape of environmental policy from the 1980s with the third programme of 1983, and even then still weakly. Among the various areas in which, according to the third programme, Community actions are to be carried out, it is indicated in letter c) that the reduction of pollution and harmful effects should happen, possibly at the source, within a setting such as to avoid the transfer of pollution from one media to another.[98] Thus, in the European context, the issue concerning the fragmented structure of environmental regulation is formally formulated; that is, it highlights the so-called *media-shifting phenomenon*. The Action Plan clarifies in this regard that the Commission will give

98 Resolution of the Council of the European Communities and of the Representatives of the Governments of the Member States, Meeting within the Council of 7 February 1983 on the Continuation and Implementation of a European Community Policy and Action Programme on the Environment (1982–1986), Letter C of the preamble.

particular importance to the coordination of actions. To this end, the Commission will study, among other things, how to regulate all the discharges that can damage different environments in order to avoid any possible pollution transfer resulting from partial measurements.[99] The awareness of the limits of a purely sectorial approach to pollution control tools is even clearer in the subsequent 1987 programme, in which self-criticism is made of the previous way of managing environmental problems: "the tendency has been to concentrate on pollution problems as these arise in the different media: air, water, soil has predominated" and

> it is at least arguable that a sector by sector approach to pollution problems is not necessarily the most economically efficient solution, i.e. it does not necessarily achieve the maximum pollution reduction (taking all media into consideration) for a given economic cost.[100]

Furthermore, the Council of the European Communities opens up the possibility of resorting to a different approach, with "the aim … to determine whether any rationale can be worked out which would provide useful guidance as to the preferred approaches to be adopted in future Community legislation".[101] This objective outlined in the fourth programme starts with the exploitation of an approach based on the consideration of the pollution sources, which is "aimed at individual industries or target groups of industries, and covering all discharges to air, land, or water and including the generation of solid as well as liquid or gaseous wastes"; an approach which, in the specific field of chemical treatment, is finally qualified by the expression "integrated approach".

> An integrated substance-oriented approach to chemicals will: take account of the occurrence of a particular substance from whatever source; proceed towards an integrated risk assessment, which takes into account the different routes through which people and the environment are exposed; lead to choices regarding the most effective and efficient solution to the problems caused.[102]

Hence, starting from these first statements, the issue of overcoming a sectorial approach to environmental problems has acquired ever-greater importance within the Community's policy objectives and has begun to manifest itself also in concrete normative provisions, within some directives as well as various environmental programmes.

99 Id. point 15.
100 Resolution of the Council of the European Communities and of the Representatives of the Governments of the Member States, Meeting within the Council of 19 October 1987 on the Continuation and Implementation of a European Community Policy and Action Programme on the Environment (1987–1992), Paragraphs 3.2.1. and 3.2.3.
101 Id. Paragraph 3.6.2.
102 Id. Paragraphs 3.4.2. and 3.3.3.

Although over the years several regulations containing aspects of an integrated approach have been introduced, there are in particular three directives that mark the emergence of this new way of conceiving environmental protection in the European legal system, which, as have I tried to show previously, is not only characterised with a multi-sector approach to the issue of polluting emissions but also extends to other numerous aspects and issues.

The first is EIA Directive (85/337/EEC) which entered into force in 1985 followed by IPPC Directive (96/61/EC) and the Seveso II Directive (96/82/EC), both of 1996.[103] The EIA Directive introduces physical measures to allow the principle of unity to become part of the integrated approach.[104] Also, it is the Directive that introduces for the first time the instrument of Environmental Impact Assessment (EIA), which will become a key element whenever the realization of given public or private projects are at stake.[105] While not expressing the terms "integration" or "environment as a whole" in the text, the Directive is clearly based on a holistic approach to environmental protection, as can be seen from Article 3, which requires the "inter-action between factors", such as human beings, fauna and flora, soil, water, air, climate and the landscape, material assets and the cultural heritage.[106] The concept of "interaction between factors", even if not specified by the Directive, clearly implies that the environment must be seen as a system of different elements.[107]

Similarly, the Seveso II Directive, although also not specifically using the term "integrated approach", provides in Article 1 that its purpose is "the prevention of major accidents which involve dangerous substances, and the limitation of their consequences for man and the environment, with a view to ensuring high levels of protection throughout the Community in a consistent and effective manner".[108] In this sense, this Directive betrays its holistic approach when it comes to the problem of major accidents, as is the case in many other provisions. For example, Article 7, Paragraph 1: "The major-accident prevention policy established by the operator shall be designed to guarantee a high level of protection for man and the

103 Respectively, Council Directive 85/337/EEC of 27 June 1985 on the Assessment of the Effects of Certain Public and Private Projects on the Environment; Council Directive 96/61/EC of 24 September 1996 Concerning Integrated Pollution Prevention and Control; Council Directive 96/82/EC of 9 December 1996 on the Control of Major Accident Hazards Involving Dangerous Substances (Seveso II).

104 The first time in which EIA was introduced dates back to 31 December 1969 when the USA Congress approved the National Environmental Policy Act (NEPA), through which it imposed a pre-assessment of the possible negative effects on the ecosystem deriving from the realization of projects. See Eberhard Bohne, *The Quest for Environmental Regulatory Integration in the European Union: Integrated Pollution Prevention and Control, Environment Impact Assessment and Major Accident Prevention* (Kluwer Law International, 2006), 15–60.

105 Id. 55.

106 Council Directive 85/337/EEC of 27 June 1985 on the Assessment of the Effects of Certain Public and Private Projects on the Environment, Article 3.

107 Eberhard Bohne, *The Quest for Environmental Regulatory Integration*, 26–45.

108 Council Directive 96/82/EC, Article 1.

environment by appropriate means, structures and management systems" or Article 9, Paragraph 1(a), sets out that the operator is required to produce a safety report "demonstrating that a major-accident prevention policy and a safety management system for implementing it have been put into effect [in accordance with the information set out in Annex III]".[109] As argued by Vardi,

> The importance of European environmental policy has grown in a pattern that followed the growth of the European Community, from its origins as a pure economic market, to its present status as a Union involved in different policies. What is particularly interesting to observe is how the European Union (at the time the European Economic Community) implemented several legislative measures concerning the environment even in the absence of explicit powers to do so.[110]

In the recent history of the evolution of environmental legislation a primary role must however be recognized as belonging to Directive 96/61/EC (Integrated Pollution Prevention and Control) – known as the IPPC Directive – concerning the integrated prevention and control of pollution caused by certain categories of industrial plants and agricultural activities. This regulatory intervention has highlighted in many respects an acceptance of the radical change in the way of dealing with environmental issues that, as argued previously, has characterized the European law of recent years; i.e. a paradigm shift from considering all environmental media as separate entities to regarding them as integrated with each other and thus seeing the environment as a whole. It is in fact only with the IPPC Directive, as stated in the following paragraphs, that an environmental regulation system was set up, and in which all the qualifying elements of what can be considered a true example of an integrated approach to pollution are present.

1.5.2 The IPPC Directive and the integrated approach

The achievement of a directive expressly formulated to guarantee an integrated approach to the problem of polluting emissions was not immediate. Indeed, it took several years, after this need was first declared in the IV Action Programme of the European Communities as an important objective to be met.

The beginning of the Commission's work in this direction dates back to 1991, and began to materialize only in September 1993 with the presentation of a proposal for a directive that preceded its adoption in its final formulation of 1996.[111] The Directive on Integrated Pollution Control constitutes precisely, as already anticipated, the first attempt at the European level to achieve what is called a holistic approach to the matter of emissions harmful to the environment, thus

109 Id. Articles 7 and 9.

110 Noah Vardi and Vincenzo Zeno-Zencovich, "From Rome to Nice: A Historical Profile of the Evolution of European Environmental Law," *Environmental Law Review* 1 (4) (2004), 219.

111 See the Proposal of Council Directive COM(93) 423 def. on the Integrated Pollution Prevention and Reduction of 17 November 1993.

considering the phenomenon of pollution in its complexity and facing it from all points of view across the board.

The novelty represented by the IPPC Directive in the field of environmental regulation is also underlined by North American studies which, in analysing the characteristics and limits of the US discipline, look at Europe as an example of the application of a necessary integrated approach to the subject of pollution, considered a tool "more effective in protecting environmental quality".[112]

In contrast with past/traditional laws and regulations on pollution – which were focused on the removal of already formed contaminants from a stream of air, water, waste and products in general (i.e. at the end of the production cycle, also defined as end-of-line/end-of-pipe/command and control methods) – the Integrated Pollution Prevention and Control (IPPC) Directive presents, as already clear from its name, two elements of particular interest. On the one hand, there is the objective of emission prevention, which goes alongside that of their reduction; on the other hand, there is the fact that both goals are pursued in an integrated way. Considering the first aspect, it can be observed that the objective of preventing the phenomenon of pollution is already in itself an important factor, as it marks the detachment from the traditional method of environmental protection based on the ex-post reduction of emissions. This is the so-called "end-of-pipe" or "end-of-cycle" model, which intervenes on the treatment of pollution only after it has been produced, thus acting downstream of the production process and limiting itself to imposing the adoption of measures for the abatement of emissions. On the contrary, the Directive envisages that the problem of pollution should be dealt with starting from the polluting source and throughout the production process, immediately imposing the adoption of those measures proven necessary to reduce the formation of harmful emissions. Moreover, this commitment aimed at prevention is the concrete transposition – in the regulation of polluting emissions – of two general principles of environmental protection: the principle of prevention and that for which "the polluter pays".[113]

The second aspect, which constitutes the qualifying factor of the entire IPPC Directive, is the adoption of an integrated approach; the weight given to it in the provisions of the Directive is evidenced by the numerous "whereas" clauses. Among several, it is worth mentioning the third, which states that "the implementation of an integrated approach to reduce pollution requires action at Community level in order to modify and supplement existing Community legislation concerning the prevention and control of pollution from industrial plants". The eighth clarifies that "the objective of an integrated approach to pollution control is to prevent emissions into air, water or soil wherever this is practicable, taking into account waste management, and, where it is not, to minimize them in order to achieve a high level of protection for the environment as a whole." Though not using the expression "integrated approach", the fifteenth "whereas" also implies

112 Clarence Davies and Jan Mazurek, *Pollution Control in the United States: Evaluating the System (Resources for the Future)* (Washington, D.C.: Routledge, 1998), 17.
113 Eberhard Bohne, *The Quest for Environmental Regulatory Integration*, 23–26.

such a concept when it refers to "the competent authority or authorities will grant or amend a permit only when integrated environmental protection measures for air, water and land have been laid down".[114]

Integration, then, is considered as a fundamental modality in view of the achievement of one of the guiding principles of the whole European environmental policy, namely the principle of sustainable development. The second "whereas" of the Directive acts as a reminder that the European policy "accords priority to integrated pollution control as an important part of the move towards a more sustainable balance between human activity and socio-economic development, on the one hand, and the resources and regenerative capacity of nature, on the other"; in this respect, also the ninth "whereas" underlines that "application of the principle of sustainable development will be promoted by an integrated approach to pollution control".[115]

This integrated approach, which is expected to characterize both the prevention and the reduction of emissions, is not however identifiable in a specific measure of the Directive, but it manifests itself in different ways which, as discussed above, can be identified within the general concept of integration. In fact, though the Directive does not provide for any overall specification of the "integrated approach", it is possible to identify and grasp its characteristics in the individual legislative provisions of the Directive. As for the reduction of emissions, the Directive determines the substantial overcoming of the sectorial approach by accepting instead an approach that is in line with the *principle of unity* of the environment. In fact, while in the past the control of emissions occurred with reference to every single media of diffusion of polluting substances (in particular air and water), according to the new approach, the Directive affirms the necessity to carry out this control with reference to all media, simultaneously and in a single organic evaluation, in order to avoid the media-shifting phenomenon.

As argued by Faure and Lefevere,

> a classic problem with a non-integrated pollution control system is that it does not take into account the possible interchangeability of emissions. Because of the – in practice – very fragmented and sectorial pollution control, once environmental regulation is established in one sector, one can often see a shifting of the pollution to other, less controlled or regulated sectors.[116]

This is expressed clearly by the seventh "whereas" clause which specifies the problem to be faced by highlighting that "different approaches to controlling emissions into the air, water or soil separately may encourage the shifting of pollution between the various environmental media rather than protecting the environment

114 Council Directive 96/82/EC, Preamble, "Whereas" n. 3, 8, 15.

115 Id. "Whereas" n. 2 and 9.

116 Michael Faure and Jurgen Lefevere, "The Draft Directive on Integrated Pollution Prevention and Control: An Economic Perspective," *European Environmental Law Review* 4 (1996), 113.

as a whole"; on the other hand, "whereas" n. 14 declares a solution to such an issue by pointing out that the "full coordination of the authorization procedure and conditions between competent authorities will make it possible to achieve the highest practicable level of protection for the environment as a whole".[117]

The premises contained in the "whereas" clauses are then developed in the provisions of the Directive, which in different Articles refers to the aspects examined. In this respect, it is worth focusing, for example, on Article 8 which provides, inter alia, that "All permits granted and modified permits must include details of the arrangements made for air, water and land protection as referred to in this Directive"; or on Article 9, Paragraph 3, according to which

> the permit shall include emission limit values for pollutants, in particular, those listed in Annex III, likely to be emitted from the installation concerned in significant quantities, having regard to their nature and their potential to transfer pollution from one medium to another (water, air and land).[118]

Moreover, it is necessary to underline that Article 7 of the IPPC Directive generally establishes that

> Member States shall take the measures necessary to ensure that the conditions of, and procedure for the grant of, the permit are fully coordinated where more than one competent authority is involved, in order to guarantee an effective integrated approach by all authorities competent for this procedure.[119]

By not specifying whether or not a single permit is required to be subjected to the polluting activity, the provision leaves the decision of how to define the authorization procedure to the individual Member States.

> As long as full coordination is achieved, the requirements of the IPPC Directive may be met through the joint effect of different permits, rather than just a single authorization. Even though, the requirements for permit applications are written in the singular form, Member States must ensure an application: hence, this could be understood as creating a requirement for single, integrated applications, even if separate bodies carry out different authorisation tasks.[120]

The precise way in which to obtain an integrated approach and to identify the conditions to which the permit must be submitted is not explicit. The IPPC Directive can thus be satisfied with different degrees of intensity, from simple forms of coordination to more incisive forms of procedural concentration. The

117 Council Directive 96/82/EC, Preamble, "Whereas" n. 7 and 14.
118 Council Directive 96/82/EC, Articles 8 and 9 (Paragraph 3).
119 Id. Article 7.
120 Neil Emmott and Nigel Haigh, "Integrated Pollution Prevention and Control: UK and EC Approaches and Possible Next Steps," *Journal of Environmental Law* 8 (2) (1996): 307.

measure through which the Directive proposes to achieve a unitary evaluation of the various environmental media is therefore entrusted to a procedural solution, through which the above-mentioned formal (or procedural) integration can be achieved. If considered in the perspective of prevention, the integrated approach not only leads to overcoming the problem referred to above as media shifting, but it also leads to significant changes in the way we deal with environmental problems. This strict relation between the integrated approach and prevention is underlined in the doctrine as follows: "Prevention for stationary pollution sources usually involves changes in plant process rather than end-of-pipe solutions, and such process changes would be much feasible under an integrated approach".[121]

This aspect clearly emerges from the type of requirements identified by the Directive and the competent authority (or authorities) that must be taken into account in order to issue the permit. Indeed, the latter must contain, in particular, the emission limit values set for the pollutants that may be emitted in significant quantities from a given plant. Article 6 stipulates that there are several specific pieces of information and data – including the description of the raw and secondary materials, substances and energy used or produced and the conditions of the site where the plant is located – that need to be provided by the plant operator to the competent authority. All these elements must be taken into account before the environmental permit is issued. Also, these indications concern aspects that are normally overlooked by a sectorial and "end-of-cycle" approach, typical of the regulations existing before the Directive, and demonstrate the variety and relevance of the factors that the administration is called upon to evaluate.[122] Furthermore, Article 9, Paragraph 4, entitled "conditions of authorization", establishes that the emission limit values defined by the permit "shall be based on the best available techniques, without prescribing the use of any technique or specific technology, but taking into account the technical characteristics of the installation concerned, its geographical location and the local environmental conditions".[123] The provision refers to the concept of "best available techniques" (BATs) which, following Article 2 of the Directive, is defined as

> the most effective and advanced stage in the development of activities and their methods of operation which indicate the practical suitability of particular techniques for providing in principle the basis for emission limit values designed to prevent and, where that is not practicable, generally to reduce emissions and the impact on the environment as a whole.[124]

The setting of the limit values, in which a good part of the operating conditions of the authorized system is realized, is therefore based, on one hand, on the

121 The strict link between the prevention and integrated approach is highlighted also in the doctrine, see for example Clarence Davies and Jan Mazurek, *Pollution Control in the United States*: 17.

122 Council Directive 96/82/EC, Article 6.

123 Id. Article 9 (Paragraph 4).

124 Id. Article 2.

identification of the BAT – namely a technological parameter suitable to reduce emissions and the impact on the environment, considered as a whole, and, on the other hand, on the consideration of the particular technical and geographical conditions in which the polluting plant to be authorized is placed, essentially embodying, for both these aspects, the spirit of the integrated approach.

The assessment of environmental compatibility, set out by the IPPC Directive as a requirement to issue the authorization to carry out certain polluting activities, is therefore not limited to considering the different environmental media at the same time, but it also examines all the possible factors that contribute to determining the pollutant effect on the environment taken as a whole. Among these factors, it is worth highlighting in particular, for the innovative aspect, that of the quantity and the modality with which the energy is used in the single production process: indeed, also the ways in which energy is utilised affects the environmental performance of a certain productive activity. This leads us to a fundamental principle contained in Article 194 of the Lisbon Treaty, dedicated precisely to energy, where the first Paragraph states that

> in the context of the establishment and functioning of the internal market and with regard for the need to preserve and improve the environment, Union policy on energy shall aim, in a spirit of solidarity between Member States, to: … c) promote energy efficiency and energy saving and the development of new and renewable forms of energy.[125]

The assessment of environmental compatibility is not simply a unitary assessment; i.e. the result of a formal integration of separate administrative activities. Instead, it is a real organic assessment of the various elements to be considered. In this way, it accomplishes – in particular through the parameter of the best available technique – what can be considered a *substantial* integration. Put another way, it is possible to argue that the IPPC Directive is not satisfied with the usual forms of control, downstream of the production cycle, disjointed for types of emissions (atmospheric, water, soil, noise, waste, etc.), separately conducted, but it expands its attention to the characteristics of the industrial process, such as energy expenditure, direct and indirect consumption of natural resources and raw materials, production and recycling of waste, interaction between the various types of pollution and their overall influence on the components of the ecosystem.[126]

125 Lisbon Treaty, Title XXI, Article 194.
126 Maurizio Cafagno, *Principi e Strumenti di Tutela dell'Ambiente* (Torino: Giappichelli, 2007), 386–387.

2 The EU legislation on integrated environmental permits

Scope, regulatory instruments and application of Integrated Pollution Prevention and Control and Industrial Emission Directives

2.1 The Integrated Pollution Prevention and Control and Industrial Emission Directives

Directive 96/61/EC on Integrated Pollution Prevention and Control (the IPPC Directive) has received repeated modifications and additions over the years and was later codified in Directive 2008/1/EC (European Parliament and Council of 15 January 2008). These amendments provided a consolidation of the text of the IPPC regulations without substantially changing the original structure of the legislation.[1]

The issue of polluting emissions has undergone further and more incisive regulatory change with the adoption of the recent Directive 2010/75/EU on Industrial Emissions, known as the Industrial Emissions Directive (IED), through which the legislator put in place a so-called *recasting* in a single legal text of seven directives, all concerning the problem of emissions produced by industrial plants, which, even if referring to specific sectors, present fields of application that are sometimes contiguous and sometimes partially overlap.[2]

1 Council Directive 96/61/EC has been amended in several occasions, particularly by: Council Directive 2003/35/EC of 26 May 2003 Providing for Public Participation in Respect of the Drawing up of Certain Plans and Programmes Relating to the Environment and Amending with Regard to Public Participation and Access to justice Council Directives 85/337/EEC and 96/61/EC; Council Directive 2003/87/EC of 13 October 2003 Establishing a Scheme for Greenhouse Gas Emission Allowance Trading within the Community and Amending Council Directive 96/61/EC; EC Regulation n. 1882/2003 of 29 September 2003 Adapting to Council Decision 1999/468/EC the Provisions Relating to Committees which Assist the Commission in the Exercise of its Implementing Powers Laid Down in Instruments Subject to the Procedure Referred to in Article 251 of the EC Treaty, Annex III, (61) Concerning Article 19 of Council Directive 96/61/EC; EC Regulation n. 166/2006 of 18 January 2006 Concerning the Establishment of a European Pollutant Release and Transfer Register and Amending Council Directives 91/689/EEC and 96/61/EC.

2 The directives subject to this re-casting are, in particular, Council Directive 2008/1/EC, Council Directive 2001/80/EC on the Limitation of Emissions of Certain Pollutants into the Air from Large Combustion Plants, and Council Directives 78/176/EEC, 82/883/EEC and 92/112/EEC Concerning the Reduction of Pollution Caused by Waste from the Titanium Dioxide Industry, as well as Council Directive 1999/13/EC on Volatile Organic Components (VOCs) and Council Directive

The new IED is not just limited to accomplishing a work of reunification, rationalization and simplification of the extensive sector of EU environmental legislation in terms of pollutant emissions, but, what is more interesting, it also introduces significant changes as part of the IPPC framework, the text of which was lastly amended in Directive 2008/1/EC.[3] The "whereas" n. 46 of Directive 2010/75/EU clarifies in this regard that "The obligation to transpose this Directive into national law should be confined to those provisions which represent a substantive change as compared with the earlier Directives. The obligation to transpose the provisions which are unchanged arises under the earlier Directives".[4]

Also, the new legislation exercises its repealing effect on the IPPC rules only from 2014; that is, 3 years after its formal entry into force in 2011, thus determining the substantial and formal coexistence (albeit for a short period) of different provisions regarding the same subject. It is for this reason that during the course of this study, I decided to maintain as a main reference the consolidated body so far expressed by the IPPC Directive in its most updated version of 2008, eventually highlighting – on a case-by-case basis – the individual provisions replaced or supplemented by the 2010 IED.[5]

2.1.1 The scope of application

The purpose and scope of the IPPC Directive, concerning integrated pollution prevention and control, is to

> lay(s) down measures designed to prevent or, where that is not practicable, to reduce emissions in the air, water and land from the abovementioned activities, including measures concerning waste, in order to achieve a high level of protection of the environment taken as a whole[6];

therefore, the reduction of emissions is the key objective by which it is intended to guarantee the achievement of greater environmental protection. From the reading of some "whereas" clauses, it is possible to draw useful indicators for a better understanding of the modalities through which the Directive intends to achieve the aforementioned purposes, the extent and complexity of the measures, and the reasons for the planned intervention in the control and prevention of polluting emissions.

As far as the scope of the intervention is concerned, "whereas" n. 2 recalls the environmental principles pursued by the European Union in ex-Article 174 of the

2000/76/EC on the Incineration of Waste. Maria Lee, "The Industrial Emissions Directive," *Journal of London University College* (2012): 1–4.

3 Id. 5–8.

4 Directive 2010/75/EU, Official Journal L334/17, "whereas" n. 46.

5 At the end of this chapter and in Chapter 3, I will discuss the reasons why the EU legislator eventually amended and updated the IPPC Directive.

6 Council Directive 2008/1/EC of 15 January 2008 Concerning Integrated Pollution Prevention and Control, Official Journal L 24, Article 1.

Lisbon Treaty by affirming that the objectives and principles of the Community's environment policy consist in particular "to prevent, reduce and as far as possible eliminate pollution … giving priority to intervention at source (and) ensuring prudent management of natural resources … in compliance with the 'polluter pays' principle and the principle of pollution prevention".[7] This "whereas" holds a particular importance as it represents the only proposition of the Directive from which explicit connections can be made to the fundamental principles of the European environmental policy (already examined in Chapter 1), allowing those principles to be connected, through a causal relationship, with the goals and objectives of the entire IPPC Directive. Indeed, references to the "polluter-pays principle" and to the principle of prevention are expressed. Also, references to other principles are present, even though not necessarily in an explicit way. In particular, the principle of sustainable development is expressed through the need to "prevent, reduce and as far as possible eliminate pollution … ensuring prudent management of natural resources"; likewise, the principle of correction at the source is evoked by the clarification that every intervention must take place "first of all at the source".[8]

In addition, with regard to the concrete measures and the modalities that the Directive itself proposes to use for achieving its own objectives, the reading of other "whereas" clauses allows delineating also the elements that characterize the environmental regulation model of the IPPC Directive.

From "whereas" n. 5 emerges the choice to adopt a general discipline that imposes an authorization before an industrial plant enters into operation or is subjected to substantial changes capable of causing pollution.[9] Thus, it confirms the preference by the European legislator for an (authoritative) instrument of environmental regulation (i.e. the permit) – or, in other words, of *command and control* – rather than for solutions considered alternative and innovative, such as the so-called market-based tools, which in the last few years have also found a lot of acceptance in the environmental field (such as the market for green certificates or environmental taxes). "Whereas" n. 17 and 18 clarify, respectively, that such a "permit should include all necessary measures to fulfil the authorisation conditions in order thus to achieve a high level of protection for the environment as a whole" and that the authorization conditions consisting of "Emission limit values, parameters or equivalent technical measures should be based on the best available techniques".[10] This formulation identifies and substantially indicates the three elements that most characterize the IPPC Directive, namely: the integrated approach (to which also other "whereas" clauses refer to), herein understood as referring to the protection of the environment "as a whole"; the setting of

7 Council Directive 2010/75/EU of 24 November 2010 on Industrial Emissions (Integrated Pollution Prevention and Control), "whereas" n. 2.

8 Ibid.

9 "Whereas" n. 5 refers explicitly to Council Directive 84/360/EEC of 28 June 1984 on the Combating of Air Pollution from Industrial Plants, as the first piece of regulation which imposed the need to have a permit to run a polluting facility.

10 Council Directive 2010/75/EU, "whereas" n. 5, 17 and 18.

emission limit values (ELVs) for certain polluting substances, also a tool traditionally used in environmental protection systems inspired by the command and control model; and, finally, the criterion of the best available techniques (BATs), on the basis of which the limit values need to be identified.

Lastly, it is worth mentioning "whereas" n. 21, according to which the BATs evolve over time, above all in relation to technical progress, and it is therefore appropriate that the competent authorities follow these developments and keep up to date.[11]

In this regard, the IPPC Directive underlines the need to take into account the temporal dimension in order to be able to grasp the various changes that may affect both the pollution phenomenon and the tools to combat it. It should be added that this consideration concerning the need to constantly update the BATs conceals an implicit reference to a further aspect, already highlighted in Chapter 1 – that is, the relationship between two criteria of European policy development: technological development and the related market of clean technologies. As it can be seen from "whereas" n. 2, 5, 17, 18, and 21, an entire logical path is outlined – which may also suggest the order to be followed in the reconstruction of the Directive.

The present chapter is therefore structured following this path. Hence, it will initially focus on the permits and their recipients – identifying their scope of application and subject – and then focus on the phases and the steps that lead to the issue of a permit. Indeed, they represent a key stage: the identification of the BATs and of the consequent setting of the ELVs for a single authorized installation.

2.1.2 The steps of application

As mentioned above, the IED has carried out the work of recasting several previous directives in a single text. Hence, it is organized as follows: Chapter I is dedicated to some brief common provisions (including those first relating to the subject and scope of the whole Directive) and then in Chapters II to VI the provisions relating to those already contained in the previous directives are merged. In other words, identification of the scope of application of the regulation concerning the pollutant emissions produced by production plants can no longer be found in a single provision. For example, the initial information about the subject and the scope of application of the whole Directive, offered by Articles 1 and 2 (in Chapter I), needs to be integrated with the more detailed specification provided by Article 10 (i.e. the first Article of Chapter II), dedicated to the subject previously stated in the IPPC Directive.

Regarding the subject matter, Article 1, Paragraph 1 of the IED provides that "This Directive lays down rules on integrated prevention and control of pollution arising from industrial activities" and then clarifies that the final aim of the contained norms is to

11 Id. "whereas" n. 21.

> lay(s) down rules designed to prevent or, where that is not practicable, to reduce emissions into air, water and land and to prevent the generation of waste, in order to achieve a high level of protection of the environment taken as a whole.[12]

The wording thus proposed in Article 1 is not substantially novel, and more or less re-proposes the text of Article 1 of the IPPC Directive in the 2008 version (Directive 2008/1/EC). That said, the very fact that integrated prevention and reduction of pollution is now the first rule of the "common provisions" emphasizes the importance it has acquired; it is no longer a provision referred to exclusively in the IPPC Directive but also in all the different regulations now merged into the text of the IED. In this sense, the integrated approach promoted by the IPPC Directive could acquire the character of a general statement or reference principle in the panorama of anti-pollution provisions dedicated to production activities. However, it would be still too early to say whether this statement – more general in scope and valid for the different parts of the Directive – would be actually followed by a change in approach in the individual sectors. For example, a central element in the integrated approach promoted by the IPPC framework, i.e. the use of the BATs as a benchmark for setting ELVs, to which the granting of an environmental permit is subject to, does not seem to be repeated in the other provisions relating to specific sectors of different polluting activities.

As far as the scope of the Directive is concerned, Article 2, Paragraph 1 simply states that "This Directive shall apply to the industrial activities giving rise to pollution referred to in Chapters II to VI", and therefore refers specifically to the single issues addressed in such Chapters and, as far as this study is concerned, to Article 10 (which is the first Article of Chapter II), where it is stated that "This Chapter shall apply to the activities set out in Annex I and, where applicable, reaching the capacity thresholds set out in that Annex". As an example, Point 1 of Annex I clarifies the criteria on the basis of which threshold values are given and beyond which a polluting activity falls under the IPPC Directive. In particular these refer to ***production capacities*** or ***outputs***. "Where several activities falling under the same activity description containing a threshold are operated in the same installation, the capacities of such activities are added together". Put another way, as already foreseen by the IPPC Directive – both in its 1996 and 2008 versions – the document contains a list of threshold limits for polluting activities divided by type for installations specified by their production capacities or outputs, which can then be combined to give an overall level.[13]

The various activities that are subject to the application of the Directive are divided into six main sectors, which in turn are divided into more specific subcategories. These sectors are: 1. Energy Industries; 2. Production and Processing of Metals; 3. Mineral Industry; 4. Chemical Industry; 5. Waste Management; and 6. Other Activities. With reference to 'Other Activities' it is useful to highlight that

12 Council Directive 2010/75/EU, Article 1, Paragraph 1.
13 Council Directive 2010/75/EU, Article 2 (Paragraph 1), Article 10, Annex I.

among the sub-categories considered is the inclusion of the intensive rearing of poultry or pigs; something which would hardly seem attributable to the subject matter of the Directive, i.e. industrial activities. However, this is because farms have always been part of the nomenclature of the French *installations classées*, which – as shown in Chapter 1 – was one of the national environmental regulations that had already presented innovative features in the approach to polluting emissions prior to the IPPC Directive.[14]

Regarding the scope of the Directive, Article 2, Paragraph 2 sets an important demarcation by stating that the Directive "shall not apply to research activities, development activities or the testing of new products and processes". Also, in this respect, the scope of the legislation remains substantially unchanged despite all the amendments made over the years on the IPPC Directive. What has changed is the formulation adopted, in that results – as mentioned – are now divided into several Articles. Moreover, this reference to the plants for the production of new products and processes is now inserted directly in the text of Article 2 instead of being part of Annex I as in the previous versions. Taking both these points into consideration, it is possible to argue that both those plants that are destined for the research and development of new products/processes (regardless of the level of pollution produced) and the plants that do not reach "significant" production levels and yield, are not subjected to the IED (as well as the IPPC).[15]

These exclusions are perfectly consistent with some of the objectives that the EU environmental policy aims to achieve (as seen in Chapter 1), and of which the Directive is a faithful expression. On the one hand, there is the goal of not limiting innovation or technological development and all the activities that aim to achieve such innovation/technological development. As already highlighted, these factors are considered fundamental for the economic and social development of the Union. Indeed, including plants destined for the development of new products and processes under anti-pollution legislation that aims to prevent and reduce emissions harmful to the environment would risk directly undermining this type of activity and with it the positive effects that may derive from it. On the other hand, for the same reason, there is a need not to burden economic activities with excessive costs due to the adoption of measures to prevent and reduce pollution. It is in consideration of this (and not only for the evidently less polluting impact they exert) that the Directive is not applied to production facilities with reduced yield, for which it would be difficult to sustain the costs related to the technologies required by the parameter of the BAT, and which would therefore be strongly conditioned and limited, with the consequence that the Directive would end up negatively affecting the achievement of an adequate level of development in the overall well-being of the production system.[16]

14 Ibid.
15 Id. Article 2, Paragraph 2.
16 Charalampos Koutalakis, Aron Buzogany and Tanja Borzel, "When Soft Regulation Is Not Enough: The Integrated Pollution Prevention and Control Directive of the European Union," *Regulation and Governance* 4 (3) (2010): 329–333.

Therefore, the economic factor plays a direct role from the moment in which the field of application of the Directive is defined, thus orienting, from the beginning, all the legislation towards the protection of the economic initiative, according to the specific approach of the sustainable development principle. Such a principle, as already underlined in the first chapter, does not subordinate economic development to the needs of environmental protection, which in no case can be considered to have an absolute value, and instead always have a conditional and therefore relative value.

Hence, in order to obtain a correct and complete identification of the area of intervention of the integrated prevention of pollutant emissions in relation to production activities, it is necessary to refer to other provisions which, although not formally aimed at delimiting the applicative scope of the legislation, end up affecting it, above all with regard to the moment of its actual application. I refer in particular to the distinction made by the Directive between existing plants, new plants and substantial modifications.

Under Directive 2008/1/EC the "existing plant" was defined as the installation which, as of 30 October 1999 and under the legislation in force before that date, was in operation or authorized or had been the subject of a request for full authorization by the competent authority, and provided that it then entered into service no later than 30 October 2000. The legislation thus distinguished, in Articles 4 and 5 respectively, between the authorization of new plants and the conditions for the authorization of existing plants, for which in particular it set the deadline for adaptation to the requirements of the Directive as of 30 October 2007.[17] The new IED regulation no longer presents this distinction, limiting itself to regulating, in Article 5, the granting of a permit in the case of new plants or of substantial modification of plants already completed. This is because at the time the IED came into force[18] all plants defined as "existing" under Directive 2008/1/EC should have already obtained an authorization whose content met the regulatory requirements. The current legislation, therefore, only foresees two types of plants (now called "installations"): the "new plants" and the "[existing] plants subject to substantial changes". According to the definition given in Article 3, Paragraph 9, a "substantial change" means "a change in the nature or functioning, or an extension, of an installation … or … plant which may have significant negative effects on human health or the environment".[19]

Again, with regard to the modification of installations by the operators, Article 20, Paragraph 3 clarifies that changes concerning the nature, or operation or extension of the installation are considered substantial if the modifications or extensions in themselves reach the thresholds foreseen in Annex I. This case is thus noticeably equivalent to the authorization of a newly constructed plant, as can be seen from the reference to the current legislation on environmental impact

17 Council Directive 2008/1/EC, Articles 4 and 5.

18 Council Directive 2010/75/EU entered into force on 7 January 2011, but the deadline for its implementation by EU Member States is 7 January 2013.

19 Council Directive 2010/75/EU, Article 3 (Paragraph 9) and Article 5.

assessment. The reference to such legislation is in fact explained since in both the hypothesis of the opening of new plants (which therefore require the issue of an environmental permit for their operation) and in that of substantial modification of an existing plant, the realization of the work may fall – at the same time – under the scope of the legislation aimed at requiring an assessment of its environmental impact.[20]

Hence, this aspect of the IPPC Directive, which I have focused on here, is significant, since it contributes to further outline the concrete scope of application of the legislation. From the time of its entry into force, the legislation became operational not only for the years to come, i.e. for plants still to be built, but also for all the already existing plants which, at that time and at that stage, were numerous and thus had to be considered as the main subject of the Directive.

Currently, its fundamental role is to foresee and regulate the possible substantial modification of the plants in conjunction with the dynamic and evolutionary nature of the pollution phenomenon. As it will be examined later in this study, substantial modification constitutes in fact a possible element in need of revision to achieve the conditions of authorization for the management of the polluting activity. In addition, such a revision hides, to a different extent, the wish to ensure the maximum possible application of the provisions aimed at preventing or reducing the polluting emissions of production activities, while meeting the needs of the economic initiative. Indeed, the latter naturally tend towards an ever increasing development in the economic performances of the plants, which may therefore require an increase in production capacity or a change in the structure of the plant.

The importance of these provisions on the concrete determination of the scope of application of the legislation was very clear in the first case of transposing the IPPC Directive in Italy. Instead of being carried out in a unitary way, this process occurred in two distinct phases, which were completed a few years apart, precisely following the distinction between existing plants and new plants.[21] In fact, the text of Article 21 of the IPPC Directive 96/61/EC gave the deadline of 30 October 1999 for transposition by the Member States; a term formally respected by Italy with the enactment of the Legislative Decree n. 372 of 4 August 1999.[22] Indeed, the decree originally provided for a scope of application limited to existing plants only, whereas the regulation concerning new plants was postponed with the aim of incorporating, via integration, the provisions relating to the new Directive on environmental impact assessment 97/11/EC and those related to the IPPC Directive for the part concerning new installations.[23]

20 Id. Article 20.

21 Teodora Marocco, "La Direttiva IPPC e il suo Recepimento in Italia," *Rivista Giuridica dell'Ambiente* 1 (2004): 35–45.

22 Council Directive 96/61/EC, Article 21.

23 Mario Medugno, "Il recepimento da parte dell'Italia della direttiva 96/61 (c.d. IPPC)," *Rivista Giuridica dell'Ambiente* (2001): 1100–1101; Massimo Gori, "Attuata la direttiva sulla prevenzione e riduzione integrate dell'inquinamento," *Rivista Giuridica dell'Ambiente* (1999): 1127.

Only with the adoption of Legislative Decree n. 59 of 18 February 2005, which repeals Decree n. 372 and extends the regulations to the newly-built plants, was the process of transposing the IPPC Directive in Italy completed.[24] Currently, following the intervention of Legislative Decree n. 128 of 29 June 2010, the Directive in question was merged into the so-called "Consolidated Law on Environment" (TUA), which now includes a dedicated title 111-bis, thus providing for the first time an integrated and coordinated version of the various environmental regulations in force in the Italian legal system.[25] The application of the IPPC (and IED) Directive in Italy will be the subject of Chapter 3 of the present study, which will analyse the Italian legislation on permits by focusing on their releases and management procedures, ultimately identifying the key legal principles of permitting in Italy.

2.1.3 The rise of 'best available technologies' and 'best available techniques' (BATs)

The regulatory model foreseen by the IPPC Directive is based on the issuing of a permit that imposes ELVs on individual plants, with reference to specific polluting substances. Such values are not pre-determined at a regulatory level, as had been usually the case in previous environmental regulations, but are established on a case-by-case basis, starting with the identification and application of BATs and taking into consideration the technical characteristics of the specific plant and the environment in which it is located. Alongside these requirements, more generally the model also encompasses the possibility of imposing all the measures necessary to minimize pollution over long distances (see the so-called cross-border pollution), and ensuring a high level of protection of the environment as a whole (see Article 9, Paragraph 4, Directive 2008/1/EU). If the aforementioned essential elements are considered individually, i.e. the setting of ELVs, the use of the BATs and the local conditions of the authorized plant, they do not reflect, as it will be discussed shortly, anything new in environmental regulation. Rather, it is in the particular combination of those same elements within the Directive in which one must look for the peculiar characteristics of this piece of regulation. Indeed, it is not so much the tools that make the IPPC Directive innovative, but instead the (integrated) way in which they are used. Put another way, what makes the real difference in the EU regulation on permits is the integrated approach to environmental protection.[26]

Before the advent of the IPPC Directive, at the European level two main positions on environmental regulation competed with each other to influence EU environmental legislation. The first is normally defined as "technical or emission-

24 Mario Medugno, "Il recepimento da parte dell'Italia": 1101.

25 Ibid.

26 Gertrude Lubbe Wolff, "Efficient Environmental Legislation. Different Philosophies of Pollution Control in Europe," *Journal of Environmental Law* 13 (1) (2001): 79–87; Council Directive 2008/1/EU, Article 9, Paragraph 4.

oriented", and it is known as the German approach; the other is called "quality or emission-oriented", and it is known as an English approach.[27] The first establishes the imposition of binding emission standards with rules that specify the amount of polluting substances that can be released into the environment by a given installation: therefore it sets a level that cannot be exceeded (namely, the so-called emission limit values – ELVs) and in some cases it also specifies a single technology to be adopted to reduce pollution. The second approach implies the adoption of qualitative standards aimed at establishing the quality of the environmental receptor in which the polluting emissions are released, establishing for this purpose the maximum concentration levels of the polluting substance taken into consideration and including a case-by-case determination of the emission values allowed for the individual plant. Both approaches have limitations.

On the one hand, the setting of limit values for the individual sources of pollution – at first glance an effective and easy-to-apply solution – proved over time to be excessively rigid and unable to adapt to the everchanging environmental conditions such as the presence of additional sources of pollution that cannot be taken into account. Indeed, the problem was that the sum of emissions from several authorized plants could as a whole be harmful to the environment. Also, this rigidity did not allow for a progressive reduction of emissions and was not compatible with the objective of prevention, failing to trigger in this sense an incentive function for the development and application of new and more efficient anti-pollution technologies. As argued by Faure:

> specification standards may become obsolete very rapidly; they also give no incentive for technological innovation since all the licensee has to do is to comply with the prescribed specification. In addition specification standards may have important anti-competitive effects, in fact providing a monopoly to the producer of the prescribed technology.[28]

On the other hand, the use of qualitative standards favours an overall assessment of the level of pollution in a given environmental context, without burdening operators with specific limits or particular technologies. In this respect, it is more flexible and can encourage the development of different technological solutions. However, this second orientation is characterized by the difficulties faced by the administration in determining the emission levels of the individual plants in relation to their compliance with the environmental standards. Indeed, in this case, an opposite problem arises compared with that of ELVs: once the overall environmental quality level has been established, difficulties arise in identifying the limit values to which a new plant, being constructed in the same area of reference,

27 Id. 82–84.

28 Michael Faure, "Optimal Specificity in Environmental Standard-Setting," in *Critical Issues in Environmental Taxation, International and Comparative Perspectives*, Vol. VIII, eds. C. Dias Soares, J.E. Milne, H. Aschiabor, L. Kreiser, K. Deketelaere (Oxford: Oxford University Press, 2010), 735.

needs to respect. In fact, the risk is that such new plants could be subjected to much stricter conditions than those imposed on the plants that have already been authorized. Moreover, because this second approach limits the measurement of environmental quality to that in the immediate vicinity of the source of pollution, it does not take into account those emissions that are pushed or dispersed elsewhere (e.g. in the atmosphere by winds or in water bodies by currents) and which could result in the overall level of pollution being higher than set by the standard itself.[29]

It should be considered that another element constituting the regulatory model set by the IPPC Directive – the use of the BAT – is not in itself an entirely new concept in European environmental legislation: the benchmark, initially referred to as the Best Available Technology (as well as its German counterpart named Stand der Technik[30] or state of the art), initially found acceptance in the American and English systems[31] and later became more widespread and popular in European environmental protection regulations, mainly – but not exclusively – in the field of atmospheric emissions.[32]

Furthermore, prior to the IPPC regulation, there were directives that referred directly to the concept of BAT and linked it to the issuing of environmental permits. For instance, Directive 84/360/EEC of 28 June 1984 on the Combating of Air Pollution from Industrial Plants, states in its Article 4, Paragraph 1, that a permit may be issued only when it is possible to ensure that "all appropriate preventive measures against air pollution have been taken, including the application

29 Id. 735–736.

30 An analysis of the German regulation on air pollution based on the Stand der Technik is provided by David Currie, "Air Pollution Control in West Germany," *University of Chicago Law Review* 49 (1982): 355–393.

31 As regards the English system, it is possible to encounter the concept of "best available technology" as far back as the Environmental Protection Act of 1990 that explicitly refers to BATNEEC (Best Available Technology Not Entailing Excessive Cost), which relates to the recommendation of the Royal Commission of 1976 on the possibility to adopt the concept of Best Practicable Environmental Option (BPEO), indeed very similar to the BAT concept; see John Gray, Tim James and John Dickson, "Integrated Regulation": 69–70. As regards the American system, the Clean Air Act foresees, following the amendments of 1976, a Reasonably Achievable Control Technology (RACT), which evolved after the update of 1990 into the formula "Best Available Control Technology", defined as "an emission limitation based on the maximum degree of reduction of each pollutant subject to regulation under this chapter emitted from or which results from any major emitting facility, which the permitting authority, on a case-by-case basis, taking into account energy, environmental, and economic impacts and other costs, determines is achievable for such facility through application of production processes and available methods, system, and techniques, including fuel cleaning, clean fuels, or treatment or innovative fuel combustion techniques for control of each such pollutant"; see Clean Air Act section 169(3), 42 U.S.C. §7479(3).

32 Council Directive 76/464/EEC of 4 May 1976 on Pollution Caused by Certain Dangerous Substances Discharged into the Aquatic Environment of the Community. At Article 6 it declares "The limit values applicable to the substances within List I shall be laid down mainly on the basis of: toxicity, persistence, bioaccumulation, taking into account the best technical means available".

of the best available technology, provided that the application of such measures does not entail excessive costs"[33]; such a reference then also recurs in other provisions, such as Articles 8, 12 and 13 of the same Directive.[34]

Also, Council Directive 88/609/EEC of 24 November 1988 (On the Limitation of Emissions of Certain Pollutants into the Air from Large Combustion Plants) in Article 6 provides that

> Member States may authorize plants burning indigenous lignite to exceed the emission limit values fixed in accordance with Article 4 if, notwithstanding the application of best available technology not entailing excessive costs, major difficulties connected with the nature of the lignite so require and provided that lignite is an essential source of fuel for the plants.

Additionally, Council Directive 89/369/EEC of 8 June 1989 on the Prevention of Air Pollution from New Municipal Waste Incineration Plants, provides in Article 3, Paragraph 4, that

> The competent authorities shall lay down emission limit values for pollutants other than those mentioned in paragraph 1 when they consider this to be appropriate because of the composition of the waste to be incinerated and of the characteristics of the incineration plant. For the purposes of laying down these emission limit values, the authorities shall take account of the potential harmful effects of the pollutants in question on human health and the environment and of the best available technology not entailing excessive costs. In particular, the competent authorities may fix emission limit values for dioxins and furans until such time as a Community directive concerning this specific question is adopted.[35]

Finally, the BAT concept is also recalled by the Council Regulation (EEC) n. 1836/93 of 29 June 1993 allowing voluntary participation by companies in the industrial sector in a Community eco-management and audit scheme, through its Article 3, letter a), where the company is required to "provide … with a view to reducing environmental impacts to levels not exceeding those corresponding to economically viable application of best available technology".[36]

It is worth emphasizing too that in all the aforementioned regulations, prior to the IPPC Directive, a definition of what is a "best available technology" is lacking. In other words, such a concept is only mentioned in the various provisions, without allowing the reader to able to clearly ascertain its significance and scope.

33 Council Directive 84/360/EEC, "whereas" n. 13.

34 See Council Directive 87/217/EEC of 19 March 1987 on the Prevention and Reduction of Environmental Pollution by Asbestos. At Article 3 it recalls the above mentioned provisions of Council Directive 84/360/EEC.

35 See Council Directive 89/429/EEC of 21 June 1989 on the Prevention on Air Pollution from Existing Municipal Waste Incineration Plants, Article 3.

36 Council Regulation EEC n. 1836/93 of 29 June 1993, Article 3, letter a).

Secondly, it is important to observe that there is no close connection between BATs and ELVs; this is particularly evident with regard to Directive 84/360/EEC, where "limit values" and the "adoption of the best technology" constitute separate and autonomous conditions for the issuing of permits to plants. A confirmation of the fact that the instrument of the BAT was previously applied without an immediate and direct connection to the ELVs comes from the ruling of the European Court of Justice, section II of July 7, 2005, proceeding C-364/03 with reference to a case of non-compliance by the Hellenic Republic with the provisions of Directive 84/360/EEC, for not having defined policies and strategies to gradually adapt steam turbines and gas from the power plant to the best available technology and thereby infringing Article 13 of the Directive. In fact, Article 13 notes that:

> In the light of an examination of developments as regards the best available technology and the environmental situation, the Member States shall implement policies and strategies, including appropriate measures, for the gradual adaptation of existing plants belonging to the categories given in Annex I to the best available technology, taking into account in particular: the plant's technical characteristics, its rate of utilization and length of its remaining life, the nature and volume of polluting emissions from it, the desirability of not entailing excessive costs for the plant concerned, having regard in particular to the economic situation of undertakings belonging to the category in question.

A similar case is provided by Directive 88/609/EEC where it is expected that under certain conditions the limit values may be exceeded despite the application of the best available technology.[37]

Even when a connection between these two parameters seems to exist, as in Directive 89/369/EEC according to which the authorities, when setting ELVs, have to "take into account" the best available technology that does not lead to excessive costs, it is still not clear in which way the parameter of the best available technology has to be applied and how it can affect the environmental regulation system adopted by the single legislation. Particularly, it is worth noting that, in the fight against pollution, the BAT was usually (and specifically) aimed at ensuring the compliance with the standard values, whether they were of environmental quality (in which case the permit was issued whenever the overall level of pollution resided within the established value) or, instead, of emission (in which case compliance with the emission value was verified, independently of the technology adopted). In the European legislation just mentioned, therefore, the application of the best available technology seemed optional and/or a mere possibility: it represented only one of the possible "measures" employed to prevent the emission of pollutants into the environment, but it did not play a fundamental role in the

37 Council Directive 84/360/EEC, Article 13; European Court of Justice, section II of July 7, 2005, proceeding C-364/03 with reference to a case of non-compliance by the Hellenic Republic; Council Directive 88/609/EEC.

issuing of the environmental permit, which was in no way dependent on its application.[38] In other words, eventually the application of the BAT was not a *conditio sine qua non* for the issue of the environmental permit.

Therefore, in order to have a definition of "best available technology", one needed to refer to the regulations of the single Member States and, in particular, as regards to the Italian legal system, to the Decree n. 203 of May 24, 1988, laying down rules on "Air Quality in Relation to Specific Pollutants and on Pollution Produced by Industrial Plants", which in Article 2, point 7 identified BAT as the "adequately verified and tested technological system that allows the containment and/or reduction of emissions to acceptable levels for the protection of health and the environment, provided that the application of these measures does not lead to excessive costs" (also referred to as BATNEEC – Best Available Techniques Not Entailing Excessive Costs).[39] From this definition we also learn that the BAT refers essentially to abatement measures, that is to emission reduction instruments intervening at the end of the cycle, according to an ex-post approach with respect to the production of the harmful substances emitted in the environment. Indeed, it is no coincidence that the Decree refers to emissions abatement, specifically consisting of filters for the treatment of fumes and hence located downstream of the production phase.[40] The regulation mechanism adopted by the IPPC Directive is therefore unique in the landscape of environmental regulation known up to now, because, as I will try to show, it aims to achieve a synthesis between the different styles of environmental regulation and, in doing so, it re-states only their most successful features/aspects: not only does it establish a close relationship between setting ELVs and the need to apply the best available technology, but, with reference to BAT, it also proposes a new and revisited concept of best available technology in the light of the integrated approach.

Lange states that "there are some differences between the legal definitions of 'Stand der Technik' and BATNEEC on the one hand, and the new IPPC BAT concept on the other hand". The author clarifies that on one hand "the German 'Stand der Technik' concept did not refer explicitly to costs as one criterion for determining the 'Stand der Technik' in a licence for a specific installation", and on the other hand that

> BAT under IPPC deals with a wider range of issues in pollution control, including energy efficiency, prevention of waste, as assessment of the consumption and nature of raw materials used as well as accident prevention and site restoration. The BATNEEC concept under section 7(2) of EPA 1990 did not grant powers to the regulator to deal with these issues.[41]

38 Bettina Lange, *Implementing EU Pollution Control. Law and Integration* (Cambridge: Cambridge University Press, 2008), 149 and 180.

39 Italian Decree n. 203 of May 24, 1988, laying down rules on "Air Quality in Relation to Specific Pollutants and on Pollution Produced by Industrial Plants", Article 2, Point 7.

40 Bettina Lange, *Implementing EU Pollution Control*, 152–153.

41 Id. 180–181.

It is only with the IPPC Directive 96/61/EC that the BAT concept is in fact better formalized and definitively consolidated at the European level, not only filling the defining gaps of previous directives but above all attributing to this parameter the fulcrum role around which to build the whole system of regulation of the environmental directive. As already mentioned several times, the Directive provides that the permit should establish limit values for pollutants, in particular for those listed in Annex III (Article 9, Paragraph 3), and also that these ELVs are based on BATs, without the obligation to use a specific technique or technology (Article 9, Paragraph 4). This scheme has been substantially maintained also in the subsequent IED, which came to replace the IPPC Directive: Article 15, Paragraph 2 proposes that

> Without prejudice to Article 18, the emission limit values and the equivalent parameters and technical measures referred to in Article 14(1) and (2) shall be based on the best available techniques, without prescribing the use of any technique or specific technology.[42]

Therefore, even though the connection between ELV and BAT has remained unchanged, the nature of this connection has undergone significant changes, as it will be further argued in the following paragraphs. For the first time, the IPPC Directive uses the expression "best available techniques" and defines it as

> the most effective and advanced stage in the development of activities and their methods of operation which indicates the practical suitability of particular techniques for providing the basis for emission limit values and other permit conditions designed to prevent and, where that is not practicable, to reduce emissions and the impact on the environment as a whole.[43]

From this definition of BAT, which is evidently more articulate and full of implications and of greater substance compared with the previous one, it is possible to draw some considerations highlighting how the IPPC Directive has revolutionized, through the very new concept of BATs, the way to intervene in environmental regulation. First of all, as already mentioned, it has now established an unavoidable relationship between the BATs and the ELVs, stressed by Article 9, Paragraph 4, according to which the former act as a reference for the latter. Such a relationship is so intrinsic to the concept of BAT itself that it cannot be avoided or merely made optional.

Moreover, it is necessary to highlight the preventive purpose (versus the previous ex-post "containment" function) of the best techniques and related limit values with respect to pollutant emissions, as well as to the context of reference, which is no longer limited to a single environmental medium but includes the

42 Council Directive 96/61/EC, Article 9 (Paragraphs 3 and 4) and Article 15 (Paragraph 2).

43 Ibid.

environment as a whole. In other words, clear reference is made, respectively, to the principle of prevention and the integrated approach to environmental protection. In particular, these observations are supported by the reading of the additional specifications that the Directive provides in the text dedicated to the definitions, where it is clarified that "techniques" (a term that replaces that of "technology") refer to "both the technology used and the way in which the installation is designed, built, maintained, operated and decommissioned", while "best" means the "most effective in achieving a high general level of protection of the environment as a whole".[44]

Hence, what emerges from the overall reading of these definitions is that the concept of BATs turns out to be strictly functional, and not merely procedural, for the achievement of "substantial integration", which is a key element of the new integrated approach to environmental protection. Substantial integration means, as argued above, the willingness to tackle the phenomenon of polluting emissions in the environment in an organic way, with the objective of obtaining the best environmental performance in the management of a given activity, taking as a reference the overall production process – from the use of raw materials, to the consumption of energy, up to the management of waste – without focusing attention either on only the final phase in which the pollution manifests itself or a specific environmental media.

The very use of the term "techniques", adopted to replace the previous term "technologies", indicates a plural set of methods (such as the construction, maintenance and operation, etc. of plants and facilities) and it marks the transition to an overall vision of the phenomenon of pollution, which from now on is tackled not only "ex-post" with the aim of eliminating harmful emissions but also "ex-ante" by intervening upstream during the single phases of the emission formation process, so as to realize not only the simple abatement or reduction of the emissions themselves but also an activity of prevention. It should be noted that this overall and comprehensive approach is then further strengthened by the reference to "best" techniques, understood as the most effective in view of achieving a high level of protection of the environment "as a whole".[45]

2.2 The BATs Reference Documents (BREFs) under the Sevilla Process

A fundamental aspect of the technological parameter represented by the BATs (and also of its predecessor – the best available technology or, as was the case in

44 Council Directive 2008/1/EC, Article 2, Paragraph 12 (a) and (c); Valerie Laforest and Remi Bertheas, "Ambiguité entre Technologies Propres et Meilleures Techniques Disponibles," *La Revue Electronique en Sciences de l'Environnement* 6 (2) (2005): available at https://journals.openedition.org/vertigo/9657.

45 As argued by Lee, "Best is 'the most effective in achieving a high general level of protection of the environment as a whole', reinforcing the holistic (whole environment) aspirations of BAT". Maria Lee, *EU Environmental Law, Governance and Decision-Making* (Oregon: Hart Publishing, 2014), 111.

Germany, the so-called "state of the art") is its intrinsically dynamic and evolutionary nature, explicit from its definition, and which has an impact on the text of the Directive and the regulatory system referred to therein.

Starting from the basic consideration expressed in "whereas" n. 21, providing that "because best available techniques will change with time, particularly in the light of technical advances, the competent authorities should monitor or be informed of such progress", the IPPC Directive contains provisions aimed at enhancing and at the same time regulating this tendency towards evolution and the continuous technical and scientific progress that characterizes the BAT parameter. In this sense Article 11 of the Directive requires the individual Member States to take action to ensure that "the competent authority follows or is informed of developments in best available techniques".[46]

Such a provision is then supplemented by Article 17, which covers the exchange of information. This exchange takes place between the Member States and the European Commission and it is expected to happen every 3 years with information on the ELVs set in the granting of permits, with particular reference to the BATs from which they were drawn. As can be seen in Paragraph 2 of Article 17, such an exchange is expected to take place among different Member States: "The Commission shall organise an exchange of information between Member States and the industries concerned on best available techniques, associated monitoring, and developments in them". The reasons for such a provision are clarified in "whereas" n. 27 of the Directive , by stating that

> the development and exchange of information at Community level about best available techniques should help to redress the technological imbalances in the Community, should promote the worldwide dissemination of limit values and techniques used in the Community and should help the Member States in the efficient implementation of this Directive.[47]

The intention of the information exchange organized by the Commission is therefore primarily aimed at increasing the level of training and dissemination of knowledge in the field of environmental technologies, so that innovation is stimulated. The development of innovation in the environmental field is characterized by scale and learning effects: the more the techniques/technologies spread and experience accumulates, the greater the information and the data that "return" to the producers, thus allowing them to make improvements compared with the original technologies. Thus, the dynamic nature of innovation tends to favour an incremental improvement that can lead to an evolutionary change in a specific technological paradigm as opposed to radical leaps.[48]

46 Council Directive 2008/1/EC, "whereas" n. 21 and Article 11.

47 Id. "whereas" n. 27 and Article 17.

48 Andrew Gouldson and Joseph Murphy, *Regulatory Realities* (London: Routledge, 1998), 28.

However, innovation is generally beset by difficulties in accessing information: companies may not be aware of the *range* of technical solutions available to solve specific problems as a result of the lack of communication networks that limit the spread of information about the successful application of new technologies (a phenomenon that can be further aggravated by national differences and language barriers).[49] Technical and technological changes, on the other hand, play a central role in achieving sustainable production, enabling a reduction in consumption of non-renewable resources and in the production of non-recyclable waste by private individuals. It is therefore understandable that the intent of the Commission is to promote, through the exchange of information, the technological progress in the environmental field as an element that is considered fundamental and strategic for the achievement of the general objectives of the environmental policy of the European Union (and beyond), including in particular that of sustainable development.[50]

At the same time, the IPPC Directive aimed to achieve, in compliance with the principle of sustainable development, the further objective of economic growth, by encouraging the growth of a European environmental technologies market, so as to build environmental technological standards capable of being competitive and able to influence other markets. Indeed, this is in line with the Lisbon strategy on the development of knowledge as a factor of economic progress of the Union. As argued by Gislev: "The importance of technological development for competitiveness is generally accepted by the scientific community, industry and policymakers. Consequently, the European Community and its Member States seek to develop policy instruments that foster innovation". Moreover, "the regulatory requirement to apply BAT is essential if the European eco-industry is to see strong growth and fight off global competition (from countries such as the United States). The core eco-industry in the European Union represents about half of the world market".[51]

In pursuing these objectives, the Commission therefore also wished to establish, in parallel with the IPPC Directive, a mechanism for standardizing and elaborating those very BATs on which the implementation of the environmental protection objectives, set out in the Directive, must be based, eventually aiming to achieve the harmonization of technical regulations on environmental protection. However, it is necessary to take into consideration that, as will be even more evident later in this study, the "best available techniques" is an elastic parameter and therefore it is susceptible by its nature to be subject to different interpretations and applications which are not always uniform. This is even more the case when

49 C. Ganzleben, "Integrated Pollution Prevention and Control: A Driver for Innovation in the European Community," (PhD diss., Oxford University, 2003), 5.

50 Cristopher Freeman and Luc Soete, *The Economics of Industrial Innovation* (Cambridge: MIT Press, 1997), 413–419.

51 Magnus Gislev, "European Innovation and Exchange of Information about BAT" in the Sevilla Process: A Driver for Environmental Performance in Industry (paper presented at European Conference, Stuttgart, April 6–7, 2000), 78–79.

national laws are at stake, since they are characterized by environmental regulations based on radically different approaches.[52]

It is common knowledge that the same draft of the text of the Directive in favour of a formulation of the BAT parameter, distinguished by its "open norm" (general, flexible exception) nature, has also been shaped by the original conflicts between the member countries, i.e. by the opposing needs linked to the their different levels of industrial development. On the one hand, the Northern and more industrialized European countries favoured the imposition of strict BAT-based emission standards so as to guarantee as far as possible the so-called *level playing field*; that is, the need to compete on equal terms between the different Member States. On the other hand, the countries of Southern Europe (above all Portugal and Spain), less developed from the point of view of industrial and environmental performance, strongly opposed the aforementioned imposition, given their inability to bear the unacceptably high costs required by the adjustment to the (too rigid) BAT-based emission standards. In this respect, Faure argues:

> Special interest groups representing industry understandably lobbied strongly in favour of harmonization of European limit values. They may have incentives to extend their strict (national) regulation to the European level, forcing their foreign competitors (in the south) to follow the same strict regulation with which they already comply.[53]

Because the wording of the Directive was the result of all these compromises, it was not guaranteed that BAT-based emission standards would be uniformly adopted by the Member States' respective legal systems. The risk would have been to face very different outcomes at the time of its concrete application and the danger that, consequently, different conditions could be originated both in terms of guaranteed environmental protection and, above all, in terms of competition between companies in different countries. This would have also undermined the achievement of one of the primary objectives of the European Union – the single market. It is on the basis of all these premises and considerations that the European Commission therefore established a Technical Working Group (TWG) for each industrial sector affected by the Directive, made up of representatives of the Member States and industries and coordinated by the Environment Directorate General of the same EU Commission. The technical groups meet at the European IPPC Bureau, based in Seville, from which originated the expression *Sevilla Process* that precisely indicates the set of elements that integrate this complex activity of exchange and processing of information. The European IPPC Bureau is the body specifically created for the preparation of the so-called *BAT Reference Documents*,

52 Id. 80. By triggering the Sevilla Process the European Commission aimed at an ambitious objective, i.e. the drafting of "high-quality reference documents that will exert a kind of a magnetic force on EU Member States and their authorities so that they will really want to use them when determining BAT and BAT-based permit conditions apart from their legal obligation to do so".

53 Michael Faure, "Optimal Specificity": 745.

more commonly referred to as BREFs, which consist of community documents identifying the various technologies and techniques normally used by operators for the individual fields of activity.[54]

Over the years, the Sevilla Process has overseen the drafting of approximately 35 BREFs; both "vertical" reference documents, concerning one or more industrial sectors or activities (for example, the BREF dedicated to Mineral Oil and Gas Refineries or the Iron and Steel Production) and "horizontal" reference documents, related to problems common to the various industrial sectors (for example, the one dedicated to Energy Efficiency or the Economics and Cross-media Effects). Each BREF has a similar structure, with a preface and then six sections dedicated, respectively, to: 1) General information, relating to the sector; 2) Processes and techniques used, with the description of the sequential steps typical of a production unit; 3) Current consumption/emission levels, relative to the levels of consumption of energy, raw material and water of each activity; 4) Techniques to be considered for the identification of BAT, in which the so-called "candidate BATs" are indicated, namely the techniques currently commercially available for the prevention and limitation of emissions and waste; 5) BAT, with the list of those among the "BAT candidates" that are considered suitable; and 6) Emerging techniques, in which are mentioned, where present, techniques still in the phase of experimentation and study that may become "BAT candidates" in the future.[55]

The BREFs therefore provide useful information for the correct identification of the BAT to be adopted in each physical case and, where possible, expressly indicate the emission levels that can be reasonably achieved through the use of individual technologies. These documents obviously do not have to be considered either obligatory or exhaustive in terms of the techniques that can be used in the various installations, otherwise they would be in direct contrast to the Directive which does not stipulate a specific technology to be imposed when setting the conditions for releasing environmental permits. Rather, the purpose of these documents is to provide specific reference points which the competent authorities can use to identify the best technique that can be employed in the concrete and specific case at stake.[56]

To confirm this, Annex IV to the IPPC Directive also includes, among other factors to be taken into account when determining the BATs, the information published by the European Commission pursuant to Article 17, Paragraph 2, which refers precisely to the BREF documents. This provision was also maintained in the text of the IED, which directly in relation to the provisions concerning the drafting of BREF documents had already been operational since January 2013. The IED has also focused on this aspect, resulting in the drafting of an additional

54 Per Sørup, "The European IPPC Bureau; What Is It, Where Is It and What Does It Do" in The Sevilla Process: A Driver for Environmental Performance in Industry (paper presented at European Conference, Stuttgart, April 6–7, 2000), 83–87.

55 Harald Schoenberger, "Integrated Pollution Prevention and Control in Large Industrial Installations on the basis of Best Available Techniques – The Sevilla Process," *Journal of Cleaner Production* 17 (2009): 1526–1529.

56 Ibid.

more simplified document taken from the BREF documents: the "conclusions on the BAT (Best Available Techniques)". This document summarizes the essential points on the single applicable BAT or on the BAT combinations, including the data on the ranges of emission limit values linked to the BAT.[57]

As it will be analysed later, the most interesting aspect originating from the introduction of this document consists in the fact that the "conclusions on the BAT" are adopted directly by the Commission, and not simply in the framework of the Sevilla Process as up until then had been the case for BREFs. This is done through a specific *comitology* procedure that reinforces and institutionalizes the role of the directive in the control of industrial emissions. The term "comitology" indicates the procedures through which the European Commission carries out its so-called implementing powers, which the Community legislator (European Parliament and/or Council) may entrust to it by allowing the Commission itself to approve a legislative act of Community law for regulating a given matter. In other words, this mechanism allows the Commission to issue regulations aimed at completing, clarifying and/or supplementing the legislation established in the basic regulatory act governing the matter – principally a regulatory act of general application, such as a regulation or a directive.[58]

2.2.1 The function and importance of BREFs

The so-called BREFs are the European reference documents identifying the various technologies and techniques normally adopted by the operators, and which therefore provide useful information for the correct identification of the best available technique to be adopted in a given and concrete case.

The reference to BREFs documents – as tools of public administrations in the issue of integrated environmental permits – only became part of the Italian Environmental Code in the modification made by Legislative Decree no. 128 of 29 June 2010, which introduces a specific Article 29-bis expressly dedicated to this subject and entitled "Identification and Use of the Best Available Techniques".[59]

With regard to the determination of the conditions regulating the issuing of environmental permits, it has often been discussed in the doctrine what the real extent of this type of document should be. Generally, the literature on this subject has clearly excluded that any obligation deriving from the above-mentioned documents could arise for Member States. For the same reason, the authorities responsible for issuing environmental permits could therefore have a margin of flexibility vis-à-vis the compliance with the indications contained therein. Also the Italian administrative judge, in line with the prevailing interpretation of the legislation, has confirmed on several occasions that "neither in the European nor in the

57 Council Directive 2008/1/EC, Article 17 (Paragraph 2); Council Directive 2010/75/EU, see "BAT Conclusions".

58 Giandonato Caggiano, "Il consolidamento della disciplina delle misure di esecuzione e della comitologia a trattato invariato," *Studi sull'integrazione europea* 3 (2006): 505–525.

59 Ibid.

Italian national legislation, is there any mandatory indication or provision of specific techniques to be used in a given context and at a given time", therefore leaving a discretionary assessment to the proceeding administration (naturally supported by suitable preliminary activity) for the identification of the BATs.[60]

That said, there would seem to be no further space for discussion on the non-binding nature and mere function of reference of the BREFs with regard to the BATs; and yet, if one looks at the recent administrative jurisprudence, while awaiting the implementation of the innovative aspects introduced by the IED, there are enough elements to suggest that the indications contained in the BREFs (namely the emission limits related to the therein recalled BAT) exert a certain degree of influence over the public administrations responsible for issuing environmental permits.[61]

Despite the scarcity of decisions that address this aspect, justification for this argument can be clearly found in the analysis of two recent judgments in which the Italian administrative judge, who was called to express first and second degree judgements on this same issue, initially excluded the binding nature of the European reference documents for the identification of the BAT, and then took a significantly different approach on appeal.

In the first case example, the question submitted to the judicial review concerned the assessment of environmental compatibility for the construction of a thermoelectric power plant fuelled by coal and biomass, in place of the previous fuel oil plant. Among the numerous objections raised against the issuing of the environmental permit and brought to the attention of the judge was the violation of the precautionary principle with regard to the measurement of emission limits of the main pollutants (sulphur oxides, particulate matter, CO_2, etc.) since requirements imposed on the construction of the plant, on such issue, would not have been in line with the BAT. It is this very (asserted) divergence between the values resulting from the best techniques, as identified in the BREFs, and those imposed by the administration in the real-world case, that constitutes the starting point for a reconsideration of the relevance of such documents. In this regard, the Court of First Instance took a position by arguing that the provisions "imposed by the EIA Decree on … can not be said to be in themselves contrary or divergent to the BREFs (guidelines) for large combustion plants, and correlatively, not based on the observance of the precautionary principle", thus demonstrating that it does not recognize these guidelines to be of particular significance with regard to the actual determination of the emission limits.[62] It was in fact considered that "these

60 Michael Faure, "Optimal Specificity": 730–738; Almut Reichel, "Introduction and Summary of Discussion" in The Sevilla Process: A Driver for Environmental Performance in Industry, (paper presented at European Conference, Stuttgart, April 6–7, 2000), 7.

61 Don Litten, "BAT Reference Documents: What Are They and What Are They Not" in The Sevilla Process: A Driver for Environmental Performance in Industry, (paper presented at European Conference, Stuttgart, April 6–7, 2000), 92.

62 Regional Administrative Court of Lazio Region, Rome, Section H, 14 October 2010, n. 32824.

guidelines should not be carried out *tout court*, but applied in a calibrated way to the type and characteristics of the plant and the site in which it is placed ... in order to obtain the desired improvement in terms of emission values". The judge therefore affirms

> not so much the *a priori* constraints of such data as if they were always and in any case maximum emission values, but more properly the need to consider them as objectives to be achieved in the necessary time, so that they can be reconciled with all (local, environmental and economic) situations, in which the plant is located or, in simpler words, in order to realize an adjustment towards realistic and achievable emission limits.

Excluding the binding scope, the conclusion is that

> the values reported in the BREFs represent an average reference value ... which indicates the practical suitability of technical data to constitute the logical base of the emission limit values preordained to avoid or ... to generally reduce emissions and the impact on the environment as a whole; so unlike those that the law actually sets as limit values, which must never be exceeded under any operating condition of the plant.[63]

As highlighted by Hagstrom,

> the BREF provides a general BAT on the sector level, which means that the presented BAT is considered to be appropriate for the sector as a whole, but not necessarily appropriate, nor even technically possible for immediate implementation at all individual sites.[64]

On the basis of these considerations, the judge, concluding for the rejection of the grievance, therefore admitted that the administration responsible for issuing the environmental permit may deviate from the references contained in the BREFs and may thus impose higher and more permissive emission limits than those indicated in them.

However, the matter was thoroughly reviewed by the judge in our second case example. Here the judge, though in agreement with the initial premises adopted by the Regional Administrative Court, partially reformed the "relative" ruling by giving a different emphasis to the values contained within the BREFs. Also the Council of State agreed that "those listed in the BREF constitute an average reference value; which implies that they are not immediately binding"; but stressed that

63 Ibid.

64 Petra Hagstrom, "BAT Process Selection and Split Views" in The Sevilla Process: A Driver for Environmental Performance in Industry, (paper presented at European Conference, Stuttgart, April 6–7, 2000), 124.

> this does not mean at all however – especially when, as in this case, peculiar environmental protection requirements are at stake in relation with the specificity of the site where the power plant is to be built – that the rules in question can be considered irrelevant, having to justify the reason to deviate from them.

Although not a direct restriction, excluded by the non-normative nature of these documents, the data contained in the BREFs would therefore impose on the relevant administration, if it considers having to deviate from them in the concrete case, a "reinforced" motivation burden. The necessity of such a burden had been underlined on a previous occasion by the administrative judge, where it was stated that

> on the contrary, the repeated imposition by the Administration of a (mere) result to be achieved (the abatement of emissions, the reconditioning of emissions within acceptable limits, or other definitions of equivalent generic content), effectively subtracts the provision for each syndication with respect to the normative parameter.[65]

This need for motivation is felt even more so when, as in this case, the competent administration, after highlighting the need to study particular solutions to ensure minimum overall impacts, and while noting that the values guaranteed by the project of the applicant would be in line with the sector BATs, nevertheless decided to set, with no apparent justification, emission limits significantly more permissive than the range indicated by the corresponding BAT.[66]

The overall indication that can possibly be derived from these rulings is that the information contained in the BREFs involves, at the expense of the public administration, at least a burden of particular motivation, which makes it possible to consider these documents as an instrument. Despite not having the formal effectiveness of binding Member States and operators in the sector with the respect to their contents, BREFs nevertheless exert a decisive influence on the process of harmonization of national legislation and administrative procedures, according to the objectives set at the European level and pursued through the aforementioned Sevilla Process.[67] In other words, here we have confirmation of the specific relevance of the Guidelines, which inevitably link themselves to the directives. This technical document, which from the juridical point of view is not binding, is however extremely significant and valuable since it contains pointers on

65 Italian Regional Administrative Court of the Umbria Region, Perugia, 10 January 2003, n. 10, point 4.5.

66 Italian Council of State, Section VI, 23 May 2011, n. 3107. See also Francesco Fonderico, "Valutazione d'impatto ambientale e amministrazione precauzionale," *Giornale di Diritto Amministrativo* 1 (2012): 70–77.

67 Michael Faure, "Optimal Specificity": 744, where the author affirms that "these BREFs, even though they formally are non-mandatory documents as to what these BATs are, de facto lead to a harmonization of BATs in Europe".

regulatory requests that have a strong capacity to make operators comply with the environmental standards.

These conclusions anticipate, at least in spirit, those novelties concerning the role of the BATs, and in particular the value of the BREF documents, which were introduced by the IED in force since January 2011, and which have been incorporated into the national laws of the Member States, as it will be seen in the next section.

2.2.2 The Emission Limit Values (ELVs) vis-à-vis BATs and BREFs

Within the integrated permit, the setting of ELVs is the result of a complex assessment, which refers to two distinct phases: a first one, aimed at identifying the best technology among those applicable to the plant in question, with the indication – where possible – of the limit values expected from it; and a second one, dedicated instead to the consideration of the factors related to the particular location of the plant, with the consequent possibility, in setting the limit values, to deviate from those associated with the BATs – in some cases towards a more rigorous approach (by further lowering the limit values) and in other cases in a more permissive sense (i.e. allowing more emissions).[68]

With reference to the first phase, I have showed that the competent authority has at its disposal more instruments that can be used to identify the BAT. However, with regards to the second phase – that is the one on which the basis of the BAT is defined for a specific case and additional factors are taken into account in order to determine the ELVs to be set in the integrated permit – it should be noted that there is almost no specification of parameters or criteria to which the administration can refer. This lack of specification occurs both at the regulatory level and at the level of steering documents or guidelines. As a result, a wider margin of discretion is entrusted to the proceeding administration on this specific point. Put another way, on one hand the legislation provides that, in fixing the limit values on the basis of BAT, the administration must take into account "the technical characteristics of the installation in question, its geographical location and the local environmental conditions" (Article 29-sexies, Paragraph 4), also establishing that the integrated permit may "include other specific conditions ... deemed appropriate by the competent authority" (Article 29-sexies, Paragraph 9); on the other hand, the General Guidelines are limited in that they only state that "when in the area where the industrial plant is located there are critical environmental conditions ... the competent Authority may request the achievement of specific environmental performance" and that "the Authority issues the permit prescribing any further requirements that may have become necessary with regard to the environmental framework and the state of the art of the plant".[69]

As for the provision of Paragraph 4, Article 29-sexies, it is not clear, for example, how the reference to the technical characteristics of the plant should be

68 Michael Faure, "Optimal Specificity": 745.

69 General Guidelines of the Italian Ministerial Decree of 2005, points 111.3 and 111.5.

interpreted, especially since this aspect should be already assumed and endorsed in the assessment aimed at identifying the applicable BAT. Indeed, such an assessment presupposes that the BAT is "sustainable" not only *economically* but also technically. The latter aspect, in fact, necessarily requires taking into account the peculiarities of the plant, starting from the design stage and data, up to the aspects related to the management of production processes.[70]

The reference to the technical characteristics of the plant could therefore be seen as superfluous and redundant compared with the previous evaluation phase aimed at identifying the BAT. However, it acquires an autonomous relevance either when this evaluation has not given positive results (for example, when a BAT does not exist for the specific type of installation), or when ELVs are not strictly associated with the applicable BAT and therefore "equivalent measures" must be adopted. In such cases, in which the lack of references may in some way constrain the decision-making autonomy of the authority responsible for issuing the integrated permit, it is possible to fill the gap, albeit indirectly, through the Guidelines and BREFs. Within those documents there is indeed a special section dedicated to the analysis of the applicability of the techniques, clarifying that among the features of the plant useful for identifying the BAT and fixing the limit values, one should consider the size, the age and the remaining life-time of the plant itself.

Therefore, the administration can derive useful indications from the Guidelines or BREFs; yet, the same cannot be argued for the *geographic location of the plant* and the *local conditions* – namely the two other aspects that the legislation requires to keep into consideration when the ELVs need to be defined in practice. It is not possible to find the slightest reference to these two aspects, either of a regulatory or non-normative nature. Hence, the discretionary margin already enjoyed by the administration appears to be even greater if it refers to these two elements that it must assess, and which are configured, within the regulatory mechanism set up by the directive, as two clauses specifically introduced to allow for case-by-case decisions on the limit values to be respected, thus enhancing the elastic and adaptive dimension of the entire environmental protection system.[71]

2.3 The new legislative (binding) features of the IED

Starting from the IPPC Directive and its environmental regulation mechanism, the European legislator implemented the IED which introduces some significant provisions: on the one hand to confirm and consolidate certain aspects of the existing Directive, and, on the other, to modify the basic indications that, since Directive 96/61/EC, characterized the legislation on integrated prevention and control of pollution produced by industrial plants. First of all, and as has already been mentioned, the IED contemplates, in the "definitions" of ex-Article 3, two terms and two notions previously not directly present in the texts of the IPPC Directive: the

70 Ibid.

71 Maurizio Cafagno, *Principi e Strumenti di Tutela dell'Ambiente* (Torino: Giappichelli, 2007), 398–399.

"BAT reference document" and the "BAT conclusions". For the first time then, it devotes, in Article 13, a specific provision to these subjects, as well as a number of references to it in the Articles that follow (Articles 14 and 15).[72]

Article 13, "BAT reference documents and exchange of information", after having clarified in the introductory paragraphs the mechanism that regulates the exchange of information useful for the drafting of the reference documents on the BAT at the EU level (i.e. BREFs),[73] states in Paragraph 5 that the "decisions on the BAT conclusions shall be adopted in accordance with the regulatory procedure referred to in Article 75 (2)" of the Treaty and in Paragraph 6 that "after the adoption of a decision in accordance with paragraph 5, the Commission shall without delay make the BAT reference document publicly available and ensure that BAT conclusions are made available in all the official languages of the Union".[74]

Article 3, Paragraph 12, of the IED also provides that the "BAT conclusions" are to be understood as

> a document containing the parts of a BAT reference document laying down the conclusions on best available techniques, their description, information to assess their applicability, the emission levels associated with the best available techniques (i.e. BAT-AEL), associated monitoring, associated consumption levels and, where appropriate, relevant site remediation measures.[75]

In consideration of these provisions, it can be argued – on the one hand – that the BAT reference document ceases to be contemplated exclusively in the perspective and texts of the Sevilla Process, thus obtaining a formal investiture directly from the IED, which in this way "institutionalizes" with a regulatory provision the mechanism of the Sevilla Process and of the EU BREFs. On the other hand, as already mentioned above, a radical change in the approach from the IPPC Directive is determined through the provision of the comitological method, applied to reach the approval of decisions on the "conclusions on BAT". This last provision, if read in the context of the appropriate definitions present in Article 3, implies that the content of the "conclusions on BAT", as approved by comitology procedure, assumes a formal binding effect on Member States.[76]

72 Council Directive 96/61/EC, Article 3; Council Directive 2010/75/EU, Articles 13, 14, 15.

73 Paragraph 1 of Article 13 of the Directive 2010/75/EU provides that "In order to draw up, review and, where necessary, update BAT reference documents, the Commission shall organise an exchange of information between Member States, the industries concerned, non-governmental organisations promoting environmental protection and the Commission".

74 Council Directive 2010/75/EU, Article 13, Paragraphs 5 and 6.

75 Id. Article 3, Paragraph 12.

76 See Féderation Européenne des Activités de la Dépollution et de l'Environnement (FEAD), "The European Commission's Proposal for the Industrial Emission Directive," (2008): 2. Moreover, the Article highlights that the IED "completely changes the spirit in which the BREFs were designed: instead of being reference guidance documents describing BATs, they become prescriptive making them binding".

The implementing provisions issued by the European Commission on the basis of the received mandate are in fact normative in nature and are hence able to complete, specify or supplement the regulations established by the EU legislator with the basic act. Having made such documents binding is certainly one of the major innovations introduced by the IED as it directly affects the heart of the IPPC Directive – i.e. the system for determining the conditions to which the issue of environmental permits is subject to.

In this respect, Article 14 of the IED provides, in its Paragraph 3, that the "BAT conclusions shall be the reference for setting the permit conditions"; the generic reference to the BATs is thus supplanted as a reference parameter for the definition of the environmental measures imposed on the operator, and it is now replaced by this specific reference to binding European documents. Article 15, Paragraph 3, specifies that the competent administrative authority should set ELVs so that emissions do not exceed the levels that are associated with the BATs and that are indicated in the BAT conclusions.[77]

More specifically, the competent authority has the possibility to set either ELVs not higher than those associated with BAT, or different limit values (in terms of values, periods of time and reference conditions) provided that the results of annual controls show that, in normal operating conditions of the plant, the ELVs associated with the BATs have not been exceeded.[78] The Directive therefore requires administrations to set ELVs which are in line with those associated with the use of the BAT, as expressed in the BAT conclusions.

The nature of a binding regulatory act acquired from the BREF documents raises the question of the direct grievance of these acts as provided for in the current Article 263 of the Treaty on the Functioning of the European Union (TFEU). The provisions establish that it must be possible for any natural or legal person to be able to challenge the acts that directly and individually affect them as well as "a regulatory act which is of direct concern to them and does not entail implementing measures". Any regulatory act that establishes bans or imposes obligations to a general category of subjects therefore becomes attackable, pursuant to Article 263, Paragraph 4, if it is shown that it directly affects the subject and does not require specific implementing measures.[79]

According to the view proposed by some scholars, within the category of regulatory measures that can be challenged pursuant to Article 263, Paragraph 4, Part II, it is possible to include both the delegated legislative acts, expressly qualified as non-legislative by Article 290 of the TFEU and aimed at implementing and

77 Council Directive 2010/75/EU, Article 14 (Paragraph 3) and Article 15 (Paragraph 3). Moreover, Article 14, Paragraph 5, provides that "the competent authority shall ensure that the technique referred to in the first subparagraph ensures a level of environmental protection equivalent to the best available techniques described in the BAT conclusions".

78 See the Reference Document on the General Principles of Monitoring of July 2003, adopted by the Sevilla Process.

79 Lisbon Treaty, Title I, Article 263 – ex Article 230 of the Treaty Establishing the European Community (TEC).

specifying the regulatory framework dictated by the legislative act, and the implementing acts having a general and abstract content, provided, of course, that they are adopted by the European institutions. The individual decision by which a general provision is applied to a specific situation should therefore be more strictly defined as an implementing measure. In this sense, all measures or denials of measures issued on the basis of the general act would constitute implementing measures.[80] On the basis of these considerations, it is therefore possible to exclude the direct contestability of BREF documents, which, although they are now general and abstract regulatory acts, are not lacking the need for implementing measures, as they are incorporated into the national laws and regulations implemented in practice by the competent public administrations.

To confirm the new role and importance assumed by the BATs and the emission values connected to them in affecting the ELVs set in the environmental permits, the IED at Paragraph 4 of Article 15 states that "by way of derogation from paragraph 3 … the competent authority may, in specific cases, set less strict emission limit values". The same provision then specifies that "such a derogation may apply only where an assessment shows that the achievement of emission levels associated with the best available techniques as described in BAT conclusions would lead to disproportionately higher costs compared to the environmental benefits".[81] Therefore, this provision directly makes explicit in the text of the legislation the real relationship that was highlighted – in the first paragraphs of this chapter – between the different interests taken into consideration by the European environmental policy: that of environmental protection, on the one hand, and that of economic development, on the other – affirming the latter's prevalence in the case of conflict between the two.

The reasons why it is considered possible in specific cases to derogate from the limit values associated with the BAT are specifically related to the geographical location and local environmental conditions of the installation concerned (Article 15, Paragraph 4, letter a) or to its technical characteristics (Article 15, Paragraph 4, letter b). Those are the same factors that had to be taken into consideration in the IPPC Directive (in addition to the BATs) in order to identify the ELVs for the individual plant. In this way, it is possible to argue that the IED aims (in part) to fill the lack of indications discussed in the previous paragraphs concerning the impact that the (environmental and technical) characteristics of the specific plant could have on the conditions of the permit.[82] Such features acquire now explicit importance in the exclusive view of cost-benefit analysis in favour of the manager of the plant. As a result, firstly the emission values connected to the BAT and contained in the "BAT conclusions" have become, as from January 2013, a standard application by the competent authorities, whose responsibility in usual circumstances is to fix ELVs so that they fall within the values expressed by the reference documents. Secondly, when the competent authority deems it should

80 Ibid.
81 Council Directive 2010/75/EU, Article 14, Paragraph 4.
82 Ibid.

deviate, in a less restrictive sense, from these values it is obliged to provide an adequate and documented reason.

The legislation thus amended does not preclude, as shown above, the possibility that administrations, in issuing environmental permits, deviate from the ELVs set as a reference. Indeed, in specific cases they are able to impose different and less severe emission levels: for instance, in the case of an imbalance between the environmental benefits and the costs necessary to obtain them; or due to the geographical location of the installation concerned, its technical characteristics or local environmental conditions. Also, in Article 14, Paragraph 4, the IED provides single Member States with the possibility to put forward rules allowing the competent authority to set stricter permit conditions than those achievable by the use of the BATs as described in the BAT conclusions.[83] In other words, it is possible to argue that the new IED enhances the application of BAT as required by the BREFs, in particular by limiting the divergence from the BAT of specific cases, and by giving greater emphasis to the justification of the conditions set in the permits.[84]

The mechanism foreseen by the IED for the setting of the permit conditions has thus abandoned the original approach which was able to grasp and reconcile, in a new and balanced combination, the positive aspects already present in the previous environmental regulation systems, such as the fixation of binding ELVs (based on the German model), the recognition given to the specific plant conditions (based on the English model) and the reference to the best technology parameter (present in both models in terms of "Stand der Technik" and of "Best Available Technology"). Instead, the IED has now adopted a new approach that seems unbalanced, at least in an ordinary way, towards a regulation system based on certain and uniform references and no longer based on a case-by-case determination of pollution levels produced by individual plants.

It can be reasonably assumed that, as has already happened in other fields regulated by European Union's policies, especially with regard to the economic-financial issues, the states of northern Europe, led by Germany, eventually succeeded in inserting into the IED a more and more rigorous approach to setting emission levels for industrial plants as opposed to a more flexible one.

2.3.1 The establishment of the permit conditions: useful indications from the Italian case

Although from the aforementioned reconstruction of the Directive it is possible to draw conclusions suggesting the existence of a two-stage evaluation process leading to the identification of ELVs, in reality, when verifying the facts, it is difficult to acknowledge such a clear dichotomy in the decision-making process followed by the administration that proceeds to issue the integrated permit. This is also due

83 Id. Article 14, Paragraph 4.

84 Anne Cikankowitz and Valerie Laforest, "La directive IPPC: où en est-on et où va-t-on?", *La Revue Electronique en Sciences de l'Environnement* 10 (1) (2010): 2–5.

to the fact that there is not a single body in charge of carrying out – from the beginning to the end – all the necessary procedures, evaluations and reconciliation of the different needs at stake.[85] In fact, it cannot be forgotten that in the Italian system, for instance, the adoption of the IPPC Directive did not result in an organizational integration of the various administrations involved in the procedure for granting environmental permits, as, for example, happened in England.[86]

In the Italian legislation, in reality integration plays an important role through the procedural coordination between the various administrations concerned, which is realized through the so-called "Conferenza di Servizi", the role and function of which will be explored more deeply in Chapter 3. The latter makes it impossible to attribute directly or exclusively which stage or part of the evaluation is carried out by a particular administration (municipality, province, region, local health office, etc.).

As regards the first phase, i.e. the selection of the BAT applicable to the concrete case, there is a need to carry out a technical-scientific assessment, particularly concerning the identification of the most suitable technical solutions that would facilitate the achievement of system performances compatible with the environment. Moreover, it is necessary to analyse, with regard to the plant operator, the actual technical feasibility and economic sustainability of the potentially suitable BAT. For such a task, the competent administration in Italy is "forced" to rely on qualified bodies, such as the Regional Environmental Protection Agencies (ARPAs) and, at the national level, the Environmental Protection Agency for the technical services (APAT; now replaced by the Institute for Environmental Protection and Research, ISPRA). These bodies play a fundamental role not only in the condition-setting phase of the environmental permitting, but also in the subsequent control phase (see Article 29-quater, Paragraph 7 and Article 29-decies, Paragraphs 3 and 11) as well as in the communication of environmental data concerning installations for the purpose of the exchange of information between Member States (Articles 29-undecies, 29-duodecies and 29-terdecies). This is even more important with reference to those extra factors which, in addition to the BATs, must be examined in order to establish the limit values to which the permit must be subordinated.[87]

Also, the role of the aforementioned bodies is key to guaranteeing those additional measures that are necessary to ensure the environmental quality levels determined for the area in which the plant is based, but which would not be

85 Charalampos Koutalakis, Aron Buzogany and Tanja Borzel, "When Soft Regulation Is Not Enough": 332.

86 See Her Majesty's Inspectorate of Pollution (HMIP) which was merged in 1996 with the National Rivers Authority and the Local Regulation Authorities, giving rise to the Environmental Agency for England and Wales. Steven Sorrell, "The meaning of BATNEEC: interpreting excessive costs in UK industrial pollution regulation," *Journal of Environmental Policy and Planning* 4 (1) (2002): 23.

87 Margherita Lafergola, "Procedimenti IPPC nell'Unione Europea: assetto organizzativo e normativo, approccio e valutazione integrata," edited by the Environmental Protection Agency for the Technical Services (APAT), now replaced by the Institute for Environmental Protection and Research (ISPRA), available at www.isprambiente.gov.it.

satisfied with the simple use of BAT. It goes without saying that carrying out such evaluations requires not only a high technical/scientific competence of the administrative apparatus involved in the decision but also, and above all, high levels of information. It is in respect to this that the proceeding administration always suffers a considerable deficit; an issue connected to the traditional problem of "information asymmetry", which in particularly complex sectors characterizes the relationship between the regulatory subject and the regulated subject. To overcome the information deficit that characterizes the process of determining the BAT and emission limits, plant operators themselves play an important role by cooperating with the competent authorities to issue the integrated permit. As argued by Sorrel,

> while Inspectors need detailed technical and economic information to set authorisation requirements, they are largely dependent upon industry for this information. In this context, inspectors typically try to build a relationship of trust and cooperation with industry, preferring this to the imposition of strict standards.[88]

In other words, in drafting the application for the permit, it is up to the operators to propose the BATs that they believe they can use in order to guarantee the compliance with the environmental protection regulations. And it is precisely from these proposals provided by the private entity that the competent authority proceeds to carry out, as a result of the preliminary investigation, the assessments required to determine the emission limits and the pollution control measures that the activity of the applicant operator will be subjected to.

In this regard, there is the problem of determining which body is specifically responsible for identifying the BAT in a specific case. Put another way, debate is focused on whether it should be exclusively up to the applicant to propose a solution that the public administration can then approve or refuse, or if it should be the competent administration's role to formulate a valid alternative in cases where the solution proposed by the operator is inadequate to achieve appropriate environmental levels. The administrative judge intervened on this issue, clarifying that "the legislation does not bind, once and for all, the burden of identifying the BAT to the company, rather than to the Administration" and that therefore "an *a priori* and unidirectional solution seems contradictory to the pragmatic nature of the instrument of reconciliation of the interests at stake".[89]

It should also be stressed that the peculiarity of the procedure established for the issuance of the integrated environmental permit is based on the collaborative relationship between the operator of the plant and the competent authority. Those

88 Steven Sorrell, "*The meaning of BATNEEC*": 23–25.
89 Italian Regional Administrative Court of the Umbria Region, Perugia, 10 January 2003, n. 10, point 4.5. See also Rockware Glass Ltd. v Chester City Council, [2005] EWHC 2250 (admin), point 75–78.

two actors jointly have the task of delineating the path that can guarantee the best environmental protection, for example, through the use of the BATs.[90] Therefore, companies have to analyse and evaluate the production processes of their plants, identify the critical issues and propose how to resolve them by making use of the most appropriate BAT, while, as mentioned above, the competent authority must assess the authorization request, taking into account the overall environmental quality objectives set for the territory concerned, and then establish the conditions and ELVs of the specific plant, both based on those obtainable with the BAT and also making use of the exchange of information on them, without ever imposing the use of a particular technique or technology. Hence, operators do not have to use only process techniques (considered to be preferable both on the basis of the integrated approach and the European principles of prevention and precaution), but can choose to use ex-post purification methods instead as long as they are able to provide detailed technical and economic assessments justifying such a choice.[91]

Take, for example, the 2008 document that provides the Italian Guidelines for combustion plants, which highlights the distinction between "primary techniques", capable of ensuring a preventive and integrated action with respect to the phenomenon of pollution, and "secondary techniques" or "techniques for the control of the effluents of the combustion process", which instead intervene downstream of the process and are determined according to the characteristics and substances contained in the effluents. In this case, it is recognized that the use of primary techniques for the reduction of emissions is limited and particularly expensive (substantially entailing the transition from one type of fuel to a "cleaner" one, such as from coal to gas), and therefore the so-called "secondary techniques" are preferable and more easily implemented.[92]

The fact that the operator plays an important role in the determination of the BAT is clearly apparent from reading of the General Guidelines, where it is highlighted that there must be a continuous relationship of collaboration between the operators and the public administration. As a result, this cooperation may lead, for example, to an update of the previously defined BAT in the light of new technologies proposed by the operator, and that is still be able to guarantee equal or superior environmental performance, perhaps at reduced economic costs.[93] As a matter of fact, the BATs are always the initial and main reference in the process of assessing the environmental compatibility of a plant subject to the permit request. Thus, identification of a particular BAT and (especially) the definition of ELVs, not being subject to a rigid and well defined procedure and involving the participation of several entities (administrations and operators), represent not only, as I

90 Alessandra Maglieri, "L'emersione dell'interesse ambientale nel procedimento amministrativo: prospettive e limiti della semplificazione," *Diritto Amministrativo* 14 (4) (2006): 847–848.

91 Ibid.

92 Alfredo Pini, "L'attuazione della direttiva IPPC in Italia ed il ruolo delle agenzie ambientali," (paper presented at the International Conference 'Autorizzazione IPPC e mercato delle emissioni: i gas serra'), Turin, Italy, 16 December 2003, 1–2.

93 General Guidelines of the Italian Ministerial Decree of 2005, point 111.2.

will argue later in this study, a possible source of jurisdictional litigation – due to the wide margin of discretion enjoyed by the administration in determining the conditions of the authorization – but also the opportunity to foster "dialogue" between authorities and private parties, helping to raise awareness and making them more mindful of the importance of environmental protection.

2.3.2 Non-compliance with permit conditions and lessons from the Italian legislation

As has been argued, the regulatory instrument to which the current European and Italian national legislation entrusts the pursuit of environmental protection with regard to industrial pollution is represented by the integrated environmental permit, together with the apparatus of the relative conditions that are well-suited to the concrete needs of environmental protection. It follows that, after the permit has been issued, for a specific production activity (or the operation of a given plant) to be carried out compatibly with the requirements of environmental protection depends on both the substantial observance of the permit conditions and their permanent adequacy over time. Therefore, effective observance of the conditions of the permit during the course of the authorized activity constitutes the first objective which obviously concerns the national and European regulations.

In fact, Article 14 of the IPPC Directive required States to take the necessary measures to ensure that the operator: complies with the permit conditions in their plant and in addition cooperates with the competent authority by communicating the data related to the control activity on the emissions of their plant; provides the assistance requested by the authority in order to carry out inspections; and take samples and generally collects information on the plant itself. In this respect, it is worth recalling Article 9, Paragraph 5, of the Directive remarking that: "the permit shall contain suitable release monitoring requirements, specifying measurement methodology and frequency, evaluation procedure and an obligation to supply the competent authority with data required for checking compliance with the permit".[94]

From these indications, which appear to be rather scarce and not very significant, it can be argued that the IPPC Directive did not tackle the problem of compliance with the conditions of the permit and in particular the consequences for their violation or non-implementation, thus transferring to the individual States the task of formulating an adequate system of controls and penalties in their national laws. This issue is partly overcome through the text of the IED that in Article 8 on "Non-compliance", besides re-proposing the operator's obligation to report any violation, provides that the Member States shall ensure that the operator will immediately take the measures necessary to restore the compliance of the installation to the operating conditions as soon as possible, and requires the competent authority to impose any appropriate additional measures which it deems necessary to restore compliance.[95] Therefore, in addition to that already and

94 Council Directive 2008/1/EC, Articles 9 (Paragraph 5) and 14.
95 Id. Article 8.

normally carried out in determining the conditions of the environmental permit, the administration is given a further conforming power over the operator's activity. In this perspective, the final Paragraph of Article 8 provides that

> where the breach of the permit conditions poses an immediate danger to human health or threatens to cause an immediate significant adverse effect upon the environment, and until compliance is restored in accordance with points (b) and (c) of the first subparagraph, the operation of the installation, combustion plant, waste incineration plant, waste co-incineration plant or relevant part thereof shall be suspended.

This provision is particularly important as it foresees a case in which – even though temporarily – the *economic aspects* are clearly moved to the background compared with those of *environmental protection*.[96]

As for Italy, it is possible to argue that the Italian legislation is in this respect already in line with the most recent European legislation (see the IED), having somehow anticipated and in some cases even foreseen with greater rigor the possible consequences following the violation of the requirements contained in the integrated environmental permit. Article 29-decies, Paragraph 3, of the TUA entrusts the Institute for Environmental Protection and Research (ISPRA) and the regional and provincial agencies for the protection of the environment (ARPA and APPA) the tasks of supervising on the proper functioning of the plant; ascertaining possible non-compliance of the permit conditions; and communicating this to the competent authority, which is then given the power to adopt progressive measures of corrective intervention.[97]

Article 29-decies, Paragraph 9 declares that, depending on the intensity and danger deriving from any violation, the administration may, in a *crescendo* of reactions: 1) warn the plant operator, assigning a deadline within which they must overcome the irregularities (letter a); 2) warn and at the same time impose the suspension of the plant's activity, if the violation of the permit conditions leads to situations of danger for the environment (letter b); and 3) revoke the authorization and order the closure of the plant, in cases where the previous measures have not been sufficient – that is, in the event of the failure to comply with the requirements imposed with the warning and in the event of repeated violations involving situations of danger and damage to the environment (letter c).[98]

This last measure, while responding to the understandable need for a gradual intensification of the response to behaviour that violates the protection provisions, seems to go beyond the same principles that inspire the European reference legislation. As highlighted on several occasions, the latter often tries to reconcile very

96 Id. Points b) and c).

97 Italian Law 152 of 3rd April 2006 (TUA), Article 29-decies, which entered into force in its current formulation through the Italian Legislative Decree n. 128 of 29 June 2010, Article 2, Paragraph 24.

98 TUA, Article 29, Paragraph 9; Maurizio Cafagno, *Principi e Strumenti di Tutela dell'Ambiente*, 259–260.

disparate interests, such as the economic one, on the one hand, and the environmental one on the other, so that neither of them should prevail over the other, and, in many cases, with an implicit preference for the needs related to economic development and business activity. To enforce a revocation of the permit or a termination of its effects, with the related and simultaneous closure of the concerned plant, would indeed constitute an unbalanced solution, albeit in favour of environmental interests at the expense of the economic ones. In other words, this would contravene one of the cardinal principles of European policy – sustainable development.

2.4 The update of integrated permits

In addition to respecting the conditions of the permit, and always with the aim of ensuring the effectiveness of environmental protection, the EU legislation is also – and above all – concerned with maintaining a fundamental assumption, i.e. the permanent adequacy over time of the initial conditions prescribed through the permit. Such adequacy needs to be verified both with regard to the type of activity/plant actually in operation as well as in relation to the many types of technical and environmental aspects initially considered for the issuing of the permit.

Within the framework of anti-pollution regulations, the legislation on industrial emissions is distinguished by the presence of this dynamic aspect, to which the IED dedicates a large amount of space and which is one of the characteristics of the regulation that make the latter potentially very effective even years after its first enactment.

Similar attention to the temporal adaptation is demonstrated in practice by taking into account changes that can refer to different factors. These include: the BATs that are developed over time and which can thus progressively allow the achievement of lower pollution levels; the environmental conditions of the area in which the plant is located, which could change, for example, following the opening of new neighbouring plants; and the authorized facility, which can undergo structural changes capable of influencing its ability to pollute, i.e. an expansion of the plant or its capacity could result in a corresponding increase in the levels of pollution produced.[99]

In all these circumstances, in which the levels of pollution directly or indirectly connected to the existence of an authorized plant can undergo significant variations, the legislation provides, and in some cases imposes, a reconsideration of the permit and the conditions originally levied so that the operating conditions of the plant are always adequate to the space–time context in which the production activity takes place, allowing them to be as efficient as possible from the point of view of the reachable environmental performance.

As I will further underline later, the resulting legislation becomes strongly dynamic and adaptive in nature. Such a dynamism and adaptability trigger an

99 Charalampos Koutalakis, Aron Buzogany and Tanja Borzel, "When Soft Regulation Is Not Enough": 333–334.

improvement of the legislation, which is now not solely based on a rigid command and control approach. That said, these two characteristics do not solve all problems and in some cases the application of the legislation may still be open to dispute.

Alongside the corrective measures that in the event of non-compliance affect the authorized installation, there are other envisaged measures that (again in the period following the issue of the permit) affect the initial conditions or the permit itself. Those measures impact on the documents related to the permit and/or on its relative effectiveness, and consist of any changes and variations that could be introduced, at the initiative of the operator, into the facility or plant that has been authorized. More specifically, Article 12 of the IPPC Directive is concerned with the management of such cases. In its Paragraph 1, the Article lays down an obligation of prior notification by an operator wishing to implement any change, thus enabling the competent authority to update the permit or its conditions where it considers it necessary; in Paragraph 2 it is stipulated that no "substantial modification" can be carried out without the issue of a (new) permit in compliance with the IPPC regulations.[100]

These provisions are transferred into the Italian law by Article 29-nonies, Paragraph 1, pursuant to which, once the planned and communicated changes are known, "the competent authority, if it deems it necessary, updates the integrated environmental permit or the relative conditions"; while, according to Paragraph 2, "in [cases where] the planned modifications … are substantial, the operator must send a new application for permit to the competent authority". This implies that in the case of non-substantial changes, the update is merely possible. It is up to the competent administration to assess whether or not those changes require an amendment to the permit conditions. In either case, once communicated and found to be non-substantial, the operator may carry out the modification without the need for any approval by the administration.[101]

On the other hand, with regards to the substantial changes – that is, those capable of significantly affecting the environment – the operator is required to apply for the issue of a new integrated environmental permit and the administration is required to carry out all the activities normally stipulated by the issuing procedure. This is because, in the presence of a substantial change such as a modification or expansion of the plant that results in an increase in the produced pollution, the plant itself substantially changes its characteristics and therefore a simple update of the existing conditions of the permit is no longer sufficient. Indeed, a new assessment of the impact of the plant on the environment is necessary – as, incidentally, is also true in the renewal of the permit.[102] On such issue, Article 20, Paragraph 3 of the IED specifies, "any change in the nature or

100 Council Directive 2008/1/EC, Article 12, Paragraphs 1 and 2.

101 Silvano Di Rosa, "A.I.A. Modifiche non sostanziali, ricevibilità o irrecivibilità?" (2012), available at www.ambientediritto.it.

102 Alberto Muratori, "La 'modifica sostanziale' di impianti e progetti tra definizioni normative, giurisprudenza e ricadute pratiche," *Ambiente e Sviluppo* 2 (2012): 147–150.

functioning or an extension of an installation shall be deemed to be substantial if the change or extension in itself reaches the capacity thresholds set out in Annex I". Indeed, the possibility to make changes concerning the subject of the authorization is not a specific characteristic of integrated permits; rather, it is a common feature to all administrative permits characterized by a *duration* – that is to say an efficacy extended over time.[103]

In the EU and Italian legislation on industrial pollution, more widespread attention is instead given to the eventuality that the initial permit conditions may come to be no longer adequate over time to the requirements of environmental protection. This is a possibility that takes place not in relation to changes in the activities carried out or to the existing plant, but rather to changes that occur in the overall context of reference. Such a specific aspect acquires considerable importance in the current EU and Italian legislation, which foresees the possibility – and in some cases the obligation – for the competent administration to update over time the conditions of the environmental permit issued to the individual plant. This is a fundamental pillar of the legislation on integrated pollution prevention and control, laid down in the IPPC Directive and then maintained in the subsequent IED. Indeed, it is here worth recalling that the purpose of the IPPC Directive was to avoid and, where this was not possible, reduce emissions deriving from polluting activities, with the aim of achieving a high level of protection of the environment as a whole. In addition to Article 1, this purpose emerged on several occasions in the text of the Directive and in particular in the provisions related to the permit conditions.[104] In this regard, Article 9, Paragraph 1, remarks that "Member States shall ensure that the permit includes all measures necessary … for the granting of permits in order to achieve a high level of protection for the environment as a whole by means of protection of the air, water and land", and Paragraph 4 of the same Article states that "in all circumstances, the conditions of the permit shall contain provisions on the minimization of long-distance or transboundary pollution and ensure a high level of protection for the environment as a whole". In this light, the IPPC Directive includes in Article 13, Paragraph 1, a general provision affirming that States must adopt measures allowing the periodical review of a permit and, if necessary, an update of the conditions therein contained.[105]

The provision in Article 13, Paragraph 1 is configured as instrumental to the achievement of its pollution reduction purpose, which the Directive does not limit itself to wanting to satisfy once and for all when issuing the permit, but rather identifies as a goal to strive for constantly and progressively over time so as to raise from time to time the ideal threshold of environmental protection reachable for a given plant.[106] Although this provision is generic, inasmuch as it does not indicate

103 Council Directive 2010/75/EU, Article 20, Paragraph 3.
104 Alberto Muratori, "La 'modifica sostanziale' di impianti": 149.
105 Council Directive 2008/1/EC, Article 9, Paragraphs 1 and 4 and Article 13, Paragraph 1.
106 Charalampos Koutalakis, Aron Buzogany and Tanja Borzel, "When Soft Regulation Is Not Enough": 340–342.

precise timing or deadlines, or specific reasons for making the update (such elements are therefore identified independently and freely by each Member State), it represented an important change compared with the previous European legislation on the matter of pollutant emissions. Indeed, the latter lacked a provision that delimited the temporal efficacy of the permit or which imposed a reconsideration and a planned adaptation of the conditions of the permit.[107]

In particular, it should be noted that no explicit provision is present in the directives that preceded Directive 96/61/EC with regard to a "planned" revision or updating mechanism of environmental protection measures contained in the permits previously issued to operators. Taking as an example Directive 84/360/EEC on the Combating of Air Pollution from Industrial Plants, which was the reference directive from which the IPPC Directive developed, it is possible to argue that the only provision that somewhat allowed for the updating of the conditions for the management of the polluting activity was given in Article 12 according to which

> the Member States shall follow developments as regards the best available technology and the environmental situation. In the light of this examination they shall, if necessary, impose appropriate conditions on plants authorized in accordance with this Directive, on the basis both of those developments and of the desirability of avoiding excessive costs for the plants in question, having regard in particular to the economic situation of the plants belonging to the category concerned.[108]

Even the following European directives on pollutant emissions, such as Directive 88/609/EEC on the Limitation of Emissions of Certain Pollutants into the Air from Large Combustion Plants, or Directives 89/369/EEC and 89/429/EEC, respectively, on the Prevention of Air Pollution from New Municipal Waste Incineration Plants and on the Reduction of Air Pollution from Existing Municipal Waste Incineration Plants, do not contain any reference to the temporary nature of the permit, or to periodic or exceptional revision tools. The only relevant provisions regard the controls on ELVs.[109]

The periodicity of the verification and the possible consequent updates of the conditions for the authorization, contemplated in Article 13, Paragraph 1 of the IPPC Directive, has usually been transposed within internal regulations through the provision of a temporary authorization, whose effectiveness over time is limited by the imposition of a deadline, after which the possibility of renewal of the permit is expressly provided for.[110]

107 See Council Directive 2008/1/EC, Article 13, Paragraph 1.

108 Council Directive 84/360/EEC, Article 12.

109 See Council Directive 88/609/EEC on the Limitation of Emissions of Certain Pollutants into the Air from Large Combustion Plants; Council Directive 89/369/EEC on the Prevention of Air Pollution from New Municipal Waste Incineration Plants; and Council Directive 89/429/EEC on the Reduction of Air Pollution from Existing Municipal Waste Incineration Plants.

110 Maurizio Cafagno, *Principi e Strumenti di Tutela dell'Ambiente*, 255.

2.4.1 The substantial modification, renewal and revision/re-examination of permits under EU and Italian regulations

The Italian legislation, in line with the European one, also provides in Article 29-octies, Paragraph 1 of the TUA, that the competent authority shall renew the integrated environmental permit on a 5-year basis, starting from the issue date of the permit. This provision applies also to those environmental authorizations/ permits which do not undergo a periodic renewal. As a result, the permit conditions are renewed.[111]

With reference to the Italian legal system, the legislation prior to the IPPC Directive had been implemented with the Decree n. 2013 of May 24, 1988, which did not present different or more specific indications on this issue. This is apparent from Article 11 which states that "the requirements of the permit can be modified following the evolution of the best available technology, as well as the evolution of the environmental situation".[112] On the occasion of the renewal, which entails the issuing of a new permit, the competent authority is therefore able to verify whether the measures contained in the original provision are still suitable to meet the environmental compatibility requirements of the plant concerned, being able to confirm them, or to affirm whether they need to be modified or integrated, and therefore updated, in order to ensure the maintenance of a high level of environmental protection. The operator of the plant is required to apply for the permit renewal 6 months before the expiry date of the existing permit, so that the competent administration can make a decision within a period of 150 days, adopting the same procedures followed for the first issuing of the integrated environmental permit. The legislation also specifies that the operator can continue their activity on the basis of the previous permit until the competent authority reaches a decision; in this way the operator is not forced to interrupt the plant operation while awaiting the pending decision or the renewal, which may indeed come after the expiry date.[113]

However, European (and Italian) legislation does not only provide for a general obligation to periodically update the conditions of the permit, but also provides for certain specific circumstances or scenarios, the presence of which require the competent administration to reconsider the permit in any case. Put another way, there are situations, other than the "ordinary" ones just described, in which it is necessary to verify and update the conditions of the permit. This verification must occur when: 1) it is ascertained that the pollution produced by the plant requires the modification or integration of the ELVs; 2) there have been substantial changes in the available techniques that are able to significantly reduce emissions without weighing too heavily in terms of costs; 3) the security linked to the management of the activity requires the use of other techniques (other than those

111 TUA, Article 29-octies, Paragraph 1.

112 Legislative Decree n. 203 of 24 May 1988.

113 Rosario Ferrara, "La protezione dell'ambiente e il procedimento ambientale nella società del rischio," *Diritto e Società* 4 (2006): 507–512.

available); or 4) it is required by EU or Italian national legislation, i.e. in the cases provided for by law (Article 13, Paragraph 2).[114]

It is not surprising that the first circumstance in which a verification obligation is imposed is when the level of pollution produced by the plant makes it necessary. As already underlined above, according to the IPPC regulation (Article 9, Paragraph 4), precisely the need to modify the existing emission values or to add new ones constitutes the most relevant condition for the issue of the environmental permit. Moreover, modified or new ELVs are the only tools able to quantify and limit the impact of the polluting installation on the surrounding environment.[115]

The second considered circumstance refers instead to the fundamental element that is relevant in determining the conditions of permit, namely the ELVs, which are represented – as highlighted previously – by the parameter of the BAT. In addition to what has been argued above, such a parameter has been adopted, in the construction of the environmental regulation mechanism of the IPPC Directive, also to ensure that technological progress can be identified and optimized in the determination of the environmental performance to be achieved for the single plant.[116]

Hence, the use of the BAT is not aimed exclusively at obtaining lower levels of emissions but rather aspires to make the industrial process or productive activity of the plant concerned more efficient – giving importance to other factors such as energy consumption, exploitation of raw materials, and the production and management of waste. Thanks to the BAT, the authorized plant must always apply the best and most up-to-date technologies, available at the time of the issuing of the permit, for the management of the polluting facility. With reference to the necessary flexibility needed by a system of environmental regulation, the Italian Constitutional Court put forward the sentence n. 250 of 24 July 2009, which stresses that

> the need to protect the undertaking of the company regarding the stability of the conditions set by the permit is certainly recessionary vis-à-vis a possible compromise, if necessary induced by the change in the environmental situation, of the 'absolute and indefectible limit represented by the tolerability for the protection of human health and the environment in which a human being lives' (sentence n. 127 of 1990). Moreover, such a need cannot prevail over the pursuit of a more effective protection of these higher values, where the technology offers solutions whose costs are not disproportionate to the obtainable advantage: a certain degree of flexibility of the plant operating regime, oriented towards this direction, is therefore inherent to the particular constitutional relevance of the legal good that, otherwise, could be offended, as well as to the inevitably, and often unpredictably, changeable nature of the environmental context of reference.[117]

114 Nicola Lugaresi, *Diritto dell'Ambiente*, 234.
115 Council Directive 2008/1/EC, Article 9, Paragraph 4.
116 Nicola Lugaresi, *Diritto dell'Ambiente*, 235.
117 Italian Constitutional Court sentences n. 127 of 1990 and n. 250 of 24 July 2009.

Such flexibility, which made the BAT method preferable compared with the rigid setting of the standards, is further enhanced and amplified by the need to revise the conditions of the permit where the available techniques have recorded substantial changes that allow for further reduction in the pollution produced by the plant (obviously without burdening the operator with excessive costs). Indeed, this provision not only ensures that from the very beginning any new plant is authorized to operate with the most advanced techniques, but also that the same plant may use again, at any time, the BATs in order to achieve a progressive reduction in the emission of pollutants and more generally an improvement of its environmental performance.[118]

Point 3) of Article 13 requires revision of the permit and its conditions and it refers generically to situations in which the issue of *safety* (of the plant) is at stake. In these cases, other techniques other than the best available ones are necessary, even though this change could negatively affect environmental performance and will entail an update or modification of the permit already in place.[119]

As regards the Italian national legislation, which applies the different term "re-examination" (or "review"), it provides that such re-examination may be ordered by the authority also following the proposal of other administrations competent in environmental matters, and it clarifies that the re-examination does not imply the release of a new integrated environmental permit.[120]

In confirmation of this, it is worth noticing that each ministerial decree of re-examination follows a well-established scheme in which the related Article 5, dedicated to the "duration and update of the permit", specifies that the duration of the "re-examination" measure, indicated with the expression "the present permit", shall start from the date of publication of the decree granting the integrated environmental permit, while Article 7, entitled "replaced permits", indicates that the "present permit" replaces the previous integrated permit, keeping the original deadline referred to in Article 5, Paragraph 1. Ultimately, the "re-examination" provision replaces the provision of the integrated environmental permit with regard to its content, while with regard to its effects, which start *ex nunc*, their duration continues to be counted from the issuance of the integrated permit.[121]

Therefore, the re-examination intervenes directly on the already released permit by modifying and integrating its conditions. The extent of the changes made by the "re-examination" provision to the content of the integrated environmental permit originally issued may differ – thus requiring varying degrees of commitment during the preliminary investigation phase by the competent authority. The "re-examination" may in fact require the operator to make simple changes to the plant (even just changes that pertain to the management of the plant and not to its conformation) and in this case it takes the form of updating the conditions of the

118 Antonio Barone, "Le fonti di energia tra gestione precauzionale e diritto giurisprudenziale," *Federalismi* 16 (2013): 7.
119 Council Directive 2008/1/EC, Article 13, Paragraph 2 (c).
120 See TUA, Article 29-octies.
121 Id. Articles 5 and 7.

permit, following a simplified preliminary activity. In other instances, the re-examination may involve a more incisive and therefore substantial change, after which the action of the administration is not limited to a simple updating but also involves performing a comprehensive re-assessment of the environmental impact of the plant through the preliminary investigation activity, typical of the procedure for issuing integrated permits. In this sense reference is made to Article 1, Paragraph 1 of the Legislative Decree of April 24, 2008 on the "methods, including accounting, and tariffs to be applied in relation to investigations and controls by Legislative Decree n. 59 of 18 February 2005", which at c) equates the preliminary activity required in case of a new issuing of an integrated permit to that to be carried out in case of re-examination that gives rise to substantial changes, while at d) equates the preliminary activity necessary in case of update due to non-substantial change communicated by the plant operator to that requested in case of re-examination involving non-substantial changes.[122]

Apart from the formula used by the legislator, the above-explained mechanism is somehow similar to the *ius variandi*, to which the administration can always appeal in the presence of the specific conditions provided for by the law.[123] This may occur through substitutive and/or additional reform, through which part of the content of the measure, subject to the intervention of the public administration, is modified by replacing or adding one or more elements.[124]

It should be added that the regulation concerning the various circumstances requiring the adaptation of the conditions of the integrated permit is supplemented by Article 9, Paragraph 6 (re-proposed in TUA Paragraph 5 of Article 29-octies), which provides for the possibility for the administration to establish temporary derogations to the conditions set in its provision if the plant operator submits to the approving administration a modernization plan to reduce pollution and ensure compliance with these requirements within a period no longer than 6 months. This possibility, which is applied with regard to all the circumstances just considered (i.e. substantial change, renewal and "re-examination"), makes it feasible and favours the entire mechanism of continuous updating that represents, as mentioned, the essential tool to pursue the purpose of prevention and the achievement of ever higher levels of environmental protection. The derogation to the obligation of complying with the conditions of the permit puts the operators in a position to carry out the technical and management adjustments required by the competent authority.[125] This is indispensable in making sure that the plant's activities comply with the prescriptions indicated by the permit, not least allowing the operator to keep the plant operational without the risk of incurring penalties – due to the unavoidable violations of the regulation which it would incur until the

122 Legislative Decree of 24 April 2008, Article 1, Paragraph 1; Antonio Barone, "Le fonti di energia tra gestione precauzionale": 7–10.

123 Massimo Giannini, *Istituzioni di diritto amministrativo* (Milano: Giuffre, 2000), 418–420.

124 Ibid.

125 Council Directive 2008/1/EC, Article 9, Paragraph 6; TUA, Article 29-octies, Paragraph 5.

complete implementation of the modernization plan. From this point of view, the IPPC Directive demonstrated once again its flexibility and attentiveness to the needs of operators, by constantly reconciling the two constituent milestones of sustainable development – the economic initiative and environmental protection.

2.4.2 The IED's new solutions for the update of permit conditions

From the analysis of the regulatory framework given so far, it is possible to argue that the IED, made to replace the IPPC Directive while maintaining the same scheme of its predecessor, gives a more articulated and partly different framework. Indeed, with regard to the verification and updating of the environmental permit conditions, Article 21, Paragraph 1, of the new Directive also imposes a general periodic review obligation for the competent authority, with respect to which it explicitly establishes some operative indications that serve to better delineate the activity that the administration has to perform at this stage.[126]

Moreover, Article 21, Paragraph 2, mentions that in general terms

> at the request of the competent authority, the operator shall submit all the information necessary for the purpose of reconsidering the permit conditions, including, in particular, results of emission monitoring and other data, that enables a comparison of the operation of the installation with the best available techniques described in the applicable BAT conclusions and with the emission levels associated with the best available techniques.

Therefore, the "BAT conclusions" and the related data become here the main reference parameter, not only in the phase of setting the conditions of the permit, but also – and consequently – in that of their periodic review.[127]

Another specific indication regarding the reconsideration of environmental permit conditions is obtainable from Article 15, Paragraph 4, which states that "the competent authority shall re-assess the application of the first subparagraph as part of each reconsideration of the permit conditions pursuant to Article 21".[128] In this respect, reference is made to the way in which the ELVs are applied, which must take place at the point of release of the emissions from the installation and whose determination is made net of any dilution occurring before that point.

Furthermore, evidence of the provision playing a key role as regards the adaptation of the conditions of permit is given by Article 21, Paragraph 3, which sets up a revision and updating mechanism focused on the events related to the "BAT conclusions", establishing that

> within 4 years of publication of decisions on BAT conclusions in accordance with Article 13(5) relating to the main activity of an installation, the

126 Council Directive 2010/75/EU, Article 21, Paragraph 1.
127 Id. Paragraph 2.
128 Id. Article 15, Paragraph 4.

> competent authority shall ensure that: a) all the permit conditions for the installation concerned are reconsidered and, if necessary, updated to ensure compliance with this Directive; b) the installation complies with those permit conditions.[129]

In particular, it is a matter of ensuring compliance, if applicable, with Article 15, Paragraphs 3 and 4, of the IED, which govern the setting of ELVs so that they do not exceed the BAT-associated emission levels contained in the BAT conclusions, as well as the cases in which it is possible to derogate from these values. With this provision, the Directive identifies the publication of documents containing the BAT conclusions as the starting point of a 4-year long period. Within such a deadline the competent authority must adjust the previous conditions contained in the environmental permit for each plant concerned. At the same time, the competent authority must ensure that the installation is compliant and therefore adapted to the conditions thus revised. Put another way, within the period of 4 years the new conditions must not only be provided for by the permit but also be realized in the plant.[130]

Unlike the IPPC Directive, it can be observed – on the one hand – how the competent administration is no longer left "alone" to assess if there are substantial changes in the BATs capable of causing a significant reduction in emissions and thus triggering the obligation to revise. This obligation is in fact now derived from the same publication of documents with the new BAT conclusions. On the other hand, however, the competent authority enjoys a period of 4 years to fulfil the task of adapting the conditions of permit, which is definitely a sufficient period of time. In this way, the IED does not provide an indication of the periodicity of the revision and updating commitment, which in fact is not imposed every 4 years. Indeed, the new legislation limits itself to "linking" the procedure to the processing of the European documents certifying the BAT conclusions.

Thus, the new Directive introduces a further element of uniformity with the environmental regulation model applicable by the Member States, which, under the previous IPPC rules, had remained free to independently determine – and in fact with considerable differences – the frequency of revision and updating activities. Moreover, the IED does not require the Member States to change the temporal validity of the environmental permit and the forecast of its renewal, a mechanism which, as previously mentioned, is normally used internally to guarantee the periodic updating of the permit conditions.

This is also confirmed by the Final Report of the Commission on the Implementation of Directive 2008/1/EC Concerning Integrated Pollution Prevention and Control and Directive 1999/13/EC on the Limitation of Emissions of Volatile Organic Compounds Due to the Use of Organic Solvents in Certain Activities and Installations of 25 October 2010, in which it is stated that

129 Id. Article 21, Paragraph 3, letters a) and b).
130 Id. Article 15, Paragraphs 3 and 4.

> Many Member States lay down specific rules for the reconsideration and updating of permits in their legal systems, although these rules vary substantially. Some Member States have established a time span for the IPPC permits, after which renewal is mandatory. For example, permits are valid for 10 years in Austria and Romania, and 8 years in the Czech Republic, Slovakia and Spain,

whereas "the IED lays down more detailed rules on the review of permits and, in particular, provides for the compulsory reconsideration of permits within four years of publication of decisions on BAT conclusions".[131]

This mechanism does not apply however to the last provisions of Article 21, in which the mandatory revision hypotheses already contemplated by the IPPC Directive are substantially re-proposed. Indeed, Paragraph 4 notes that if an installation is not covered by any of the BAT conclusions, the permit conditions shall be reviewed and updated "where developments in the best available techniques allow for the significant reduction of emissions". Also, in Paragraph 5, it is then prescribed that the permit conditions shall be reconsidered and, where necessary, updated at least when: a) the pollution caused by the installation is of such significance that the existing ELVs of the permit need to be revised or new values need to be included in the permit; b) the operational safety of the installation requires the use of other techniques; c) it is necessary to comply with a new or revised environmental quality standard.[132]

Focusing on the general framework of the examined regulation, it becomes clear that the features of *renewal, revision, substantial modification*, and more generally all those modifications that allow the updating of the permit conditions, work as instruments through which the legislator may ensure the objective of an ever-increasing level of environmental protection. This objective is pursued through the constant reduction of polluting emissions produced by plants subject to the IPPC regulations. Therefore, through these measures the competent administration carries out a prevention activity that does not end with the issue of the permit, but which develops into a continuous and progressive regulation of the administrative relationship that does not allow distinctions between first- and second-degree proceedings. On a more specific and operational level, these measures confirm and further reinforce the regulatory mechanism based on the variable parameter of the BAT, which in this way amplifies its stimulating effects on the market of clean technologies and acts as a dynamic reference to achieve continuously up to date and efficient environmental performance. The parameter of the BATs ultimately assumes a primary role also in carrying out the power of review and update of the environmental permit, confirming – under this particular aspect – that the integrated permit does not operate on a merely procedural level

131 Final Report from the Commission on the Implementation of Directive 2008/1/EC Concerning Integrated Pollution Prevention and Control and Directive 1999/13/EC on the Limitation of Emissions of Volatile Organic Compounds Due to the Use of Organic Solvents in Certain Activities and Installations, available at https://eur-lex.europa.eu/legal-content/EN/TXT/HTML/?uri=CELEX:52010DC0593&from=IT
132 Council Directive 2010/75/EU, Article 21, Paragraphs 4 and 5.

and with a simplifying function, but rather constitutes a substantial innovation that can constantly increase the efficiency (and effectiveness) of the environmental protection system.[133]

On the contrary, the single environmental permit, established in the Italian regulatory framework by Legislative Decree no. 59 of 29 May 2013, differs from the integrated permit in that it is a measure to simplify the administrative burdens on small and medium-sized enterprises, as was explained in the Chapter 1. Also, from the point of view of its temporal validity, the single environmental authorization, which does not apply the BAT parameter, is characterized by a considerably longer duration (usually equal to 15 years from the time of release) than that foreseen by the integrated permit.[134]

2.5 Competent administration assessments and judicial review

As already noted above, both the BAT parameter and the other factors that must be considered in each specific case by the competent administration issuing the integrated environmental permit, represent concepts that are not well defined and are to a certain extent generic. The formula "local environmental conditions", for instance, provides an example of a concept in which the real scope and margin of action remains difficult to delineate. Indeed, it is the very way the provisions are formulated that makes these concepts deliberately flexible and open.[135]

This flexibility, or elasticity, certainly represents a positive aspect of the legislation. Indeed, first of all it allows pollutant emissions to be tackled even when there are trade-offs between different objectives that are not directly compatible with each other. In this respect, the need to obtain the highest level of environmental protection might clash with that of not burdening the economic initiative with (too high) costs, which may undermine the continuation of production activities. This is, as a matter of fact, what makes the objective of the IPPC Directive so difficult and complex to achieve. Hence, it is possible to see how the factor of technological evolution that is "captured" and exploited in the concept of BAT gives the administration in charge the possibility of issuing the environmental permit to simultaneously satisfy two typical needs of modern administrative action: on the one hand, the *effectiveness*, by obtaining the achievement of lower and lower emission levels; on the other hand, the positive trend of the *proportionality* principle, namely allowing operators to implement – among the most advanced technologies – only those that are economically sustainable for them.[136] In other words, the operators are put in the position where they can undertake an economic effort proportional to and commensurate with the effective increase of the achievable environmental performances.

133 Bettina Lange, *Implementing EU Pollution Control*, 142–146.
134 Alberto Muratori, "L'autorizzazione (quasi) unica per PMI e stabilimenti non-AIA: il regolamento definitivo," *Ambiente e Sviluppo* (2013): 305.
135 Bruno Tonoletti, *L'accertamento amministrativo* (Padua: Cedam, 2001), 129–130.
136 Ibid.

Secondly, this flexibility/elasticity allows at the same time that the adopted compatibility measures are subject to constant updates, thus ensuring the environmental protection legislation is always up to date. It is important here to underline the key role played by some general clauses in environmental law (such as the best available technique) that are particularly useful in relation to technical issues because they allow for the establishment of rules of environmental protection without freezing the legislation to a specific historical period. This makes it possible to update the environmental compatibility requirements as the result of developments in science and technology.[137]

The other side of the coin is that these very characteristics, namely generic and flexible references, result in an indeterminacy that can give rise to difficulties and problems at the time of their application in the specific individual cases. In this respect, Sorrel underlines that "such framework concepts can be appropriate where the regulatory target is complex, but they also devolve potentially controversial decisions to the level of the individual site regulator (the Inspector in the UK)".[138] Indeed, the competent administration finds itself having to use some of the so-called "indeterminate legal concepts" which allow it, by their nature, at the time of the concrete application, to have an area of action and choice that is not well defined and difficult to qualify.[139]

As already mentioned, the overall activity carried out by the competent authority responsible for issuing the integrated permit is ultimately aimed at setting the ELVs of the polluting plant which applied for the authorization. Therefore, this is the fundamental core of the administrative procedure that is also the subject of the judicial review by the administrative judge. Hence, it is crucial to further define the nature and juridical qualification of such an administrative procedure.

If one focuses, first of all, on the parameter of the BAT, it is possible to point out that there is certainly a general clause with respect to which, on the one hand, the legislation indicates criteria for implementing the technique to be applied (contained in Annex XI) and, on the other hand, explicitly calls for the content of BREFs to which to refer to. Put another way, the European as well as Italian legislator has provided/now provide all the legislative instruments enabling (the proceeding administration) to make the assessment. The other side of the coin is that the margins of action in the hands of the proceeding administration have been considerably reduced. This seems even truer following the IED and the binding reference to the "BAT conclusions".

In this sense, some scholars argue that

137 Domenico Amirante, *Diritto ambientale italiano e comparato* (Napoli: Jovene, 2003), 70.

138 Steven Sorrell, "*The meaning of BATNEEC*": 26–28.

139 Massimo Giannini, *Istituzioni di diritto amministrativo*, 425; Bruno Tonoletti, *L'accertamento amministrativo*, 111–115.

> when the regulation contains qualifications and descriptions of facts following general categories, and at the same time it offers the criteria for making the concretization, it must be denied that there can be a space for evaluations in favour of the public interest in the concrete case and, therefore, these evaluations should be subject to a legitimacy check.[140]

These scholars argue that the boundary line separating the assessment from discretion has faded, above all, in the field of the overall assessments required for the application of indeterminate general categories that contain qualifications of facts according to value judgments. A typical example of a case in which this check requires an overall assessment is the prohibition of restrictive concentrations of competition as referred to in Article 6 of Italian Law n. 287 of 1990, with respect to which it is highlighted that

> the provision, however, after having outlined the case with the general clause above, fully establishes the criteria for the overall assessment. In this way, the relevant facts of the situation as a whole are punctually predetermined by the legislator with a list that, rather than representing the simple framework, provides the criterion of the assessment made to the public administration.[141]

In the light of these considerations, it could therefore be argued that the administrative activity concerning the identification of the BAT applicable to a specific case should be configured as a mere technical assessment and therefore it should be fully verifiable by the administrative judge.

However, even these additional criteria, provided by the law in order to make more substantial and concrete the concept of the general clause of the BAT, may be not enough to exclude *a priori* the certain degree of discretion used by the competent administration in order to protect the public interest. In other words, a certain degree of discretion (albeit technical) may persist, as the competent authority responsible for issuing the integrated permit or proceeding administration requires further clarifications and specifications, as it is evident from the concepts of "technical feasibility" and "economic sustainability", which – as it has been highlighted above – play a central role in the selection of the applicable BAT.

In more general terms, it is in fact possible to argue that the margin of non-questionability should depend on a careful consideration of the degree of completeness of the regulation; that is to say of the maximum possible exploitation of the preceptive capacity of the substantive legislation. Where there is a legal criterion of decision, non-questionability should not be at stake. Indeed, one of the main problems to be faced with regard to interpretation should therefore be that of identifying the criteria for concretization offered by the normative provision to

140 Italian Law n. 287 of 1990, Article 6; Translation from Bruno Tonoletti, *L'accertamento amministrativo*, 323.
141 Id. 130 and 323.

be applied: an interpretation which, on the contrary, is almost always a prerogative of the jurisprudence.

On the other hand, the assessment aimed at setting ELVs is not reduced, as mentioned, only to the identification of the applicable BAT but it also covers other factors (such as the technical characteristics of the plant, the geographical location and local environmental conditions) that contribute to complete the environmental compatibility assessment of the facility applying for the authorization. Even with respect to these elements, it is possible to observe the generic and indeterminate nature of the provisions of the regulation. Nevertheless, in this case there are no further specifications or instructions contained in annexes or other reference documents or guidelines. In this regard, the legislator has therefore given no useful instrument to delimit as far as possible the margin of uncertainty of the regulation and the assessment of these factors made by the competent administration. As a result, a margin of discretion by the latter is therefore present.[142]

Within the overall process of determining the ELVs to be set for an integrated environmental permit, it is possible to identify two distinct phases which are different from each other not only in logical terms but also and above all in terms of the discretional nature of the evaluation operated by the administration.

A similar consideration, albeit to a different extent, has been made by some scholars observing how in the process leading to the final decision of environmental proceedings it is possible to distinguish a *preparatory phase* (outside the environmental compatibility assessment) and a *constitutive phase.* The former is characterized by an assessment of compliance with the regulations dictated to protect the various components – naturalistic, historical-cultural, landscape, healthiness – of the environment or to guarantee compliance with technical or (anyhow) binding rules. The latter instead includes the evaluation of "reference parameters" (technical prescriptions, economic rules, etc.) which would characterize the judgment of environmental compatibility as "necessarily permeated" with discretionary elements.[143]

The technical rules that operate as evaluation parameters in the assessment of environmental compatibility in the EIA, are present in the legislation either as technical specifications in a specific field (for example, in the field of construction) or as rules imposed by law or otherwise as binding limitations (for instance, emission limits) or, still, as guidelines for the application of the best available technology. Indeed, the EIA would have as a reference general provisions that are not strictly established and defined by the law and in this resides its discretionary nature, unlike the situation where directives set detailed rules, in which case the public administration would carry out an activity of simple verification.[144]

142 Id. 324.

143 Peter Wathern, *Environmental Impact Assessment: Theory and Practice* (London: Routledge, 2013), 35.

144 Id. 40.

Nevertheless, it should be noted that the difficulty of splitting the BAT identification phase applicable to a given case from the assessment of these additional factors, on the one hand, and the fact that the two phases are intertwined in a single assessment, on the other, make the environmental compatibility assessment – through which the public administration shall set the emission limit values – to be qualified overall by an exercise of technical discretion by the jurisprudence. It is therefore necessary to specify that the qualification of the activity carried out by the administration in issuing the integrated environmental permit inevitably affects also the nature and intensity of the judicial control exercisable by the administrative judge.[145]

As regards the nature of the assessments made by the public administration in carrying out the procedures for issuing the environmental permit, it may be argued that the jurisprudence indicates that where an industrial plant is subject both to the integrated permit and the EIA (as may happen, for example, in the case of the opening of a new plant or of modifications of an existing plant), the characteristics of administrative discretion that characterize the EIA end up also impacting on the evaluation aimed at issuing the integrated environmental permit, thus generating the perception that the diversity of nature between the two types of assessments is not so clear and may hence be perceived as confused. In this regard Milone underlines that according to the regional administrative court of Italy the programming and planning phase carried out by the EIA allows in any case for the subsequent political evaluation by the integrated environmental permit, concerning the mediation between interests of constitutional importance, such as those of environmental protection and other interests that the central and local administrations involved in this procedures, are in charge of.[146] The difficulty of separating the two phases and of distinguishing the two natures of the overall assessment is well expressed in a Italian Council of State ruling, which generally noted that it is indeed frequent to find a very elusive demarcation line between the technical evaluation in question and the weighting of the public interest. In short, it transpires that the technical evaluation and the weighting of public interest on occasions cannot be separated – appearing to be merged into a unitary logical process. Also, this difficulty in separating these two phases is, to a large extent, accentuated by the development of the technology and by the organizational and functional changes of the administrative action.

The two above-mentioned aspects are indeed closely connected and specular: simply, it can be argued that the greater the detail with which the law governs the exercise of power attributed to the public administration, the smaller the degree of choice that it has available in the exercise of its function and therefore the greater the intensity of the control operable by the administrative judge; vice versa, the more general, incomplete and essential the regulation is, the greater the margin of manoeuvre that the administration enjoys in terms of the elements to take into

145 Id. 41

146 Silvano Di Rosa, "A.I.A. Modifiche non sostanziali", 5.

account in the assessment of a specific case, and consequently the more reduced and circumscribed will be the role played by the administrative judge.[147]

At the same time, it is possible to state that the *technical discretion*, to which administrative assessments refer to while issuing the integrated environmental permit, is traditionally handled by the jurisprudence according to an approach aimed at excluding an overriding control of the decisions made by the administration, in which at least, initially, the aspect of choosing between several applicable solutions is strengthened, thus assimilating the technical and administrative discretion and hence establishing the same type of external and indirect management for both. As time went by, first the doctrine and then the jurisprudence allowed for a different position. Indeed, starting from the verdict of the Italian Council of State n. 601 of 1999, the principle that

> the judicial review of technical appraisals can take place ... on the basis of not merely the formal and extrinsic control of the logic followed by the administrative authority, but instead, of the direct verification of the reliability of the technical operations in terms of their correctness as to technical criterion and application procedure

was affirmed, hence admitting that the administrative judge can go so far as to directly verify "the de facto elements of the administration, whether they are simple or complex".[148]

This principle, reaffirmed on several occasions by successive judgments, is however not confirmed as regards the assessments by administrative authorities that exercise functions related to the protection of specific constitutional values, including the technical appraisals by the authorities responsible for environmental protection.[149] And indeed the judges of the Italian Council of State have stressed that

> the difficulty of separating conceptually between questionability and administrative opportunity is accentuated precisely in cases where the assessment presents characters of objective complexity, linked to the relevance of interests of primary rank; [such] interests [are] protected by constitutional rules intended to prevail in the balancing judgment that pits them against the interest deduced by the claimant;

all elements "that induce to configure the administrative power as a subject of a weak type".[150]

147 Id. 26.

148 Italian Council of State n. 601, Section IV, 9 April 1999, (2001), 11.

149 See Council of State n. 4000, Section IV, 17 July 2002; Council of State n. 4071, Section IV, 30 July 2002; Council of State n. 6575, Section IV, 29 November 2002; Council of State n. 1259, Section IV, 1 March 2002; Council of State n. 3212, Section VI, 6 June 2000.

150 See Council of State n. 5287, Section IV, 6 October 2001.

In relation to these last considerations, the modification made by the IED must then be positively considered. By binding the proceeding administrations to respect the ELVs associated with the BAT and contained in the "BAT conclusions", the Directive indeed determines a tendentious transformation of the power of the administration from a discretionary (technical) one to a restricted one, at least as regards the identification of the emission limit values under standard environmental conditions, i.e. when "the geographical location or local environmental conditions of the installation concerned" or its "technical characteristics" do not lead to "a disproportionate increase in costs compared to environmental benefits" (thus justifying an exemption from the aforementioned BAT-AELs).[151]

In the light of what has been argued so far, it is possible to state that the regulation confirms the path displayed in this study with regard to the IPPC Directive. Indeed, concerning the logical process followed by the competent administration in assessing the environmental compatibility of a plant, Article 15 of the IED distinguishes explicitly the time of the identification of the ELVs, now necessarily aligned to the BAT-AEL regulated by Paragraph 3, from the one regulated by Paragraph 4 in which the discretionary factors related to a specific plant eligible to receive the permit (hence, to be authorized) come into play. Such a distinction is further highlighted not only by the fact that the second step of the evaluation is a possibility, but also by the fact that it now requires adequate supporting reasons, consisting of a specific documentation that must be attached to the permit conditions.

Moreover, the new IED has a decisive impact, as mentioned, on the extent of discretion enjoyed by the competent administrations, which have to accept limited margins for manoeuvre in the assessment leading to the setting of ELVs. Indeed, once the BAT applicable to the specific case has been identified, no limit values exceeding the levels associated with the BAT can be established in the BAT conclusions document. That said, it is still too early to be able to say whether this reduction in the manoeuvring space will actually be carried out by the competent authorities, given that: 1) the IED legislation does not provide further elements to better delineate the BAT selection process applicable to a specific case; and 2) the emission values associated with the BAT represent only an upper limit, which cannot be exceeded by the proceeding authority, thus still leaving to the administration a certain margin of choice equal to the spectrum of emission values in which each individual BAT-AEL materializes. It should also be noted that – on the one hand – Article 14, Paragraph 5 allows for the possibility for the administration to impose the use of a BAT not described in any of the BAT conclusions, as well as the inverse case of a BAT expressly foreseen but for which no emission level is specified. On the other hand, letter b) of Article 15 allows the proceeding authority to deviate from the limit values associated with the BAT and to set "different emission limit values … in terms of values, periods of time and reference conditions", establishing that in this case "the competent authority shall, at least annually, assess the results of emission monitoring in order to ensure that emissions under normal operating conditions have not exceeded the emission levels

151 Council Directive 2010/75/EU, Article 3, Paragraph 12.

associated with the best available techniques".[152] The overall indication deriving from such provisions is therefore that, also in light of the new IED, the level of discretion exercised by the competent administrations will remain high, thus making the control carried out by the administrative judge in judicial review still fundamental. Finally, it is possible to argue that the task of the judge will be greatly facilitated by at least some of the new regulatory provisions.

2.5.1 BATs, self-restraining and litigation cases

The indeterminacy which characterizes the exercise of administrative power on the subject of integrated environmental permit may often lead, as it has been analysed above, to a review by the administrative judge. In the concrete implementation phase of the Directive, such an indeterminacy has so far led to the occurrence of two divergent and antithetical phenomena and scenarios. On the one hand, the indeterminacy resulted in an excessive rigidity of the proceeding administrations in the determination of the limits and measures to tackle polluting emissions. This is mainly due to a distorted use of the BAT. On the other hand, a distorted use of the reference documents of the BAT allows for an excessive flexibility in the acceptance of conditions and values that are more favourable for operators than those that can actually be requested on the basis of the IPPC legislation.[153]

Indeed, there are some concrete cases providing clear evidence of these two scenarios. With regard to the first case, there are several examples of how administrations tend to use the BAT parameter without always making it consistent with the provisions of the IPPC Directive (and now of the IED).

In judgement n. 10 of 10 January 2003, the Regional Administrative Court of the Umbria region in Italy ruled on the case of a permit in which adjustments were required for a previously authorized olive oil processing plant, imposing, inter alia, specific requirements for the purpose of containing odour emissions. The complaints of the applicant company about the provision concern both its failure to comply with the identification of air quality limit values or polluting agents, and the lack of conditions for the modification of the permit (represented by the evolution of the BATs or the environmental situation), as well as the non-definition, if not in a very generic way, of the content of the prescribed formalities, in any event considered impossible to be satisfied due to the characteristics of the plant.[154]

In his analysis of the case, the judge underlined that with regard to the "factors relevant to the issue of the permit ... both the Administration and the applicant company have correctly identified the focal point in the introduction of the best available technology", and then concludes that "the logical approach of the acts ...

152 Id. Article 14, Paragraph 5, and Article 15, Letter b.
153 Steven Sorrell, "*The meaning of BATNEEC*": 26–30; Domenico Amirante, *Diritto ambientale*, 71.
154 Italian Regional Administrative Court of the Umbria Region, Perugia, 10 January 2003, n. 10, point 4.5.

that have considered the obligations which can be imposed on the applicant company to avoid the problem of odour emissions, does not appear to be free of criticism".[155] Given that, in relation to the odour emissions, the content of the prescriptions consists of imposing the design and implementation of "adequate works of collection, conveyance and abatement in order to minimize the problem of odoriferous disturbance", the judge notes that

> the formulation … limits itself to identifying a result, even generically defined. On the other hand, it does not give any indication of the types, characteristics, technical specifications of the structural and management adjustments that may be envisaged, nor of the relative technical and economic sustainability of the company.[156]

Another example of how the administration can toughen excessively the conditions for issuing the permit, thus betraying the spirit of the Directive (sometimes with the endorsement of the same jurisprudence), emerges from the sentence n. 214 of the Regional Administrative Court of the Piedmont Region, section I, of January 15, 2010. The verdict concerned the regional resolution with which the permit for two diesel power units for the production of electricity and heat was modified, imposing a temporal limitation on its duration and establishing that, in order to continue the self-production of electricity, the company would then have to install a plant with the capacity to contain emissions within the limits of those deriving from gas-powered engines. Among other remonstrations, what the operator complains about is an excess of power due to lack of investigation and motivation on behalf of the administration "because it would be shown that the applicant has always maintained the emission values within those imposed by the regional permit and, indeed, the emissions from the motor groups in question would be below the regional values".[157]

Although operating under the application of the previous legislation, the concept of the best available technology is substantially re-read by the judge in the light of the IPPC Directive and its principles, thus giving to the Directive a different and more meaningful scope compared with what was actually implemented in Italy up until then.[158] This is demonstrated by considering the judge's sentence, wherein they claimed that "there were indeed techniques for adapting the plant or replacing it with a methane plant" and then concluded that there were "no contradictions nor missing preliminary investigations, since the provision focuses on the need of containment of pollutants; such a containment can take place on the basis of new adaptation techniques or new plants"; and yet, as previously mentioned, the emissions in question were below the regional values. That said,

155 Ibid.

156 Id. Point 4.6

157 Italian Regional Administrative Court of the Piedmont Region, Turin, 15 January 2010, n. 214, point 2.

158 Id. Chapter 3, Paragraph 3, Note 31.

accordingly it could be argued that the existence of cleaner technologies would be sufficient to make their imposition legitimate by the competent administration, even if the activity concerned is already compatible with the ELVs established by the environmental legislation. Moreover, the conclusion reached by the judge does not appear convincing, since, by endorsing the administration's intervention, it is accepted that whenever a more up-to-date and cleaner technology is available, it must always be applied; such a conclusion, in the light of what has been examined above, is instead oversimplifying and not responding to the much more complex assessment which the authority shall perform at the time of issue of the environmental permit. Also, in this case, therefore, the response of the administrative judge essentially avoids the complete review of the decision-making process by the administration in support of its provision.[159]

A last example of an excessive intervention by the competent administration is related to the long-standing issue of the integrated environmental permit granted to the steel company named Ilva[160] of the city of Taranto in Italy, which was the subject of the sentence n. 1187 of the Regional Administrative Court of the Puglia region of 11 July 2012. With the permit at hand, the administration imposed further and general abatement measures on the emission of substances for which ELVs had already been set, in line with the values contained in the BREFs. Indeed, during the 3-year period 2008–2010, Ilva had already shown it had complied with such values. Among the requirements imposed by the administration, Ilva specifically challenged a requirement for the installation of abatement systems dedicated to emissions of macro and micro pollutants. Such a requirement had not been specified in the final preliminary investigation; it was not found in reference documents on the BATs (BREFs) approved by the EU Commission; and – since the Taranto plant had already complied with the limits imposed by the integrated environmental permit in the 3-year period 2008–2010 – it proved to be useless and technically unsustainable.[161] The issue had already been examined in the precautionary phase of the trial, when the prescription had been identified as

> erroneous and generically formulated, since the aforementioned emission points of the substances dispersed in the air … are subject to the limit values set by the permit … and a constant verification system that allows it to be traceable within the same limits … so that the need to introduce unspecified

159 Bruno Tonoletti, *L'accertamento amministrativo*, 114–115.

160 Ilva is the largest steelworks in Europe, and one of the biggest in the world. Indeed, it is an Italian company producing Europe's largest steel output. According to 2010 estimates, the production of dioxin by this steel industry accounted for approximately 90 per cent of the overall Italian emissions and 8.8 per cent of the European emissions. At the beginning of September 2018, while the present study was being drafted, Italy's Ministry of Economic Development approved the selling of the company to *ArcelorMittal* for 1.8 billion euro. The case-study of Ilva will be studied more closely in Chapter 3. http://www.gruppoilva.com/en/ilva-group/ilva-group/steel-plants/taranto

161 Italian Regional Administrative Court of the Puglia region, Lecce, 11 July 2012, n. 1187.

> 'abatement systems' appears without the necessary clarification regarding the specific content of the imposed obligation (both as regards the abatement methods and the identification of the micro and macro pollutants to be abated) to the applicant company, which alleges that it has already adopted the best available techniques.[162]

In the sentence, the Board then decided to confirm this assessment by stating that, once

> the obligation to contain emissions for each chimney has been set within the values established by the best available techniques, defined in the tables of the relevant paragraph, the further indication of the need for a system to reduce the emissions of macro and micro-pollutants is clearly shown to be illogical and without a specific justification.

The prescription referred to is set out in Paragraph 9.2.1.1.3 ("Cokefazione") of the definitive preliminary opinion (page 828 et seq.), after table n. 287 which, for each emission point, indicates exactly the final values allowed for each parameter (powders, NOx, SOx, etc.), in several cases setting them below the regulatory limit of Legislative Decree n. 152 of 2006 and corresponding to the BAT. The judge underlined that

> even if the introduction of further limits with respect to the BAT can be hypothesised, it is in any case necessary that the prescription has a specific content, so as to enable the producer to comply with it and to verify its compliance with the established parameters.

In this sense, it is evident that the requirement should be understood as generating the obligation to implement it "through extremely flexible tools, for example through the presentation of a feasibility study on the basis of which the subsequent comparison aimed at defining the detailed aspects not specified in the integrated environmental permit".[163]

2.5.2 BREFs and litigation cases

Moving onto the second scenario/phenomenon, represented by excessively permissive solutions, it is here necessary to highlight a different aspect, namely that of the flexibility with which the administrations can set polluting emission limits, often regardless of the data contained in the BREFs. Such flexibility sometimes runs the risk of leading to actual freedom and/or arbitrariness, which if invoked in the area of technical discretion can make it problematic to investigate and/or verify if the administration has correctly applied the normative indications or

162 Italian Regional Administrative Court of the Puglia Region, Lecce, 9 March 2012, n. 201.
163 Ibid.

whether it has disregarded the principles and informative criteria of the Directive. In this case, too, some concrete examples of unjustifiably permissive interventions can serve to illustrate with greater clarity what has just been argued.[164]

First, it is possible to recall the sentence, previously cited above, concerning the role of BREFs in the BAT identification process in which it emerged that, when issuing the integrated environmental permit, the administration had set ELVs which were much higher than those indicated in the BREFs. In particular, the competent authority had established values for carbon monoxide above 120 mg/ Nm^3 compared with values associated with the applicable BAT of between 30 and 50 mg/Nm^3. Moreover, the administration had not been able to adequately justify the choice to set emission levels so much higher than those indicated as achievable through the application of the BAT and, it is in this respect, namely that of insufficient justification, that the administrative judge requested the cancellation of the permit.[165]

On another case, however, the judge was requested to make a decision on the objections raised by the municipality concerning the legitimacy of the regional integrated environmental permit for a non-ferrous metal foundry (falling within the scope of the IPPC Directive). While noting that "the limits set by the Region could have been even stricter, in particular taking into account the 2001 BATs for non-ferrous metals" and that "even for odorous emissions the limit could have been adjusted to take into account the proximity to residential buildings", the judge rejected the appeal referring to the presence of technical discretion in the decisions taken by the proceeding administration, and essentially bypassing the logical argumentative path followed by the Region.[166] Therefore, the judge seemed to assume an attitude of deference for the discretionary choices of the administration, arguing that

> in the absence of more specific complaints, it is not considered possible to identify margins of illegitimacy, not even with regard to the precautionary principle, which still presupposes a choice among more technical solutions that are punctually described and hence comparable with each other.

Considering this case, it is possible to argue that the jurisprudence shows an attitude of *self-restraint* with regard to the assessments made by the administration on integrated environmental permits.[167] Indeed, at least on the basis of the pronouncements issued so far, there are still very few cases in which the judges, given the objections raised against the issue or denial of the integrated permit, try to overcome the obstacle represented by the intrinsic indeterminacy of the concept of

164 Massimo Giannini, *Istituzioni di diritto amministrativo*, 425.
165 Italian Council of State, Section VI, 23 May 2011, n. 3107.
166 See Italian Regional Administrative Court of the Lombardy region, Brescia, Section I, 22 January 2010, n. 211, available at www.giustizia-amministrativa.it
167 Cristina Videtta, "Le valutazioni tecniche ambientali tra riserva procedimentale e self-restraint del giudice amministrativo," *Foro Amministrativo* 4 (1) (2005): 1359–1365.

BAT, and to verify instead the concrete and correct use by either the administration or the operator of the authorized plant.[168]

In this regard, in the sentence n. 2121 of the Regional Administrative Court of the Lazio region, section III, of 5 March 2008, the judge's sentence states at Paragraph 6 that

> it is known that the prevailing jurisprudence accepts – when complex technical evaluations are at stake, based on the application of proper rules of inexact sciences and with margins of opinion – a prognostic evaluation of the effects of a given activity and a judicial review which does not allow a substitute power of the judge, so as to overlap its own technical evaluation (equally questionable) or its logical model of implementation of the indeterminate concept to the authority's work, but which is limited to a control of reasonableness, logicalness and coherence.[169]

Precisely on the basis of this orientation the judge rejects the objections of illegitimacy made against the contested provision and, at point 12, further clarifies that "it is necessary to move from the consideration that the positive judgment of environmental compatibility, for the reasons set out in the previous point sub 6, can not be questioned here" and that "any other consideration exceeds the limits of what can be performed by the administrative judge on the complex technical evaluations, such as those that occur during the verification of the environmental impact of an electricity production plant".[170] It can be observed that the administrative judge already had to face in the past an indeterminate concept such as that of the BAT, referring in particular to concept of best available technology that, as previously mentioned, is already present in the Italian legal system within the Decree n. 203 of May 24, 1988, concerning emissions into the atmosphere. However, it should be also emphasized that in such a different context, the concept – while posing the same problems – did not prove decisive for the legitimacy of the issue of the permit as the object of the verification was the compliance with the emission standards, which, at that time, were not bound to the BAT. As a consequence, to assess the legitimacy of the permit, it was sufficient to ascertain the compliance with the emission standards without having to verify the concrete use of this or that best technology.[171]

For the same reasons, and even to a higher extent, the judge faced difficulties in taking care of what had previously been indicated as the second phase of evaluation and which leads the administration, once the BAT has been identified, to set emission limits that have to be complied with. In this phase, as already argued, the

168 Rosario Ferrara, "La valutazione di impatto ambientale fra discrezionalità dell'amministrazione e sindacato del giudice amministrativo," *Foro Amministrativo* (2010): 3179–3184.

169 Italian Regional Administrative Court of the of the Lazio region, Section III, 5 March 2008, n. 2121.

170 Ibid.

171 See Legislative Decree n. 203 of May 24, 1988.

administration enjoys even wider margins of manoeuvre, which as a consequence represents an obstacle to the activity of the judge. Unlike what may happen in other sectors, such as those in which regulatory authorities operate, the administrative judge does not verify the accuracy of the technical assessments made by the administration on environmental matters; the control of the "reasonableness and technical coherence of the administrative decision" in environmental or landscape-territorial matters takes place then through the simple verification of the non-existence of clues from which the illegitimacy of the discretionary choice of the administration is revealed.[172] On the other hand, it is worth noting that such an attitude of the administrative judge concerning decisions by the competent authorities to issue environmental permits is also highlighted in the UK experience, where "the courts have adopted a relatively 'hands off' approach, interfering only where the decision-maker can be shown to have acted irrationally".[173]

Particularly emblematic in this respect is the English case Thornby Farms Ltd vs. Daventry District Council, in which a permit was granted to the company Time Right Incineration for the installation of two incinerators for the disposal of animal carcasses. The company Thornby Farms claimed in its appeal that the administration had erred in identifying the BAT for the specific case, having considered a simple transposition of the maximum emission levels indicated in the guidelines of reference to be sufficient to ensure that the BAT was going to be used in the specific case. The incinerators were in fact authorized to emit levels of polluting emissions at higher concentrations than those that they were able to achieve, in line with the levels set by the Guidance note PG 5/3 (95) which provides at Paragraph 17 that "the following concentrations of pollutants must not be exceeded in any atmospheric emissions". The court of second instance did not agree with the thesis presented by the administration. The latter argued that the levels set by the specific Guideline mirrored the applicable BAT: the fact that they cannot be overcome does not ensure that they are actually the best levels that can be guaranteed in this specific case. Indeed, the court recalled that the objectives of the Directive and of the national legislation, on one hand, "will not always be met by prescribing the highest emission permitted by paragraph 17 of the guidance note" and, on the other, that the proceeding authority "must address itself to what is the best available technique" so that "the emission levels in PG 5/3 are not, and are not intended necessarily to be, coincident with use of the best available techniques". The assessment leeway available to the administration should not therefore weaken its obligation to ensure that the BAT is adopted. In its conclusions, in Paragraph 61 the Court goes on to clarify that

172 Italian Regional Administrative Court of the of the Lazio region, Section III, 5 March 2008, n. 2121.

173 See Levy v Environmental Agency, [2002] EWHC 1663; Thornby Farms Ltd v Daventry District Council, [2002] EWCA Civ 31; Steven Tromans, "Environmental Judicial Review," 6 March 2006: 13–14, available at www.39essex.com/docs/articles/STR Judicial_Review_seminar_paper_060306.pdf.

> neither does the discretion to specific conditions which the 'enforcing authority considers appropriate' limit the obligation to achieve the objective when considering the issue in the present case. It confers a discretion to decide how most appropriately to achieve the objective but does not weaken the obligation to ensure that BATNEEC will be used.

With regard to what was eventually implemented by the competent administration the judge states that "this case reinforces the need for a properly documented process to be undertaken at the time of the decision and not only when litigation arises", precisely underlining the need for greater clarity in the decision-making process that administrations should follow in determining the conditions for granting environmental permits. Despite this, the court does not conclude by arranging for the cancellation of the issued permit but claims to be "not however prepared to quash the authorisation or to make a formal declaration".[174]

174 Ibid.

3 The application of the IPPC and IED in Italy

Towards the achievement of sustainable development

3.1 The IPPC in Italy: procedural vs. substantial integration

The IPPC Directive was not implemented in the Italian legal system via a single piece of regulation but, on the contrary, followed a path of progressive acceptance of the legislation. This path has determined, through continuous and subsequent editing and amendment, the transposition of the whole EU regulation into Italian national law, including the changes that in the meantime have taken place at the European level.[1] Initially, the regulation on the prevention and reduction of emissions was implemented in Italy, albeit partially, by Legislative Decree n. 372 of 1999; after a few years, this regulation achieved full implementation through Legislative Decree n. 59 of 2005. At present, following the implementation of Legislative Decree n. 128 of 29 June 2010, the regulation of reference can be found directly in the so-called *Testo Unico dell'Ambiente* – TUA (i.e. "Consolidated Law on Environment"), which now provides a title III-bis dedicated to integrated pollution prevention and control. Since the first regulations, the solution adopted by the Italian legislator in implementing the EU directive has been to provide a unique permit, which "replaces every other authorization, visa, clearance, opinion on environmental matters provided for by the provisions of the law and by the relevant implementing rules".[2]

In Italy, application of the IPPC Directive was at first performed only in relation to newly constructed or newly authorized plants and not to existing plants and installations. An extension to the scope of application of the legislation took place only many years later with the adoption of Legislative Decree n. 59 of 2005, which made the integrated permit regulations compulsory for existing plants too. This choice was made – as already noted – without the imposition of any single and/or specific obligation deriving from the IPPC Directive. Indeed, Article 7 of Directive 2008/1/EC provides that:

> Member States shall take the measures necessary to ensure that the conditions of, and procedure for the grant of, the permit are fully coordinated where more than one competent authority is involved, in order to guarantee

1 Teodora Marocco, "La Direttiva IPPC": 35–38.

2 Alfredo Scialò, "L'integrazione dell'AIA nel procedimento di VIA nel secondo decreto correttivo del TUA," *Ambiente e Sviluppo* 6 (2008): 524–525.

> an effective integrated approach by all authorities competent for this procedure.[3]

Indeed, the European legislation does not introduce the tool of integrated permits into the legal systems of the Member States, as sometimes it is misleadingly argued; in fact, the Community legislation does not impose any obligation on the member countries to set up a single procedure, or to identify a single competent administration, or to replace the different qualifications with a single permit. This point is also confirmed by "whereas" n. 15 of the Directive, which declares that the "full coordination of the authorisation procedure and conditions between competent authorities should make it possible to achieve the highest practicable level of protection for the environment as a whole".[4] It is mainly with reference to this choice, namely to make integrated permit regulations compulsory for existing Italian plants, that experts and scholars have argued about the *fundamental characteristic* of the IPPC Directive (as it is) adopted in Italy. Moreover, scholars have recognized that through this choice the Italian legislator allowed for the implementation of the integrated approach that, as mentioned above, is precisely the key innovative characteristic of the IPPC Directive.[5]

Recalling what previously has been observed with reference to the concept of "integration", and to its role within the text of European permitting legislation, it is then necessary to focus on the specific modality which can be attributed to the integrated permit, thus establishing whether it represents a model of effective substantive integration, in the spirit of the Directive, or just an example of organizational or purely procedural integration. In this respect, it is necessary to recall Paragraph 5 of Article 29-quater of the Consolidated Law on Environment (TUA),[6] which discusses "the convening by the competent authority, for the purpose of issuing the integrated environmental permit, of a special 'Conferenza di Servizi',[7] to which the competent environmental administrations are invited". At the same time, Paragraph 3 of Article 29-sexies states that

> the integrated environmental authorization must include emission limit values set for the polluting substances ... that may be issued by the concerned plant in significant quantities, considering their nature, and their potential for transferring pollution from one environmental media to another, such as water, air and soil, as well as the limit values under the current legislation on noise pollution.[8]

3 Id. 525; Council Directive 2008/1/EC, Article 7.
4 Id. "whereas" n. 15.
5 Teodora Marocco, "La Direttiva IPPC": 39–41.
6 Italian Legislative Decree n. 152 of 3 April 2006.
7 Literally the expression "Conferenza di Servizi" means "Service Conference" or "Conference of Services". In practice, it is a "collegial body made of different administrations" or, in other words, a "decisional process among competent agencies". The "Conferenza di Servizi" is also mentioned in Chapter 2, Section 2.3.1, of the present study.
8 Translation from TUA, Article 29-sexies, Paragraph 3 and Article 29-quater, Paragraph 5.

On one hand, some of the arguments present in the doctrine are aimed at stressing the mechanisms of integration and procedural simplification that characterize the issue of the integrated environmental permits, with particular reference to the role of the "Conferenza di Servizi" – a *collegial body made of different administrations* or, in other words, a *decisional process among competent agencies.* The usefulness of this decisional process lies precisely in the possibility of concentrating in a single logistical and temporal context the evaluations and positions of the individual public interest authorities involved in an administrative procedure, in order to allow their coordination and to favour agreements between them, in accordance with Article 15 of Law n. 241/1990. In fact, among the different simplification models, the "Conferenza di Servizi" is – through its single office ("sportello unico") – the only tool able to ensure that diverse interests are taken into account and are consistent with the fundamental principles of guaranteeing the legality and good performance of the administrative action.[9]

On the other hand, some other arguments present in the doctrine are aimed at stressing the problems connected to the relationship between this specific (integrated) permit and the other environmental authorizations envisaged in the Italian legal system. In particular, I refer to the relationship between integrated permits and Environmental Impact Assessment (EIA), but also more generally between integrated permits and other environmental procedures, such as the Strategic Environmental Assessment (SEA), as well as further proceedings authorizing renewable energy production plants, waste production plants, etc.[10] An integrated approach is therefore guaranteed as the different measures that were previously issued by different administrations are now concentrated in a single assessment procedure under a special collegial body (i.e. "Conferenza di Servizi"). In fact, the latter is considered the legal instrument through which integration takes place, because

> the separate and detailed evaluations of the various public interests at stake, typical of the ordinary administrative procedures, fall into a single, global and contextual evaluation, so that each public subject participating to the 'Conferenza di Servizi' must consider, in addition to its own, the public interests represented by the other administrations in order to reach a final solution able to satisfy, in the best way, all the public interests involved.[11]

Now, though from the procedural point of view it can be certainly argued that the "Conferenza di Servizi" constitutes an instrument of integration chosen by the

9 Alessio Scarcella, *L'Autorizzazione Integrata Ambientale* (Milano: Giuffrè, 2005), 190. Maria Alessandra Sandulli, "Tutela dell'ambiente e sviluppo economico e infrastrutturale: un difficile ma necessario contemperamento," *Rivista Giuridica dell'Edilizia* 1 (2000): 10.

10 Alberta Milone, "Il procedimento autorizzatorio degli impianti di produzione di energia rinnovabile: rapporti con VIA e AIA," *Ambiente e Sviluppo* 12 (2009): 1123–1124.

11 Franco Gaetano Scoca, "Analisi giuridica della conferenza di servizi," *Diritto Amministrativo* 2 (1999): 262.

Italian legislator, it must be clarified that – at the same time – such a decisional process manages integration from an organizational point of view. In fact, there are two possible approaches to integration: one seeks to entrust the task of issuing the permit to a given subject, while maintaining the substantial competences subdivided among several administrations; the other assigns to a single authority the individual environmental competences previously exercised by separate entities, thereby putting in place a full organizational concentration of tasks. The text of the Italian law does not operate this second type of integration, and therefore it is not possible to recognize in the choice of the "Conferenza di Servizi" the will by the legislator to achieve a comprehensive organizational integration. Indeed, the competences remain distinct among the various administrations and are directly addressed to them; and this remains true despite the role played by the "Conferenza di Servizi" in the decision-making process. The attribution of the competence to issue the integrated permit to the ministerial (or regional) authority inevitably requires the use of cooperation and coordination mechanisms between the various competent administrations: this confirms the procedural and non-organizational value of the "Conferenza di Servizi".[12]

This argument is also corroborated by the outcome reached by the doctrinal and jurisprudential debate on the nature of the "Conferenza di Servizi". Indeed, both the doctrine and the jurisprudence have recognized the "Conferenza di Servizi" as a collegial body resulting from the temporary, extraordinary or mixed contribution of the various administrations involved, each of which, therefore, remaining the holder of its competence and participating in the management of its function. The output of this ongoing autonomous exercise of competences and functions is that the production of the effects of the collegial body is not to be attributed to the "Conferenza di Servizi" itself, but to the individual participating administrations. Thus, the "Conferenza di Servizi" cannot be considered an "agency" and therefore its actions cannot be challenged in jurisdictional offices.[13]

Therefore, because the attention of the Italian doctrine is focused on the procedural aspects of the integrated environmental permit, one could argue that integrated permits in Italy can or should be qualified simply as an act of formal or procedural integration rather than a matter of substantial integration. Given this type of operational solution, through which the integrated approach to the environment is manifested in the Italian legal system, it is no coincidence that many scholars associate with it the progressive simplification of administrative action, a topic on which more and more attention has been placed in the last few years.

Part of this simplification process is provided, for example, by Legislative Decree n. 5 of 9 February 2012 on the "Urgent provisions on simplification and development", which also intervenes, through Article 23, on environmental matters by providing for the introduction of the "Single environmental authorization for small and medium-sized enterprises". The discipline of this new environmental permit is set out in a regulation issued within 6 months of the entry into force of

12 Franco Gaetano Scoca, "Analisi giuridica": 262–266.
13 Id. 264; Alessio Scarcella, *L'Autorizzazione Integrata*, 192.

the Decree and adheres to the following guiding principles and criteria: a) the permit replaces any communication, notification and authorization required by the current legislation on environmental matters; b) the environmental permit is issued by a single authority; c) the issuing procedure must be based on the principle of proportionality of the administrative obligations in relation to the size of the company and the business sector, and it must avoid the introduction of greater burdens for companies.[14]

According to some scholars, the integrated permit also represents, in fact, "a good example of functional simplification"; others consider integrated permits as "an innovative form of simplification". More recently, there are also scholars who warn about the risks of considering integrated permits as part of "the broader strand of those policies of simplification that have affected the productive activity sector in recent years". Such scholars highlight how under this specific meaning such simplification mainly satisfies a new and different interest, not only that of better authorization procedures for operators but also that of better care of the protected public good.[15] The argument of "simplification" in reference to the integrated permits does not refer to the need to simplify in the traditional sense, i.e. as a tool to make the procedure smoother or to overcome procedural stalls. Rather, simplification here indicates the application of suitable measures to achieve the legal result to which the norm tends. Indeed, such a result is the adequate protection of the environmental assets involved.

It is therefore important to emphasize that it is not sufficient to refer to the procedural concentration – which determines the replacement of a plurality of sectorial authorizations with an integrated permit – in order to be able to maintain that the integrated permit fully fulfils the principles of *substantial* and not merely *formal* integration of the IPPC Directive. If this was enough, it would not be a real integrated approach towards the environment and pollution, or at least it would not be an actual substantial integration. In other words, the integrated permit would represent only "an additional multimedia permit", thus frustrating the rationale of the EU directive by resulting in a mere sum of several authorizations – each related to a single context of pollution considered individually (air, water, soil, etc.). Erling puts this as follows: "many innovative permit programs only achieve lesser forms of substantive integration".[16]

As a matter of fact, the element characterizing the European legislation which better represents the new system based on the integrated approach is rather to be found, as it was broadly highlighted in the previous chapter, in the parameter of best available techniques (BATs), to which one has to refer to when setting the emission limit values (ELVs) of the authorized plant/installation. More than any other, this aspect demonstrates the not mere procedural and simplified nature of

14 Legislative Decree n. 5 of 9 February 2012, Article 23.

15 Alfredo Scialò, "L'integrazione dell'AIA": 526; Alberta Milone, "Il procedimento autorizzatorio": 1125.

16 Uwe Erling, "Approaches to Integrated Pollution Control in the United States and the European Union," *Tulane Environmental Law Journal* 15 (1) (2001): 19.

the innovation introduced by the integrated permit; rather, the purpose of the latter is to achieve a genuine substantial integration in the environmental assessments underlying the issuing of environmental authorizations or permits. In fact, it is in the very moment in which the competent subjects establish the limit values and the measures for the reduction of polluting emissions that the integrated approach operates, not least by imposing to keep in mutual consideration all the effects produced by the activity on the environment as a whole, in a unitary – and no longer sectorial – way.

3.2 The (concrete) identification of the BAT in Italy

To analyse the functioning of the BAT concept, and to be able to grasp its most interesting and controversial aspects, it is very useful to examine this issue starting from the implementation of the contents of the IPPC Directive in Italy and in Italian legislation. As already mentioned, the regulation on the integrated prevention of pollutant emissions from industrial plants (i.e. the IPPC Directive) has been fully implemented in the Italian legal system through Legislative Decree 59/2005, which was subsequently integrated with some modifications into the text of Legislative Decree n. 152 of 3 April 2006 on "Environmental Regulations" – also known as the Consolidated Law on Environment (TUA).[17] Moreover, Italy has formally adopted and made operational the changes introduced by the IED (Directive 2010/75/EU) thanks to Legislative Decree n. 46 of 4 March 2014 on "Industrial Emissions". More specifically, from EU law n. 96 of 6 August 2013 ("Enabling Act to the Government for the Transposition of European Directives and the Implementation of other European Union Acts – European Delegation Law 2013"), Italy adopted, inter alia, the provisions included in Article 3 indicating the guiding principles and criteria for the implementation of Directive 2010/75/EU and, in particular: a) the reorganization of the responsibilities regarding the issue of permits and controls; b) the provision, for certain categories of installations and after consultation with the most representative associations at national level of the operators of the installations concerned, of permit requirements in the form of binding general provisions; c) the simplification and rationalization of the permit procedures, including the preliminary investigation phase, also in relation to other procedures aimed at issuing measures having the value of integrated environmental permit; d) the use of the proceeds of administrative sanctions for purposes related to the enhancement of extraordinary environmental inspections provided for in Directive 2010/75/EU and those aimed at verifying compliance with the permit obligations for existing plants without authorization, in order to allow greater effectiveness in preventing permit violations foreseen by the 2008/1/EC of the European Parliament and of the Council of 15 January 2008; and e) the review and rationalization of the

17 The inclusion of the integrated environmental permit into the TUA took place through Legislative Decree n. 128 of 29 June 2010.

sanctions system, in order to allow greater effectiveness in preventing permit violations.[18]

Hence, Italian national legislation regarding the implementation of BATs, stated within Article 29-sexies of the TUA that "the integrated environmental permit must include emission limit values set for polluting substances" (Paragraph 3), and that

> the emission limit values, the parameters and the equivalent technical measures referred to in the preceding paragraphs refer to the application of the best available techniques, without the obligation to use a specific technique or technology, taking into account the technical characteristics of the installation in question, its geographical location and local environmental conditions.
> (Paragraph 4)[19]

As often happens, in particular in those countries where the regulation of a given sector is introduced for the first time as a result of a European directive, the norms implementing the European legislation reproduced almost literally the text of the provisions of the reference directive, and more precisely – in the case of Italy – the text of Article 9, Paragraphs 3 and 4, concerning the "conditions of a permit". The regulatory framework is then completed by Article 29-bis, specifically dedicated to the "Identification and use of the best available techniques", pursuant to which the integrated environmental permit is issued taking into account: the indications present in Annex XI; the information disseminated pursuant to Article 29-terdecies, Paragraph 4; as well as the BREF documents (BAT Reference Documents) published by the European Commission "in compliance with the guidelines for the identification and use of the best available techniques".[20] It should be borne in mind that the application of these European documents in the Member States may indeed be *direct* (in the English text or in its translation, as it was the case of the BREFs on "monitoring principles") or *indirect* (through the issuing of reference or national guidelines, which refer to the indications contained in the BREF documents). In this second case, it was not possible to simply transpose them into the national language concerned; instead in many cases this mechanism gave rise to different solutions as a result of the unique characteristics of the individual countries and the sectors concerned.[21]

Looking more closely at the above concepts, it is possible to observe how in the field of the BATs, and their related identification, the competent administration finds itself in the presence of precepts and links whose scope and dynamics are not easy to determine and that, despite of this, it is obliged to consider. In this respect, Faure

18 See Legislative Decree n. 46 of 4 March 2014 on "Industrial emissions"; EU Law n. 96 of 6 August 2013; Council Directive 2010/75/EU, Article 3.

19 Translation from TUA, Article 29-sexies, Paragraphs 3 and 4.

20 Article 29-bis was introduced in the TUA through Legislative Decree n. 128 of 29 June 2010, Article 2, Paragraph 24. Alfredo Pini, "L'attuazione della direttiva IPPC in Italia", 2; Alessio Scarcella, *L'Autorizzazione Integrata*, 28.

21 Eugenio Lanzi and Alfredo Pini, "I principi generali del controllo ambientale nella normativa europea IPPC," (paper presented at the conference "L'evoluzione dei controlli ambientali, in Italia ed in Europa," Bologna, Italy, February 2004, 3).

underlines that: "the required BAT, in itself, does not offer significant guidance to an agency or to the regulated industry. The vagueness is obvious".[22] In addition to providing a notion of the BATs (see TUA, Article 5, dedicated to "definitions") accompanied by further clarifications aimed at clarifying the meaning of individual terms (*techniques, available techniques* and *best available techniques*), the TUA refers to its Annex XI. This Annex literally reproduces the contents of Annex IV of the IPPC Directive (referred to in Article 2, point 12), with an indication of further "considerations" to be taken into account, "in general or in a particular case" in the determination of the BATs. In this respect, it is possible to mention the use of low-waste production techniques (n. 1) or the time required to use a BAT (n. 8), including the consumption and nature of raw materials, or water used in the process and energy efficiency (n. 9), or the need to prevent or minimize the global environmental impact of emissions and hazards (n. 10).[23]

As a matter of fact, it is possible to argue that not taking into account these additional elements helps to better delineate or clarify what should be identified as the "best available technique". Indeed, the above-mentioned considerations are rather vague and merely indicative statements, which therefore do not provide useful references suitable to be directly applied as criteria of choice in the identification of one technique with respect to another. Likewise, they do not enable the derivation of any hierarchical criteria that can in some way be adopted in the process of identifying the best among the available techniques. It is therefore clear that these reference criteria are very general indications that, for a more effective application of the IPPC Directive, require further procedural and technical analysis, as well as the development of a hierarchical approach, especially for the most complex cases.[24]

Although not decisive, a contribution towards a better understanding of the boundaries of the BAT is nevertheless offered by the jurisprudence which, even though to a much lesser extent compared with the attention reserved for other aspects (such as those strictly linked to the procedures and coordination among the different permits), has also addressed the topic of the BATs, examining in particular the question of how a BAT should be concretely used by the public administration in the evaluation process aimed at setting emission limits. The administrative judge has first of all clarified how "the use of BAT is an alternative or complementary tool, compared to that consisting in the direct setting of mandatory limits for the release of polluting substances. Through it, the supervisory administration is provided with a more complex and significant tool".[25]

22 Michael Faure, "Optimal Specificity": 740.
23 Translation from TUA, Annex XI.
24 Alfredo Pini, "L'attuazione della direttiva IPPC in Italia", 5.
25 See Italian Regional Administrative Court of the Umbria Region, Perugia, 10 January 2003, n. 10; Italian Regional Administrative Court of the Piedmont Region, Turin, 26 July 2007, n. 2866; Italian Regional Administrative Court of the Lazio Region, Perugia, 14 October 2010, n. 32824; Italian State Council, Section VI, 23 May 2011, n. 3107.

As was discussed in Chapter 2, BATs are certainly a very complex and significant parameter compared with the environmental quality standards that may be set once and for all by a given law. This is because BATs are (by definition) continuously subject to changes/updates; a characteristic that allows BATs to grasp and enhance both technical evolution and variables of cost (differently from fixed standards). Discussing the different nature of the "best available techniques" with respect to environmental quality standards or emission standards, Beijen affirms that

> normatively descriptive goals and standards can be used as an alternative way to set standards, instead of use of environmental quality standards or product standards. Examples are the concept of best available techniques in Article 9 of the IPPC Directive or the good status of water in the Water Framework Directive.[26]

In fact, the technological progress applied to production processes and to the tackling of emissions triggers two virtuous mechanisms: on the one hand, it guarantees an increasingly greater level of environmental performance with progressive emission reduction values; and, on the other hand, it allows for lower costs in the implementation of the technical solutions used to contain emissions. Thus, the resulting environmental protection measures are more sustainable, also from a financial point of view.[27] In this respect, it is possible to argue that through the new European regulatory system, a step forward has been made in comparison, for instance, with the aforementioned so-called German approach, in which the imposition of predetermined values at a regulatory level resulted in greater difficulties in adapting the regulation to both technological developments and achievable environmental improvements.

Equally persuasive is the relevance gained by the BATs, understood as an alternative (or complementary) tool for the establishment of absolute limits or standards. Indeed, BATs represent a parameter of indirect determination of environmental performance. Though not completely replacing the specification of emission limits, BATs "prepare the ground" for them by providing the reference data from which to start to take into consideration those additional specific factors (such as, for example, the geographical situation in which the plant is located) that contribute to the identification of the most appropriate ELVs (and the additional measures to be taken) in relation to that specific activity and in that specific production context. Put another way, BATs trigger a virtuous cycle that leads to the definition of ELVs, which eventually includes elements related to the case in question.[28]

26 Barbara Beijen, "The Implementation of European Environmental Directives: Are Problems Caused by the Quality of the Directives?," *European Energy and Environmental Law Review* 20 (4) (2011): 157–158.

27 As regards this issue, the focus of the Directive has already been highlighted in Chapter 2, Section 2.5 in which the BAT reference documents and the exchange of information are discussed.

28 Roger Dijkmans, "Methodology for Selection of Best Available Techniques (BAT) at the Sector Level," *Journal of Cleaner Production* 8 (1) (2000): 11–21.

The preliminary problem faced by the proceeding authority is therefore that of identifying what is *in practice* the BAT from which to start the assessment leading to the establishment of the emission limits that must be respected by the plant operator. This step is however made more difficult by the further point that the BATs, as mentioned above, do not refer only to the specific technological solutions that are applicable but also to the organizational and procedural measures that the plant operator can adopt to achieve the appropriate levels of environmental performance, which considerably widens the number of elements to be taken into consideration.[29]

3.2.1 Technical feasibility and economic sustainability

As part of the whole process of identifying the applicable BAT for a concrete case, a critical and almost decisive aspect is represented by the assessment of the technical feasibility and (especially) the economic sustainability of a certain solution. This emerges clearly from the reference contained in the definition provided in Article 2, Paragraph 12, letter (b) of the IPPC Directive, which refers to the concept of "best available techniques" as

> those developed on a scale which allows implementation in the relevant industrial sector, under economically and technically viable conditions, taking into consideration the costs and advantages, whether or not the techniques are used or produced inside the Member State in question, as long as they are reasonably accessible to the operator.[30]

The elements of technical feasibility and economic sustainability are two of the four steps identified by the so-called Vito methodology, which is a selection procedure for identifying the BAT developed by the Flemish Institute for Technological Research (Vito). This selection procedure is divided into four steps: the first is aimed at identifying environmental criticalities and a list of applicable BAT "candidates"; the second provides for the analysis of the technical feasibility of the identified techniques; the third step, evaluates the environmental benefits connected to the adoption of a given technique; and, finally, the last step of the procedure consists of the analysis of the economic sustainability of the identified BAT. Only after these four steps is it possible to identify the BAT applicable to the specific case, after having thus proceeded to discard in succession: those techniques that have proved to be technically unfeasible; those techniques that, though feasible, cannot guarantee the achievement of significant environmental benefits; and finally those techniques which, although feasible and effective, are not sustainable from an economic point of view.[31]

29 Id. 15.

30 Council Directive 2008/1/EC, Article 2, Paragraph 12, letter b); Council Directive 2010/75/EU, Article 3, Paragraph 10, letter b).

31 Thierry Brechet and Henry Tulkens, "From BAT (best available technique) to BCAT (best combination of available techniques)," Discussion Papers 2006105, Université Catholique de Louvain, Center for Operations Research and Econometrics (CORE), 2006, 1–31.

Moreover, neither the IPPC Directive nor its transposition into the Italian legal system, present other provisions giving further evidence or in-depth analysis to clarify this aspect, so that it seems to fall back on the utmost discretion of the public administration to evaluate, for example, when a technique can be considered to be applicable in economically and technically valid conditions or what should be understood as "reasonable conditions" of access to it by the individual operator.

As argued in Chapter 2, in the case of Directive 84/360/EEC on the Combating of Air Pollution from Industrial Plants (characterized by the use of the different but very similar concept of BATNEEC), the European legislator had likewise devoted little space to the economic evaluation of the technical solutions to be adopted, which are indeed present only in Article 4, Paragraph 1, imposing to ensure that "all appropriate preventive measures against air pollution have been taken, including the application of the best available technology, provided that the application of such measures does not entail excessive costs", and of Article 12 which requires "the desirability of avoiding excessive costs for the plants in question, having regard in particular to the economic situation of the plants belonging to the category concerned" to be taken into account.[32] And yet, the problem posed by the application of the principle of economic sustainability of a technical solution had already emerged in relation to the best available technology adopted in the Italian legislation by Decree n. 233 of 24 May 1988, wherein Article 2 subordinated the adoption of the best technique available to the non-excessive costs incurred by the company. With reference to this provision, a question of constitutional legitimacy was raised in contrast to the fundamental right to health enshrined in Article 32 of the Constitution, as well as the principle expressed in Article 41 for which the economic initiative is subordinated to the social utility.[33]

That said, more references regarding the relevance of the economic evaluation of the technical solutions to be adopted on a case-by case basis can be found in other pieces of Italian legislation currently available to operators. On the one hand, additional references may be found in general terms in the ministerial guidelines issued in 2005 (see ex-Article 3) of the Legislative Decree n. 372/99 which also contain the criteria for the identification and use of the BATs (simply called the *General Guidelines*); on the other hand, much more information is provided by the so-called *Sectorial Guidelines.*

3.2.2 The General *and* Sectorial Guidelines

The *General Guidelines* suggest that one of the basic criteria to refer to in order to identify the BAT is the "sustainability" of its application. This is in accordance with the *Guidelines'* principle that states that the application of the provisions of the IPPC Directive must be aimed at obtaining the best environmental

32 Council Directive 84/360/EEC, Article 4, Paragraph 1, and Article 12.

33 Amedeo Postiglione, "Migliore tecnologia disponibile e costi eccessivi in materia di inquinamento atmosferico," *Rivista Giuridica dell'Ambiente* 5 (1990): 303–310.

performance from each plant, without compromising the unsustainably of the production levels of the sector, even from an economic point of view. In this regard, the *General Guidelines* also provide operational guidance when they suggest that

> in particular, it should be assumed that the techniques indicated as possible best available techniques in the Sectorial Guidelines have passed the economic feasibility test with reference to the average state of the art of that given sector, and therefore, when technologically applicable, such BAT can be introduced in economically sustainable conditions.[34]

Basically, in the *Sectorial Guidelines*, a BAT is presumed to be economically sustainable and considered to be applicable to the average situation found in the production sector being considered. This suggests that the competent administration could limit itself to request the adoption of a certain "best technique" indicated in the *Sectorial Guidelines*, as long as it is technically feasible, leaving to the operators the burden of proving the non-economic sustainability of the related solutions and of demonstrating that in the present case alternatives equally suitable to guarantee adequate environmental performances in the specific territorial context are available.[35]

Instead, the *Sectorial Guidelines* address as a matter of fact both the issues of technical feasibility and related economic sustainability in a much more precise way. Indeed, such guidelines provide tangible pointers for each existing solution, so as to effectively put the operators and the competent administrations in a position to grasp the pros and cons of one or other technique as a "BAT candidate". The apparent simple presumption of economic sustainability of the BAT present in these documents is therefore overcome. In other words, sustainability must always be assessed on a case-by-case basis in relation to the characteristics of the single plant subject to the evaluation.[36] Therefore, there is no possible automaticity in considering the economic sustainability of a given technique, and hence applying a BAT just because it is technically feasible.

The sustainability criterion is not, however, the only "economic" parameter that the competent authority is required to take into consideration when identifying the BAT applicable to the single plant to be authorized. Once "sustainability" has been verified, the other parameter that comes into play is the "cost–benefit ratio". Indeed, the proceeding public administration must identify, among the BAT candidates that are economically sustainable, the one that, with the same achievable environmental performance, imposes lower costs on the concerned plant.[37] Particularly clear on this point are the *Sectorial Guidelines* on combustion plants, in which a further specific

34 Riccardo Fuzio, "Il bilanciamento di interessi costituzionalmente protetti nella nuova normativa sull'inquinamento atmosferico," *Foro italiano* 11 (1991): 39–43.

35 Id. 42.

36 Italian Regional Administrative Court of the Umbria Region, Perugia, 10 January 2003, n. 10, point 4.5.

37 Uwe Erling, "Approaches to Integrated Pollution", 20.

indication is provided by stating that "for an existing plant, with performances already close to those expected with the use of BAT, it is therefore necessary to consider the additional cost-effectiveness margin of the implementation of a new technique that allows the achievement of the BAT level".[38] Put another way, the assessment that the competent authority has to perform is therefore more delicate when it comes to identifying the BAT applicable to an existing plant of which environmental performance (for instance its levels of polluting emissions) is slightly lower than that achievable with the application of the "candidate" technique. This is because the possible benefit in terms of environmental quality could easily be considered lower than the cost necessary to obtain it.

Finally, with regard to the identification of the best available technology to be applied in a given case, an interpretation emerges from these guidelines, which is not immediately verifiable by the reading of the European legislation and which greatly enhances the economic needs of the companies affected by the technical adaptation imposed by the IPPC Directive. Thus, the authority responsible for issuing the permit appears to be invested with the task of not only protecting the achievement of high environmental quality standards but also of safeguarding the economic performance of the company that manages the plant, with the aim of reconciling these two values when they are potentially in conflict. In particular, the reference to the "additional cost-effectiveness margin" seems to refute that the objective is mainly that of improving environmental performance "as far as possible", so much so that when the levels reachable through a BAT prove to be excessively onerous, it would be possible to put in place measures and to sustain economic efforts aiming to reach those levels, even without fully satisfying them.[39]

3.3 A case study of the Ilva Company

Since 2012, the Italian legislative framework on the compliance and revision of the limits and restrictions imposed by the integrated environmental permit has been enriched by new provisions following the enactment of Legislative Decree n. 207 of 3 December 2012[40] and of Legislative Decree n. 61 of 3 August 2013.[41] Indeed, these pieces of ("special") regulation are dedicated to plants of strategic national interest. The purpose of such regulations, which leave unchanged the provisions of Legislative Decree n. 152/2006 analysed above, is to regulate those scenarios that are not covered by the general legislation. The reason for the approval of the two Decrees comes from the strong and specific need to remedy and give a solution to the problematic issues resulting from the (mal-)functioning of the Ilva steel plant located in Taranto, a

38 Annex I of the Ministerial Decree of 2008, Official Gazette n. 51 of 3 March 2009, 149–150.

39 Italian Regional Administrative Court of the Abruzzo region, Pescara, section I, 28 November 2012, n. 507.

40 Decree published in the Official Gazette n. 282 of 3 December 2012, converted into Law n. 231 of 24 December 2012 (see Article 1, Paragraph 1).

41 Decree published in the Official Gazette n. 129 of 4 June 2013, converted into Law n. 89 of 3 August 2013.

city in the South of Italy. As briefly mentioned in Chapter 2, Ilva is the largest steelworks in Europe, and one of the biggest in the world. According to 2010 estimates, the dioxin produced by the plant accounted for approximately 90 per cent of the overall Italian emissions and 8.8 per cent of European emissions. It was as the result of such massive polluting emissions, that the Italian government registered increasingly higher numbers of fatalities among workers and citizens in the city of Taranto and, in 2012, this situation came to a head.[42]

3.3.1 Ilva and its violations of EU and Italian environmental law

The Ilva case starts in 2012 when the judiciary of Taranto ordered the seizure of the steelworks for serious environmental violations, and the consequent closure of the iron and steel plant. Although the first investigations and legal actions against Ilva started as far back as the 1980s, the violations and serious problems related to pollution only became known much later. As argued by Bonelli in reconstructing the story of the Ilva case,

> the proportions of health and environmental drama in Taranto, since the early 1990s, were evident both to the population and to the doctors who noted an increase in mesothelioma diseases, leukaemia, cancer and thyroid diseases. Although there were signs of concern from the point of view of health, related to the serious environmental pollution, institutions proved to be immobile and elusive.[43]

On 26 July 2012, the judge in charge of the preliminary investigations signed the seizure order for the Ilva installations in Taranto and put in place precautionary measures against the managers under investigation. Because of the extremely serious environmental violations and the hundreds of consequent deaths, in the same year the company's top management was arrested, including: the president of the Ilva Company, the director of the Taranto plant, the chief executive of the coking department as well as the area manager. The accusation was of culpable and intentional disaster, poisoning of food substances, intentional omission of precautions against accidents at work, aggravated damage to public goods, spills and release of dangerous substances and atmospheric pollution.

However, since the Ilva Company had for decades played a fundamental role in the Italian economy and was a key asset in Italy's industrial output, the Italian government tried to continue to carry out the production at the company. To do so, *ad hoc* laws were passed to circumvent the permitted levels of pollution, postponing the deadline by which the company should have been brought into compliance with environmental standards and ELVs.[44]

42 See Chapter 2, Section 2.5.1, footnote n. 160 of the present study.
43 Translation from Angelo Bonelli, *Good Morning diossina* (Brussels: Green European Foundation, 2014), 15.
44 Id. 20.

In fact, the health and environmental disaster caused by the Ilva Company of Taranto is one of the most serious in Italian and European history. In 2010, according to court reports and Ilva declarations, 4,159 tons of dust, as well as 11,000 tons of nitrogen dioxide and sulphur dioxide were released into the surrounding environment. According to other reliable sources, between 2010 and 2015, 93 per cent of all the dioxin and 67 per cent of all the lead produced in Italy was sent into the atmosphere by the Ilva iron and steel plant. The appointed appraisers of the Taranto Public Prosecutor have calculated that in 11 years 11,550 people died as a result of the emissions, in particular from cardiovascular and respiratory causes.[45]

With the Ministerial Decree of 21 January 2015 an "extraordinary administration procedure" was opened and a government-appointed "board of directors" was assigned to manage the Ilva Company. The extraordinary commissioners had the task of reorganizing the company, both environmentally and economically, and then reselling it. Hence, after the launch of the investigation in 2012 and the subsequent extraordinary administration procedure of 2015, the Italian government launched an international tender and at the beginning of September 2018 – while the present study was being drafted – Italy's Ministry of Economic Development approved the selling of Ilva to the Indian multinational corporation ArcelorMittal for 1.8 billion Euros.[46]

Indeed, this is the starting point and general context from which to move on to consideration of the new regulations introduced by the Italian legislator.

3.3.2 The "revision" procedure of Ilva's environmental permit

The case of the Ilva Company can be examined starting from the decree of 15 March 2012 through which the Italian Minister for the Environment, Land and Sea initiated, pursuant to TUA's Article 29-octies, Paragraph 4, the revision procedure of the integrated environmental permit for the steel plant owned by the Ilva Company in Taranto.[47]

The issuing of the integrated environmental permit took place through Decree n. 450 of 4 August 2011, following an exceptionally long procedure. Indeed, the application for an integrated environmental permit was presented by the Ilva Company back on 28 February 2001, considerably more than 4 years before the date in which it was actually issued, and hence contravening the maximum time limit of 300 days. Article 29-quater, Paragraph 10, indeed provides that

> the competent authority shall make its determinations on the application for integrated environmental permit anyhow within one hundred and fifty days from the submission of the application, that is, in the case referred to in

45 See INES Database (i.e. National Register of Polluting Emissions): 563; available at http://www.isprambiente.gov.it/files/aria/ines-eper-prtr.pdf

46 Nicola Barone and Andrea Gagliardi, "Ilva, siglato accordo al Mise. Da Arcelor ok a 10.700 assunti," *Il Sole 24 Ore*, September 5, 2018.

47 See Ministerial Decree n. 325 of 15 March 2012 and Ministerial Decree n. 547 of 26 October 2012.

paragraph 8, within one hundred and eighty days from the submission of the application.

Moreover, Paragraph 15 declares that the aforementioned terms shall be doubled in the presence of specific agreements stipulated between the State, the regions, the provinces and the territorially competent municipalities as well as the operators "in consideration of the particular and significant environmental impact, complexity and of the pre-eminent national interest of the plant, in compliance with the provisions of this decree".[48]

The revision procedure of the environmental permit of Ilva Company was instigated after numerous and different requests from multiple parties. For example, the decree included measures for solving the critical situation in the area surrounding the Ilva plant – both at the level of environmental health and at the sanitary level. The criticalities had been reported on several occasions, with separate claims made by the judiciary of the city of Taranto,[49] the Mayor of the city[50] and the Puglia Region.[51] All those requests pushed for and triggered the (necessary) modification of the operational conditions of the plant, with particular reference to the treatment of polluting emissions. These claims (made by judiciary, city mayor and region) are perfectly in line both with Article 13 of IPPC Directive and its application into the Italian legislation, that is Article 29-octies of Legislative Decree n. 152/2006. Those Articles state that the competent authority must review the conditions of the integrated environmental permit. In this respect, Paragraph 4, letter a) of Article 29-octies notes that this procedure of revision shall take place when "the pollution caused by the plant is such as to make it necessary to revise the emission limit values set in the permit or the inclusion in the latter of new emission limit values".[52] Such a circumstance was found both in the appraisals drafted by the Taranto Public Prosecutor's Office and in the environmental monitoring report carried out by the Regional Agency for Environmental Protection of the Puglia Region (ARPA Puglia), on which the Region's notification was based.

In another way, the revision procedure of the environmental permit of the Ilva Company came after a request from the Ministerial Commission on IPPC-integrated permit (an *ad hoc* body set up by the Ministry for Environment). In particular, the "review" or "re-examination" provision puts forward measures to adjust the operating conditions of the plant to the new BATs[53] (and the related ELVs)

48 Angelo Buonfrate, "A.I.A. e impianti di rilevante impatto e preminente interesse nazionale: l'accordo dell' 'area industriale di Taranto' (parte seconda)," *Ambiente e Sviluppo* 7 (2009): 733–736.

49 Stefano D'Angiulli, "Caso Ilva di Taranto: adesso o mai più," *Ambiente e Sviluppo* 217 (2) (2013): 117–118.

50 Italian Regional Administrative Court of the Puglia region, Lecce, 19 September 2012, n. 1550.

51 Stefano D'Angiulli, "Caso Ilva di Taranto": 118.

52 Council Directive 2008/1/EU, Article 13; Translation from TUA, Article 29-octies, Paragraph 4, letter a).

53 Id. Letter b).

contained in the so-called "BAT conclusions" for the production of iron and steel, adopted by the European Commission.[54] The norms of Legislative Decree n. 207 of 3 December 2012, issued not too long after the conclusion of the "re-examination" procedure, regulate the subject through Article 1, Paragraph 1, which states that

> in case of a plant of strategic national interest … the Minister for the Environment, Land and Sea may authorize, during the review of the integrated environmental permit, the continuation of the production activity for a fixed period of time not exceeding 36 months, and on condition that the provisions contained in the review of the same permit are fulfilled, according to the procedures and terms indicated therein, in order to ensure the most adequate protection of the environment and health according to the best available techniques.[55]

Furthermore, Article 1, Paragraph 1 of Legislative Decree n. 207 considers a plant to be of strategic national interest when it is

> identified by decree of the President of the Council of Ministers (i.e. Prime Minister), in which it is operational a number of subordinate workers (not less than two hundred for at least a year), including those admitted to the treatment of 'unemployment benefits', in which there is an absolute necessity to safeguard employment and production.[56]

Article 1, Paragraph 1 of the same Legislative Decree was also the main provision of the regulatory framework that immediately allowed for the lifting of the block on productive activity (i.e. seizure orders) that had been put on the Taranto plant by the judicial authority. The following Paragraph 4 of Article 1 indeed announces that

> the provisions referred to in paragraph 1 shall also apply when the judicial authority has taken seizure orders on the assets of the company that owns the factory. In this case, the seizure orders do not prevent, during the period of time indicated in the permit, the functioning of the business activity pursuant to paragraph 1.

Then, in Paragraph 2 of the same Article it is specified that "the measures aimed at ensuring the continuation of the production activity are exclusively and to any effect those contained in the provision of integrated environmental permit, as well as the provisions contained in the re-examination provision".[57]

54 See Commission Implementing Decision n. 2012/135/EU of 28 February 2012 Establishing the Best Available Techniques (BAT) Conclusions under Directive 2010/75/EU of the European Parliament and of the Council on Industrial Emissions for Iron and Steel Production. See also Chapter 2, Section 2.5.1, of the present study.
55 Translation from Legislative Decree n. 207 of 3 December 2012, Article 1, Paragraph 1.
56 Ibid.
57 Id. Article 1, Paragraphs 2 and 4.

In this way, further elements are introduced with regard to the review and update of the legislation for the national strategic plants according to a relationship of apparent compliance with the Legislative Decree 152/2006. In fact, production activity is allowed to continue even if the plant in question is no longer complying with the law, and this can be done because of the provisions contained in the integrated environmental permit and/or in the "re-examination" measure, even when the seizure orders adopted by the judicial authority are pending. This mechanism not only guarantees the continuity of production but also prevents any other public entity – apart from the competent authority (upon issuance of the integrated permit) – from subjecting the plant concerned to further conditions.[58]

That said, in the light of the examination of these provisions, which also present a certain degree of generality and abstraction, it is possible to argue that – far from satisfying general needs – Legislative Decree n. 207 of 2012 was specifically introduced to solve the problematic intertwining of administrative and criminal aspects that emerged in the Ilva case. This is confirmed by Article 3, entitled "Effectiveness of the integrated environmental permit issued on 26 October 2012 to the Ilva Company controls and guarantees", which has specific provisions specifically dedicated to the plant of Taranto.[59]

In particular, while Paragraph 2 does not recall the general provision of Article 1, reiterating that the integrated permit of the Ilva plant issued after the result of the "review" procedure contains the provisions aimed at ensuring the continuation of the production activity of the plant, Paragraph 3 provides that for a period of 36 months the Ilva Company "is in possession of the assets of the company and is in any case authorized … to continue the production activity in the establishment and marketing of the products, including those made before the date of entry into force of this decree". Indeed, this is a provision substantially *tailored* to the specific case of Ilva, particularly when it authorizes the continuation of the marketing of the products, including those already produced before the legislative decree, on which a judicial seizure was pending.[60]

Furthermore, it should be added that originally Article 3 included additional measures specifically dedicated to the Ilva Company by establishing, in Paragraph 4, the existence of "a Guarantor, of undisputed independence, competence and experience, in charge of overseeing the implementation of the provisions of this decree" for a period not exceeding 3 years. The powers of such a Guarantor were aimed at ensuring the monitoring of the implementation of the provisions contained in the integrated environmental permit. In particular, he was granted the power to propose "appropriate measures, including the possible adoption of

58 Alberto Muratori, "Decreto salva ILVA: scelte difficili," *Ambiente e Sviluppo* 1 (2013): 8–12.

59 Luca Geninatti Satè, "Caso Ilva: la tutela dell'ambiente attraverso la rivalutazione del carattere formale del diritto," 16 May 2013; available at www.forumcostituzionale.it.

60 Valentina Cavanna, "Caso ILVA e conflitto di attribuzione tra poteri dello Stato," *Ambiente e Sviluppo* 4 (2013): 326–329.

extraordinary administrative measures also in consideration of articles 41 and 43 of the Italian Constitution".[61]

On the basis of Article 3, Paragraph 6, the Guarantor could use the Institute for Environmental Protection and Research (ISPRA) as well as regional and provincial agencies for environmental protection (ARPA – APPA) to acquire the necessary information and documents/papers that the company, administrations and interested bodies should have provided, having to report to the President of the Council (Prime Minister) and the competent Ministers (Minister of the Environment, Land and Sea, and Minister of Health) any criticality found in the implementation of the measures contained in the integrated environmental permit. In this way, the Guarantor was assigned with certain functions that, according to the general regulation pursuant to Legislative Decree n. 152/2006, are now exercised by the competent administrations in environmental matters. In fact, pursuant to Article 29-decies, Paragraph 3, the tasks of ascertaining the compliance with the conditions of the integrated permit (letter a), the regularity of the checks to be carried out by the operator (letter b) and the compliance with the communication obligations (letter c) are currently up to ISPRA and the national and provincial agencies.[62] Also, it is worth highlighting that the appropriate measures and any extraordinary administrative measure were not directly attributable to the Guarantor, but could only be proposed by this entity: it is not clear, however, whether it was up to the competent authority, that is the Minister for the Environment, Land and Sea, to adopt the appropriate acts as a result of the operator's failures detected by the Guarantor, or whether this was to be reported to the President of the Council of Ministers together with the Minister of the Environment, Land and Sea and the Minister of Health. In any case, the new subject introduced by Article 3, Paragraph 4, (i.e. the Guarantor) did not reflect the role of the commissioner, but rather the role of a body of connection and integration between the supervisory and control functions, normally managed by complex bodies, and the competent authority charged with adopting those provisions regarding the integrated environmental permit. This consideration is also supported by another provision that is included in Paragraph 6, according to which the "activity carried out by the Guarantor, as well as the criticalities and defaults found, are an integral part of the half-yearly report" with which the Minister for the Environment, Land and Sea reports to the Parliament about the compliance with the provisions contained in the re-examination of the integrated environmental permit (Article 1, Paragraph 5).[63]

61 Translation from Legislative Decree n. 207 of 3 December 2012, Article 3, Paragraph 4.

62 Fabio Di Cristina, "Il decreto salva ILVA", *Giornale di Diritto Amministrativo* 4 (2013): 369–373; Translation from Legislative Decree n. 207 of 3 December 2012, Article 3, Paragraph 6; TUA, Article 29-decies, Paragraph 3.

63 Fabio Di Cristina, "Il decreto salva ILVA": 373; translation from Legislative Decree n. 207 of 3 December 2012, Article 1, Paragraph 5 and Article 3, Paragraphs 4 and 6.

3.3.3 Additional legislative measures for plants of strategic national interest

The provisions just analysed in the previous section were subsequently repealed during the conversion of Legislative Decree n. 207 into legislative Decree n. 61, i.e. the so-called "saving Ilva decree".[64] Nevertheless, they still carry great importance because they have, to a certain extent, anticipated what was essentially the predictable outcome of the Ilva case.

Indeed, a few months after the first legislative act, the Italian government intervened again with the adoption of the Legislative Decree n. 61 of 4 June 2013, with which were adopted, in partial continuity with the Legislative Decree 207/2012, "new urgent provisions to protect the environment, health and labour in the operation of companies of strategic national interest". Such a decree provides that the Council of Ministers, on proposal of the President of the Council, can thus decide to appoint an extraordinary commissioner (that is an external administration) of a company, when the number of subordinated workers is not lower than one thousand, in order to manage at least one plant of strategic national interest pursuant to Article 1 of Legislative Decree 207/2012, whose production activity has entailed and involves serious and significant dangers for the integrity of the environment and health due to the repeated failure to comply with the integrated environmental permit.[65]

Moreover, Legislative Decree 61/2013 in Article 1, Paragraph 1-bis, specifies that the solution of the commissioner/external administration is implemented "upon verification of the non-observance of the provisions contained in the integrated environmental permit by the Institute for Environmental Protection and Research (ISPRA), with the support of the Regional and Provincial Agencies for Environmental Protection (ARPA) – in contradiction with the company concerned". As regards the inspection and assessment carried out by ISPRA and ARPA, Article 1, Paragraph 13-bis, states that "the Minister for the Environment, Land and Sea submits to the Parliament a report every six months on the state of the environmental controls, so as to prove also the adequacy of the activities carried out by ISPRA and ARPA".[66]

Then, Legislative Decree 61/2013 introduces a new administrative measure to be applied in the case of non-observance of the provisions contained in the integrated environmental permit. Such a measure has a different and lesser value if compared with those already and generally regulated by Article 29-decies, Paragraph 9 of Legislative Decree n. 152/2006.[67] Indeed, it goes without saying that the goal of the commissioner/external administration is obviously to preserve business continuity and ensure the allocation of the company's resources to cover the costs needed to carry out the health and environmental remediation measures (resulting from the dangerous situations subsequent to the repeated failure to comply with the integrated permit).

64 See Legislative Decree n. 61 of 4 June 2013, i.e. the so-called "saving Ilva decree".
65 Giulia Avanzini, *Il commissario straordinario* (Torino: Giappichelli, 2013), 57–62.
66 Legislative Decree n. 61 of 4 June 2013, Article 1, Paragraphs 1-bis and 13-bis.
67 TUA, Article 29-decies, Paragraph 9.

As regards Legislative Decree 61/2013, Article 1, Paragraph 2, is reinforced by the provision of Paragraph 11 of the same Article, according to which

> the competent judge shall release the financial resources for which the seizure has been ordered, also pursuant to Legislative Decree n. 231 of 2001, to the detriment of the subjects against whom the administrative authority has ordered the implementation of the obligations to implement the provisions … . The aforementioned financial resources are made available to the commissioner and bound to the purposes indicated in the previous period.[68]

The reference to the hypothesis of sequestration of sums of money ordered by the magistrate against the holders of the integrated permit originates once again from the specific case of the Ilva plant. Indeed, against the Ilva Company two seizures were ordered of 1.2 billion euros and 8.1 billion euros, respectively. By freezing the financial resources of the company, such seizures had put the continuation of the company's production activity in serious danger. It is worth noticing that the duration of the seizures is fixed at 12 months, extendable up to a maximum of 36 months, i.e. a period of time equal to that within which a plant of national strategic interest may be authorized to continue production, as provided for by Article 1 of the Legislative Decree n. 207 of 2012 – albeit pending compliance with the methods and timescale established in the "review" procedure for adapting the plant throughout the implementation of the best available techniques.[69]

It should also be noted that alongside the special commissioner/external administration, who is assigned all the powers and functions of the normal management bodies of the company (i.e. replaces the management of the company), the Minister for the Environment, Land and Sea – in conjunction with the Minister of Health and Ministry of Economic Development – nominates a committee of three experts who, following a discussion with the special commissioner, prepares and proposes to the Minister the plan of measures and activities for environmental and health protection that identifies the actions and time schedule needed to ensure compliance with the legal requirements of the integrated environmental permit (Legislative Decree 61/2013, Article 1, Paragraph 5). The peculiarity of the plan thus prepared is its ability, once approved, to modify the content of the integrated permit as regards the definition of the time schedule within which to implement the prescriptions contained therein, so that the completion of the measures is guaranteed to be carried out within 36 months from the entry into force of the Law 61/2013. On the basis of the plan drafted by the committee of experts and approved by decree of the Minister for the Environment, Land and Sea, the extraordinary commissioner/external administration has the task of preparing an industrial plan that concurrently guarantees compliance with the environment and health requirements set out by the experts *and* the

68 Legislative Decree n. 61 of 4 June 2013, Article 1, Paragraph 11.

69 Michele Massa, "Il commissariamento dell'ILVA e il diritto delle crisi industriali," *Quaderni Costituzionali* 3 (2013): 617–620.

continuation of business and production activities (L.D. 61/2013, Article 1, Paragraph 6).[70]

That said, the start of the implementation of the provisions belonging to the integrated environmental permit, according to the timing set out in the experts' plan, needs to be approved within the industrial plan drawn up by the extraordinary commissioner. For this reason, in a very initial stage it was established that, until that moment, it was up to the commissioner themselves to guarantee the progressive adoption of the measures envisaged by the integrated environmental permit and by the other authorizations and requirements for environmental and health protection (L.D. 61/2013, Article 1, Paragraph 8).

However, Legislative Decree 61/2013 was indeed modified and supplemented by a subsequent amendment by the legislator which, through Legislative Decree n. 136 of 10 December 2013, made further changes to the original text of the so-called "second saving Ilva decree". A first series of changes had in fact been implemented already with Legislative Decree n. 101 of 31 August 2013, which introduced specific provisions related to the profile and the powers of the extraordinary commissioner with regard to contracts, liabilities and budget (Paragraphs 3, 4 and 5-ter), together with other provisions dedicated to the construction and management of landfills for special waste (Paragraphs 1, 2 and 6).[71]

Going back to the amendments introduced by Legislative Decree 136/2013 it is firstly worth noticing that Article 1, Paragraph 8, sets out that the commissioner must guarantee the adoption of the measures put forward by/included in the integrated environmental permit and by/in the other environmental and health authorizations and regulations. According to the same Article, this must happen until the completion of the plan drafted by the committee of experts (so, no longer until the approval of the consequent business plan drafted by the very same committee, as it was established before the amendment).[72]

Secondly, the so-called "second saving Ilva decree" establishes that the progressive adoption of the prescribed measures is considered to be achieved if simple compliance with two specific conditions is made: a) the air quality in the area outside the plant needs to comply with the limits established by the current European and Italian laws, or at least the air quality shall not have deteriorated since the start of the work of the commissioner; b) at the date of approval of the plan proposed by the committee of experts, at least 80 per cent of the needed actions to comply with the requirements contained in the integrated permit must have been initiated, without prejudice to the non-application of the terms envisaged by integrated permits and their conditions. The decree concludes by specifying the duty/obligation by the commissioner of sending to the Institute for Environmental Protection and Research (ISPRA) an analytical report of the aforementioned interventions within 30 days since the approval of the plan drafted by the committee of experts and referred to in Paragraph 5.[73]

70 Ibid.
71 Legislative Decree n. 101 of 31 August 2013, Paragraphs 1–6.
72 Translation from Legislative Decree n. 136 of 10 December 2013, Article 1, Paragraph 8.
73 Legislative Decree n. 136 of 10 December 2013, Article 2.

A first significant aspect of the new provisions is given by the fact that the task of guaranteeing the "progressive adoption" of the necessary measures is substantially meaningless since the commissioner simply imposes the duty of "starting" – and therefore not fully implementing – a substantial part of the requirements contained in the integrated permit. But there is more. Indeed, in fulfilling these tasks the commissioner is not even required to respect the time schedule indicated by the provisions (originally) contained in the integrated permit. This implies that for all the time necessary to formulate and adopt the plan containing the measures and activities for environmental and health protection, proposed by the committee of experts and finally approved by the President of the Council of Ministers, the extraordinary commissioner/external administration may allow the continuation of the (polluting) activities of the plant without in fact having to impose compliance with either the contents of the conditions and requirements imposed by the integrated environmental permit or the time schedule provided for their implementation.[74] Moreover, it should be highlighted that the time required for the approval of the plan referred to in Article 5 can reach a total of 60 days from the day of the proposal made by the committee of experts. Article 1, Paragraph 7 of Legislative Decree 136/2013 stipulates that within 45 days from the receipt of the plan by the committee of experts, the Minister for the Environment, Land and Sea shall formulate a proposal that must be approved by the President of the Council of Ministers within 15 days from that time, after deliberation of the Council itself.[75]

Furthermore, Article 1, Paragraph 9 of the same Legislative Decree 136/2013 regulates the possibility for the Ministry for the Environment, Land and Sea to convene a "Conferenza di Servizi"

> for the purpose of receiving the permits, agreements, opinions, clearance and assents, issued by local and regional authorities, the competent ministries, and all the other administrative bodies involved, needed to carry out the works envisaged by: the integrated environmental permit; the plan of measures and activities for the environmental and health protection; the industrial plan of production activities.

This is, on one hand, a way to apply a procedural simplification and acceleration but, on the other hand, also another additional step slowing down the overall process. In other words, it may be argued that Paragraph 9 allows for a further cause of delays or nevertheless additional time required for the activation of the initiatives necessary to implement the adaptation of the plant to the various prescriptions foreseen by the integrated environmental permit. Such a provision also contemplates the possibility that the works necessary to carry out the environmental and health protection measures and consequent compliance of the productive activities may fall within the scope of the environmental impact assessment (EIA) of the works, meaning that the 60

74 Michele Massa, "Il commissariamento dell'ILVA": 619.
75 Legislative Decree n. 136 of 10 December 2013, Article 1, Paragraph 7.

days from the convocation, within which the "Conferenza di Servizi" must express itself, may be suspended for up to 90 days, extendable only once for a period of 30 days in case of technical complexity.[76]

In consideration of all these elements, it is clear that the specific legislation under examination, even if it does not seem to present a general and abstract approach, ends up introducing a special treatment, which entails a considerable expansion of the power to disapply (in essence) the contents of the integrated environmental permit, ordinarily foreseen by Italian Law 152/2006, in implementation of the European legislation. As already mentioned, the IPPC Directive allows the competent authority responsible for issuing an environmental permit to derogate from the environmental compatibility requirements if the plant operator implements a modernization plan that allows, within a period of 6 months, the plant to meet those same requirements and to make a reduction in pollution. Of course, here the legislator does not express themselves in terms of a "derogation" but of a "modification" in the timing of implementation of the integrated environmental permit; also, it affirms and strengthens – for plants of strategic interest – the possibility that the competent administration may override (and with this in essence to derogate) the immediate application of the requirements prescribed in the environmental permit on a case-by-case basis.

Therefore, it is possible to argue that, in the case of companies of national interest, the provision of an extraordinary commissioner represents, as already noted, a special solution to be used in cases of serious non-compliance with the provisions of the integrated environmental permit. In this way, it is applied as a different and additional measure than those already provided for in Article 29-decies, Paragraph 9, of Legislative Decree 152/2006; and such measure is actually set up precisely to avoid the application of the most incisive measure – that is, the revocation of the permit and the consequent cessation of productive activity.

However, the committee of experts, which acts within the scope of the external administration, has the power to re-define the timing of implementation of the conditions of the integrated permit. Also, such a committee introduces a sort of possible "improper" revision of the permit's content, which allows postponing the implementation of the prescriptions at times other than those normally established, up to a maximum of 36 months. It should be noted that the maximum 36-month deadline for the implementation is set "in concrete", and starts from the moment of entry into force of the conversion law. In this sense, in fact, the final part of Paragraph 7 in its last amendment provides that "the decree approving the plan referred to in paragraph 5 concludes the review procedures envisaged by the integrated environmental permit, [and] provides an integration to the integrated environmental permit". The provision then clarifies that, since the plan includes the provisions of the integrated permit, "its contents may be modified by the procedures referred to in articles 29-octies and 29-nonies" of the TUA, and therefore it may still be subject to the ordinary legislation analysed above.[77]

76 Id. Article 1, Paragraph 9; Franco Gaetano Scoca, "Analisi giuridica": 263.
77 Legislative Decree n. 136 of 10 December 2013, Article 1, Paragraph 7.

In this way the concrete and timely realization of the measures prescribed in the integrated environmental permit is made even smoother and does not appear definitively defined at the time the permit is issued.

3.4 Reflexive regulation, access to information and public participation

The provisions examined above, as well as at the end of Chapter 2,[78] establish mechanisms for the periodic review and updating of the permit conditions, and intervention measures in case of non-compliance with the limits set by the permit. Those provisions are therefore one of the aspects of the IPPC regulation which, together with the other elements already examined in the previous paragraphs, contribute to characterize it in a highly innovative way compared with the previous European legislation on polluting emissions.

In this respect, the IPPC Directive also marks a further breakthrough from previous environmental regulation solutions. The latter were characterized by the rigidity and immutability of the prescriptions, which were the expression of a classic command-and-control intervention model, unable to effectively deal with the complexities put forward by the (dynamic and changeable) environmental matters.[79] Instead, the regulatory model implemented by the IPPC Directive presents a set of specific elements that make it an alternative to the traditional command-and-control public intervention, as well as to the use of market-based regulation tools. In addition to the temporary nature of permits, and the related discipline of renewal and revision of the conditions contained therein, it is indeed worth underlining the key role played by the operators thanks to the establishment of the Sevilla Process, as well as the presence of provisions concerning the acknowledgement, management and use of information, which pervades and supports the entire Directive and which is a fundamental tool for its functioning.[80]

As far as the operators are concerned, it has already been noted how they maintain a relationship of real collaboration with the administration throughout the whole process leading up to the issue of the integrated environmental permit – in particular during the phase of recognition of the BAT applicable in each case. This collaboration, guaranteed by provisions that emphasize the importance of the participatory aspect within the procedure, does not represent an exclusive peculiarity of the IPPC Directive or more generally of single environmental matters, but is also found in different contexts and can hence be understood as a common feature to all modern legislative acts in which the recipients of the administrative action are more involved in the downward phase of implementation of the measures. An example, in this respect, is provided by the antitrust proceedings;

78 See Chapter 2, Sections 2.4 and 2.4.1 of the present study.

79 For more debate on the limits of and criticism to the command-and-control pollution control model, see Richard Stewart, "A New Generation of Environmental Regulation?," *Capital University Law Review* 1 (2001): 21–25.

80 Adrienne Heritier, "New Modes of Governance in Europe: Policy Making without Legislating?," *Political Science Series*, Institute for Advanced Studies, Vienna 2002, 13–18.

another example is the proceedings of the regulators of public services, wherein the participation of the interested parties is at the basis of the legitimation of the independent administrative authorities' tasks.[81]

However, one distinctive element of the IPPC Directive is that operators are directly involved in the Sevilla Process, namely in the process of drafting the BAT reference documents: indeed, it is through the participation of their own representatives in the individual Technical Working Groups that the operators can directly contribute to the definition of the BATs for the different productive sectors and thus influence the formulation of the BREF documents.[82]

Now, as already underlined, the technical indications contained in the BREFs have always been conceived as fundamental reference parameters for the identification of the BAT and the ELVs connected to them, and this role has become even more decisive from the moment in which, with the entry into force of the IED, the documents on the "BAT conclusions" derived from the BREFs have become binding. The participation of the operators in the process of elaboration of the technical rules on which the whole industrial emissions regulation is based shows that the IPPC regulation model is not based on a top-down logic, as it was the case of the traditional command-and-control systems. Instead, it is bottom-up oriented, so that those who are the final recipients of the rules do participate in the drafting of such rules.[83]

Another element that characterized the IPPC Directive, and its distinctiveness from the environmental regulation models that preceded it, is then – as anticipated above – the set of rules that ensure the knowledge and the know-ability of the decisions and of the environmental assessments by the public through the *information* tool, which can perform various functions and therefore be configured in a variety of ways.[84] In this respect, the matter of public participation has been amended and supplemented by Article 4 of Directive 2003/35/EC of the European Parliament and of the Council of 26 May 2003 ("Providing for Public Participation in Respect of the Drawing Up of Certain Plans and Programmes Relating to the Environment and Amending with Regard to Public Participation and Jccess to justice Council Directives 85/337/EEC and 96/61/EC") and it is indeed the first implementation in the European legislation of Article 6 of the Aahrus Convention of 25 June 1998 on access to information, public participation in decision-making and access to justice in environmental matters.[85]

81 Id. 15.
82 Magnus Gislev, "European Innovation": 78.
83 In particular, as regards the bottom-up approach in the environmental field, see Yohannes Mariam, "Environmental Sustainability and Regulation: Top-Down Versus Bottom-Up Regulation," *Munich Personal RePEc Archive Paper*, 2001, 5.
84 Valerio Scarone, "La specialità del diritto all'informazione ambientale," *Foro Amministrativo* (2004): 77.
85 Council Directive 2003/35/EC, Article 4; United Nations Economic Commission for Europe, "Convention on Access to Information, Public Participation in Decision-Making and Access to Justice in Environmental Matters," Aarhus, Denmark, 25 June 1998, Article 6.

Indeed, Article 4, Paragraph 1 of Directive 2003/35/EC remarks that the "Member States shall ensure that the public concerned are given early and effective opportunities to participate in the procedure" and refers to Annex V for the specification of the procedures through which this is to be exercised.[86] Following the same rationale, Article 15, Paragraph 1 of Directive 2008/1/EU clarifies that the *procedure* refers to the issue of a permit for new plants (letter a), to the issue of a permit for substantial changes in the operation of an installation (letter b) and to the update of a permit or permit conditions related to an installation (letter c). Annex V then identifies in detail the different aspects on which the public must be informed, also clarifying that the information must be given to the public "early in the procedure for the taking of a decision or, at the latest, as soon as the information can reasonably be provided".[87] This information, including the advisory reports and those collected from operators and sent to the competent authority during the procedures of issuing permits, are instrumental to public participation, allowing them the right to submit observations and opinions to the authority. Eventually, the latter will duly consider the received petitions at the time of its decision.

The close relationship of instrumentality present in such proceedings between information and participation, and its relevance in the environmental field, emerged from the 1992 Rio de Janeiro Declaration, whose Principle 10 states that

> environmental issues are best handled with the participation of all concerned citizens, at the relevant level. At the national level, each individual shall have appropriate access to information concerning the environment that is held by public authorities, including information on hazardous materials and activities in their communities, and the opportunity to participate in decision-making processes. States shall facilitate and encourage public awareness and participation by making information widely available.[88]

The information as such is then called to perform a further function, ensured through obligations, that instead of being of "passive" and subsequent value, allows the public to access other relevant information on environmental matters. In particular, reference is made to the possibility by the public to acknowledge the results deriving from the control on discharges (that is, on emissions) required by the permit conditions (Paragraph 2) and, more generally, to know the content and the reasons for any environmental decision as soon as it is adopted (Paragraph 4); in this case the pursued aim is to guarantee the transparency of the decision-making process.[89] Such a substantial regulation promotes and favours as much as possible the participation in environmental proceedings and the knowledge of the information related to them. Moreover, it has a decisive role in achieving two further important objectives expressed in the "whereas" clauses n. 24 and n. 25 of the IPPC Directive, the achievement of which is a fundamental

86 Council Directive 2003/35/EC, Article 4, Paragraph 1.
87 Council Directive 2008/1/EU, Article 15, Paragraph 1.
88 UN General Assembly, "United Nations Conference on Sustainable Development", Principle 10.
89 Id. Article 15, Paragraphs 2 and 4.

condition for the proper functioning of every modern mechanism of environmental regulation: that of promoting public awareness of environmental problems and acceptance of the decisions adopted, and that of promoting the environmental education of the public.[90]

It is here worth noticing that the characteristics just analysed seem to recall some aspects of so-called *reflexive environmental regulation*, an expression adopted by the doctrine which applies the concepts expressed by the legal theory known as "reflexive law" to environmental matters. The theory promotes, within a given social context, the establishment of self-reflexive and self-critical procedures with regard to the negative effects produced on the natural environment, as an instrument to achieve the environmental protection objectives to which a community aspires. The basic idea of this operational approach is that law and regulation should not be used directly, with the imposition of specific orders or commands, but rather indirectly, establishing incentives and procedures capable of inducing the social organizations themselves to verify in a critical and creative way the impact of their activity on the environment, as well as the way to improve performance in terms of lower environmental impact.[91] The fundamental elements of the environmental regulation models that follow this approach are: voluntary participation; disclosure of information to the public; the participation of associations in order to protect (widespread) public interests; and the provision of institutional procedures for self-analysis and self-criticism.[92]

3.4.1 The Eco-Management and Audit Scheme

An example of such a reflexive approach in the environmental field is provided by the European legislation that, through EEC regulation n. 1836/1993, established the so-called "Eco-Management and Audit Scheme (EMAS)"; a system of eco-management that companies carrying out industrial activities can voluntarily join for the evaluation and improvement of the environmental efficiency of (non-) industrial production and for the presentation of the relevant information to the public (Article 1, Paragraph 1).[93] According to the EMAS regulation, any (public

90 Council Directive 2008/1/EC, "whereas" n. 24 and 25.

91 Eric Orts, "A Reflexive Model of Environmental Regulation," *Business Ethics Quarterly* 5 (1995): 780.

92 Id. 788, where Orts highlights the connection with the concept of "responsive law" used by Selznick who states, "there is no escaping the need for institutional self-awareness and self-criticism"; Philip Selznick, *The Moral Commonwealth: Social Theory and the Promise of Community* (Berkeley, CA: University of California Press, 1992), 236.

93 Council Regulation (EEC) No 1836/93 of 29 June 1993 Allowing Voluntary Participation by Companies in the Industrial Sector in a Community Eco-management and Audit Scheme, then replaced by the Regulation (EC) No 761/2001 of the European Parliament and of the Council of 19 March 2001 Allowing Voluntary Participation by Organisations in a Community Eco-management and Audit Scheme (EMAS), and lastly by the Regulation (EC) No 1221/2009 of the European Parliament and of the Council of 25 November 2009 on the Voluntary Participation by Organisations in a Community Eco-management and Audit Scheme (EMAS), repealing Regulation (EC) No 761/2001 and Commission Decisions 2001/681/EC and 2006/193/EC.

or private) organization that pursues an environmental policy may request to register its environmental management system. This registration implies that the (public or private) organization voluntarily will: 1) comply with specific requirements, including that of providing an environmental analysis related to the impacts of the activity performed; 2) carry out internal environmental audits, i.e. a systematic, documented, periodic and objective assessment of the installation/facility's performance, of its environmental management system and of the processes designed to protect the environment, respecting the procedures and objectives set in Annex II and III; and 3) draft an environmental declaration, containing all the relevant information concerning the organization and its management system, and make it available to the public.[94]

The EMAS states that all these documents must be verified and validated by an accredited or qualified "environmental verifier", to be then presented to the competent authority for registration, which entitles the user to display a special EMAS logo. Because of this configuration, the EMAS regulation is hardly ascribable to a command-and-control regulation model, and at the same time it cannot be compared with market-based regulation. Although its success depends very much on market factors, its main instrument of action is identified as the dissemination of information, so that, on the one hand, the public becomes aware of the fact that the registered subjects have actually adopted behaviours and measures to ensure the environmental compatibility of their business, and, on the other hand, the registered organizations have received a certificate that differentiates them from those that have not taken on the same environmental commitments. The EMAS regulation seeks in essence to encourage organizations to be accountable to the environment. To do so, it does not require the achievement of predetermined and binding targets but it is limited to requiring compliance with procedures that companies must follow when adopting their decisions regarding the environment. This very focus on the procedural aspects is considered a characteristic element of the reflexive law. In this respect, Orts clarifies that

> in whatever form, reflexive strategies of law reform emphasize the role law plays in structuring the rules of the game for other institutions. The procedural approach of reflexive law means that regulators cannot control the precise nature or direction of the change that will result from a particular strategy.[95]

Even though it cannot be linked to such a model of reflexive regulation, which the voluntary aspect lacks, the IPPC Directive shares with the EMAS system (and with the different system of ISO 14001) some elements that have a typically reflexive nature. Moreover, some of the IPPC Directive's provisions show common features with the EMAS regulation system, thus allowing the mitigation of the typically

94 Regulation (EC) No 1221/2009 of 25 November 2009.
95 Eric Orts, "Reflexive Environmental Law," *Northwestern University Law Review* 89 (1995): 1267 and 1312.

rigid characteristic of a command-and-control model – also to which the IPPC Directive belongs to, since it eventually allows for the issue of a permit. Hence, the "reflexive" element shared by the EMAS regulation and the IPPC Directive is certainly the one pertaining to the so-called public disclosure, i.e. the transparency and public access to the relevant environmental information.[96] The latter is guaranteed, as argued above, through the provision of specific obligations concerning not only the plant operators (obliged by the permit issuing procedure to publish the relevant information regarding the installation concerned) but also the competent administration (which is obliged to communicate with the public both before and after the decision on the issuing of the permit, as well as to the Member States which periodically must transfer to the EU Commission the data on ELVs and the BATs referred to in the permits issued by their administrations). In this respect, Article 17, Paragraph 1 of Directive 2008/1/EU asks that:

> With a view to exchanging information, Member States shall take the necessary measures to send the Commission every three years ... the available representative data on the limit values laid down by specific category of activities in accordance with Annex I and, if appropriate, the best available techniques from which those values are derived.[97]

Another element of "reflexive" regulation shared by the IPPC Directive is the direct participation of the plant operators in the environmental regulation system. Though the IPPC Directive does not put forward voluntary participation as in the EMAS, such participation plays a particularly important role, being able to decisively influence the drafting (and implementation) of the technical rules on which the system is based. Although, according to the EMAS regulation, plant operators can decide freely whether or not to undertake the adoption of an environmental management system, in the framework of the IPPC Directive the operators are obliged to undertake the regulatory mechanism based on the BATs, having in turn the possibility to directly influence the application of this crucial parameter. In both cases, the outcome is "reflexive" in its effect, since it directly empowers from below the subjects that are most directly involved in environmental matters. Not least, it should be borne in mind that in 1990 the EMAS registration system was originally proposed as a mandatory system; only after highly negative reactions by the operators did the European Commission opt for a voluntary membership scheme.[98]

Moreover, some provisions of the IPPC Directive directly connect the two different models to each other, thus creating synergies, albeit limited to certain aspects. Indeed, a first implicit reference to the EMAS regulation is "hidden" in the Directive, which in Article 6, Paragraph 2 states that

96 Id. 1267–1268.

97 Council Directive 2008/1/EC, Article 17, Paragraph 1.

98 Juergen Franke, "Political Evolution of EMAS: Perspectives from the EU, National Governments and Industrial Groups," *European Environment* 5 (6) (1995): 155–159.

> where information supplied in accordance with the requirements provided for in Directive 85/337/EEC or a safety report prepared in accordance with Council Directive 96/82/EC of 9 December 1996 on the Control of Major-accident Hazards Involving Dangerous Substances or other information produced in response to other legislation fulfils any of the requirements of this Article, that information may be included in, or attached to, the application.[99]

Since, as mentioned above, the EMAS regulation requires the operator, for the purposes of registration, to provide a series of very detailed and informative reports on the plant and the manner in which its activities are carried out, this provision allows the operators of the plants to easily satisfy the request of information for the issue of the permit, as long as the applicants are "certified" according to the EMAS regulation. As a result, adherence to the voluntary environmental management system is encouraged, thanks to the resulting procedural simplification.

Then, if one takes into account the IED, which represents the continuation and evolution of the IPPC regulatory system, a further link with the EMAS regulation can be identified in Article 23, Paragraph 4, on the issue of environmental inspections, which notes that "the systematic appraisal of the environmental risks shall be based on ... the participation of the operator in the Union eco-management and audit scheme (EMAS), pursuant to Regulation (EC) No 1221/2009".[100]

As part of the provisions on environmental inspections, a further example of a measure to guarantee the public disclosure of environmental information can be found in Paragraph 6 of Article 23 of the IED, pursuant to which, after each on-site visit, the competent authority draws up a report that

> shall be notified to the operator concerned within two months of the site visit taking place. The report shall be made publicly available by the competent authority in accordance with Directive 2003/4/EC of the European Parliament and of the Council of 28 January 2003 on public access to environmental information within 4 months of the site visit taking place.[101]

Lastly, as regards the public disclosure of environmental information, the Italian national legislation directly refers to the EMAS and ISO regulations. It does so through specific provisions which not only confirm the procedural advantages resulting from the duty to release information but also introduce a substantial advantage, that is the extension of the duration of the integrated environmental permit for those subjects who obtained the (EMAS/ISO) certification. Article 29-octies on the permit renewal and review sets out, in Paragraph 2, a longer duration term of the integrated environmental permit "in the case of a plant which is registered pursuant to Regulation (EC) 761/2001", whereby the "renewal ... is

99 Council Directive 2008/1/EC, Article 6, Paragraph 2.
100 Council Directive 2010/75/EU, Article 23, Paragraph 4.
101 Id. Article 23, Paragraph 6; Juergen Franke, "Political Evolution of EMAS": 157.

carried out every eight years" and not every five, while Paragraph 3 provides that the renewal is carried out every 6 years "in the case of a plant that is certified according to the UNI EN ISO 14001".[102]

Thus, the analysis of these regulations and provisions, which recall alternative environmental management models, finally confirms the fact that even though the IPPC Directive (and later the IED) is based on a command-and-control model, it does embrace some of the features of reflexive environmental regulation, thus determining the construction of a substantially unprecedented system in the (EU) field of environmental protection legislation.

3.4.2 The effectiveness of environmental judicial protection

As mentioned in the previous chapter, the BAT parameter is the fundamental turning point from which the whole IPPC Directive was developed. BAT determines the main characteristics of the IPPC Directive and IED, particularly with regard to two aspects: the type of the assessment made by the competent authority when the integrated environmental permit is to be issued; and the "reflexive" capacities of the legislation of reference, which result – inter alia – in a system of periodic review of the permit conditions. With regard to the first aspect, it was previously highlighted that the indeterminacy of the concept of BAT ends up in connoting the decisions of the administration as a *technical discretion*, or even as a mixed discretion. As regards the second aspect, however, I have already shown how the reference to the BAT, as an evolving parameter, is the key element requiring the complex process of continuous updating of environmental protection measures, starting from the Sevilla Process up to the revision of the issued permit. Both these aspects affect in turn a third element – the judicial protection achievable in each specific case – in which the administrative court represents the ultimate instrument for guaranteeing the correct application of the IPPC Directive.[103]

Different, but still connected to the effectiveness of the judicial protection, is the problem of the effectiveness of environmental protection. Although the instruments of judicial protection can influence it, the effectiveness of environmental protection is mainly determined by the regulatory framework in which the principles and rules expressed are transposed – at a more general level – by the European legislation. In this respect, the Italian provisions analysed above with regard to the review of the conditions of the integrated environmental permit for plants of national strategic interest raise some concern. Indeed, throughout a 36-month period, an Italian plant is still authorized to exercise its production activity, with the additional possibility that, in the presence of an extraordinary commissioner, the timing for the implementation of the plant adjustment measures can be further modified and extended. In fact, it can be argued that the stability and certainty of the requirements of the integrated environmental permit are significantly reduced, as well the actual level of environmental protection guaranteed

102 Translation from TUA, Article 29-octies, Paragraph 2.
103 Eric Orts, "Reflexive Environmental Law,": 1271–1273.

through the permit. Such a regulatory arrangement does not seem to be able to ensure the effectiveness of the environmental protection because it allows the continuous postponement of the deadline within which a plant must operate in conditions of full compliance with the environmental compatibility parameters set by the administration. Put another way, what should be a derogation regime, limited in time, is substantially transformed into an ordinary regime, so much so that a plant operator may eventually prefer the emergency/derogation regime to the "business as usual" one.[104]

As highlighted above during the analysis on jurisprudence, making the evaluation put forward in the integrated environmental permit into a discretionary activity by the competent authority, in many cases ends up weakening the guarantor role played by the court in checking for "substantial" compliance with the regulation. In fact, with the presence of technical discretion, the judge has lost a substantial degree of control on decisions concerning pollution regulation; their task is thus confined to the verification of the formal and procedural legitimacy, having to adopt a self-constraint approach that is not found in other sectors. From this perspective, the actual reflexive characteristics of the IPPC Directive may influence the outcome of the work carried out by the administrative judge towards the ultimate adoption of a self-constraint approach. A similar obeisance to the assessments of the administration, which somehow draw a common line between the Italian and the English jurisprudence, can indeed be explained and be partly justified with regard to that typically reflexive aspect of the integrated environmental permit that consists of being temporary and subject to revision.[105]

This argument can clearly be seen, for example, in the final part of the sentence of the aforementioned Regional Administrative Court of the Italian city of Brescia.[106] In this case, the judge acknowledges that "in a reasonably broad time perspective, the highlighted criticalities (especially the presence of coarse powders and bad smells) pose the problem of the extension of the monitoring of the values of concentration of pollutants", and concludes that

> the five-year duration of the integrated environmental permit allows the Region to improve the monitoring requirements over time and redefine the limits to the various forms of pollution towards a more precautionary sense, taking into account the new BAT and data progressively gathered on the efficiency of the various mitigation systems,

thus also overcoming the complaint put forward by the applicant in this regard. Indeed, the judge acknowledged the elements that contributed to the questionable outcome of the assessment made by the administration, when he clarified that

104 Ibid.; Richard Stewart, "A New Generation": 22–23.
105 Marc Pallemaerts, "The Proposed IPPC Directive: Re-Regulation or De-Regulation?," *European Environmental Law Review* 5 (6) (1996): 177.
106 See Chapter 2, Section 2.5.2 of the present study. T.A.R. Lombardia, Brescia, sez. I, 22 gennaio 2010, n. 211, in www.giustizia-amministrativa.it.

> the need to expand the monitoring systems has a particular importance if we consider the following aspects: (a) the concrete situation of the place and site, and in particular the absence of natural barriers between the foundry and the residential area; (b) the non-adoption in the production process of some BATs such as post-combustion solutions … able to provide greater guarantees regarding the elimination of pollutants; (c) the increase in emissions linked to the activation of the new melting furnaces.[107]

In this case, the judge not only exercised an extrinsic and non-penetrating role, but does not even seem to want to express himself on the disputed point, "exploiting" the fact that the integrated environmental permit is perceived as a temporary measure, subject to review by the competent authority, for which the recognized critical issues could in any case be solved with the imposition of more restrictive measures by the administration itself.

On this specific issue, the sentence underlines that "the balance guaranteed by the integrated environmental permit between the rights of the community and the economic initiative of the counter-party must therefore be understood as dynamic, that is, evolving towards increasingly less polluting solutions".[108] This statement effectively interprets the spirit of the IPPC Directive, which consists of seeking a balance between economic development and environmental protection, and translates it into a decision, namely that of total rejection of the appeal, which seems to be in contrast with the need of the appellant's judicial protection. In this regard, it is worth highlighting that, in reference to the Thornby company case already mentioned in Chapter 2, even the English judge seemed to base to a certain extent the non-annulment of the environmental permit on considerations related to the temporary nature of the permit itself.[109] In Thornby Farms Ltd v. Daventry District Council, the appellate court announced that a "review" of the permit would not have provided any reasons to support the need for emission standards lower than those authorized and, while confirming that this consideration did not "weaken" the imperative to apply the BAT, it believed that it allowed the issue to be addressed in a less drastic way than precluding the further business of the company; and this especially in the presence of a legal obligation requiring the revision of the permit conditions, especially if the latter should intervene a few months after the sentence. Since the administration was required to follow the developments in technologies and techniques to prevent and reduce pollution, the judge declared he was confident that the administration itself would provide in the near future an appropriate review and consequently ended up rejecting the appeal.[110] Bell underlines that, in the Thornby case, the judge

107 Translation from Ibid.

108 Ibid.

109 Thornby Farms Ltd v Daventry District Council, [2002] EWCA Civ 31, [2003] QB 503.

110 Ibid.

> refused to quash the grant of the authorisation notwithstanding its unlawfulness on the basis that there was a timely opportunity to review the existing authorisation which would enable the emissions limits to be revised to reflect the true application of the BATNEEC standard to the statutory objectives.[111]

In other words, the statement of the English judge also includes the two elements found in the judgment by the Italian court: the explicit reference to the possibility of revising the conditions of the authorization, and the reference to the problematic relationship between the opposing interests of environmental protection and economic initiative. In the Italian judgment, this relationship is expressly described in terms of a necessarily dynamic balance, so that environmental protection measures can be progressively defined over time, and this leads in the specific case to allow the continuation of the authorized plant.

In the judgment of the English court the relationship between opposing needs remains implicit and implied, but it is also resolved in favour of the economic initiative already in place. Indeed, it clearly emerges that the judge considers a less drastic solution to be preferable than the one deriving from the cancellation of the permit, and which would act as an obstacle to the continuation of the activities of the company in question. Hence, it can be argued that the temporary nature of the integrated environmental permit and the possibility for its revision can: persuade a judge to uphold the provision even in the presence of illegal activity, prevent adequate assurance from being made concerning the correct application of the principles and rules of the IPPC Directive vis-à-vis the proceeding administration and lessen the effectiveness of judicial protection. Moreover, given that it does not assure absolutely a substantial respect for the anti-pollution regulations, such an approach can indirectly undermine the very objective of the Directive, which is to achieve a high level of environmental protection.[112]

Therefore, the conclusions reached by the administrative courts on the aforementioned cases present a lack of protection: on the one hand, the critical aspects of the permit are in no way opposed (in fact, the permit is not annulled, even partially); on the other hand, there is no true guarantee that in the process of reviewing the permit conditions, the administration will intervene to remedy these problems. Hence, in the absence of the annulment of the act, the authority is not compelled, in the renewed exercise of its power, to take into consideration the content of the judge's ruling, leading to the risk of it becoming a dead letter.

In relation to the latter aspect, a recent development must be considered in the Italian administrative jurisprudence on environmental matters, which suggests an answer to the need for greater effectiveness of protection in the considered hypotheses. In particular, I refer to a controversial sentence of the Italian Council

111 Stuart Bell, "Statutory Pollution Prevention Objectives: Are They Rules or Aims?," *Journal of Environmental Law* 15 (1) (2003): 82.

112 Analysing the Thornby case and other similar ones, Bell here argues, "These cases should cause us to reflect upon the limits of pollution prevention rules in terms of their justiciability". Id. 85.

of State (Section VI, 10 May 2011, n. 2755) in which it was declared that, in the case of an contravening measure, the decision to cancel the permit is not mandatory – the perpetrator (in this case the administration) can be given the possibility to remediate within a certain period of time (in this case the Region must issue the SEA within 10 months) if so required by the judicial protection.[113] With this ruling, which was widely criticised by the doctrine,[114] the administrative judge has substantially redefined the scope of the sentence that accepts the action for annulment. Even though the judge of the Council of State acknowledged that the public administration (i.e. the Region) contravened the law, he decided to give to the administration the possibility to remediate and, at the same time, did not cancel the permit. In particular, the Council of State has in fact ruled that

> when its application would be incongruous and manifestly unjust, or contrary to the principle of effectiveness of judicial protection, ... the rule of annulment with effects *ex tunc* of the act challenged according to the circumstances must find a derogation either with the partial limitation of the retroactivity of the effects (Section VI, 9 March 2011, n. 1488), or with their effective date *ex nunc* or completely excluding the effects of the cancellation and placing only the conformation effects.[115]

There are two regulatory elements to which the judges of the Italian Council of State mainly refer to: the first one is represented by the lack of rules of internal legislation that precludes the administrative judge the possibility of actually determining the effects of his acceptance judgments; the second one is put forward in Article 1 of the Code on the administrative process of the principles of European law on the effectiveness of protection. According to the Council of State, such a reference would also allow the applicability in internal law of the current principle concerning the powers of the Court of Justice according to which "the Court, where it deems it necessary, shall specify the effects of the annulled act which must be considered definitive".[116] This principle is expressed by the Lisbon Treaty on the functioning of the European Union, in Article 264 (ex 231), Paragraph 2.[117] The possible extension to the internal judicial system concerning the power of the administrative judge to regulate the effects of the annulment would hence be corroborated by the fact that the authority on environmental issues between the EU and the Member States is of a concurrent nature and this should imply that

113 Italian State Council, Section VI, 10 May 2011, n. 2755, available at www.giustizia-amministrativa.it.

114 See Aldo Travi, "Accoglimento dell'impugnazione di un provvedimento e 'non annullamento' dell'atto illegittimo," *Urbanistica e Appalti* 15 (8) (2011): 936–939; Enrico Follieri, "L'ingegneria processuale del Consiglio di Stato," *Giurisprudenza Italiana* 2 (2012): 439–442.

115 Translation from Italian State Council, Section VI, 10 May 2011, n. 2755.

116 Aldo Travi, "Accoglimento dell'impugnazione": 440.

117 See Lisbon Treaty, Title I, Article 264, Paragraph 2 – ex Article 231 of the Treaty Establishing the European Community (TEC).

"the standards of judiciary protection may not be different, depending on whether the regulatory acts are issued at Community or national level (and, therefore, that the dispute should be decided by the EU judge).[118]

The conclusion is therefore that the granting of the appeal may also involve exclusively conformative effects, without determining the annulment of the act, which would therefore continue to be effective until the administration, renewing the exercise of its power, issues "further measures, substitutive *ex nunc* of those resulting as illegitimate". Thus, in this case the Council of State provides that within a period of 10 months from the notification or communication of the sentence, the public administration will adopt a new provision, thus warning that in case of inertia and in the case of non-compliance "the Section will be able to assess all the circumstances and exercise the powers provided for by the Code of the administrative process, including those concerning the measures of dissuasion of any non-compliance".[119]

In this respect, it is evident that even in the case of lack of protection as was previously mentioned, if the administrative judge does not cancel the environmental permit which was assessed as censurable, the permit would therefore be circumscribed, if not overcome, given the possible conformative effects and even in the absence of the cancellation of the permit itself. In other words, the concrete implementation of the permit would then be guaranteed by the possible judgment of compliance in case of inaction of the administration.[120]

It should also be noted that the possible admissibility of this new mode of intervention by the Italian administrative judge is of particular interest because the solution concretely accepted in the aforementioned case is duly reflected in a significant pronouncement by the English judge concerning the specific subject of the environmental permit issued in compliance with the IPPC Directive. The case in question (Rockware Glass Ltd v Chester County Council) concerned the appeal lodged by an industrial company against IPPC authorization that had been granted to its competitor, complaining that the ELVs set for a certain pollutant were "unduly generous" and did not reflect what could be achieved through the application of the BAT. Instead, the competitor claimed that, in the light of the IPPC Directive, alternative production processes to the one used could not be considered as "available". Indeed, the judge emphasized the indications provided by the General Guidelines (of the Secretary of State) regarding the "availability of techniques", and stated that an alternative production technology (cleaner furnaces that adopt the *oxyfuel process*) was already available and that therefore the parameters set by the BAT had not been respected. The sentence therefore upheld the appeal and ordered the annulment of the permit, although the effectiveness of the judgment remained suspended pending an appeal brought by the unsuccessful party.[121]

118 Italian State Council, Section VI, 10 May 2011, n. 2755, Translation from point 18.3.

119 Id. Translation from point 19.

120 Marco Macchia, "L'efficacia temporale delle sentenze del giudice amministrativo, prove di imitazione," *Giornale di Diritto Amminsitrativo* 12 (2011): 1313.

121 Rockware Glass Ltd., R (on the application of) v. Chester City Council & Anor, [2005] EWHC 2250.

In the second instance,[122] the Court of Appeal substantially shared the assessments expressed by the court of first instance, confirming the judgment on the illegitimacy of the permit and therefore the validity of its annulment. However, the Court of Appeal (even though confirming the illegitimacy of the permit) decided not to impose the closure of the plant given the short time between the (possible) cancellation of the permit and the issuing of a new permit to the same company. Hence, what can be observed is a decision that is substantially similar to that of the Italian court: the Court states that the annulment would remain suspended until a decision by the competent administrative authority on the application for renewal of the authorization by the company concerned; such a short delay in the effects of the annulment, would not be incompatible with what the court is required to do under the EU law.[123] It is possible to argue that in this case, just as in the decision of the Italian Council of State, the English judge, assessing the circumstances of the dispute and the substantial needs of the parties involved, formulates a more balanced and functional solution, intervening on the effects of the annulment sentence, so that these are suspended until a new decision of the administrative authority to replace the previously annulled permit.

However, it should be noted that, though from a procedural point of view, the decision of the English court can be compared with that of the Council of State, from a substantive point of view it does not fully satisfy the applicant's request, but instead rather shows the non-acceptance of the application for relief. This explains why the sentence in question falls, together with others, among those "cases in which the courts have exercised their discretion to refuse relief".[124] It should therefore be noted that in the specific field of administrative activity in the environmental sector, the application of the relevant jurisprudential guidelines can lead to an apparently paradoxical finding; namely, that the very temporary or provisional nature of the integrated permit, together with its related renewability, trigger greater stability or resistance for administrative determinations that may be even criticized because they are not in line with the IPPC Directive unlike the possible reactive intervention (through cancellation) of the judicial review.

3.5 Towards enhanced standardization of environmental standards

An analysis of the environmental regulation mechanisms focused on the parameter of the BAT stimulates further considerations that, although not directly concerned with the legal instrument used (i.e. the integrated environmental permit), regard the process of harmonization of environmental protection on the basis of the relationship between European legislation and national regulations.[125]

122 Rockware Glass Ltd v. Chester County Council, [2006] EWCA Civ 992.

123 Sarah Hannett, "Significant United Kingdom Environmental Cases January–December 2006," *Journal of Environmental Law* 19 (2) (2007): 267–276.

124 Gregory Jones, "Remedies in Judicial Review Proceedings for Breaches of EU Law," ALBA Annual Summer Conference, 16–18 July 2010; available at www.adminlaw.org.uk.

125 For further examination of the factors affecting the implementation of EU environmental policies, see Cristoph Knill, *Implementing EU Environmental Policy* (Manchester: Manchester University Press, 2000).

Already in the early phases of its original formulation, the IPPC Directive has indeed gone through a long process of adjustment and balancing between the different solutions proposed. This process has been supported by Member States and some of them have tried to influence the elaboration of the text in order to introduce concepts and tools that are as similar as possible, or at least compatible, with those of their own legal tradition.[126]

As highlighted above, many of the solutions proposed by the IPPC Directive drew their inspiration from the different traditions/settings in force at the time in the main member countries. One example in this respect is the English IPC regulation which included the concepts of Best Available Technology Not Entailing Excessive Cost (BATNEEC) and Best Practicable Environmental Option BPEO.[127] Also relevant is the German experience with its basis in the use of binding technological standards and the related concept of "Stand der Technik".[128] Moreover, France influenced this process, with the tool named "installations classées", which already allowed the conditions of the permit to be tailored to individual cases.[129]

Thus, precisely because it was the result of compromises and mutual concessions, the resulting Directive 96/61/EC introduced a context and provisions that should have facilitated its implementation in national legislations, particularly in those countries that had assumed a "proactive" approach in relation to the directive. In other words, the United Kingdom, Germany and France, rather than undergo the imposition of EU environmental standards, decided to promote this process and turn a possible constraint into a competitive advantage.[130]

Furthermore, the European Commission, aware of the considerable difficulties (and differences) normally faced during the process of transposition of the Community legislation into the various national laws, established the so-called Sevilla Process. This was intended to act as a process of standardization and elaboration of the BATs. Following the process, the environmental protection objectives must be based on those very BATs, in order to maintain the role of "orientation" in the implementation of the directive by the Member States and thus eventually ensuring the harmonization of environmental technical regulations. A proof of this emerges from the document COM/2003/0354 final "on the Road to Sustainable Production – Progress in implementing Council Directive 96/61/EC Concerning Integrated Pollution Prevention and Control". Indeed, on page 7 it is stressed that

> the central role of the concept of 'best available techniques' and the lack of absolute standards laid down in the Directive imply that a functional structure for exchanging information on best available techniques and monitoring is

126 Hubert Heinelt et al. "Environmental Policy: The European Union and a Paradigm Shift," in *European Union Environmental Policy and New Forms of Governance* (Ashgate: Aldershot, 2001), 1–32.

127 See Chapter 2, Section 2.1.3 of the present study.

128 Ibid.

129 See Chapter 1, Section 1.3.1 of the present study.

130 Michael Faure, "Optimal Specificity": 742–744.

crucial to ensure a 'soft harmonisation' of environmental standards in Europe.[131]

As underlined by Pallemaerts,

> the Commission seems to have given up much of its belief in the virtues of uniform Community-wide emission standards as an instrument for achieving a high level of environmental protection as well as harmonizing the conditions of competition in the internal market.[132]

Nevertheless, many countries took advantage of the fact that the Directive gave Member States considerable margins of freedom in implementing its content, ultimately keeping their environmental regulation systems (in terms of emissions) as unaltered as possible or, at least, avoiding their complete compliance with the European model. In this regard, Pallemaerts argues,

> The Commission in its explanatory memorandum repeatedly stresses that the proposed Directive will lay down only a general legal framework for integrated pollution control, and that it will be for the Member States to determine the actual emission limit values to be imposed in individual permits".[133]

In fact, as it has already been highlighted, the Directive introduced norms and formulas that, once incorporated into the national law, have left ample room for interpretation, specification and regulation.

3.5.1 The transposition of the Directive

For some years now, the European Union has tended to approve environmental legislation that leaves more and more room for specific implementation choices to be carried out by the Member States, including technical and scientific decisions. A clear example of this trend is given by the IPPC Directive of 1996, which instead of setting new ELVs established that the aforementioned permit must include ELVs based on the BATs; all this resulted in, if not a marked lack of homogeneity of the normative dispositions adopted by the single Member States, certainly a few divergences with regard to the modalities of implementation of the measures conceived by the Directive, and therefore of the operative solutions put in place. In particular, among those countries that already had integrated permitting systems, some (e.g. United Kingdom and France) limited themselves to

131 COM (2003) 354 Final Communication from the Commission on the Road to Sustainable Production, 7.

132 Marc Pallemaerts, "The Proposed IPPC Directive": 177; Paola Biondini, "Evoluzione, consistenza e prospettive di 'norme' e 'regole' tecniche nell'ordinamento europeo," *Studi parlamentari e di politica costituzionale* 151–152 (2006): 100.

133 Ibid.

making minor changes to their existing legislation, with the consequence that the specific methods of transposing the IPPC Directive were very disparate.[134]

The experiences of transposition into foreign laws have shown how effectively the transposition of the IPPC Directive in the individual Member States has in each individual case assumed very different characteristics and assumed very different outcomes. Indeed, on one hand, in Italy and France (as well as in other countries) considerable difficulties and delays occurred in the complete and correct adoption of the provisions of the Directive; on the other hand, in other contexts such as that of the United Kingdom, it was possible to find a significantly higher level of adhesion to the IPPC standard. Retrospectively, to get a better idea of the phenomenon, it seems useful here to refer to two actual experiences concerning the transposition of the Directive, and which have led in an emblematic way to diametrically opposed outcomes at least in terms of, most importantly, the application of the BATs according to the values expressed in the European BREFs documents.

The transposition of the Directive into the English national law initially encountered some delay, due in part to a rigorous analysis of the specific requirements introduced by the IPPC Directive with respect to the preceding legislation. However, this did result in a better acceptance of the "philosophy" of the new rules compared with what happened in other Member States.[135] In particular, if one refers to the most problematic aspect, that is the use of the BATs and, together with it, the uncertain value of the indications contained in the BREFs for the determination of ELVs, it is possible to recognize the English experience as an example of a certain success with regard to the actual fulfilment of the IPPC Directive.[136] In fact, by reading the conclusions of a 2008 report on the implementation of the IPPC Directive in the United Kingdom, it emerges that in most of the installations subject to environmental permit the prescribed requirements are "demonstrably based on BAT", i.e. they are based on the BATs.[137] In other words, it is possible to argue that the English experience was immediately characterized by its high recourse to the information contained in the European reference documents (BREFs) and which, therefore, despite not being formally binding in the Member States (at least until the adoption of the IED), were

134 COM (2005) 540 Final "Report from the Commission on the implementation of Directive 96/61/EC concerning Integrated Pollution Prevention and Control," 3.

135 Patrick ten Brink and Andrew Farmer, "Implementation of the IPPC Directive (96/61): Analysis and Progress of Issues," *Institute for European Environmental Policy (IEEP)*, October 2003, 6.

136 Id. 6. Also, the authors here clarify that "ELVs in permits issued to date largely fall within the range indicated in the BREFs".

137 "Assessment of the implementation of the IPPC Directive in the UK", Final report, edited by the Department for Environment, Food and Rural Affaire (DEFRA), January 2008, 99. The Report focuses on ten cases, in eight of which "Permit conditions were determined against the indicative BAT within the relevant Sector Guidance Note. These 8 permits all contained appropriate ELVs and/or equivalent technical measures for the main sources of emissions that appeared to be commensurate with the indicative BAT as detailed within the UK Sector Guidance Notes".

substantially incorporated into the national law, through the Guidelines, thus acting as essential parameters in determining the ELVs for the issue of environmental permits.[138] In the few UK cases in which the assessment of the competent authority diverged from the indications contained in the BREFs, the judges have highlighted the wide margin of discretion recognized by the legislator to the administration in areas such as the geographic location and environmental context of the plant, which according to the provisions of the Directive itself, legitimized the setting of limits other than those achievable through the application of the BAT indicated in the BREFs.[139]

As for French law, according to the regulation of "activities and plants whose operation presents risks to the environment" (Installations Classées), contained since 2000 in the Code de l'environnement, which in Articles L.511-1 and following has definitively codified the norm of the law of 19 July 1976 (and the related implementing Decree n. 1133 of 1977), it was generally required for such activities to undergo a prior check in the form of a special permit of the prefect, which entailed the imposition of requirements capable of preventing environmental hazards or inconveniences. The regulations thus envisaged concerned only new permits, and nothing was available in relation to the plants previously authorized and still active.[140] Similar to Italy, in France the extension of the European regulations to existing plants took place at a later stage, with the Arrété of 29 June 2004; the latter established the obligation to submit a 10-year budget (*bilan de fonctionnement*) for the commencement of the update of the permit already issued. Such a change also entailed greater clarification and specification regarding the content that must characterize the *bilan de fonctionnement*: the plant operator was required to provide information on the methods by which they achieved the objectives of prevention and reduction of polluting emissions that, following the requirements of implementation of the IPPC Directive started to be compared with the BATs indicated in the European BREFs reference documents. In determining these requirements (i.e. pollution thresholds), in principle a considerable margin of discretion was left to the proceeding authority, which could take into account, in addition to the characteristics of the installation, on one side

138 John Gray, Tim James and John Dickson, "Integrated Regulation": 71.

139 Levy v. Environment Agency & Anor, [2002] EWHC 1663 (Admin). On the defecting approach by the UK judges on environmental issues, see Stephen Tromans, "Environmental Judicial Review", Monday 6th March 2006, in www.39essex.com/doci/articles/STR_Judicial_Review_seminar _paper_060.306.pdf, 14. Here he recalls the following cases: R (Bedfor and Clare) v. London Borough of Islington, [2002] EWHC 2044 (Admin); R (Burkett) v. London Borough of Hammersmith and Fulham, [2003] EWHC 1031; R (PPG 11 Limited) v. Dorset County Council, [2003] EWHC 1311 (Admin); R (Kent) v. First Secretary of State, [2004] EWHC 2953 (Admin); Humber Sea Terminal Limited v. Secretary of State for Transport, [2005] EWHC 1289 (Admin).

140 Eberhard Bohne, *The Quest for Environmental Regulatory Integration in the European Union: Integrated Pollution Prevention and Control, Environment Impact Assessment and Major Accident Prevention* (Amsterdam: Kluwer Law International, 2006), 166–168.

its actual and overall environmental context, and on the other side the "state of the art" methods, which allowed the imposition of the BATs (having to refer to the BAT that is also economically acceptable). However, this margin of manoeuvre was very limited because of the obligation for the prefect to take into account the technical standards (pollution thresholds) set out in greater detail by numerous (autonomous) ministerial decrees or by decrees transcribing the objectives or norms established from European directives.[141] In fact, the French Government implemented the provisions of the IPPC Directive often through the binding ministerial decrees (arrétés ministériels). This was carried out in line with the provisions of Article 9, Paragraph 8, of the IPPC Directive, which allowed Member States to "prescribe certain requirements for certain categories of installations in general binding rules instead of including them in individual permit conditions".[142] For this reason, the French national regulation is very precise and detailed and normally requires different ELVs for different types of production. At the local level, for instance, the variation in the ELVs is very limited, since the prescribed values are in most cases those of the national regulation and are not frequently modulated according to the characteristics of the plant (depending, for example, on the its geographical location or the specific environmental context): almost all of the arrétés préfectoraux respect the applicable provisions established in the arrétés ministeriels.[143]

It should also be noted that, in the comparison of the ELVs set by the national sectorial regulations and those indicated in the BREFs BAT, very often the French values were significantly higher than those that according to the European documents could be achieved through the BATs, and this has led the European Commission to initiate infringement proceedings against France (which is not the only country to have been found in default).[144] It is precisely in order to avoid further infringements and to speed up the process of adaptation to the IPPC Directive that the French Ministry of the Environment took the initiative to amend some existing sectorial decrees so that the ELVs provided for therein would correspond with the performance obtainable using the BAT indicated in the BREFs.[145] In this way, companies that according to their permit are compliant with these new parameters are considered to be "IPPC compatible". In reality, however, this happens without ensuring the use of the BATs for a company's activities. Hence, this solution adopted by the French Ministry is in reality inadequate for meeting the principles of the IPPC Directive: an approach of automatic adjustment of emission values to those indicated for the BAT in the BREFs betrays the very spirit of the Community legislation, which instead requires a case-by-case analysis of the

141 Id. 166–167. Moreover, he argues "The substantive permit requirements concerning environmental protection are primarily specified in the Integrated Order of 2 February 1998 and in several sectorial statutory orders. These orders set binding uniform minimum requirements for permit conditions".

142 Council Directive 2008/1/EC, Article 9, Paragraph 8.

143 Rapport Installations IPPC en France et valeurs limites d'émission, *INERIS* (2004): 55.

144 Id. 56–59.

145 Anne Cikankowitz and Valerie Laforest, "La directive IPPC", 9–15.

performance of the plant compared with those obtainable through the BAT. Such an analysis must refer obligatorily to the use of the techniques indicated in the BREF documents. Still, this is not necessary if the permit is considered in itself compatible with the Directive, simply on the basis of the limit values. Finally, also disputable is the fact that this method of automatic adjustment eliminates completely the incentive to develop innovative prevention and reduction techniques; one of the objectives, albeit of a more general nature, that the European Union pursues within its own environmental policy. In this way the "best available techniques" are substantially and automatically converted into "Emission Limit Values" without their possible use being taken into concrete consideration by the companies in the formulation of their "operating budget".[146]

The inhomogeneous solutions that have thus emerged, not only between the United Kingdom and France, but more generally across several other Member States, have justified and necessitated a further commitment by the European Commission in addition to that already laid down at the time of the first formulation of the IPPC Directive in 1996. The aim of this commitment was to achieve a greater level of harmonization between the various national regulations. The monitoring activity on the implementation of the IPPC Directive in the various Member States has been instrumental to this objective, as prescribed by Article 17, Paragraph 3, which first requires that Member States send a report to the Commission every 3 years, and also provides for the Commission's obligation to draw up its own report. The latter must not only be published, but also be submitted to the European Parliament and the Council, together with the submission of possible proposals.[147] This fact-finding activity is therefore not so much, or not only, aimed at allowing the European Commission to verify the correct transposition and effective application of the provisions of the Directive – an indispensable prerequisite for the Commission to sanction, as indeed it has done, the defaulting States – but it is rather directed towards acquiring the necessary information for intervening directly on the critical issues that have emerged in the various national reports. Thanks to the obligation to issue periodic reports on the implementation of the legislation, the IPPC Directive itself operates as a *reflexive* procedure, which encourages the Commission's self-learning about the limits of the adopted legislation. At the same time, the need to issue periodic reports acts as a stimulus to make the institutions accountable for the implementation of the legislation and the adaptation of its internal rules and provisions.[148]

Moreover, this process of continuous revision of the IPPC Directive is supplemented by an effort to progressively standardize the legislation on pollutant emissions that involves, in addition to the IPPC Directive, numerous other specific directives with the aim of providing an increasingly clear and consistent framework of reference for the Member States in the fight against pollution from production

146 Id. 10–12.

147 Council Directive 2008/1/EC, Article 17, Paragraph 3; Council Directive 91/692/EEC of 23 December 1991 "Standardizing and Rationalizing Reports on the Implementation of certain Directives Relating to the Environment".

148 Daniel Farber, "Environmental Protection as a Learning Experience," *Loyola of Los Angeles Law Review* 27 (1994): 791–798.

activities. This regulatory reorganization first manifested itself in the codification of Directive 96/61/EC and of its amendments in the text of Directive 2008/1/EC (again concerning IPPC) and further in the subsequent re-casting of six different directives in the text of the IED 2010/75/EU.[149]

As it refers to the activity of policy-making, this process is adequately described by the expression "policy learning", the most evident manifestation of which, in the context of the regulation of polluting emissions, was the adoption of the new IED. In fact, the latter is, as already noted, the positive evolution of the IPPC Directive and it aims precisely to tackle the criticalities detected in the phase of concrete implementation of the IPPC Directive within EU national laws. Even within this evolving and constantly improving situation, the concept of policy learning obviously manifests itself; in particular Listokin clarifies how

> Before implementing a policy, policymakers may have only a dim idea about the effects of the policy. After implementing the policy and observing its effects, policymakers will often have a much better sense of the outcomes associated with the policy in current and future periods. Thus, policymakers will have 'learned' about the policy and have a much greater ability to predict the policy's impacts.[150]

3.5.2 The verification of compliance

Through the regulatory changes introduced by the IED, the European Commission amended the provisions of the IPPC Directive in several ways; in some cases clarifying their meaning or further specifying their content and in other cases by replacing or integrating them with entirely new provisions. All amendments have been made with the aim of reducing the room for manoeuvre of individual Member States during the transposition and implementation phases of the Directive, since such margins were in many cases larger than usual due to the ambiguity of some concepts or the generality of the expressions used (and their consequent limited prescriptive content).[151]

Once again, the main subject of this revision has been, the concept of the BAT or, to put it more accurately, the role that BAT must assume within the process of identifying the ELVs contained in the integrated environmental permit. As a result, the IED has not only provided for the first time at a regulatory level a definition of BAT reference documents (i.e. BREFs) but it has also introduced a series of substantial changes, such as the introduction of data (now contained in BREFs documents), and in particular the data/parameters set by the "BAT conclusions". The conclusions now perform the function of setting unavoidable

149 Daniel Fiorino, "Rethinking Environmental Regulation: Perspectives on Law and Governance," *Harvard Environmental Law Review* 23 (1999): 441–445.

150 Yair Listokin, "Learning Through Policy Variation," *The Yale Law Journal* 118 (2008): 483, footnote n. 1.

151 Daniel Fiorino, "Rethinking Environmental Regulation": 442.

parameters for those administrations that need to determine in practice the ELVs. Put another way, the IED addresses an issue that was previously a subject of debate and often led to different interpretations by Member States.[152]

As a result of these changes, apart from the discretional assessment process that is normally carried out on a case-by-case basis by the authorities responsible for issuing authorizations and which has been substantially shifted to before the application phase, the margin of choice left to the States and their administrations during the implementation of the legislation has become more limited. This is a novelty underlined several times in the European Union documents that followed the implementation of the 1996 IPPC Directive: e.g. COM/2003/0354 final "Communication from the Commission to the Council, the European Parliament, the European Economic and Social Committee and the Committee of the Regions on the Road to Sustainable Production – Progress in Implementing Council Directive 96/61/EC Concerning Integrated Pollution Prevention and Control"; COM/2005/540 final, "Report of the Commission on the Implementation of Directive 96/61/EC Concerning Integrated Pollution Prevention and Control"; COM/2007/843 final, "Towards a More Effective Policy on Industrial Emissions"; and SEC/2007/1679 Impact Assessment, COM/2010/593 final, "Report from the Commission on the Implementation of Directive 2008/1/EC Concerning Integrated Pollution Prevention and Control and Directive 1999/13/EC on the Limitation of Emissions of Volatile Organic Compounds Due to the Use of Organic Solvents in Certain Activities and Installations".[153] Whereas prior to the IED it was up to the individual administration, collaborating with the plant operator, to identify the best available and applicable technique and, consequently, to set the ELVs after taking into account the characteristics of the site, it is now possible to argue that this assessment takes place in two stages at two different levels: 1) the Member States and the European Commission; and 2) the competent administrations. The Member States and the European Commission set, once and for all through the comitology procedure – within the "BAT conclusions" – the emission values associated with the individual BAT. Consequently, the ELVs of the issued individual permit must be adjusted accordingly. On the other hand, it is up to the competent administrations to verify, when issuing the permit, whether the technical and environmental conditions of the plant require different and less stringent emission ELVs to be set than

152 Id. 444–445.

153 See COM (2003) 354 Final Communication from the Commission on the Road to Sustainable Production; Council Directive 96/61/EC Concerning Integrated Pollution Prevention and Control; COM (2005) 540 Final "Report of the Commission on the Implementation of Directive 96/61/EC Concerning Integrated Pollution Prevention and Control"; COM (2007) 843 Final, "Towards a More Effective Policy on Industrial Emissions"; COM (2010) 593 Final "Report from the Commission on the Implementation of Directive 2008/1/EC Concerning Integrated Pollution Prevention and Control and Directive 1999/13/EC on the Limitation of Emissions of Volatile Organic Compounds Due to the Use of Organic Solvents in Certain Activities and Installations".

those established in the "BAT conclusions". This has the inevitable positive consequence of triggering greater harmonization or, even better, standardization in the use of the parameter of the BATs within the different Member States.[154]

In this way, the overall system of the regulation on polluting emissions seems to become more rigid and moves away from its fundamental characteristic, that is flexibility, understood not only as the ability to adapt to the single local environmental contexts (possibility that will still be allowed), but rather also in its capacity to stimulate the spontaneous development of environmental technologies by operators that was one of the implicit goals of the IPPC Directive.

That said, the role played by the IED is in no way less incisive, particularly taking into account further delicate and problematic aspects concerning the functioning of the integrated environmental permit system such as those relating to the verification of the compliance with the authorization conditions and its periodic updates. In particular, with regard to the verification of the compliance of the permit conditions, the already mentioned Article 8 of the IED expressly concerning the "violations" contemplates the suspension of activity at least for the most serious cases of non-observance of the permit conditions, such as those accompanied by imminent dangers to human health or the environment. More specifically, Article 8, Paragraph 2 of Directive 2010/75/EU states that:

> Where the breach of the permit conditions poses an immediate danger to human health or threatens to cause an immediate significant adverse effect upon the environment, and until compliance is restored in accordance with points (b) and (c) of the first subparagraph, the operation of the installation, combustion plant, waste incineration plant, waste co-incineration plant or relevant part thereof shall be suspended.[155]

The introduction of this remedy, which was not present in the text of the IPPC Directive either in its 1996 or 2008 formulations, is testament to a greater concern for the effective observance of the conditions of the permit, with which noncompliance was not initially assessed. Under the IED, each Member State keeps the right to freely determine/set which measures to adopt. However, this "freedom" may result in the application of (different) measures/solutions that vary in intensity from one State to another. As previously noted, for example, the Italian legislation provides in addition to suspension an even more incisive measure – the revocation of the integrated environmental permit with the consequent closure of the plant.[156]

There are then new requirements that have been introduced with regard to the verification of compliance. Article 23 specifically dedicates some of its paragraphs to "environmental inspections". These paragraphs provide in a detailed and timely manner the contents of the environmental inspection plans, which must be

154 Daniel Farber, "Environmental Protection": 793–794.
155 Council Directive 2010/75/EU, Article 8, Paragraph 2.
156 See Council Directive 2008/1/EC and Council Directive 91/692/EEC.

prepared by the competent administrations identified by the individual Member States (Paragraph 3); the different timescale within which the inspections are to be carried out, depending on the risks of the installation concerned (Paragraph 4); and finally the consequences deriving from the findings made on any failure to comply with the permit conditions (Paragraph 6).[157] The IPPC legislation has thus been able to evolve autonomously with respect to the systems from which it had drawn inspiration and example, proceeding in the direction of a model capable of standardizing the regulatory framework of individual Member States in terms of pollutant emissions as well as other relevant fields of environmental protection, as it will be argued, inter alia, in the next section.

3.6 Economic growth vs. environmental protection: room for improvement

From the analysis conducted so far, it has emerged that a significant difference exists between the IPPC Directive (now IED) and the anti-pollution regulations that preceded it and how the IPPC was not limited to adopting previous mechanisms and solutions, but it rather put forward a completely different legislative model for tackling pollution. As highlighted in the previous sections, this is true despite the fact that some of the fundamental concepts on which the IPPC Directive was based had already been elaborated earlier, so much so that many of the IPPC features cannot be considered as completely novel in the legal solutions adopted in the field of environmental protection.

The first truly novel factor that permeated the entire IPPC Directive, and also had an innovative influence on already existing instruments, was that of the *integrated approach*. The second, which contributed to the IPPCs' breakthrough approach as compared with previous environmental regulations, was the introduction of *reflexive law* principles in the adopted regulation system. In particular, reference is made to those mechanisms and procedures that favour the revision and correction of the choices made by the institutions in environmental matters, such as: the mechanism of the BATs and the related updating process according to the Sevilla Process; the procedures of renewal and re-examination of the environmental permit issued or of the modifications to the already authorized plant; and the monitoring of the application of the directive which has stimulated, at regulatory level, the evolution from the IPPC Directive to the IED.

Hence, the intervention model put forward by the IPPC Directive is the combined result of many diverse tools used in environmental regulation (i.e. *command and control, market based, reflexive*), in an attempt to build a system to combat pollution and protect the environment; one that includes the positive and most effective aspects of preceding models without re-proposing the limits of the past. Holm puts it in this way:

157 Council Directive 2010/75/EU, Article 23, Paragraphs 3, 4 and 6.

> The IPPC directive balances between all three types of standards mentioned: ambient, emission and technology. It contains efforts to counter-balance problem-shifting by aiming for integrated pollution prevention measures, and besides normal emission focus it contains aims for energy and raw material inputs but also recycling.[158]

Thus, the IPPC Directive satisfies a need that has been stressed by the doctrine. Given the difficulties encountered in tackling environmental problems and the phenomenon of pollution, the public regulator cannot limit itself to use only one type of intervention tool in preference to others by considering each tool as an alternative to the other. Instead, they should elaborate more articulated solutions capable of integrating all available tools in a complementary way, bearing in mind the challenges posed by the complexity of environmental problems.[159]

In other words, the IPPC regulation provides a complex and articulated environmental regulation model that, by setting ELVs connected to the use of the BATs, allows it to simultaneously meet the different and opposed interests involved in the exercise of an economic activity (especially if it is also polluting) – something that did not occur in the past. On the one hand, the system is in fact aimed at achieving the best possible level of environmental protection without compromising or excessively limiting production activities and operators' interests; on the other hand, it is designed to ensure maximum adaptability to the individual concrete situations to which it is intended to be applied (whether these are conditioned by technical, economic or geographical elements), without however renouncing a suitable level of uniformity of the operating conditions within individual Member States and for each sector, thanks to the harmonization mechanisms of the legislation within the European Union.

Moreover, the legislation on the prevention of polluting emissions aims to achieve its environmental protection objectives through the creation and development of a Community market of green technologies, thus becoming a stimulating factor for new economic initiatives generating innovative contents rather than a regulatory one. These objectives, which have always been considered antithetical and mutually exclusive, find their joint realization thanks to the use of the BATs, taken as a reference for setting the conditions for the authorization of the plant.

As it emerges from the present analysis, such a mechanism presents characteristics that allow reconciliation between the values of environmental protection, production, efficiency, innovation and economic development. Ultimately, it can therefore be argued that by associating the integrated approach with that of reflexive law, the IPPC Directive implements a regulatory model capable of realizing the concept of sustainable development in a positive system of norms; a

158 Jesper Holm, *Modernisation and Flexible Environmental Regulation* (Bielefeld: Zentrum für Interdisziplinäre, 1999), 11.

159 Giulio Spina, "Strumenti di tutela dell'ambiente. Dal diritto penale ai sistemi (volontari) di gestione ambientale," *Ambiente e Sviluppo* 7 (2012): 649.

concept which is usually perceived as a mere abstract and rhetorical enunciation. Indeed, there are numerous critical considerations regarding the vagueness of the concept expressed by the formula "sustainable development". Peck, for instance, underlines that "sustainable development has become a buzzword largely devoid of content … a concept [that] provides little policy traction"; Hodas states that "a sceptic very well might describe the rapid, universal adoption of the language of sustainable development as simply a brilliant, politically expedient compromise between the forces of economic growth and those of environmental protection"; finally Smith considers the definition of "sustainable development" provided by the Brundtland report as "so vague that one cannot even discern from it the conceptual connection between sustainable development and the finite carrying capacity of the Earth's ecological systems and natural resources".[160]

The reconciliation between the requirements of environmental protection and those of economic development and private initiative (as well as, according to the most recent conception, those of a social nature) that characterizes the concept of sustainable development, is effectively guaranteed and achieved by virtue of an articulated normative *corpus*, which among other things tends to assume more and more prescriptive capacity over time, not least showing a strong expansive tendency, as evidenced by the evolution of the IPPC Directive in the form of the current IED. Indeed, during the above analysis it has been possible to observe how the new Directive has enriched the regulation of integrated pollution prevention and control with binding provisions, which regulate in a more rigorous way the process through which ELVs of individual permits are established, with the consequences both of restricting the Member States' scope for action in transposing the European legislation and that of the competent administrative authorities in applying it effectively.[161]

Concerning the expansive capacity of the environmental regulation model that characterizes the IPPC Directive in the framework of public pollution control interventions, one may highlight two main aspects. First, the IED extended the scope of application of the norms regulating the prevention of polluting emissions to additional production sectors. Second, and above all, the IED merged the provisions of six different previous directives on pollution and emissions, giving rise to a set of rules of general application substantially recalling those of its predecessor, the IPPC Directive. This regulatory framework seems to be able to represent a significant factor in the expansive trend of the model, which may further be extended in the future thanks also to the fact that all the different specific regulations share now the same "glossary", formulated by the common provisions

160 Alison Peck, "Sustainable Development and the Reconciliation of Opposites," *St. Louis University Law Journal* 57 (2012): 151; David Hodas, "The Role of Law in Defining Sustainable Development: NEPA Reconsidered," *Widener Law Symposium Journal* 3 (1998): 1–2; Susan Smith, "Ecologically Sustainable Development: Integrating Economics, Ecology, and Law," *Willamette Law Review* 31 (2) (1995): 277.

161 Andrew Farmer, "Revising IPPC: Incremental Change Rather Than a Radical Overhaul of EU Industrial Emissions Policy," *Environmental Law Review* 10 (4) (2008): 258–259.

on "definitions". In practice, defining uniformly the concepts and terms used by the various sectorial regulations, opens the way to the increasingly easy adoption of measures and intervention mechanisms common to the various sectors.[162]

Yet, the analysis of the IPPC model has shown how "sustainable development" is also pursued through the weighting of the different needs; because of this, the result may not necessarily represent a perfect balance and in many instances de facto pre-eminence is given to economic interest over that of environmental protection. In spite of what is provided by Article 1 of the IED, which states that its final objective is to

> lay(s) down rules designed to prevent or, where that is not practicable, to reduce emissions into air, water and land and to prevent the generation of waste, in order to achieve a high level of protection of the environment taken as a whole,

indeed the Directive itself presents some provisions which clearly show how the attention paid to the economic aspects of the authorized activities is maintained at times higher than that dedicated to environmental protection.[163]

It has already been highlighted that the provision contained in Article 8, Paragraph 2 of the IED (according to which "where the breach of the permit conditions poses an immediate danger to human health or threatens to cause an immediate significant adverse effect upon the environment, and until compliance is restored in accordance with points (b) and (c) of the first subparagraph, the operation of the installation, combustion plant, waste incineration plant, waste co-incineration plant or relevant part thereof shall be suspended")[164] can be read as intended to never completely undermine the economic initiative and the production activity of the plant operator, unlike what happens in Italian law in which a serious violation of the conditions of the integrated environmental permit can lead to the revocation of the permit and the simultaneous closure of the plant. This particular focus is immediately detectable in the definition of "available technique" – also intended as an "economically viable" technique which is to be determined by "taking into consideration costs and benefits" and with respect to which the manager must have access "on reasonable terms". Moreover, the intrinsic focus on the economic aspect of the authorized plants also finds further and numerous confirmations in the Guidelines or general specifications for a certain sector, from which it is inferred that the economic sustainability and the cost–benefit analysis of the single technique examined orientate in a critical way the assessments of the public administration in determining the best available concretely applicable technology.[165]

162 Id. 260.
163 Council Directive 2010/75/EU, Article 1.
164 Id. Article 8, Paragraph 2.
165 See the present study, Chapter 2, Section 2.3.

In this respect, even more significant are the contents introduced by the IED in Article 15, Paragraph 4, which gives the competent authority, in specific cases, the power to set lower ELVs than those indicated in the BAT conclusions "only where an assessment shows that the achievement of emission levels associated with the best available techniques as described in BAT conclusions would lead to disproportionately higher costs compared to the environmental benefits". Put another way, if the emissions of a given plant do not greatly exceed the emission levels achievable with the BATs, but reaching them would require them to adopt measures whose cost is rather significant, the competent authority may allow emission values to be more permissive and therefore more favourable for the operator.[166]

Now, since it has been shown that by definition the BAT can be identified as such only if it is economically sustainable and accessible at a reasonable cost for the plant operator, it follows that the actual assessment of any disproportion between the costs of solutions to be adopted and the environmental benefit achievable happens at a later and subsequent stage; a stage where, since the economic tolerability of the measures required has already been verified and no longer in question, it becomes somewhat a matter of comparison and choice between two needs that, in truth, do not seem to be on the same level. On the one hand, there is the (non-essential) need for companies to use as few economic resources as possible; on the other hand, there is the (fundamental) need to protect the environment through the compliance with certain pollution standards. Among those two requirements, the legislation seems to give priority to the economic one, admitting that the level of pollutant emissions may in actuality be higher than that which would be achievable through the best available and practicable technique (as attested in the BAT conclusions). The same reference to the disproportion of costs with respect to benefits seems to betray a notion of the principle of proportionality not entirely in line with the more rigorous one generally accepted in administrative law: namely, that the proportionality of a measure is assessed first of all with regard to its suitability to satisfy the public interest and its necessity compared to other less burdensome methods of intervention. In reality, the principle of proportionality implies that it is the duty of the administration to investigate all possible alternatives to its action. And it has to do so in such a way as to always seek a solution not only more suitable for the pursuit of the primary public interest, but also the mildest instrument among those at their disposal and among those that are really necessary.

In the IED, proportionality is instead invoked in order to legitimize an exemption from the principle that requires compliance with the ELVs expressed in the BAT conclusions, which are now binding and represent the level of emissions considered compatible with the primary purpose of environmental protection. That being the case, it should be noted that the reflexive nature of the IPPC Directive, expressed in particular by the norms on updating and periodic review of environmental permit conditions, also seems abstractly suitable for

166 Council Directive 2010/75/EU, Article 15, Paragraph 4.

effectively reconciling the two opposing and underlying requirements of sustainable development, and can in some cases actually reveal the anthropocentric vision that has characterized this notion from the beginning.[167] Indeed, if it is true that environmental protection is better guaranteed by the IPPC Directive through the possibility of continuously modifying the authorization conditions and therefore the permitted emission levels (evidently in the sense of reducing them with the passage of time and advancing technology), and if, on the other hand, the economic initiative and the productive activity are safeguarded thanks to a certain flexibility enjoyed by operators in the commitment to adapt their plant to the conditions of the permit (which in fact, they do not require to be immediately satisfied at the time of issue, thus allowing a fulfilment that does not affect the continuity of production), it is also true that the implementation and concrete application of these rules in the EU (and Italian) legal system have also revealed the possible occurrence of risks as regards the effectiveness of environmental protection, and therefore the incapability of the system to realize the economic objective and that of environmental protection to the same extent – which are included in the paradigm of sustainable development.[168]

In the jurisprudence, it has been observed that EU judges (including Italian ones) can in some way put their focus on the "provisional" nature of the permit so as not to revoke the authorization, even though there would be grounds for it. Given that the environmental permit can or must be re-examined periodically or in specific cases by the competent authority, the argument used is that "possible environmental inadequacies can be corrected by the permit itself", so hence the annulment of the authorization (which would have the effect of blocking the production/functioning of the installation) can be avoided.

At the regulatory level, the recent Italian national provisions regarding the review of permits introduced by the Decree on the aforementioned Ilva plant, can in some cases prevent the competent authority from being able to demand the rapid implementation of the provisions contained in the permit and/or to be able to react quickly through measures such as warning, suspension or revocation in the case of non-observance of the prescriptions of the permit.

Therefore, at both these levels (the jurisprudence and the regulatory), the continuity of the production activity of the authorized plant/installation appears to be safeguarded, even at the expense of an effective and timely protection of the environment and in spite of the irregularities or serious non-compliance with the environmental permit at stake. The representation of the sustainable development that derives from this analysis leads me to argue that a complete implementation of the concept, understood as an effective balance between development and the environment, is still far from being achieved.

167 Sanford Gaines, "Reflexive Law as a Legal Paradigm for Sustainable Development," *Buffalo Environmental Law Journal* 10 (1) (2002): 1–4.

168 "In some cases, it may even reduce the need for making tradeoffs between values of economic growth and environmental protection by encouraging new solutions that provide gains for both". Eric Orts, "A Reflexive Model": 779.

As discussed in Chapter 1, the concept of sustainable development was historically born in a period of great ferment (i.e. the 1970s) in respect to the theme of environmental protection. This resulted from the awareness that the pursuit of an increasingly high economic well-being clashed with the limitation of the natural resources, and at both the doctrinal and legislative levels it was widely believed that the conflict between the economy and the environment could be resolved. The belief was that sustainable development was able to satisfy both needs without having the pursuit of one sacrificing the other. With reference to these first enthusiastic theories Pallemaerts observed,

> it is not surprising that such a concept (as sustainable development) has received widespread support from leaders of the North and South alike, environmental and Third World movements, international bureaucrats and enlightened managers of financial and economic institutions and structures in both capitalist and socialist countries. This is explained by the artful vagueness which the new paradigm of 'sustainable development' casts upon their respective responsibilities.[169]

In the long path towards the attainment of sustainable development, it is possible to argue that only a first – though essential – step has been carried out; i.e. the one indicated by the principle of integration, according to which in order to effectively address the requirements of environmental protection, the latter must be integrated into the instruments and policies implemented to promote economic development.[170] Yet, even so, it is still lacking a criterion allowing it to achieve an "equal" integration between the needs of the economic growth and those of environmental protection, once both have been taken into account in the adoption of a specific regulation.[171]

That said, the IPPC Directive and IED mark a significant step forward in this direction, offering a solid normative basis worthy of serious debate of its pros and cons and a springboard from which to start the process of elaborating and consolidating the concept of sustainable development. Such a concept needs to be conceived in accordance with a vision that deviates substantially from its

169 Marc Pallemaerts, "International Environmental Law from Stockholm to Río: Back to the Future?," *Review of European Community & International Environmental Law* 1 (1992): 261.

170 Barnhizer is sceptical on the real possibility to achieve sustainable development due to the predominance of people's personal interests. See David Barnhizer, "Waking from Sustainability's 'Impossible Dream': The Decision-Making Realities of Business and Government," *Georgetown International Environmental Law Review* 18 (2006): 45–48.

171 Luis Aviles, "Sustainable Development and the Legal Protection of the Environment in Europe," *Sustainable Development Law & Policy* 12 (3) (2012): 29. Aviles also argues that in the historical period prior to the rise of the "sustainable development" concept, "Environmentalists hoped … that the concept of sustainable development would spawn legal rules and principles that would resolve legal disputes without sacrificing the interests of either the environment or development".

anthropocentric nature, thus achieving a clearer and more sincere formulation of the objectives that one really wants to pursue and that can actually be accomplished.[172]

172 Peck argues in positive terms about the "dichotomy" between *development* and *environment*, which is rooted in the concept of sustainable development. In this respect, he refers to the Carl Jung's "principle of opposites", as well as to the "Tao principle" of Taoism, according to which the opposing forces play a fundamental role in the transformation process leading to an overall improvement of the system. See Alison Peck, "Sustainable Development": 151–155.

4 Potential and constraints of China's regulatory framework on environmental permits

4.1 Sustainable development vs. ecological civilization

In Chapter 1, I showed why and how sustainable development is one of the cardinal principles of European policy and how this concept evolved, starting from 1987, first at an international level and then within multinational and national contexts.[1] In this respect, it was worth noting that the Italian law on environmental protection provides one of the most balanced definitions of the concept of sustainable development. Indeed, the aforementioned TUA, in its Article 3-quater, Paragraph 4, goes beyond the mere integration between environmental demands and economic dynamics, by emphasising that the resolution of questions regarding environmental issues needs to be addressed so as to guarantee sustainable development, and hence ensure the proper functioning and evolution of natural eco-systems and prevent the risk of negative impacts possibly caused by human activity.[2] Moreover, in Paragraph 2, the same law introduces the duty of public authorities to "primarily take into consideration" the environmental protection issues when public and private interests are at stake, consequently establishing a hierarchy among the involved interests and providing a practical action rule which makes the set-out principle ready to be implemented.[3]

In the chapters that followed, the possible achievement of sustainable development was elaborated further, in particular, with an analysis of the key characteristics, applications and implications of the IPPC Directive and its successor, the IED. As a result, it is possible to argue that sustainable development is not a merely abstract and rhetorical notion, as it is often perceived in literature, but that such a concept is pursued through the weighting of socio-economic and environmental needs, though not necessarily leading to a perfect balance between them.

1 The concept of *sustainable development* was first introduced at the global level in 1987 within the Report of the World Commission on Environment and Development (the so-called Brundtland Commission), which defined it as "a development that meets the needs of the present without compromising the ability of future generations to meet their own needs". See Report of the *World Commission on Environment and Development: Our Common Future* (Oxford: Oxford University Press, 1987), 41.

2 Italian Law 152 of 3rd April 2006 (known as TUA, Testo Unico dell'Ambiente – i.e. Consolidated Law on Environment), Article 3-quater, Paragraph 4.

3 Id. Paragraph 2.

This incapability to realize the *economic* and *environmental protection* objectives to the same extent – which are both included in the paradigm of sustainable development – ends in many instances with a *de facto* pre-eminence being attributed to the economic interest to the detriment of environmental protection.

When it comes to China, however, rather than arguing about the *paradigm of sustainable development* and its implications, it is possible to argue about the *development paradigm of ecological civilization.* It is true that the concept of sustainable development does appear in China's environmental protection legislation, explicitly in Article 1 of the Environmental Protection Law of 2014:

> This Law is formulated for the purpose of protecting and improving environment, preventing and controlling pollution and other public hazards, safeguarding public health, promoting ecological civilization improvement and facilitating economic and social sustainable development.[4]

Nevertheless, although mentioning the need of "facilitating economic and social sustainable development", it does not elaborate or specify how sustainable development should be facilitated and what the balance should be between its economic and social meaning. Instead, in Article 1, the concept of sustainable development is linked to, and to a certain extent overcome by, the concept of *ecological civilization.*[5]

Akin to "sustainable development", the concept of "ecological civilization" was coined in the 1980s, precisely in 1984 by the agricultural economist Ye Qianji. Ye looked at ecological civilization through the lens of ecological philosophy and initially used this formula to emphasize the importance of sustainable agriculture in China, eventually arguing about the crucial contribution of ecological agriculture to the future sustainable development of the country. Three years later, in 1987, the scholar urged action on the progressive deterioration of China's ecological environment and launched his call to arms "vigorously promoting the construction of eco-civilization" at the national level. In particular, he specified that ecological civilization meant that "humanity can both benefit from nature, and also act in the interest of nature, since this is the only way for man and nature to maintain a harmonious and unified relationship".[6] Ecological civilization emerged in this way as a concept opposed to industrial civilization; as the need to respect nature and achieve ecological justice versus the utilitarian, profit-driven world resulting from the industrial revolution.[7]

4 Environmental Protection Law of the People's Republic of China 2014: Article 1.
5 Ibid.
6 Maurizio Marinelli, "How to Build a 'Beautiful China' in the Anthropocene. The Political Discourse and the Intellectual Debate on Ecological Civilization," *Journal of Chinese Political Science* 23 (2018): 373.
7 Arran Gare, "From 'Sustainable Development' to 'Ecological Civilization': Winning the War for Survival," *The Journal of Natural and Social Philosophy* 13 (3) (2017): 140–141.

However, ecological civilization has far more profound philosophical roots that date back throughout Chinese history, philosophy and development. Over 2500 years ago, the founder of Taoism, Lao Tze, stated that "Man takes his law from the Earth; the Earth takes its law from Heaven; Heaven takes its law from the Tao. The law of the Tao is its being what it is". According to the commonly accepted interpretation, the meaning is that

> people live, work and reproduce according to the law of the earth; the earth changes seasons and produce various life according to the laws of heaven; the heaven operates and changes according to the major 'Tao'; while the major 'Tao' follows the law of nature and lets nature takes its course.[8]

Put another way, Lao Tze scrutinised the rules and the relationship between human beings and nature focusing on the key concept of *law*. Law acquires different connotations such as "following the example", "depending on", "being up to" and "complying" and eventually leads the philosopher to conclude that human beings are not supposed to transform and control nature; they should instead respect nature and comply with its laws. The Chinese philosopher, Zhuangzi then further elaborated this precept into the philosophy of the "harmony between humans and nature", which for more than 2000 years has characterized the history of Chinese farming, ultimately contributing to the development of world civilization in spite of human mistakes and natural disasters.[9]

In the course of history, ecological civilization was often conceived exclusively from a cultural point of view, and became the synonym of shared values. Following such a view, the human being is part of nature and for this reason it should respect nature and treat it rightly. As a consequence, all human activities should entirely respect the laws of nature and humans should pursue development in harmony with nature. This is what is commonly defined as the "narrow" understanding of ecological civilization and which I would rather identify as "classical ecological civilization". Classical ecological civilization is characterized by two key objectives. The first is (ecological and social) *justice*, which encompasses the respect of the rights and interests of nature and at the same time the protection of human interests and rights. The second is *harmony*, understood as the need to reach compatible and mutual interests between human beings and nature and eventually between individuals and society. In sum, it is possible to argue that this understanding of ecological civilization implies a sort of passive accommodation between humans and nature, where the former is required to restrain its desire of unnecessary material occupation and consumption in order to preserve the balance of the latter.[10]

8 Pan Jiahua, *China's Environmental Governing and Ecological Civilization* (Beijing: China Social Sciences Press, 2014), 35.
9 Ibid.
10 "China Human Development Report. 2013 Sustainable and Liveable Cities: Toward Ecological Urbanisation", compiled by the United Nations Development Program (Beijing: China Translation and Publishing Corporation, June 2013), 100–102.

On the other hand, a "broader" interpretation of ecological civilization is not only confined to the respect and co-existence of human beings towards nature, but it also includes the governance systems, such as production patterns based on the shared value, economic development and social stability. In this respect, besides the two aforementioned objectives, this form of ecological civilization aims for the achievement of *high efficiency* and *human development*.[11] High efficiency is understood as the need to preserve natural eco-systems both through ecological and efficient productivity capable of minimizing the input and maximizing the output, and through the establishment of social efficiency – achieved via a comprehensive system of laws and norms. Human development implies aiming for key and ultimate goals, such as quality of life and dignity. Thus, the development paradigm of ecological civilization is the combination of the above-mentioned four elements: justice, harmony, high efficiency and human development. Put another way, *justice* is the foundation of ecological civilization, *harmony* is the original philosophy behind it, (high) *efficiency* is the means for its achievement, and *human development* is its ultimate objective.[12]

In broad terms, ecological civilization comprises a clear social component that embraces both the material and spiritual achievements of society, including the accomplishment of increasingly greater harmony between human beings and nature, the enhancement of non-polluting (or less-polluting) productivity, the increase of social prosperity and eventually the attainment of human development.[13] In other words, this wider understanding emphasizes the ultimate objective of what can be defined as the ecological civilization of the modern era or "modern ecological civilization", which is to combine comprehensive development while securing people's health and quality of life. This no longer implies a passive reconciliation between human beings and nature; instead, the harmony between humans and nature (hence, human development) arises from the active application of modern science and technology along with the implementation of the laws and regulations that go with it. In this light, the modern meaning of ecological civilization includes multiple dimensions and presents *sustainability* as its most prominent characteristic. Indeed, ecological civilization safeguards the sustainability of natural eco-systems and, as shown above, requires sustainability in both economic and social development.[14] In this respect, it is possible to argue that (modern) ecological civilization is very similar to – if not overlapping with – the concept of sustainable development, analysed in the previous chapters.

However, over time, the Chinese philosophy of "harmony between human beings and nature" became weaker, mainly as the result of China's industrial

11 Werner Hans Keller, Xia Zhang and Yong Liu, "Functions of Law in the Sustainable Development of China and a Model for Environmental Legislation," *European Business Review* 29 (4) (2017): 10.

12 Arran Gare, "From 'Sustainable Development' to 'Ecological Civilization': 148; Chun Xu, "The Position of Ecological Civilization in the Human Civilization" Conference Proceedings of Ecological Civilization, Globalization and Human Development, Sanya, China, June 2009, 158–161.

13 Pan Jiahua, *China's Environmental Governing*, 37.

14 Werner Hans Keller, Xia Zhang and Yong Liu, "Functions of Law in the Sustainable Development": 2 and 13.

development. Indeed, starting from the 1950s' Great Leap Forward and the 1960s' Campaign of Following the Example of Dazhai in Agricultural Development, China followed in its own way the path traced by western industrialization and, together with it, the belief that – despite all – humans could ultimately get the better of nature.[15] It goes without saying that this drastic change from the pursuit of "harmony between humans and nature" to that of industrial development had negative impacts on the environment with dramatic consequences not only in terms of resource depletion (i.e. water degradation and soil erosion) but also for the balance of the ecosystem. This is also the reason why in the 1980s, following and in parallel with the strong debate occurring at the international level and described in previous chapters, China studies and academic discussions on ecological civilization and ecological economics resurfaced as a prominent topic. Yet, in those years the degradation of ecological resources was still *reversible* – thanks to the country's relatively low energy consumption and pollution levels.[16]

However, from its start, the twenty-first century has been characterized by China's large-scale and rapid industrialization, so much so that the ecological imbalance was severely threatened and the reversibility of ecological degradation put at high risk.

Fully based on the exploitation of fossil fuels and linear production patterns "from raw materials to waste", in this stage of history Chinese industrialization fostered an incredibly fast enhancement of social productivity which, through the creation of a huge material wealth, ultimately allowed it to tackle – inter alia – the problem of poverty. According to the National Bureau of Statistics, between 1978 and 2017 China was able lift out of poverty more than 700 million people living in rural areas, at an average of approximately 19 million people per year. Moreover, in 2018, official data showed that almost 14 million people were taken out of poor living conditions and in the following 2 years the Chinese government helped another 20 million people to further eliminate poverty in the country. According to the United Nations and the World Bank, China's poverty-relief accomplishments have addressed more than 70 per cent of global poverty alleviation in the past four decades. This is the only case worldwide in which a country has been able to increase the living conditions of so many people over such a relatively short period of time.[17]

15 Zhihe Wang, Huili He and Meijun Fan, "The Ecological Civilization Debate in China," *Monthly Review*, November 1, 2014, 1–3.

16 China Council for International Cooperation on Environment and Development, "Roundtable on Global Governance and Ecological Civilization," Roundtable Proceedings, Brussels, Belgium, June 2018, 37–38.

17 Weiping Tan, "Chinese Approach to the Eradication of Poverty: Taking Targeted Measures to Lift People out of Poverty" (Speech given at the Expert Panel on the Implementation of the Third UN Decade for the Eradication of Poverty (2018–2027), Addis Ababa, April 18, 2018); Carolina Sanchez, "From Local to Global: China's Role in Global Poverty Reduction and the Future of Development" (Speech given by the Senior Director for Poverty and Equity of the World Bank at Taobao Village Summit, Heze – Shandong, China, December 7, 2017); Christine Loh, "China's Poverty Relief Approach is Exemplary," *China Daily*, April 4, 2019.

The consolidation of this process produced major changes in the development paradigm, eventually benefitting all aspects of human social development such as the economy, politics and culture, as well as the quality of life of the Chinese population. However, the price to be paid for all this has been a dramatic – and sometimes *irreversible* – depletion of natural resources, environmental pollution and the consequent degradation of the ecosystem.[18]

China's total consumption of commercial fuel moved from the 650 million tonnes of coal equivalent in 1980 to 3.75 billion tonnes of coal equivalent in 2013; moreover, the country transformed itself from being a net exporter of crude oil at the beginning of the 1990s to that of a net importer with a surplus of approximately 330 million tonnes for both oil and coal. China's environmental quality (i.e. air, water and soil quality) has also been negatively affected and is paying a remarkable – and often irredeemable – price of such fast industrialization and its consequent socio-economic development.[19]

According to the 2016 Report by the Ministry of Environmental Protection (MEP) – now the Ministry of Ecology and Environment (MEE) – despite the deterioration having reversed its negative trend after years of steady decline in quality, polluted Chinese water is still a critical problem. The report shows that 60 per cent of groundwater quality is graded "bad" or "very bad" and the current state of the rivers still represents an emergency situation. For instance, 30.5 per cent of the Yellow River Basin's shallow groundwater stations have been found to be of "very bad" quality, while almost 90 per cent of the stations in the Songhua and Liao River Basins report "bad" quality or worse; additionally, the proportion of rivers with water "unfit for human contact" stands at 28.8 per cent. Finally, of the 27 major monitored lakes and reservoirs, 34 per cent were unsafe for any use and 30 per cent were safe for industrial and irrigation uses only, leaving just 36 per cent safe for human consumption after treatment. As a consequence, today almost all Chinese provinces have limited quantities of water (particularly in certain seasons) and many of them are as dry as the countries of the Middle East.

This scarcity of water resources is made worse by their uneven geographical distribution. As an example, the North of the country has only 16 per cent of the total national water, yet it is home to 47 per cent of the overall population and produces 49 per cent of the gross regional product. Moreover, this deficit of surface water in the Northern regions has led to the overexploitation of groundwater, ultimately causing the progressive depletion of groundwater reserves.[20]

From polluted groundwater to contaminated soil is a short step. According to the National Soil Pollution Survey carried out in 2014 by the Chinese Academy for Environmental Planning, over 16 per cent of the total soil in China is contaminated, and nearly 20 per cent of its total farmland is contaminated by heavy

18 Pan Jiahua, *China's Environmental Governing*, 36.
19 Ibid.
20 China Water Risk, Ministry of Environmental Protection 2016 State of Environment Report; available at http://www.chinawaterrisk.org/resources/analysis-reviews/2016-state-of-environment-report-review.

metals.[21] With 7.2 per cent of the world's cultivated soil area, China feeds approximately 22 per cent of the world's population. Hence, Chinese agricultural production is a key issue strictly linked to both the national economy and the livelihood of the Chinese population. Furthermore, the large population, the urbanization process and above all the rapid industrialization, human over-exploitation and natural phenomena (e.g. acid rain), have led to the contamination of 5.392 million km^2 of land, accounting for approximately 56.2 per cent of the total national area. Of this area, soil degradation resulting from land erosion and water loss accounts for 1.8 million km^2, desertification for 0.33 million km^2, soil salinization for 0.99 million km^2, pasture degradation for 2 million km^2 and soil pollution for 0.26 million km^2.[22]

Though, in fact, possibly not the most serious issue, air pollution is commonly perceived as China's most prominent environmental problem. The significant debate on this and the subsequent measures undertaken by the Chinese government in the last decade, has meant that this area has seen greater improvement than those of water and soil. Over the last 40 years, China has become the world's biggest carbon emitter, so much so that it nowadays emits more carbon dioxide than the USA and EU combined. Nevertheless, as already mentioned, efforts by the Chinese government in tackling this very tangible and dramatic problem have, in recent years, inverted the negative trend.[23] As recorded by the Ministry of Environmental Protection in 2017, the average level of particulate matters less than 10 micrometres in diameter (PM10) in 338 Chinese cities fell to 75 micrograms per cubic metre – a decrease of 5.1 per cent compared with 2016, and the average level of PM2.5 in those cities was of 43 micrograms per cubic metre – a decrease of 6.5 per cent from 2016. Even so, the World Health Organisation recommends a maximum average exposure of 25 micrograms per cubic metre in a 24-hour time period so the situation is still far from rosy. In addition, because air pollution has plagued China for many years this has, as discussed, led to dramatic consequences for soil and water contamination (e.g. the phenomenon of acid rain).[24]

In other words, by espousing industrial production patterns, China triggered four decades of breakneck economic growth but which, on the flipside, gave rise to a critical – and often irreversible – ecologic imbalance. Referring back to the modern meaning of ecological civilization, it is therefore possible to argue that each of its four dimensions (justice, harmony, high efficiency, and human development) were somewhat overlooked in the name of economic prosperity, which in turn was beneficial also for the promotion of social stability.

21 Financing Models for Soil Remediation in China; available at https://www.iisd.org/sites/default/files/publications/financing-models-soil-remediation-china.pdf.

22 Xiangzheng Deng et al., "Growth, Population and Industrialization, and Urban Land Expansion of China," *Journal of Urban Economics* 63 (1): 96–100.

23 UN Environment, "Ecological Civilization: Our Planet," United Nations Environment Programme, Zhu Guangyao, Nairobi, Kenya, March 2016, 2–4.

24 Xinhua, "China Sees Fast PM 2.5 Reduction in 2017," *China Daily*, January 18, 2018.

As a result, in 2002, the 17th Congress of the Chinese Communist Party eventually reintroduced into the government agenda the need to promote and build ecological civilization. On that occasion, the Congress decided to "build ecological civilization and generally establish the production structure, growth approach, and consumption pattern of energy resource saving and ecological environment protection" so as to promote the re-foundation of ecological civilization. Therefore, from 2002 onwards, ecological civilization has been recognized as being as important as material, spiritual and political civilization. This change for the future, which takes into account one of the philosophical principles of the past, i.e. one of the founding principles of Taoist philosophy, was very well expressed by President Hu Jintao in his speech at the Congress: "Building ecological civilization, in essence, is building a resource efficient and environmental friendly society that is based on resource and environment carrying capacity, complies with natural laws and aims at sustainable development".[25]

Since the beginning of the twenty-first century, ecological civilization has constituted, together with material, spiritual and political civilization (and social culture), one of the "five dimensions" of socialism with Chinese characteristics, in which each dimension complements the other and none of them should be overlooked. In this way, the creation of ecological civilization is a comprehensive and integrated concept, which ultimately calls for the inclusion of key concepts from material, spiritual and political civilization. In one way, ecological civilization contains topics belonging to material civilization, such as ecological economy, green recycling technologies and ecological welfare; and, at the same time, it encompasses subjects pertaining to spiritual and political civilization, such as ecological justice and awareness as well as laws and policies. In another way, social, political, economic and cultural development are all closely interlinked with the realization of modern ecological civilization, and hence it needs to be incorporated at all levels within the economic, political, cultural and societal realms.[26]

In this light, the ecological economy, recycle economy, low-carbon economy and green economy all contribute to the realization of ecological civilization albeit from different angles. Ecological economy is an economic system aiming at fulfilling the desire of development by human beings while preserving the balance of the ecosystem via the application of advanced technologies. In this respect, strong emphasis is given to the concept of sustainability. Recycle economy is focused on the need for co-existence between humans and nature by means of the reduction, recycling and reuse of resources and products at every stage from processing to consumption and from exploitation to disposal. Hence, the paradigm of traditional economics with its linear rises in resource utilization is exchanged for an economic system based on virtuous recycling. Low-carbon economy refers to a form of economy that prioritizes human development and highly efficient productivity. Therefore, the main objective of such an economy is to decrease the emissions deriving from greenhouse gases and, in line with the objective of the Paris

25 UN Environment, "Ecological Civilization: Our Planet", 2–4.
26 Pan Jiahua, *China's Environmental Governing*, 40.

Agreement, keep the global temperature well below a 2 per cent rise from pre-industrial levels. Finally, green economy applies the principle of green development to both production and consumption stages, encouraging the use of renewable energies to accomplish abatement and, more generally, the protection of the ecosystem as a whole.[27]

In sum, given the modern definition of ecological civilization discussed above, it is possible to argue that all these four forms of economic systems do lead to the achievement of ecological civilization by promoting the reduction of pollution and discharge, and fostering the use of efficient energy sources and technologies – with the ultimate goal of the realization of *sustainable development*.

In classical terms, ecological civilization is indeed a different concept from sustainable development; with its meaning derived from the term *ecology*, it represents a passive accommodation between humans and nature, as well as the reining in of the human desire for unnecessary materials and consumption, to ultimately preserve a natural balance. The same cannot be said for modern ecological civilization.[28] From the above argument, it is possible to see that sustainable development and (modern) ecological civilization are very similar concepts, if not overlapping ones. One concept stresses from its very name the importance of the need for sustainability, including that of economic stability over the long term; the other – particularly in its classical form – is more a sociological concept and is focused on achieving a harmonious relationship between humans and nature.[29] However, even though the former (i.e. sustainable development) emphasises the economic dimension and is a "less sociological concept", this does not imply that it does not take into account the importance of social development. On the flip side, despite the latter (i.e. modern ecological civilization) putting its focus on the need to achieve an harmonious relationship between humans and nature, this does not imply that the economic dimension is overlooked. For all these reasons, therefore, I understand ecological civilization in its broadest sense. Ultimately, the differences between these two concepts lie in the different cultural, philosophical and historical traditions that generated them and in the consequent way ecological civilization gives more strength to the importance of human development.

To a certain extent, it is possible to argue that this strong emphasis on the need to prioritize human development and environmental protection, thus moving any economic consideration to the background, may allow China to do better than the EU (and Italy) in achieving the desired balance between environmental protection and human activities towards the goal of *sustainability* – which is in fact a key

27 Kunmin Zhang and Zongguo Wen, "Review and Challenges of Policies of Environmental Protection and Sustainable Development in China," *Journal of Environmental Management* 88 (2008): 1249–1251.

28 Zhihe Wang, Huili He and Meijun Fan, "The Ecological Civilization Debate in China", 10–14; Arran Gare, "From 'Sustainable Development' to 'Ecological Civilization'": 130–133.

29 Mette Halskov Hansen, Hongtao Li and Rune Svarverud, "Ecological Civilization: Interpreting the Chinese Past, Projecting the Global Future," *Global Environmental Change* 53 (2018): 195–203.

feature common to both concepts. Following this intent, the Minister of Ecology and Environment, Mr. Li Ganjie, has stressed on several occasions that the environment should not be "sacrificed" for economic growth.[30] As he argued,

> while some people say one-size-fits-all approaches in environmental law enforcement have damaged economic development, others say local governments have relaxed their efforts in environmental protection as the country experiences an economic downturn ... . We resolutely oppose those tendencies. Once we find such cases, we will resolutely stop them and hold officials fully accountable.[31]

That said, and going back to the comparison between sustainable development and ecological civilization, the differences between the two concepts – which have profound roots, particularly in Chinese history – are not a determining factor for the ultimate achievement of environmental protection and the laws governing it. Though not the same, the two concepts ultimately have the same objectives, such as human development, environmental protection and sustainability; hence, they do not and should not require the use of different implementation tools or different laws governing the impact of human activities towards nature. From this line of reasoning, this chapter will proceed in using the two concepts – namely, ecological civilization and sustainable development – as synonyms.

Finally, given the very balanced definition of the concept of sustainable development provided by Italian environmental law, it is possible to argue that here the definition of sustainable development is much closer to the current Chinese conceptualization of ecological civilization compared with the more vague definitions of the same concept present in EU legislation. Indeed, in line with the concept of ecological civilization and the aforementioned declarations by the Chinese Minister of Ecology and Environment, Italian law states that the duty of public authorities is to "primarily take into consideration" the environmental protection issues when public and private interests are at stake, consequently establishing a hierarchy among the involved interests and providing a practical action rule which makes the set-out principle ready to be implemented. In this light, the focus and objective of the present study acquires even more importance and, as a result, this ecological perspective shared by the Italian and Chinese approaches to environmental protection and sustainable development is fully in line with the ecological definition of the environment given at the end of Chapter 1, eventually proving its consistency and coherence. Indeed, the theoretical foundations towards effective environmental regulation are solid both in Italy and China, and the matter is now to determine the legislative structure and means that need to be embraced by China in order to strengthen environmental protection and efficiently tackle pollution.

30 Liqiang Hou, "Ecology Should Not be 'Sacrificed'," *China Daily*, March 12, 2019.
31 Ibid.

4.1.1 The Beautiful China goal and the guide for ecological environment protection in the new era

As discussed above, unlike sustainable development, the concept of ecological civilization was not widely used until 2002, when President Hu Jintao reintroduced it in the government agenda on the occasion of the 17th National Congress of the Communist Party of China. In 2007, ecological civilization became one of the five key objectives of the country's overall development plan, and 5 years later, in 2012, its critical role was restated and further strengthened at the 18th National Congress of the Communist Party of China, when President Xi Jinping was elected General Secretary of the CPC Central Committee. On this occasion, the construction of ecological civilization was recognized as a major objective of the party and was written into the party constitution, ultimately enhancing the government's focus on this fifth dimension and affirming the need to give increasing centrality to such a concept in the future development plans of China.[32]

In fact, as China embarked on its 13th Five Year Plan in 2015, the commitment to environmental protection issues appeared more solid than ever. Two years later, in his 2017 address at the Davos World Economic Forum, President Xi Jinping pronounced that it was impossible for China's growth to continue to be at the expense of the environment and talked about the need to foster ecological civilization: "It is important to protect the environment while pursuing economic and social progress so as to achieve harmony between man and nature and between man and society" [towards the] "shared future of mankind".[33]

More recently, on the 18 May 2018, China's commitment to ecological civilization was further strengthened at the 8th National Conference on Ecological Environment Protection held in Beijing. The Conference, attended and addressed by both President Xi Jinping and Premier Li Keqiang, is of historical significance for accelerating the realization of ecological civilization in the new era. The key outcome of the Conference was President Xi's Thought on Ecological Civilization, which delineates the higher and broader positioning of ecological civilization in national development and the process of reform.[34]

In his speech, President Xi argued that building an ecological civilization is of vital importance for the sustainable development of the country. Since the 18th CPC National Congress, he argued, China had carried out a number of essential, ground-breaking and long-term tasks to stimulate historical and global changes to ecological environment protection. He then argued that developing an ecological civilization necessitates compliance with six principles: harmony between humans

32 Zhilin Mu, Shuchun Bu and Bing Xue, "Environmental Legislation in China: Achievements, Challenges and Trends," *Sustainability* 6 (2014): 8976–8977.

33 See China Water Risk, Ministry of Environmental Protection 2016 State of Environment Report; available at http://www.chinawaterrisk.org/resources/analysis-reviews/2016-state-of-environment-report-review.

34 China Council for International Cooperation on Environment and Development, "Shocks, Innovation and Ecological Civilization. A 'New Green Era' for China and for the World," CCICED Issues Paper 2018, 1–2.

and nature; that lucid waters and lush mountains are invaluable assets; that a good ecological environment is the most inclusive wellbeing for people; that mountains, waters, forests, farmlands, lakes and grasslands form a life community; the conservation of the ecological environment through the strictest system and rule of law; and pursuit of global ecological progress. Additionally, efforts should be made to guarantee that the quality of the ecological environment will be drastically enhanced and the objective of building a Beautiful China basically accomplished by 2035 through accelerated construction of ecological civilization systems.[35]

In line with the origins and development of the concept of ecological civilization that was discussed at the beginning of this chapter, President Xi addressed critical questions such as why one should build ecological civilization, what it should be and how it should be built. President Xi also recalled the five dimensions discussed above by claiming that by the mid-twenty-first century, material, political, spiritual, social and ecological civilizations will be upgraded in all respects, green development models and lifestyles fostered, harmony between humans and nature preserved, a national governance system and capacity for ecological environment fully restructured and a Beautiful China built. From that day onwards, this became the long-term fundamental ideology for further developing ecological civilization and constructing a Beautiful China, thus advancing ecological civilization to a new stage.[36]

Moreover, the Conference elevated the status given to the development of an ecological civilization from that of "great importance" for the sustainable development of the Chinese nation, as stated in the report to the 19th CPC National Congress, to being of "fundamental importance". The Conference also highlighted, with three affirmative Chinese words, the great steps that had been made in building an ecological civilization following the 18th CPC National Congress, translated as: historical, watershed and global change. Nevertheless, it also indicated that China's ecological environment is still very fragile and that the results achieved so far, in spite of the fact that the quality of the ecological environment is constantly improving, are not enough.[37]

Also, three considerations emerged from the Conference with regard to the current state of the construction of ecological civilization: first, it is going through a critical phase of different pressures and loads; second, it has entered a key period that entails more quality ecological goods to encounter people's higher and higher demands for a beautiful environment; third, it has come to a time in which China is definitely capable of tackling prominent ecological and environmental challenges.

Besides the aforementioned six principles, the Conference also stressed five requirements needed to enable the development of an ecological civilization in a

35 Liang Yu, "Xi Vows Tough Battle against Pollution to Boost Ecological Advancement," XinhuaNet, 20 May 2018; available at http://www.xinhuanet.com/english/2018-05/20/c_137191762.htm.

36 Id. 3; Mette Halskov Hansen, Hongtao Li and Rune Svarverud, "Ecological Civilization": 196–198.

37 Maurizio Marinelli, "How to Build a 'Beautiful China'", 380–381.

new era: 1) to foster the construction of ecological civilization systems; 2) to encourage green development in all respects; 3) to prioritize the solving of prominent ecological and environmental problems so as to guarantee people's livelihoods; 4) to efficiently prevent risks to the ecological environment; 5) and to raise the level of environmental governance.[38] It goes without saying that all these five realms are inevitably touched, more or less directly, by the implementation of an effective permitting system.

Consequently, five ecological civilization systems should be fostered:

> an eco-culture system based on ecological values; an eco-economic system led by ecology-based industrial development and ecological industrialization; a target responsibility system with improvement of ecological environment quality at its core; an ecological civilization system guaranteed by the modernization of governance system and capacity; and an ecological security system focusing on virtuous cycle of the ecological system and effective prevention and control of environmental risks.

Those developments should be accompanied by the increased responsibilities by local Party committees at all levels as well as government leaders, whom accept primary responsibility for ecological environment protection in their respective administrative regions.[39]

In other words, mid-2018 heralded the rise of a major theoretical accomplishment, namely President Xi's Thought on Ecological Civilization, which became the theoretical guide for Beautiful China Construction. The 8th National Conference on Ecological Environment Protection strengthened the determination and willingness by Chinese authorities to keep building ecological civilization and to keep fighting against environmental pollution and ecological damage, making progress towards the realization of the national strategic goal of constructing a Beautiful China. Not least, this signals that important steps are being taken in delivering, as President Xi puts it, "people's longing for a beautiful life".[40]

In his address to all participants at the conference (i.e. government officials and civil servants), Premier Li Keqiang suggested they study carefully, understand and implement the spirit of the key speeches delivered by General Secretary Xi Jinping and, guided by Xi's Thought on Socialism with Chinese Characteristics for a New Era,[41] build ecological civilization systems, foster a system and rule-of-law construction, stay committed to ecological advancement and environmental protection, and struggle to win the hard war on pollution.

38 China Council for International Cooperation on Environment and Development, "Shocks, Innovation and Ecological Civilization," 4–6.

39 Id. 7.

40 Yuanchao Xu, Debra Tan and Woody Chan, "Two Sessions, Five Highlights for Water," March 2018; available at http://chinawaterrisk.org/resources/analysis-reviews/two-sessions-five-highlights-for-water.

41 See Zhikui Zhao, *Socialism with Distinct Chinese Characteristics* (Beijing: Beijing Times Chinese Press, 2014), 15–33.

4.1.2 War on pollution: striving to win the battle of (air, water and soil) pollution prevention and control

A few years before his 2018 speech at the 8th National Conference on Ecological Environment Protection, specifically in 2014 at the National People's Congress, the Chinese Prime Minister, Mr. Li Keqiang stated in front of the 3000 delegates of the assembly that China had declared "war on pollution". Hence the "war" was not only one of the instruments for supporting the achievement of ecological civilization, but also a key step in focusing – in an unprecedented manner – on the need to protect the environment and prioritize this need over that of economic growth.[42]

Since mid-2016, this "war on pollution" started to show its first results particularly in the field of air pollution, where a reduction by 20 per cent in PM2.5 was registered in numerous Chinese cities, including Beijing. A year later, during the 19th National Congress of the Communist Party of China (CPC) of October 2017, in his speech President Xi Jinping mentioned the word "environment" 80 times, many more than the word "economy".[43]

More recently, in mid-June 2018, the CPC Central Committee and the State Council released the "Opinions on Comprehensively Strengthening Ecological Environment Protection and Resolutely Fighting for Pollution Prevention and Control". This document established that by 2020, there will be a general improvement of the quality of ecological environment, a remarkable decrease in the total amount of major pollutants released and a more efficient control over environmental risks, so that the level of ecological environment protection will boost the achievement of building a moderately prosperous society in all respects.[44] The Opinions also affirms that China should attain a fundamental improvement of ecological environment quality – hence the basic realization of the objective of constructing a Beautiful China – by speeding up the building of an ecological civilization system, the reforming of the industrial structure and ways of production compatible with the conservation of resources and ecological environment protection. By 2050, ecological civilization will be upgraded in all different realms and modernization of the national governance system and capacity for ecological environment will be achieved.[45]

With regard to the promotion of sustainable production models, the document specifically required, by the end of 2018, an acceleration in the reform and in some cases the removal of heavily polluting industries, particularly if located in the proximity of urban areas or key water basins. In such instances, as for example in the case of industries producing chemicals or hazardous substances, local authorities are required to set out dedicated plans aimed at the environmental

42 UN Environment, "A Review of 20 Years' Air Pollution Control in Beijing," United Nations Environment Programme, Nairobi, Kenya, 2019, 6.
43 Id. 7.
44 At the time of writing no results had been published.
45 Ruiqiang Dong, "The General Plan for Pollution Prevention and Control for Three Years: The Problem of Environmental Protection First Accountable Provincial, Municipal, County Party Secretary?," *The Economic Observer*, June 30, 2018.

monitoring and upgrading of the given industrial facility and, when deemed necessary, the delocalization or closure of the polluting plants. To do so, the document also provided specific quantitative indexes to assist the city governments concerned to draft such special plans. This requirement also directly involves the application of permits.[46]

Finally, in order to promote energy efficiency and the conservation of resources, the document demanded the implementation of national water conservation actions able to tackle the aforementioned problems regarding water as a whole, thus: improving the water pricing mechanism; promoting the construction of a water-saving infrastructures and water-saving cities and monitoring the total water consumption at a national level to contain it within 670 billion cubic meters per year by 2020; coping with climate change; and adopting long-lasting measures to ensure the accomplishment of the action targets for controlling greenhouse gas emissions by 2020.[47]

Furthermore, in June 2018, the State Council promulgated the Three-Year Action Plan on Winning the Blue Sky Defense Battle. The Plan established that, in a 3-year period, the total of major air pollutant emissions together with greenhouse gas emissions should be consistently reduced, as well as the concentration of fine particular matters (PM2.5). In addition, it was announced that the number of heavy pollution days should be sharply lowered so as to improve significantly the quality of (ambient) air and hence obtain a general and substantial increase in the people's 'blue-sky' wellbeing.[48] By 2020, total sulphur dioxide and nitrogen oxide emissions should be reduced by more than 15 per cent compared with the 2015 levels; the concentration of PM2.5 in cities at the prefecture level and above, which exceed the relevant standards should decrease by more than 18 per cent over 2015 levels; the proportion of good air quality days in cities at the prefecture level and above should reach 80 per cent, and the proportion of days with heavy pollution and above should decline by more than 25 per cent over 2015 levels; provinces which have accomplished the objectives indicated in the 13th Five-Year Plan ahead of schedule should maintain and strengthen their achievements; those that have not should ensure attainment of required targets in a prompt way and time; and finally, air quality improvement targets for Beijing should be further enhanced on the basis of those established in the 13th Five-Year Plan.[49]

The key areas subject to the requirements set forth by the Three-Year Plan include the Beijing–Tianjin–Hebei region and surrounding areas, so that all city governments of this large area (namely, the so-called Jing-Jin-Ji region) have been, since mid-2018, seriously committed to meet the targets with concrete actions towards heavy polluting industrial facilities and sources. Taking the city of Beijing

46 Ibid.
47 Ibid. At the time of writing no results had been published.
48 Michael Greenstone and Patrick Schwarz, "Is China Winning its War on Pollution?" *Air Quality Life Index Report*, March 2018, 2–4.
49 Ministry of Ecology and Environment, "Three-Year Action Plan for Winning the Blue Sky Defense Battle," July 13, 2018. At the time of writing no results had been published.

as an example, one of the most relevant cases and problematic industrial sites to be tackled in order to comply with the Three-Year Action Plan for Winning the Blue Sky Defense Battle is that of the Sinopec Yanshan Petrochemical Plant, located not more than 50 km southwest from the city centre.[50] This industry is a large integrated refining and chemical enterprise capable of processing over 10 million tons of crude oil and producing over 800,000 tons of ethylene annually. It has more than 70 sets of production units, which inevitably discharge a large amount of waste water, waste gas and solid waste. Technical innovation and management measures adopted by the company in recent years have helped effectively control these pollutants and have significantly reduced emissions.[51]

The Three-Year Action Plan for Winning the Blue Sky Defense Battle in Beijing also aimed to further reduce pollutant discharge. Therefore, the Beijing Municipal Bureau of Ecology and Environment has accordingly enhanced the supervision on the company and their work in this respect. The possibility to apply the knowledge taken from EU and Italian laws and regulations on permits and the benefits resulting from their analysis, may in fact allow the identification of the possibly applicable BAT in a real and important case-study in China, keeping in mind the lessons learnt from the Ilva case and looking forward (and possibly providing advisory support) to the future definition of the Chinese law, regulations and administrative schemes related to environmental permits and their application.

In general, since 2014 and even more strongly since 2018, the efforts of the Chinese government and the Ministry of Ecology and Environment (MEE) have been focussed on preventing and controlling pollution in three specific realms: *air*, *water* and *soil*.

With regard to *air* pollution prevention and control, in line with the abovementioned Three-Year Action Plan for Winning the Blue Sky Defense Battle promulgated by the State Council in mid-2018 to further strengthen air pollution control measures, in 2018 the MEE released the implementation plan for air pollution prevention and control in key zones such as the Beijing–Tianjin–Hebei region and surrounding areas, the Yangtze River Delta and Fenhe and Weihe Plains, in order to provide clear directions in the fight against air pollution. As a result, from June 11 to July 8 of the same year, the MEE carried out two rounds of detailed inspections of "2+26" cities in Jing-Jin-Ji region and surrounding areas. Despite the notable accomplishments made by the cities of Beijing, Tianjin and Hebei in air pollution control, 5204 criticalities with regard to atmospheric environment were identified. The most serious problems were found in Quyang County of Hebei, followed by Tongzhou District in Beijing. The second round of inspections highlighted continuing problems in Zhaoxian County (Hebei) and the urban area of Jincheng (Shanxi), while Huixian (Henan) failed to meet the air pollution control requirements.[52] Also, around 120 critical situations with regard

50 UN Environment, "A Review of 20 Years' Air Pollution Control in Beijing", 48–50.

51 See SINOPEC Beijing Yanshan Company website page at www.sinopec.com/listco/en/about_sinopec/subsidiaries/refinery_petrochemical/20161109/news_20161109_378768480886.shtml.

52 Michael Greenstone and Patrick Schwarz, "Is China Winning its War on Pollution?" 2–8.

to atmospheric environment were identified in Quyang County of Hebei and 34 small coal-fired boilers in 28 companies were not eradicated as requested; some enterprises did not activate any pollution control facilities or had major unorganized emissions. The checking of the key areas subject to the Winning the Blue Sky Defense Battle were carried out also in August 2018, when around 200 inspection teams inspected 208 counties (prefectures and districts) in the Beijing–Tianjin–Hebei region and surrounding areas, ultimately spotting slightly more than 100 air-pollution-related environmental criticalities.[53]

More importantly, this thorough and intense activity of inspections has not been a one-time exercise. Indeed, the MEE then released the "Action Plan for Comprehensive Control of Air Pollution in Beijing–Tianjin–Hebei Region and Surrounding Areas in the Autumn and Winter of 2018–2019" and requested comments from all involved authorities and parties. Moreover, together with local authorities and concerned departments, the MEE will continue to increasingly promote clean energy heating in northern China, encourage the removal of small coal-fired boilers, facilitate bulk coal pollution control, promote the upgrading of key industries, accelerate motor vehicle pollution control and strengthen joint pollution prevention and control in key areas.[54]

Finally, the MEE made wise use of the available advanced technologies to effectively tackle air pollution and enhance the quality of its monitoring. In 2018, through the launch of a "clairvoyance project", the MEE split all administrative regions in the "2+26" cities of the Jing-Jin-Ji region and surrounding areas into grid units measuring 9 km^2 each, and utilized satellite remote sensors to screen 3600 grid units with a comparatively high annual average level of PM2.5 as hot spot areas for monitoring and eventually identifying and solving air pollution problems. Through satellite remote sensing, this project is able to estimate the average PM2.5 intensity in each grid unit and compare it with the meteorological and air quality monitoring data of the previous year. Then, it is able to establish the level of emissions under stagnant weather conditions regardless of the impact of exogeneous factors, thus completing the screening. For grid hot spots notified three consecutive times in the same year or six times in total, the MEE will require local authorities to improve the environmental conditions by means of notification, mobilizing working groups and publicly interviewing the responsible officers of local governments.[55]

Also as regards the intensification of *water* pollution prevention and control measures, the Chinese government plans to further strengthen its efforts and initiatives in the years to come. In April 2018 at the first meeting of the Central Financial and Economic Affairs Commission to define possible successful measures for winning the war of pollution prevention and control, it was stressed that the

53 UN Environment, "A Review of 20 Years' Air Pollution Control in Beijing", 25–27 and 49–52.

54 Id. 26

55 Id. 48–52; Michael Greenstone and Patrick Schwarz, "Is China Winning its War on Pollution?" 4–7.

objectives of a reduction in total key pollutant emissions and an improvement in the overall quality of the ecological environment by 2020 could be accomplished by the combination of several actions.[56] As well as securing victory in Winning the Blue Sky Defense Battle, with regard to water pollution these initiatives must aim to: 1) attain full control of urban black and odorous water bodies; 2) reach a comprehensive control of the Bohai Sea; 3) preserve and restore the ecological balance of the Yangtze River; 4) protect water sources and control agricultural and rural pollution; and 5) ensure such objectives may be accomplished in the within 3 years. Chinese authorities planned to tackle these five water challenges for supporting the battle of pollution prevention and control, giving a key role to the Party committees at all levels. The latter must in fact urge lower levels officials to implement the work and mobilize all segments of society to engage in pollution prevention and control.[57]

Among these five "water battles", at the time this book was being drafted, the one in which the MEE had already started to implement actual actions was the control of black and odorous water bodies. Together with the Ministry of Housing, Urban and Rural Development, the MEE has in fact launched a dedicated campaign concerning the control of black and odorous waters, which covers 36 key cities and some other prefecture-level cities nationwide, and will carry out a special inspection of the first batch of eight provinces, autonomous regions and municipalities, including Guangdong, Guangxi and Hainan, which started in September and October 2018. Those failing to effectively remedy the identified criticalities will be considered accountable by central environmental inspectors.[58]

Moreover, in recent years comprehensive control of ecological environment around the Bohai Sea has generated public concern. Great pressure has been put on the ecological environment in the proximity of the Bohai Sea because of its poor self-purification capability and large-scale land reclamation from the sea by the government, overexploitation of marine resources and massive mariculture in previous years. According to the latest updates by the MEE, it will continue to promote a balanced development of land and sea, as well as pollution control and ecological protection; also, it will work hand-in-hand with competent departments of the concerned provinces and cities in order to develop, as soon as possible, an action plan on comprehensive control of the Bohai Sea. Put another way, the MEE promises to intensify efforts to inspect and rectify sewage outlets to the sea, clean up illegal and unreasonable outlets, and focus on the control of ship and port pollution as well as the construction of refuse transfer and disposal facilities.[59]

56 At the time of writing no results had been published.
57 Chien Tat Low, "Key Water Policies 2018–2019," March 18, 2019, available at http://www.chinawaterrisk.org/resources/analysis-reviews/key-water-policies-2018-2019/.
58 China Council for International Cooperation on Environment and Development, "Progress on Environment and Development Policies in China and Impact of CCICED's Policy Recommendations," 2017–2018, 22–23.
59 Ibid.

Finally, water bodies as sources of drinking water will be prioritized in the list of "four water bodies" subject to water pollution prevention and control. Indeed, the MEE and Ministry of Water Resources recently jointly launched a tailored campaign on environmental protection focused on centralized drinking water sources at the national level. The two ministries established the following targets: to finalize the clean-up and rectification of county-level surface water sources along the Yangtze River Economic Belt and those at the prefecture level and above in other areas by the end of 2018; and to complete clean-up and rectification of county-level surface water sources in all other areas by the end of 2019.[60] According to the 2018 statistics, approximately 2400 surface water sources are part of this campaign, including 1160 county-level water sources along the Yangtze River Economic Belt. According to the same statistics, the most prominent problem is still the illegal discharge of sewage by industrial facilities, and in this respect the role that an efficient permitting system may play to tackle this criticality is of crucial importance.[61]

Last, with respect to soil pollution prevention and control, the MEE continues to promote and develop the so-called "Clean Soil Campaign". The key measures include: to fully implement the Soil Pollution Prevention and Control Action Plan to strengthen soil pollution risk control; to intensify the already ongoing activity of detailed surveying on soil pollution and safeguard the safety of agricultural land and construction land; to accelerate the construction of pilot zones for comprehensive prevention and control of soil pollution and pilot application of soil pollution control and remediation technology; and to improve the prevention and control of solid waste pollution and accelerate classified disposal of refuse.[62]

In 2018, MEE also released the "Provisions on Evaluation and Examination of the Implementation of the Soil Pollution Prevention and Control Action Plan", guiding annual evaluation and mid-term assessment of the implementation of such Action Plan by provincial, autonomous regional and municipal people's governments during the 3-year period 2018–2020. Then, from 2019 to 2021, the MEE will assess the implementation of the Action Plan by local governments compared with the previous years as well as the achievement of the priorities in soil pollution prevention and control set out at the beginning of each year. The evaluation and assessment will lead to the achievement of soil pollution prevention and control objectives and the completion of priorities in soil pollution prevention and control. In particular, the annual evaluation concerns the completion of priorities in soil

60 For more information about the clean-up and rectification of county-level surface water sources along the Yangtze River Economic Belt, please see China Council for International Cooperation on Environment and Development, "Ecological Compensation and Green Development Institutional Reform in the Yangtze River Economic Belt (YREB)," CCICED Research Report, Special Policy Study (SPS) May 2019; available at https://cciced.eco/wp-content/uploads/2020/06/cciced-sps-2-2-yangtze.pdf

61 Chien Tat Low, "Key Water Policies 2018–2019," March 18, 2019.

62 Mimi Lau and Frank Tang, "China's Environmental Clean-up Campaign hasn't Cost Jobs or Hit Economy," *South China Morning Post*, October 23, 2017.

pollution prevention and control; whereas the mid-term assessment concerns the completion of soil pollution prevention and control objectives and the completion of priorities in soil pollution prevention and control. Hence, the priorities in soil pollution prevention and control involve: comprehensive surveys on soil pollution, prevention from the source, classified management of agricultural land, land access management during construction, pilot demonstration, fulfilment of responsibilities of all parties and public engagement. However, soil pollution prevention and control objectives include safe utilization ratio of polluted farmland and safe utilization ratio of polluted plots.[63]

In order to lead local governments to entrust third parties to evaluate pollution control and remediation results, implement the Action Plan, accomplish soil pollution control and remediation objectives and duties, and preserve the quality of agricultural products and the safety of the living environment, in December 2017 the Ministry of Environmental Protection (now the MEE) printed and released a document called "Guidelines for Technical Evaluation of Soil Pollution Control and Remediation Results". These Guidelines shed a light on how to regulate the evaluation of soil pollution control results by third parties entrusted by the provincial (autonomous regional and municipal) people's governments or departments concerned. At the same time, such Guidelines can be considered the first and foundational document for China's evaluation of the outcomes deriving from the actions against soil pollution taken by different provinces, autonomous regions and municipalities.[64]

4.1.3 Ecological civilization governance: from organizational and judicial reform to environmental permits

In the first sections of this chapter, I have deliberately focused on the regulations and action plans put forward by the Chinese competent authorities in recent years, particularly 2018. This choice derives from two main needs: first, the need to provide the most up to date information on the most recent and relevant laws and policies related to ecological civilization, environmental protection and eventually to environmental permits; second, the need to highlight when the breakthrough occurred – the year 2018 – in China's ecological and environmental protection. Indeed, 2018 is the first year of the above-mentioned new era. It is also a year of great historical importance in that it coincides with the 40th anniversary of the reform and opening-up and the 20th anniversary of the rise of the State Environmental Protection Agency (SEPA), now the MEE. Furthermore, 2018 was the first year in which the spirit of the 19th CPC National Congress started to be realized. Last, but not least, this year witnessed the long-awaited restructuring and major reform of what was up to then called the Ministry of Environmental Protection and other key environmental departments.

63 China Council for International Cooperation on Environment and Development, "Progress on Environment and Development Policies," 23–24.
64 Ibid. 24.

Indeed, during the drafting of the present book, the Ministry of Environmental Protection of the P.R.C. (MEP) was turned into the Ministry of Ecology and Environment (MEE), as an outcome of President Xi's leadership and China's "Two Sessions" (两会) held in Beijing in March 2018. As a result, the competences of this newly renamed Ministry were expanded so as to include: climate change and reduction of emissions (previously under the National Development and Reform Commission – NDRC); prevention of underground water pollution (previously under the Ministry of Land and Resources – MLR); formation of water function zones, setting and management of discharge outlets, basin water protection (previously under the Ministry of Water Resources – MWR); prevention and control of agricultural pollution (previously under the Ministry of Agriculture – MoA); protection of the ocean environment (previously under the State Oceanic Administration – SoA); and south-to-north water diversion project steering committee office (previously under the State Council).[65]

Hence, the MEE's functions have been further upgraded and expanded and this Ministry has assumed more environmental responsibilities through adjustments in the environmental governance that – it is possible to argue – are unprecedented in intensity, depth and breadth and fully reflect an "integration of pollution governance and ecological regulation". In this respect, the integration of the NDRC department of climate change into the MEE is actually a precise change to synergize work, such as pollutant emission abatement and greenhouse gas emission reduction, to tackle climate change. Indeed, the fight against climate change involves energy utilization and carbon dioxide emission reduction, measures which go beyond pollution control as carbon dioxide itself is not a pollutant per se but causes a modification in the balance of the greenhouse gases. Since 2018, carbon dioxide emissions have been regulated by the MEE, making the regulation over emissions more comprehensive and making it easier to accomplish the overall objective of building ecological civilization. Besides being more functional and consistent towards the achievement of the environmental protection objectives, MEE organizational reform and new tasks interestingly mirror the structure of the Italian Ministry for the Environment, Land and Sea, so much so that the two structures and competences are now perfectly overlapping. In this light, the analysis of the laws and competences on environmental protection and permitting systems in the respective countries, as well as of the two ministries, acquires even more meaning. Also, this means that the replication of specific schemes, provisions and operational measures present in the Italian permitting structure will more likely be straightforwardly applicable to the Chinese context.[66]

As mentioned above, the profound organizational reform of the MEE also included the amalgamation of environmental departments with the aim of linking

65 Tianjie Ma and Qin Liu, "China Reshapes Ministries to Better Protect Environment," *China Dialogue*, March 14, 2018; available at https://www.chinadialogue.net/article/show/single/en/10502-China-reshapes-ministries-to-better-protect-environment.

66 Ibid.

each department's potential and hence force through the integration of its respective organizational functions – so as to trigger improvements in the enforcement of environmental law in the society as a whole. Such improvements include, inter alia, following up environmental legislation, improving the punishment mechanism, consolidating environmental judicial enforcement, enhancing environmental monitoring capabilities and modifying the performance assessment of governmental officials. In this light, in 2018 the Chinese judicial authority issued, as of today, the latest version of the General Provisions of the Civil Law. According to Article 9 of the so-called basic provisions of the law, the parties to civil legal relations shall conduct civil activities contributing to the conservation of natural resources and the protection of the environment.[67] Put another way, for the first time the General Provisions of the Civil Law required civil activities to be consistent with resource conservation and environmental protection, thus promoting the green principles in line with the development of the "green lifestyle" proposed at the 19th National Congress of the Communist Party of China (CPC).

Moreover, in June 2018, the Supreme People's Court of China (SPC) issued the "Opinions on Deeply Studying and Implementing the Xi Jinping Thought on Ecological Civilization and Providing Judicial Services and Guarantee for Ecological and Environmental Protection in a New Era". This important document urged local courts to prioritize the judicial function of environmental resources, strengthen judicial services and eventually ensure the building of ecological civilization. The Opinions highlighted that more efforts should be made to develop innovative trial implementation modes and foster the overall protection, system recovery, regional overall planning and widespread management of the ecology and environment. Additionally, the document stated that more attention should be paid on the necessity to solve the most relevant ecological and environmental problems, so as to serve and ensure pollution prevention and control and the protection of ecological security.[68] To help win the harsh fight against pollution prevention and control, the SPC should judge, according to the laws, cases concerning air, water, soil, solid waste management and disposal, noise and vibration pollution. Furthermore, in order to provide strong judicial support to the Winning the Blue Sky Defense Battle, the SPC should reinforce the hearing of air pollution disputes in key areas of China, including the Jing-Jin-Ji region and neighbouring areas, the Yangtze River Delta and the Fen-Wei Plain. Then, additional efforts should be made to hear disputes on water pollution in important waters, such as those of the Yangtze River, Yellow River, Poyang Lake, Dongting Lake and Taihu Lake, and to stimulate the treatment of polluted and odorous waters so as to preserve people's rights to live in a quiet and beautiful ecological environment where blue sky, clear waters and clean soils are guaranteed.[69]

67 See General Provisions of the Civil Law of the People's Republic of China, Basic Provisions, Article 9.

68 China Council for International Cooperation on Environment and Development, "Progress on Environment and Development Policies," 30.

69 Xiang-chao Pan, "Research on Xi Jinping's Thought of Ecological Civilization and Environment Sustainable Development," *Earth and Environmental Science* 153 (2018): 1–3.

Finally, the SPC should: defend marine natural resources and the environment and judge cases concerning the pollution and damage of the marine ecology according to law; facilitate the construction of a beautiful countryside; satisfy the requirements of the rural rejuvenation strategy; and hear different kinds of cases concerning rural natural resource exploitation and utilization, the overall management of rural living environment, agricultural ecological products and services – in order to foster the sustainable development of agriculture and the construction of ecologically liveable beautiful countryside. Ultimately, the SPC should continuously increase its capacity to protect biodiversity; judge cases about the damage to biodiversity according to law; preserve the diversity of species and the ecosystem, and help ameliorate the legal system of the biodiversity protection; thoroughly ensure the layout of the ecological security strategy; hear disputes related to key ecological function areas and environmentally sensitive and vulnerable areas according to law; focus on ecological protection and recovery; and build a barrier for ecological security.[70]

Besides the recent reforms in environmental governance, both at the ministerial and judicial level, in recent years China has made remarkable efforts towards the construction and implementation of a permitting system for protecting the environment through the control of pollutant emissions. Indeed, permits play a determinant role in the achievement of modern ecological civilization I discussed previously, not least by reforming and improving the management system of stationary pollution sources.

Looking at the latest standards and regulations on environmental permits, it is here worth highlighting that since the "Implementation Plan for Pollution Control and Discharge Permit System" released by the State Council in 2016, in 2017 the MEE (at that time still the Ministry of Environmental Protection – MEP) issued both the guidance document named "Catalogue for Classified Management of Stationary Pollution Sources" and the "Interim Management Regulations on Discharge Permitting", as well as the general principles of the "Technical Specifications for Application for and Issuance of Pollutant Emission Permits in Thermal Power and Paper-making Industries" and the "Technical Guidelines for Self-Monitoring by Pollutant Emission Units". Though still preliminary, these have been important steps in the way towards an increasingly complete system of regulations and technical specifications to fully support the application for and issuance of pollutant emission permits.[71]

As well as this, a national pollutant emission permit management information platform has been created and launched with the aim of allowing the application for and issuance of pollutant emission permits for enterprises in thermal power and papermaking industries. During the drafting of the present book, the Chinese competent authorities kick-started this work, so much so that local environmental bureaus are actively deploying and organizing such implementation. In particular, by May 2018, approximately 6000 enterprises had been registered on the national

70 Id. 3–5; China Council for International Cooperation on Environment and Development, "Progress on Environment and Development Policies," 30–31.

71 Id. 25.

pollutant emission permit management information platform, 1500 pollutant emission permit applications were awaiting approval and environmental authorities had issued around 70 permits subject to national unified coding.[72] Undoubtedly, these are positive and important steps in the development of a progressively robust system regulating environmental permits; however, it goes without saying, these limited fields of application as well as the modest figures involved, especially in the light of China's industrial dimensions, makes it all look it like a single drop in a limitless ocean. But there is more. Even though, in general, the issuance of pollutant emission permits is proceeding in an orderly fashion, problems such as the failure to achieve a comprehensive coverage of permit issuing and to respect deadlines, and an inadequate technical force for permit implementation, still occur country-wide. On top of this, numerous local environmental bureaus are currently struggling under the heavy tasks of systems linking and enhanced responsibilities, and this inevitably affects progress.[73]

In this view, the MEE will have to carry on with strict environmental law enforcement and environmental protection supervision and enhance its source control, and the role played by environmental permitting will be crucial. This is the reason why it is now worth making a step backward in order to analyse Chinese environmental permits from their very first steps and then focus on the law and regulations related to them. The objective is twofold. First, to identify the strengths and, above all, the weaknesses present in the Chinese laws and policy tools regulating permits; second, in the light of what has been argued in previous chapters about the EU and Italy, to draw recommendations for effectively developing the legislation regulating Chinese permitting so as to allow its full and successful implementation. If the latter were to occur, the Chinese government will ultimately be able to strengthen ecological environmental protection, also implementing the Action Plans on *air, water* and *soil* pollution control; push forward high-quality development and provide qualitatively ecological goods to satisfy people's ever-growing demands for a beautiful life; make a breakthrough in the war of pollution prevention and control, and advance the building of a Beautiful China; and foster green development and intensify the protection of ecosystems, so much so that (modern) ecological civilization will be finally built.

4.2 China's policy tools on permits

Besides some key Chinese environmental laws related to permits, which will be analysed below, the Chinese legislative scenario is composed of four major policy tools gravitating around environmental permits, which – as a matter of fact – laid the foundation for the aforementioned laws in the need of directly tackling

72 Ibid.

73 Wenhong Xu and Hui Yang, "New Measures Further Reform Pollutants Discharge Permit System," *International Law Office Broad and Bright*, April 9, 2018; available at https://www.lexology.com/library/detail.aspx?g=fd441021-26b9-49ef-85f7-bef9450ac40a.

pollution generated by industrial facilities and enterprises. These are: Emission Standards, Total Emission Control, Environmental Impact Assessment (EIA) and Emission Fee (recently replaced by the New Environmental Protection Tax).

In brief, Emission Standards is the set of legal requirements governing the *concentration* of released pollutants and it is the only document – indeed comparable to a law – for supervisory bureaus to assess whether an enterprise is complying with the rules[74]; through Total Emission Control, the central government establishes emission targets by *total volume*, at provincial or city level, of specific water and air pollutants (SO_2, NO_X, COD, NH_3-N) which are not regulated by Emission Standards[75]; EIA refers to the methodology for performing analysis, projection and evaluation on potential environmental impacts of say a construction project prior to its realization[76]; finally, Emission Fee details the fees for pollutant discharge (i.e. fees charged to companies to be able to discharge a certain amount of pollutants) and its final aim is to encourage a reduction in emissions.[77]

As I will discuss in the following pages, these four tools go some way towards providing useful information and mechanisms to regulate the permitting system in China, inevitably giving support to the government bodies in charge of enforcing the legislation related to permits and enhancing their enforcement capacity. Each of them stipulates often-indispensable standards (i.e. concentration and total volume) as well as temporal and spatial criteria towards a more comprehensive pollution management system.

4.2.1 Emission Standards and Total Emission Control

Permits were first introduced in China in the mid-1980s in the field of water pollution control. Indeed, at that time China launched, in some areas of the country, experimental versions of two very important policy tools, namely *Emission Standards* and *Total Emission Control.*

Like the EU and Italy – prior to the IPPC Directive – China too took its first steps in the fight against pollution by adopting a "sectorial" approach; that is, by tackling pollution of different environmental media, such as air or water, through the application of specific and distinct policy tools. The first of these tools was Emission Standards, which aims to establish the concentration-based standard of a given pollutant, so that a business is allowed to discharge pollutants into the

74 The MEP is in charge of developing, drafting, and approving the standards. Zhen Zhang et al., "Environmental Technology Transfer and Emission Standards for Industry in China," *The Journal of Technology Transfer* 40 (2015): 743.

75 Chazhong Ge et al., "China's Total Emission Control Policy: A Critical Review," *Chinese Journal of Population Resources and Environment* 7 (2009): 50–52.

76 Jesse Moorman and Zhang Ge, "Promoting and Strengthening Public Participation in China's Environmental Impact Assessment Process: Comparing China's EIA and US NEPA," *Vermont Journal of Environmental Law* 8 (2006): 282–283.

77 Ruonan Zhao et al., "The New Orientation of Discharge Permit System in the Environmental Management System," *Applied Mechanics and Materials* 737 (2015): 985.

environment within certain prescribed limits. In other words, Emission Standards is the set of legal requirements governing the *concentration* of released pollutants by industrial facilities and it is the only policy tool – indeed comparable to a law – which allows Chinese supervision bureaus to assess whether an enterprise is complying with the rules.[78]

As already analysed in the previous chapters, setting Emission Standards for certain polluting substances is a tool traditionally used in environmental protection systems inspired by the command-and-control model, and the key problem with such a system is that, if multiple polluters are involved, the total amount of pollutant discharged may still be harmful.

Since the 1980s, in specific areas of the country, China started to implement experimental versions of Emission Standards in the waste water sector as a means to constrain the negative impact of pollutants discharged by industrial facilities into natural water. In this first stage, the key objective was officially to protect public health and to promote the development of environmental technologies. However, it is also from the mid-1980s – specifically after the Second National Conference for national environmental protection – that the role of economic growth started to acquire greater importance, so much so that, by the end of the decade, the economic component was definitely prioritized over both the social and the environmental ones.[79]

In this context, the Water Pollution Prevention and Control Law of 1984 highlighted the importance of emission standards and required the policy-makers to ensure that the standards reflect water quality as well as economic benefits. Meanwhile, other policy tools, such as Emission Fees and EIA (which will be analysed in the next section), partially took over the role of Emission Standards.

As mentioned above, Emission Standards fix the (maximum) concentration limits for pollutants that each industrial facility may release into the environment. Nevertheless, as argued more broadly in this section, the quality of the environment is not a function of emission concentrations, but of total loadings. Indeed, even under a concentration standard, total emissions may increase due to longer operating periods, increased production and/or new emitters. Therefore, through the mere application of Emission Standards it was difficult to predict whether there would be an increase in environmental quality even when all industrial facilities complied with such concentration standards. This uncertainty was the most important shortcoming in the management of air and water quality through emission concentration standards. Put another way, even though the Chinese government published numerous Emission Standards for water pollutants tailored to different types of industries and categories, in the latter years of the 1980s and all the 1990s there was no clear relationship between Emission Standards and water or air quality.[80]

78 Zhen Zhang et al., "Environmental Technology Transfer": 743 and 749.
79 Id. 745–746.
80 Id. 746–747.

Following the introduction of the emission concentration standards policy, China's pollution control efforts then focused on Total Emission Control (TEC). The latter determines the maximum allowable amount of pollutants in each area and it allocates that load among all individual dischargers through a permit system. Since the late 1980s, through TEC, the Chinese central government established *total volume* emission targets, at provincial or city level, for specific water and air pollutants which were not regulated by the Emission Standards.[81]

The TEC approach was preliminary launched in 1988 during the Third National Conference for Environmental Protection in which the State Environmental Protection Administration (SEPA), at that time the national environmental authority of China, proposed to strengthen the fight against pollution by the implementation of a TEC approach in combination with the main pollution control policy of the time – the emission concentration standards. Since the very beginning, the implementation of the TEC involved four key elements: setting national emission targets, allocating targets to industrial facilities, collecting emission data and enforcing the policy.

In 1985, Shanghai became the first city in China to adopt the above-mentioned tools (i.e. Emission Standards and TEC) along the Huangpu River, eventually imposing restrictions on the total amount of water pollutants. Subsequently, both tools were gradually extended to other cities such as Xuzhou, Shenzhen, and Chongqing, with a certain degree of success.[82]

In 1988, the National Environmental Protection Agency, which in the same year was upgraded to the State Environmental Protection Agency (SEPA), issued an administrative regulation called the Measure on Water Pollutant Discharge Permit Management for implementing at national level the Emission Standards and TEC tools. In other words, this regulation empowered local Environmental Protection Bureaus (EPBs) to set up a plan for total pollutant load control of water and to apply pollutant discharge permits based on local conditions.

Those steps marked the beginning of a new phase of environmental water management in China so much so that, in 1991, SEPA extended its scope from water to air by implementing both tools (Emission Standards and TEC) in 16 test-cities in order to control air pollution. The application of those tools in the selected cities allowed for the collection of useful data and information in the view to ultimately extend the implementation of total pollutant load control and discharge permits all over China.[83]

This enlargement goal was far from accomplished, however. Indeed, there was no national comprehensive legislation pertaining to the total emission standards and control able to include all forms of pollutants, nor was the existing system wholly adequate for the pollutants it did oversee. Moreover, though this experimental stage targeted pollutants in both air and water sectors, water pollution

81 Chazhong Ge et al., "China's Total Emission Control Policy": 50–52.

82 Zhiping Li, "The Challenges of China's Discharge Permit System and Effective Solutions," *Temple Journal of Science Technology and Environmental Law* 24 (2005): 375–376.

83 Ibid. 376–78.

seemed to be tackled better than air pollution. In sum, some regulations had been put in place, but they were not fully developed, or were they enacted within the framework of a larger and comprehensive plan.[84]

Even so, this experimental period that was initiated in 1988 allowed the policy to be extended to the national level 8 years later, in 1996, when the TEC policy was included in the "Ninth Five-Year Plan for Environmental Protection and Environmental Targets for 2000". According to this 5-year Plan, the TEC policy set out to regulate the release into the environment of 12 pollutants, with the aim of achieving a 10 per cent reduction for those specific pollutants in the course of the next 5 years. In this respect, starting from 1996, the Chinese government set ambitious environmental goals and put the TEC policy tool at the centre of its fight against rising pollution levels on the basis of three main criteria: temporal, spatial and volume; indeed, the policy established the total authorized emissions within a given area and a given period of time.[85] Therefore, it is possible to argue that the TEC policy tool integrated the Emission Standards and tackled its very deficiency. Following the TEC, the focus of pollution control in China gradually moved from concentration to total loadings of pollutants.

Subsequently, TEC policy soon came to be considered as a basis for all upcoming environmental policies and regulations, and it played an ever more important role in the attempt to enhance the environmental quality and management of the country.[86] For decades, TEC has been one of, if not the most important, policy of China's pollution control system; a policy capable of reaching the reduction targets of 10 per cent, according to MEP statistics, and nevertheless able to reduce annual emission of targeted pollutants – consequently improving the quality of China's environment.[87]

Since the early years of their respective applications, several key differences have become clear between Emission Standards and TEC policy tools.

Indeed, the former addresses industrial facilities through a general approach, by determining uniform and nationwide concentration standards for each polluting source. In doing so – i.e. by requesting each industrial facility to attain a uniform concentration standard – this tool, though seemingly simple in its approach, generally imposes a higher overall cost on the given industry. Moreover, the application of this policy does not take into account the so-called local conditions, such as climate, the location of the facility, flora, landscape and land use. In fact, all these elements can deeply affect the capability of an environment to recover.[88] Furthermore, under a concentration standard, polluting facilities must tackle all emissions and, due to the usually limited pollution control budgets, high rates of

84 Neil Carter and Arthur P.J. Mol, *Environmental Governance in China*. New York: Routledge, 2007, 20–24.

85 Alex Wang, "The Role of Law in Environmental Protection in China: Recent Developments," *Vermont Journal of Environmental Law* 8 (2006–7): 198–201.

86 Chazhong Ge et al., "China's Total Emission Control Policy": 50.

87 Ministry of Environmental Protection of China, China's Environmental Status Report, 2006–2012; available at http://jcs.mep.gov.cn/hjzl/zkgb.

88 Chazhong Ge et al., "China's Total Emission Control Policy": 51.

non-compliance have been recorded in the application of concentration standards in China as is the case elsewhere. Finally, Emission Standards ask for the incessant monitoring of polluting emissions in order to ensure that a facility's emissions do not go beyond the established target. This is not only costly and difficult to implement uniformly across the country, but it is also less preferable compared with a policy founded on total emissions which, particularly for some pollutants, can be implemented more easily through engineering calculations based on the quality and quantity of the energy source used (i.e. fuel, coal, etc.).[89]

On the other hand, TEC has its basis in company-wide compliance; it determines an emission limit for each industrial facility; and it aims to give to the operators the flexibility to reach the standard in a cost-effective way. Specifically, it provides companies with the flexibility to prioritize investment in pollution controls on the basis of different types of pollutants at different facilities and to select the most suitable pollution control method according to each industrial facility at stake. In this light, TEC results in being a more convenient approach compared with Emission Standards, towards the accomplishment of emission reductions and environment-friendly goals. Finally, the targets for China's TEC are established from figures related to total emissions during the previous 5-year period. Hence, it is crucial to build a thorough and exact inventory from the previous 5-year period in order to set the total targets for the next lustrum.[90]

As argued above, the Emission Standards present numerous shortcomings which have been somewhat tackled by TEC. That said, the implementation of TEC over the years has also highlighted numerous deficiencies.

Overall, to regulate the total ecological capacity of a given area and consequently determine its capacity for each pollutant, the implementation of the TEC policy requires profound technical expertise as well as considerable financial resources. As a matter of fact, ensuring that polluting facilities monitor their emissions and discharges within the allowed quantities has always been a challenging task for two major reasons. First, because of the low quality of technical equipment and expertise for pollution monitoring and the lack of connection of the monitoring tools to a network; second, due to the historically scarce quantity of human resources that local EPBs are able to put towards the onsite monitoring activities to determine the actual loading of regulated pollutants.[91] As already discussed, such a deficiency has recently been tackled through the involvement of MEE teams in the thorough and intense activity of inspections in specific areas of the country; however, a comprehensive coverage at national level is still far from being accomplished. Moreover, China's environmental setting and conditions diverge considerably from one place to the other, so much so that it has often been impossible to establish the eco-capacities and sources of the many pollutants

89 Ibid.

90 Id. 52.

91 Yong Geng and Joseph Sarkis, "Achieving National Emission Reduction Target – China's New Challenge and Opportunity," *Environmental Science and Technology* 46 (1) (2012): 107–108.

throughout such a heterogeneous and large country. As a result, given the complexity and immense scale of Chinese ecological systems, it has often been difficult to establish the exact outcomes of TEC implementation. In this respect, the scope of China TEC policy tool at national level has been, and still is, too broad and it lacks a scientific and environmental rationality and solidity. This is also the reason why the TEC policy is usually treated and implemented as an ***ad interim*** and/or complementary measure for pollution reduction and control and is ideally applied in relatively confined areas or to a specific industry, for tackling a certain number of pollutant emitters.[92]

The implementation of TEC has also lacked the continuity needed to ultimately lead to consistent results. Over the years, the targeted range of pollutants recognized at the national level has been halved from 12 pollutants in the 1996–2000 period (namely, the Ninth Five Year Plan period) to 6 pollutants in the 5 years between 2001 and 2005, and then even reduced to 2 pollutants in the period 2006–2010. This progressive reduction of pollutants was due in some cases to the fact that some of them had ceased to be a national problem; however, more often it was because of the EPBs' difficulty in obtaining reliable data on given pollutants as a result of the substantial dependence on the self-reported measurements, the high number and heterogeneity of polluting indicators, the different monitoring frequency according to different areas and the fact that different production facilities used different techniques and applied diverse methods to treat pollution.[93] Though not able to provide a full picture of environmental improvement needs, the hope was that by focusing on fewer pollutants the implementation of the policy would be simpler. One way or the other, this reduction of the targeted pollutants has inevitably led over time to distorted industrial development, sometimes even resulting in increased levels of emissions for certain polluting substances. For instance, as argued by Qing Hu et al.,

> local governments have attempted to shut down industries with high COD (e.g. pulp mills) and promote the development of low COD discharging industries, e.g. mining, metallurgical and building industries. This has likely led to a rising level of heavy metals pollution since 2000.[94]

As discussed in Section 4.1.2 of the present study, since 2014 and even more intensely since 2018, the Chinese government and the MEE have made increasingly effective efforts in order to prevent, control and tackle exacerbated pollution levels in air, water and soil. As mentioned above, additional implementation and action plans have been released (on winning the blue sky defense battle and the comprehensive control of air pollution, on ground and surface water sources, as

92 Chazhong Ge et al., "China's Total Emission Control Policy": 55–56.
93 Qing Hu et al., "Total Emission Control Policy in China," *Environmental Development* 25 (2018): 127; Chazhong Ge et al., "China's Total Emission Control Policy": 56.
94 Ibidem.

well as on soil pollution prevention and control) to strengthen China's ongoing and future action. Collectively, the aforementioned plan of inspections carried out by the MEE since 2018 and the critical amendments to the Environmental Protection Law (in 2014) and the Laws on Air, Water and Soil Pollution Prevention and Control (in 2015, 2018 and 2019, respectively) demonstrate the immense remedial efforts and key institutional solutions that China has put in place in recent years for fostering ecological progress and protecting the environment as a whole.[95]

Going back to the implementation of TEC at the national level and its limitations, it is worth recalling that one of the fundamental characteristics for the execution of TEC is the assignment of TEC quotas to each provincial government, mainly on the basis of its industrialization, historical emissions data and capability of reducing emissions by its polluting industries. The problem, however, is that even though each provincial government is required to apply the same criteria to allocate the quotas to the cities under its jurisdiction, the same provincial authorities do not have the capability to collect accurate and reliable data on the levels of pollutant emissions which would allow them to establish the absorption capacities of the pollutants by the ecosystem taken into consideration. Indeed, such methodologies for accurate measurement are, to date, not available.[96]

Another deficiency of the implementation of the TEC policy tool is that it does not take into consideration the different characteristics of each ecosystem, so that similar reduction targets are set regardless of the available environmental capacity. For example, as argued by Qing Hu et al.,

> Beijing, Tianjin, the Yangtze River Delta and Pearl River Delta regions account for only 8% of the total land area of the country, but consume 42% of the country's total coal, 52% of gasoline and diesel, 55% of the iron and steel production and 40% of cement production and produce 30% of the sulphur dioxide, nitrogen oxides and soot emissions. The emissions of these pollutants per square kilometres in these areas are 5 times more than in other areas, but the reduction target is only set at 20% higher than other less polluted areas. The target reduction of a 10% for each TEC pollutant appears discretional and unscientific. This target setting has no benefit to the environment for those pollutants which have already significantly exceeded their environmental capacity.[97]

Put another way, because they are not based on scientific evaluation of the pollutant reductions needed to improve environmental quality in a particular area, achievement of TEC targets is often unrealistic. Also, the lack of consistency in the emission data used to set the TEC targets and assess compliance give rise to a

95 See Section 4.1.2 of the present study.
96 Qing Hu et al., "Total Emission Control Policy in China": 127–128.
97 Id. 128.

constant gap between the actual emissions recorded in a given 5-year Plan period and the targets set for the next one.

Finally, in view of the enormous environmental differences among China's regions, the TEC shows a lack of flexibility to achieve targets. Indeed, as stated above, the TEC policy tool should provide companies with the flexibility to prioritize investment in pollution controls on the basis of different types of pollutants at different facilities and enable them to select the most suitable pollution control method according to the industrial facility at stake. Nevertheless, empirical implementation of TEC in China has revealed that the tool has limited itself to set targets without providing the polluting enterprises with flexible mechanisms capable of facilitating them by means of the autonomous selection of the most appropriate measures to self-control pollution and so to achieve such targets.[98]

Overall, it is possible to argue that China's pollution has not exhibited a meaningful improvement since the implementation of TEC policy tool and this has undermined the previous certainties regarding the actual efficacy of the TEC tool for controlling and managing pollution. Moreover, in spite of the fact that in the same period Emission Standards started to benefit from the positive action played by the TEC tool, from the start the lack of integration between these two regulatory instruments ultimately has undermined their effectiveness. This inability to integrate has meant that Emission Standards focus mainly at the quantitative and technical level such as the concentration of released pollutants into water and air, whereas TEC has focused on the overall qualitative aspects of those environmental means.[99]

In principle, though the TEC policy is considered to be a very effective tool for pollution control, the above analysis has proved why such a tool alone hardly suits China's needs as, primarily, it is best suited to relatively closed ecosystems where pollutant capacities and emissions can be realistically identified and quantified. Setting emission quotas and targets is an innovative instrument for the implementation of the TEC, but it is crucial to clearly delineate the responsibilities and liabilities for a pollutant's control between local governments and industrial facilities and to obtain relatively reliable and accountable pollution and emission data. The scope and allocation of emission quotas have to be thoroughly assessed while the diminution of pollutant emissions must be rigorously implemented for single pollution sources.[100]

Though presenting some positive features, the TEC policy alone does not take into consideration the different characteristics of each ecosystem; it does not provide the polluting facilities with the flexibility to achieve targets; it does not have the capability to collect accurate and reliable data; it has difficulties in establishing the exact outcomes of its implementation; and it lacks the continuity needed to

98 Wenbo Xue et al., "Assessment of Air Quality Improvement Effect under the National Total Emission Control Program during the Twelfth National Five-Year Plan in China," *Atmospheric Environment* 68 (2013): 74–75.

99 Ibid.

100 Qing Hu et al., "Total Emission Control Policy in China": 128.

ultimately lead to consistent results. These have been its key deficiencies and that eventually accounted for increased levels of pollution. Instead, the TEC policy should focus on polluters and stringent concentration standards should be used as the assessment tool of environmental quality for local governments.

4.2.2 Environmental Impact Assessment and the New Environmental Protection Tax

Since the 1970s, EIA has proven to be "the most widely emulated form of environmental regulation" worldwide. Indeed, EIA is not only an instrument helping decision-makers to collect the needed environmental information, but it is also a tool able of instilling environmental values into decision-making attitudes through wider social learning.[101]

China launched its first EIA system in 1979 and it strengthened the EIA through the issuing of the Environmental Protection Law (EPL) of 1989. Still, it was only in 2003 that a law entirely dedicated to EIA entered into force with the aim of mitigating pollution and environmental damages caused by newly constructed projects or plants and promoting a more consistent development of the economy and society along with nature. Such a law was later amended first in 2016 and – more recently – in 2018.

In general, there are two types of EIA in China: plan-based EIA and construction-based EIA. As far as the latter is concerned, there are different EIA documents that need to be submitted according to the level of impact of the construction project. Therefore, there is an EIA report for considerable impact, an EIA statement for average impact and an EIA registration form for limited impact. The management of the EIA approval is scattered among different public authorities at different levels, and a set of given criteria are adopted in order to establish such a division of competences in the attempt to ensure a proper delivery of both EIA services and environmental scrutiny in China.[102]

As mentioned above, a first amendment to China's EIA Law was approved in July 2016. The amended version of the Law included a couple of key features. First, it reduced the administrative requirements for EIA acquisition, hence not obliging the applicant to obtain the EIA before the processing of any other construction permit – as was the case in the previous version of the Law. In other words, in order to enhance the administrative efficiency of EIA, the legislator decided to delete the clause of holding an EIA as a precondition for obtaining other approvals. Second, the 2016 amendment considerably enhanced the penalties for the violators of the Law.[103] Indeed, the 2003 text (see Article 31)

101 Yun Ma, "Dynamics in Central-Local Division of the Authority of EIA Approval in China," *Journal of Environmental Law* 31 (2019): 29.

102 Zining Jin, "Environmental Impact Assessment Law in China's Courts: A Study of 107 Judicial Decisions," *Environmental Impact Assessment Review* 55 (2015): 35–36.

103 Gao Qi, "Mainstreaming Climate Change into the EIA Procedures: A Perspective from China," *International Journal of Climate Change Strategies and Management* 10 (3) (2018): 352–353.

punished enterprises in violation of the legislation (i.e. carrying out construction works before receiving approval) with a fine not higher than 200,000 RMB, so much so that a fine of this scale often represented an irrelevant penalty – particularly for the medium and large enterprises and projects/plants.[104] The amendment tackled this deficiency by significantly increasing the fines given to violators, who now must consider the risk of facing extremely high costs; construction projects are now charged between 1 per cent and 5 per cent of their total investment quota, depending on the level of violations and damages.

However, the most recent amendment of the EIA Law also marked several attempts at ameliorating the administrative procedures and ultimate efficiency of the Law. In this respect, through Article 19 and Article 20, the 2018 Law attributed to EIA bodies the possibility of defining the qualification and certification requirements previously authorised exclusively by environmental authorities. Thus, if it has the capacity to do so, an enterprise may prepare the EIA registration forms itself and/or entrust and pay an EIA body or practitioner for drafting EIA reports and statements.[105]

As highlighted in Chapter 2 when focusing on the procedures for issuing integrated permits,[106] among the different permits needed for constructing a new plant or modifying an existing plant, by requiring a preliminary investigation activity, EIA approval is at the pre-construction stage. Article 22 of the EIA Law distinguishes between the three types of EIA documents and their finalization procedures: both EIA reports and statements are marked according to a "graded EIA approval system"; whereas the EIA registration form does not need any approval but needs to undergo a record-filing system.

With regard to the former, EIA reports and statements must be submitted by enterprises so as to be assessed and approved by the competent environmental authorities – the MEE at the national level and the Bureaus of Ecology and Environment (BEEs) at provincial, municipal and county levels.[107] The timing thresholds for completing the EIA approval procedures are 60 days for an EIA report and 30 days for an EIA statement.[108] During the EIA approval procedure, the costs for carrying out technical evaluations of submitted EIA documents by technical bodies may be covered by environmental authorities, when this is considered to be necessary. As a matter of fact, this very method of allowing one technical body to review a report drafted by another professional EIA counterpart is severely criticised for two reasons: first, it generates redundancy of the overall

104 Environmental Impact Assessment Law of the People's Republic of China 2003: Article 31.
105 Environmental Impact Assessment Law of the People's Republic of China 2018: Articles 19 and 20.
106 See Section 2.5 of the present study.
107 Environmental Impact Assessment Law of the People's Republic of China 2018: Article 22.
108 Ibid.

process and, second, it allows approval authorities to be considered unaccountable for their final pronouncements.[109]

Moreover, the Chinese EIA Law introduces the *veto* feature. Indeed, in cases where the environmental authorities do not approve the EIA, this implies the abortion of the project. In this respect, Article 25 states that the construction should not start in case EIA documents are not submitted for the EIA approval procedure or are rejected following the assessment of process and quality. This gives EIA a substantive regulatory trait, eventually empowering Chinese environmental authorities – by giving them the discretion of stopping unsustainable development activities – as well as the leverage for influencing other investment authorities. That said, the expected positive results do not necessarily become reality.[110]

Despite it playing an unarguably constructive role in the prevention of pollution and ecological damage, not least thanks to its improving amendments, since 2003 and over the following years EIA in China did not prove to be as efficient as expected. This is true, in particular, when the data regarding the EIA ultimate enforcement and related eventual performance are taken into account.

The total amount of EIA approvals by BEEs by all levels has more than doubled in 15 years, registering an increase from approximately 194,000 in 2001 to 440,000 in 2015. Nevertheless, the enforcement data – that is the number of projects/plants with EIA approval over the total number of projects – has proven to be inconsistent with the (increasing) environmental degradation. In fact, the very high EIA enforcement rates were not accompanied by such noteworthy and positive results in environmental quality.[111] Put another way, in spite of its improved and substantive regulatory force, in practice EIA did not often lead to more efficient environmental decision-making and enhanced environmental quality.

Similarly, the enforcement rate of EIA has moved from 56 per cent in 1993 to figures consistently above 99 per cent since 2004, reaching 99.9 per cent in 2010. As argued by Ma Yun, "the enforcement rate had not been listed as an indicator since 2011 simply because it was too high".[112] Nonetheless, such data have been challenged more than once. For instance, in 2003, six ministries carried out an *ad hoc* environmental law enforcement campaign which highlighted that 51 per cent of illegal polluting plants were newly built and, yet, the percentage of EIA enforcement in the same year reached 98 per cent. Such an incongruity between high enforcement rates and prevailing noncompliance has shown once again that EIA approval in China was often and easily circumvented.[113]

Furthermore, this situation has been worsened over time by the so-called "disassembling strategy of EIA approval". The strategy involves dividing a single

109 Gao Qi, "Mainstreaming Climate Change": 353–355.

110 Environmental Impact Assessment Law of the People's Republic of China 2018: Article 25.

111 Zining Jin, "Environmental Impact Assessment Law": 36.

112 Yun Ma, "Dynamics in Central-Local Division": 45.

113 Zining Jin, "Environmental Impact Assessment Law": 37.

project into several parts so that the competence for its EIA approval can move from the higher levels of environmental authorities to lower ones, thus increasing the rate of final approvals. The success of this strategy is facilitated by the over-bureaucratic project planning and licensing process. Made of a series of complex and separated approvals, the procedural scheme of project licensing in China repeatedly creates delays due to what some scholars define as "multi-staged approvals". Here, different approvals are linked with each other at different stages and at different rates – in some cases in a parallel mode and in others in the form of a relay race – so that they are able to further protract and complicate the whole process. As argued by Ma Yun,

> a reported extreme example is that a construction project, from the very beginning to the end, has to go through more than 100 separate procedures with 20 departments and 53 offices involved, 109 stamps and seals affixed and 36 items of fee collection charged. The duration of the whole process of approval amounts up to 2,020 days with a minimum of 799 days even if a shortcut is selected.[114]

Thus, the above-mentioned problems show that although numerous legislative efforts and amendments were made to improve and simplify the implementation of EIA, EIA approval in China has often not been taken seriously and easily circumvented. As a result, the EIA Law fails to prevent violations and in reality encourages non-compliance. In this light, recalling what was discussed in Chapters 1 and 2 with regard to the precautionary principle, it is possible to argue that the specific characteristic of EIA approval – in playing the role of a regulatory mechanism which triggers the precautionary principle – fails.

Finally, the application of an integrated approach would contribute by tackling those issues through a single assessment procedure able to combine the issuing of EIA and environmental permits, not least taking into account the public interests through legal (integrating) instruments.[115]

On January 1, 2018, following China's National People's Congress (NPC) Standing Committee approval at the end of 2016, the Chinese government implemented a new environmental tax policy, effectively replacing the existing pollution discharge fee system that had been in force since 1979.

The New Environmental Protection Tax focuses on the same four sectors as the pollutant discharge fee: water, air and noise pollution, as well as solid waste. Therefore, entities discharging pollutants in those environmental media are subject to the Environmental Protection Tax. In reference to Article 3 of the same Law, carbon dioxide (CO_2) is not present in the list of taxable pollutants.[116]

114 Yun Ma, "Dynamics in Central-Local Division": 33.

115 Reference is made, inter alia, to the special collegial body (i.e. "Conferenza di Servizi") analysed in Chapter 3 of the present study.

116 Environmental Protection Tax Law of the People's Republic of China 2018: Articles 2 and 3.

The Environmental Protection Tax aims, inter alia, to tackle the problem of inefficient collection (i.e. enforcement) of the pollution discharge fees and to increase companies' accountability towards pollution reduction. To address the former issue, the new legislation mandates the coordination of fee collection by both the environmental protection body and the tax authority, and regulates that all collected revenues must be retained at the local level.[117]

The Environmental Protection Tax is also more accurate compared with the previous Emission Fee system. Indeed, the latter did not distinguish between light and heavy polluters, so that companies did not have any incentive to reduce their emissions. In contrast, the new Law established different tax rates according to the level of pollution, thus obliging heavy polluters to pay a higher fee than light polluters.

So on the second issue – to increase companies' accountability towards pollution reduction – the Environmental Protection Tax provides more attractive tax reductions as an incentive to cut emissions: under the new law, polluters may receive a 25 per cent reduction if they are able to reduce their air or water discharges by 30 per cent below the proscribed standard.[118] Moreover, the penalties for violators have been toughened, so much so that the failure to pay can result in a fine up to five times the original tax, and criminal penalties can be brought against severe lawbreakers.[119]

Since different provinces, autonomous regions and municipalities face different environmental and economic challenges, the legislative tool allows the provincial-level authorities to establish and amend the applicable tax amount on air and water pollution within a specified range. In theory, this should produce a sort of virtuous circle where local authorities should be keener to apply the law and punish polluters; whereas companies should positively respond to the bigger incentives to "green" their production.

Though it certainly marks a step forward towards a more stringent enforcement of the polluting Emission Fees system, it is still too early to properly assess the actual impact of the Environmental Protection Tax in China. Indeed, the scale of its impact will depend on many factors and, given the flexibility foreseen at the provincial level, it may vary significantly between Chinese provinces. In other words, the fact that the pollution tax rates are set at the provincial level – pertinent since each province is subject to different socioeconomic conditions – may ultimately push polluting companies and plants to move to more tax friendly provinces of the country. This scenario is then worsened by the lack of an independent monitoring system.[120]

Furthermore, there are some critical exemptions to the Environmental Protection Tax. For instance, those plants discharging pollutants directly to centralized

117 Id. Articles 14 and 15. Under the Emission Fees scheme, only the environmental authority was in charge of the fees collection.

118 Id. Article 13.

119 Id. Articles 6, 23 and 25.

120 Laney Zhang, "China: New Law Replacing Pollution Discharge Fee with Environmental Protection Tax," *Law Library of Congress*, February 8, 2017.

sewage and waste treatment facilities and those that dispose solid wastes in facilities that respect the local and national standards are exempt from the tax. Also, pollutants discharged from agricultural production and from motor vehicles are also exempt from the Environmental Protection Tax.

Finally, the fact that CO_2 is notably absent from the list of pollutants weakens the overall impact of the Environmental Protection Tax of China. Indeed, leaving out CO_2 implies not taking into consideration very relevant fields, such as coal production and other energy producers. On the one hand, this inevitably allows coal to remain a competitive energy source and combustion engine vehicles the main method of transportation and, on the other, certainly limits the ultimate impact of the Law – particularly with regard to the mitigation phenomenon of air pollution, and the air pollution prevention and control in urban areas.[121]

In analysing China's policy tools on permits, I argued that Emission Standards, Total Emission Control, Environmental Impact Assessment and Emission Fee/ New Environmental Protection Tax provide valuable information and mechanisms for regulating the permitting system in China, inevitably supporting the institutions responsible for the enforcement of the national legislations related to permits. Indeed, each tool stipulates often-indispensable measurement criteria (e.g. concentration and total volume) as well as temporal and spatial criteria towards a more comprehensive pollution management system and, more generally, towards the accomplishment of ecological civilization.

That said, the above analysis has allowed us to look at the other side of the coin. Indeed, these environmental regulation solutions are characterized by the rigidity and immutability of their own prescriptions, which are typical of the classic command-and-control intervention model, incapable of effectively dealing with the complexities put forward by the (dynamic and changeable) environmental matters and ecosystems. Moreover, such tools often suffer from: the lack of continuity needed to eventually achieve consistent results; the scarcity of accurate and reliable data on pollution; the difficulty in establishing the exact outcomes of their implementation; the incapacity of preventing violations; and, above all, the absence of any form of integration among them – which from the start has undermined their ultimate effectiveness. Such key deficiencies eventually accounted for increased levels of pollution, so much so that China's pollution has not registered a meaningful improvement since the implementation of these four environmental regulation solutions.

Put another way, the above analysed tools create additional duplications, do not solve all gaps and, above all, do not provide a solution to, rather exacerbate, the problem of governance. The fact that they are not integrated with one another generates an overall low efficiency mainly caused by their fragmented and multifaceted rules, the (consequent) absence of clear indications on how such regulations should be fulfilled and, not least, the presence of too many departments willing to have their say on permits. This is true to such an extent that it is a complex – and sometimes impossible – task to determine which MEE or BEE

121 Ana Cicenia, "Environmental Protection Tax in China," *China Briefing*, January 18, 2018.

department is in charge of which tool and, even worse, what are the responsibilities within each tool. For instance, as argued above, the EIA department of a local BEE will supervise a new construction project, which – once terminated – will fall under the responsibility of another department, say, the monitoring one. As a result, EIA provisions and liabilities will no longer be taken into account causing, on one hand, a deficient enforcement of the legislation and, on the other, confusion or free riding by the construction company.[122]

In spite of the significant contribution made by the amended EIA Law and the indispensable complementary role played by the policy tools, overlaps, gaps and even conflicts are far from being solved. The lack of integration between these tools and the laws analysed below, along with the legislative tools themselves and the deficient institutional enforcement, are the problems that need to be tackled for improving China's permitting system. Thus, a revised framework is urgently needed and, therefore, it is paramount to determine what recommendations and best practices China should follow towards efficient environmental permitting.

4.3 Updates to the environmental (permits) legislation

The legal framework of China's environmental permits was initially established in the second half of the 1990s and in the early 2000s through national legislations, policy pronouncements and specific regulations.

In 1996, the National People's Congress approved the 9th Five-Year Plan of National Economic and Social Development, which recognized the importance of the TEC tool – thus providing a national legislative basis for environmental protection in China. In the same year, the Plan for Total Emissions Control of Major Pollutant Discharge was released, going far beyond the mere target of emissions' concentration by focusing on the TEC of 12 targeted major pollutants, including 8 water pollutants, 3 air pollutants, and 1 solid waste pollutant.[123]

A decade after its first experimental introduction and implementation, the government codified the TEC policy tool in specific laws and regulations. In 1996, the Standing Committee of People's Congress amended the 1984 Law of the People's Republic of China on Prevention and Control of Water Pollution, adding a specific Article regarding the TEC system for water pollutants. Article 16 states:

> With regard to water bodies where the standards for water environment quality established by the State still cannot be attained although the discharge of water pollutants has conformed to the discharge standards, the people's governments at or above the provincial level may institute a system for control of the total discharge of major pollutants, and a system for making an estimate

122 Jinnan Wang, "中国排污许可制度改革框架研究". 环境保护 (*Environment Protection*) 44 (2016): 11.

123 Zhiping Li, "The Challenges of China's Discharge": 376.

> before deciding on the quantity of major pollutants to be discharged by an enterprise that is charged with the task of reducing its discharge.[124]

Also, on the 20 March of 2000, the State Council promulgated a newly modified regulation called: "Implementation Rules on the Law of People's Republic of China on Prevention and Control of Water Pollution". The regulation established the implementation of the TEC for major pollutants in water bodies that had achieved the concentrative standards for the discharge of water pollutants but had not achieved the overall environmental standards of environmental water quality. In addition, it provided specific and practical rules for combining as much as possible the TEC tool with the Emission Standards, eventually strengthening the permitting structure. Finally, the regulation set up four steps for the application of a water pollutant discharge permit system. The first step was a water pollutant report and registration; the second, was the establishment of targets for the TEC in a specific area and the distribution of pollutant reduction quotas among pollutant dischargers in the area; the third step gave EPBs, at the county level or above, the authority to issue emission permits to dischargers based on the targets of the total pollutant load control in that area; the fourth and final step, was the supervision and regulation of the permit.[125] Put another way, through this regulation, EPBs were appointed and authorized to inspect the permit holder's facilities, as well as enforce punishments upon those in violation of their permit conditions. Hence, the TEC tool became the basic requirement for implementing the discharge permit system, while in turn the Emission Standards became the legal tool for implementing the TEC tool.[126]

In April 2000, the Standing Committee of National People's Congress modified the Law of the People's Republic of China on the Prevention and Control of Atmospheric Pollution. The Law allowed for the implementation of a system of TEC for air pollutants in those regions failing to meet the prescribed quality standards of the atmospheric environment, as well as in acid rain control and sulphur dioxide pollution control areas, designated as such with the approval of the State Council. The permit system for discharging main atmospheric pollutants had from then on to be adopted in areas covered by the total load of atmospheric pollutants control plan, following the decision by the State Council or the People's Government of provinces, autonomous regions and municipalities directly under the Central Government.[127]

Thus, it is during these first 15 years (2000–2014) that the legal framework of China's environmental permits was initially established through national legislation, policy pronouncements and specific regulations. Though some positive results deriving from the implementation of the TEC and Emission Standards

124 Law of the People's Republic of China on Prevention and Control of Water Pollution (1996 amendment), Article 16.
125 Alex Wang, "The Role of Law in Environmental Protection in China": 198–200.
126 Zhiping Li, "The Challenges of China's Discharge": 377–78.
127 See Article 25 of the 2000 Law of the People's Republic of China on the Prevention and Control of Atmospheric Pollution.

tools were registered at the local level in selected provinces, the system still showed too many problems. Overall, its implementation turned out to be unsatisfactory. First, the laws made during the 2000s were too "soft"; they did not bind *all* polluters to comply with the discharge permit system or did they take into consideration *all* pollutants. Second, the implementation rate was lower than expected, particularly since many provinces – for example in western China – lacked the financial and human resources to implement the permits at all; thus causing, at the very least, an uneven application of regulation and enforcement. Third, although permit applications were, supposedly, carefully examined for either approval or rejection, in practice almost no rejections were registered. Hence, the issuance of permits seemed more an *ex-post* acknowledgement of pollutant discharge rather than limiting *ex-ante* the amount of emissions.[128]

Indeed, a comprehensive legislation on permits, to be applied throughout the whole country, will turn out to be the *conditio sine qua non* for accomplishing an effective pollution management policy. The next sections will show how Chinese policy-makers tried to tackle the above-mentioned problems, particularly from 2014 onwards.

As argued above, since the second half of 1980s – when permits were first introduced in China – some scattered provisions regarding permits have been introduced in different laws, administrative guidelines and regulations. Despite some progress, however, it is possible to argue that during almost three decades the country did not provide itself with a specific law on permits and the permitting system was mainly carried out through pilot projects in selected provinces, thus serving as a complementary measure of emission reporting rather than a pollution management policy.[129]

More interestingly, even though few developments occurred over such a long period of time, since 2014 this long-standing trend has been noticeably inverted and four crucial laws on environment and pollution have heralded a new phase.[130] In 2014 and 2015, respectively, both the Law on Environment Protection and the Law on Air Pollution Prevention and Control were amended and 2018 and 2019, respectively, saw the new Law on Water Pollution Prevention and Control and the new Soil Law come into force. These key four pieces of legislation warrant a closer look as means of highlighting the steps forward recently made by China, both directly and indirectly, with regard to permitting.

128 Zhiping Li, "The Challenges of China's Discharge": 378–379.

129 Ruonan Zhao et al., "The New Orientation of Discharge Permit System": 984.

130 2014 was a turning point year. As well as the revision of the Environmental Protection Law, in the same year the MEP drafted an informal document named "Management Method", which – though ultimately not released by the State Council – was useful in persuading the local authorities to do more with regard to permits. China Council for International Cooperation on Environment and Development (CCICED), "Progress in Environment and Development Policies in China and Policy Recommendations Impact", CCICED 2014 Annual General Meeting, December 1–3, 2014: 23 and 41.

4.3.1 The 2014 Environmental Protection Law (EPL)

The 2014 Environmental Protection Law (EPL) comes 25 years after the enactment of its predecessor[131] and aims to transform China's environmental legal system mainly by strengthening pollution control requirements and liabilities. In line with the principle of ecological civilization discussed above, it is China's first legislative attempt to harmonize economic and social development with environmental protection.

The approval of the Law marks the completion of a very distinctive and divisive 3-year revision process characterized by an unusually high number of drafts. Indeed, firstly the EPL went through four different reviews by the NPC Standing Committee, even though legislative procedures usually allow for a maximum of three; secondly, several drafts were openly released to the public, and therefore they benefitted from the contribution of critical discussion and comments by experts, academicians and civil society organizations; thirdly, there was a strong debate among government authorities which explicitly disagreed on different aspects of EPL drafts, thus postponing the finalization of the definitive text of the Law. Although such a process took longer time than expected, the 2014 Environmental Protection Law was ultimately able to achieve some critical objectives capable of tackling some of the major deficiencies in the past legislation on environmental protection.[132]

First of all, the 2014 EPL enhanced the accountability of governmental bodies at all levels in the attempt to enhance both the importance of environmental protection needs over economic priorities and to strengthen the reliability and credibility of environmental data. Indeed, Article 26 of the new Law provides local governments with wider environmental responsibilities and gives them the possibility to establish more severe policies compared with the ones applied at the national level. Through Articles 42 and 68, the 2014 EPL stipulates that local authorities are from now on formally evaluated and held accountable for their environmental performance. These Articles declare that local civil servants failing their enforcement duties may face demotion, dismissal as well as criminal prosecution. Furthermore, responsible officials must resign in cases of illegal permitting, lack of acknowledgment of illegal polluting activities, the falsifying/faking of data or figures related to monitoring, and refusal to divulge environmental information. Moreover, Article 68 contains nine Paragraphs specifying a set of administrative punishments aimed at government officials carrying out ineffective or corrupt environmental enforcement. In particular, Paragraph 1 of the same Article imposes direct liability on officials granting permits illegally.[133]

131 See Environmental Protection Law of the People's Republic of China (1989).

132 Jost Wubbeke, "The Three-Year Battle for China's New Environmental Law," *China Dialogue*, April 25, 2014; Guizhen He et al., "Revising China's Environmental Law," *Science and Law* 341 (2013): 133.

133 Environmental Protection Law of the People's Republic of China 2014, *EU – China Environmental Governance Programme English Translation* (2014): Articles 26, 42 and 68.

Second, contrary to the previous Environment Protection Law (1989), the 2014 Law provides institutional bodies with powerful tools to enforce environmental regulation in China. In this respect, Article 63 introduces detention penalties of up to 15 days, inter alia, for pollution discharges in absence of permits; Article 59 allows penalties to cumulate on a daily basis from when the polluter received a compliance order.[134] In other words, the 2014 EPL – particularly through Articles 59 and 63 – moves away from the limitations on fines and one-time only penalties, by introducing a more rigorous daily fine system as long as environmental infringement continues – and with no ceiling. True, Article 45 of the EPL (1989) already included administrative punishments for (generally defined) corruption, abuse of power and negligence.[135] However, the 2014 amended Law lists the prohibited conducts and consequent penalties in detail, thus providing a legislative endorsement of the aforementioned enhanced accountability. Hence, Articles 59 and 63 of the 2014 EPL go some way towards overcoming the problem of too low environmental penalties in case of violations of the law – which have for long been identified as one of the major causes of poor performance of environmental laws and policies implementation in China – by eventually putting in place a deterrent for delayed or non-compliance by the violator. Finally, according to Articles 64 and 69, the EPBs (now BEEs) have the right to close down plants in violation of environmental laws. Hence, not only private and public parties, but also individuals are now held accountable – and are punished – for environmental violations.[136]

Third, the 2014 Law addresses one of the key features of an effective environmental permitting system and environmental governance: environmental information disclosure and (consequent) public participation. Indeed, Chapter 5 of the EPL is entirely devoted to filling the gap of the 1989 EPL in terms of public participation and environmental information disclosure. Namely, it guarantees public rights to environmental information (Article 53); requires environmental departments to disclose environmental data, regulatory information and regulatory compliance records (Article 54); and mandates industry disclosure of pollution emissions (Article 55).[137] In essence, since 2014 EPL entered into force, governmental bureaus at the county level and above that are in charge or involved in environmental protection must publish information and data on environmental quality, management and supervision.

Similarly, industrial polluting plants must publish information on their discharge of pollutants and/or operation of environment-related facilities. Also, the assessments of the environmental performances both of local environmental bureaus

134 Id. Articles 59 and 63.

135 Environmental Protection Law of the People's Republic of China (1989): Article 45.

136 Guizhen He et al., "Revising China's Environmental Law": 133.

137 See also Article 56 establishing that the drafting of environmental impact reports must engage the public and the report must be published; and Article 62 regarding the violation of disclosure requirements which is punishable by fine and subject to public disclosure. Environmental Protection Law of the People's Republic of China (2014): 11–13.

(and their responsible officials) and industries have to be released publicly. Finally, the 2014 EPL specifically states that

> violations of environmental regulations as well as environmental performances will be recorded in the credit archive of organizations/individuals – a system-in-the-making that lists all achievements and performances of individuals/organizations, to be used for promotions and demotions – and the names of individuals/organizations violating environmental regulations will be made public.[138]

In addition to these three key aspects, 2014 EPL reaffirms environmental protection as a basic national policy by strengthening environmental policy principles, strategic environmental assessment (SEA) and environmental governance implementation.

Article 4 stipulates for the first time that environmental protection is to be considered as a basic national policy, so that economic development must be matched with environmental protection, instead of the other way as was the case in Article 1 of the 1989 EPL. Moreover, Article 5 of the 2014 EPL sets out some principles for environmental protection: prevention as priority, policy integration, public participation and responsibilities for those who cause environmental, ecological and health damage.[139] As discussed above, several Articles delineate and empower state environmental authorities with the responsibilities and supervisory powers over environmental matters. And yet, the 2014 EPL does not address either the precautionary principle or environmental justice.

As regards SEA, Article 14 *encourages* ministries and provincial level authorities to take into consideration the possible environmental impacts when economic and technology development policies are drafted. Also, Article 19 provides that EIA should be carried out both on planning and construction projects. To the same extent, EIA at the project level is strengthened and further defined. Article 56 requires that complete EIA reports (and not only a summary, as was previously the case in practice) must be made available to the public and such reports need to include a chapter on how the public participated in the EIA process. Furthermore, Article 63 states that construction projects without EIA approval need to be blocked (instead of allowing for a re-submission of an EIA report), and Article 65 holds the EIA agencies (those governmental bodies responsible for evaluating and approving EIA reports) accountable for counterfeit EIA reports. That said, even though MEE and environmental specialists strongly promoted SEA during the last decade, the 2014 EPL represents a "missed chance" for SEA. Indeed, instead of being enforced, the latter is only encouraged and, in practice, this makes an enormous difference.[140]

138 Lei Zhang et al., "Power Politics in the Revision of China's Environmental Protection Law," *Environmental Politics* 22 (6) (2013): 1029–1030.
139 Environmental Protection Law 2014: Articles 4 and 5.
140 Id. Articles 14, 19, 56, 63 and 65.

Finally, in terms of enhanced environmental governance implementation, the 2014 EPL tackles the deficiencies of its predecessor – exclusively focusing on conventional regulatory methods – by giving legal basis to existing and new market-based instruments for the improvement of plants' environmental performance through an ecological compensation system (Article 31), environmental taxes (Article 43), environmental liability insurance (Article 52) and green credit (Article 54).[141]

In the light of what discussed above, the 2014 EPL is unarguably considered as the most progressive and rigorous environmental protection law in Chinese history. It defines more severe penalties for environmental polluters; it contains provisions for tackling pollution, including public participation; it allocates enhanced accountability on local and national authorities and law-enforcement bodies; and it establishes higher standards for polluting plants and enterprises. In other words, the Law enhances the accountability of governmental bodies, provides the latter with powerful tools to enforce environmental regulation in the whole country and fosters environmental information disclosure and consequent public participation and awareness. Inevitably, all such features have positive repercussions on the China's permitting system, particularly thanks to the establishment of direct liabilities for officials granting permits illegally, to the introduction of severe detention penalties for pollution discharges in absence of permits and to the measures aimed at raising public awareness and participation through the disclosure of environmental information and data related to environmental quality, management and supervision.

Yet, due to several constraints, the Law is not enough for effectively regulating the management and enforcement of permits.

As discussed above, 2014 EPL introduced, among others, a significant element: the (enhanced) liability of governmental bodies and their officials. Though making a step forward in terms of the attribution of legal liability, the Law is mistaken in its choice of who should be responsible. To better regulate the environmental behaviour of enterprises, it is the latter that should become, as observed in the case of EU and Italy, fully responsible for their polluting conduct – knowing the Law that applies to their activities and accepting legal enforcement actions in case of non-compliance with relevant permits. *Ad hoc* amendments to the examined Articles 59 and 68 of the EPL which already deal with legal liabilities of polluters, may enable this transfer of civil and penal liabilities from governmental and local institutions to enterprises, leaving to the former the sole tasks of verification, approval and supervision.

Another limitation affecting the EPL, and more generally China's overall environmental governance structure, is the legislative fragmentation, and the consequent presence of overlaps, both of which this EPL does not try to resolve. As observed in the above analysis, the EPL touches upon many aspects related to permits that are – to different extents – also the focus of the policy tools, such as EIA (see, inter alia, EPL Articles 56, 63 and 65) and environmental taxation (see, inter alia, EPL Article 43).

141 Id. Articles 31, 43, 52, 54.

This fragmentation and overlap inevitably weaken the enforcement and impact of the amended EPL and, at the very least, lead to conflicts of interest among government authorities and, also, do not solve their incapacity to handle the implementation of environmental permits by EPBs. Indeed, the MEP mainly provides guidance to these local authorities but does not have adequate authority over them. Local governments (which are often more focused on economic growth) keep a close control on the personnel and financing of the EPBs and therefore on their decision-making. In other words, in practice, the EPBs do not have the power to enforce harsh penalties on polluting companies or plants violating the environmental laws, or do the EPBs face legal or other consequences if they fail to do so.[142] As a consequence, the concrete results of, for instance, the above-mentioned Articles 59 and 63 of the EPL on penalties will depend on how local EPBs (subsequently the BEEs) or the MEP (subsequently the MEE) itself will apply and enforce such provisions.[143] Put another way, the introduction of the aforementioned modern regulatory principles, in line with the actual environmental challenges China is facing, is a necessary but not sufficient condition to secure the implementation of permits, in which enforcement strongly depends on the capacity of the institutions to put them into practice. Eventually, these aspects also undermine the positive implementation of the other virtuous features inserted in the amended Law, in terms of enhanced penalties for violators.

Finally, although the 2014 EPL undoubtedly provides the public and civil society organizations with the right to access environmental information and to participate in environmental governance, such a scheme is far from satisfactory, particularly in comparison with the level of involvement guaranteed by EU and Italian legislation. For instance, in China parties are not allowed to sue the government in cases, for example, of serious deficiencies in air, water or soil quality. The creation of a public environmental litigation system needs to be considered so as to provide a cost-effective remedy for the affected parties and, from what has already been discussed in Chapter 3, the Italian legislation can be considered a model from which to be inspired. Also, the lack of participation by the operators in the process of elaboration of the technical rules, on which – as discussed in previous chapters – the whole industrial emissions regulation is based, connotes a top-down regulation model typical of command-and-control systems.

Despite the undeniable progress in terms of legal liabilities, civil society participation and, in some cases, regulatory specificity (at least in contrast with its more generic predecessor), the new legislation on environmental protection does not provide a comprehensive framework for an effective permitting system. In particular, it does not establish the standards, volumes and fees for emissions, and does not fully regulate EIA.[144] Moreover, and even more importantly, the new

142 Alex Wang, "The Search for Sustainable Legitimacy: Environmetnal Law and Bureaucracy in China," *Harvard Environmental Law Review* 37 (2013): 365–367.

143 Jinnan Wang, "中国排污许可制度改革框架研究": 11.

144 True, the 2014 EPL contains a couple of provisions (Articles 61 and 65) defining legislative authorisations for EIA enforcement remedies, referring to the failure to submit proper EIA documentation. However, this is clearly not a full regulation on EIA.

legislation does not define how its provisions should be enforced, indirectly posing a broader problem of governance. For all these reasons the implementation of EPL up to date has not been as efficient as expected.

4.3.2 The 2015 Law on Air Pollution Prevention and Control

The latest amendment of the Law on Air Pollution Prevention and Control, which was passed in August 2015 (and entered into force on January 1, 2016), introduces new important provisions with regard to permits.

Compared with its predecessor, the 2015 amended Law was expanded from 66 Articles divided into seven Chapters, to 129 Articles and eight Chapters. Article 1 defines the Law's objective as "protecting and improving the environment, preventing and controlling atmospheric pollution, safeguarding public health, advancing ecological civilization and promoting the sustainable development of economy and society".[145] Hence, unlike its predecessor and starting from its very first Article, the amended Law establishes a direct link between air pollution and public health; and it does so by explicitly acknowledging that the national government is determined in tackling the health concerns of civil society.[146]

Article 2 further defines the scope, referring to the need to implement measures against the pollution "caused by the burning of coal, industrial production, motor vehicles and vessels, dust as well as agricultural activities". The aim is to prevent and control different sources of atmospheric pollutants, including "air pollutants and greenhouse gases, including particles, sulphur dioxide, nitrogen oxides, volatile organic compounds, and ammonia etc." and disclose to the public information on atmospheric pollution.[147] Thus, compared with the previous piece of legislation, the new air Law enlarged the list of targeted pollutants to include particulate matter, volatile organic compounds (VOCs) and greenhouse gases (GHGs). Such pollutants, previously under the control of different state agencies, now fall under the spectrum of a single law and authority.

The MEE, under the authority of the State Council, is responsible for identifying key geographical regions for air pollution prevention and control. The local provincial and municipal authorities, along with MEE and relevant bodies of the State Council, will then identify a governing body to draft a plan for the reduction and control of air pollutants, based on regional economic development and capacity. The chosen governing body will then finally manage and supervise regional air monitoring and the setting of standards.[148]

The 2015 amendment provides that China should encourage clean and efficient use of coal and, more generally, modifies the country's approach towards air

145 Air Pollution Prevention and Control Law of the People's Republic of China 2015, *Clean Air Alliance of China English Translation* (2015): Article 1.

146 Yana Jin, Henrik Andersson and Shiqiu Zhang, "Air Pollution Control Policies in China: A Retrospective and Prospects," *International Journal of Environmental Research and Public Health* 13 (2016): 1–2.

147 Air Pollution Prevention and Control Law 2015: Article 2.

148 Id. Article 4.

quality management by requesting that cities regularly issue and submit final plans to prove they are able to meet the national air quality targets. In this respect, not only are local authorities responsible for drafting and implementing such plans, which define the ways for reaching the targets, but also they are accountable for the actual achievement of the planned targets.[149] In cases where the air quality targets are not reached within a given period of time, local government leaders will be asked to elucidate on the reasons and accordingly set up adjustment plans; meanwhile, new projects in the city will be put on hold as well as their application for EIAs.[150] Thus, the local governments within each Chinese province will have the authority and responsibility to improve air quality as a whole, and throughout such practice will have to ensure transparency towards the public. Finally, the MEE will monitor the implementation and performance of these plans.

Besides submitting definitive plans, Chinese cities are also required by the Law to regularly publish updates on the development and implementation measures both to their controlling government agencies and the public. The planning process shall be open and transparent, allowing public input. Furthermore, the Law calls for

> measures to improve energy structure and popularize the production and utilization of clean energy; optimize the utilization of coal to be cleaner and more effective; and reduce the proportion of coal in primary energy consumption and the discharge of atmospheric pollutants during the production, utilization and transformation of coal.[151]

Moreover, the new Law establishes a direct link between air quality and total emissions of pollutants, hence providing a legislative basis for the above discussed "Three-Year Action Plan for Winning the Blue Sky Defense Battle", promulgated by the State Council in 2018.[152]

As far as permits are concerned, Article 19 stipulates the conditions under which enterprises and operational entities shall apply for a pollutant discharge permit. Articles 99 and 123, though partially overlapping with Article 59 of the EPL, further define the legal liabilities of the polluter: the first, sets out pecuniary fines (from 100,000 to 1,000,000 RMB) as well as suspension or closure penalties when pollutants are discharged without permits or by unofficial means and/or exceed the air emission standards; the second, lists the acts in violation of the Law, allowing authorities to issue daily penalties.[153]

In line with the improvement registered by the amended EPL, also the 2015 Law on Air Pollution requires wider environmental transparency towards the

149 Id. Article 14.
150 Id. Article 22.
151 Id. Article 32.
152 See Section 4.1.2 of the present study.
153 Air Pollution Prevention and Control Law 2015: Articles 99 and 123.

public. In Chapter III, the Law establishes that the State Council authorities must assess provincial-level governments with regard to the accomplishment of their air quality improvement targets. Also, Chapter III defines other items which needs to be publicly disclosed, such as the: air quality standards; a catalogue of major polluters; name, position and contact details of environmental authorities and supervisors; outcomes of air monitoring tests; and sources and trends of air pollution in relevant areas. In this respect, it is worth mentioning Article 91, which stipulates that relevant state environmental departments must

> observe and simulate atmospheric conditions and use new technologies of artificial satellites, photogrammetric measurement and long-distance monitoring so as to analyse the sources and future trend of atmospheric pollution in these key areas. The department shall release such analyses to the public.[154]

Additionally, Chapter III acknowledges the key role to be played by public participation in the enhancement of environmental protection. For instance, in order to encourage public contribution, Article 31 provides that regional governments should keep as confidential the information related to any person who reports about illegal polluting actions and, in case their assertions are truthful, reward the informer.[155]

In terms of legal liabilities, the law requires polluting plants to install monitoring tools and openly publish data on emissions. The fines laid down for violators are set up to RMB 200,000. Furthermore, polluting facilities are required, for the first time, to keep track of the monitoring data and digitally link computerized monitoring tools to local EPBs. This gives both national and local authorities an additional instrument to control emissions and better manage monitoring systems, finally allowing them to combine on-site investigations with remote surveillance.[156]

Up to this point, the analysis of the 2015 amendment of the Law on Air Pollution Prevention and Control is encouraging. The new Law marks a step forward in terms of (broader) objective and scope, legal liabilities, enhanced penalties for violators and public participation. That said, the picture is not totally satisfactory.

China's most recent air Law does not provide precise parameters and indications for air standards, pollution modelling and monitoring; also, the Law does not put forward a concrete framework for implementing an effective permitting system; lastly, most provisions of the Law are too general – so much so that the few instructions related to the regulatory mechanisms for emission control leave too much room for interpretation and few guarantees of enforcement.

Indeed, as argued above with regard to 2014 EPL, the 2015 Law on Air Pollution Prevention and Control does not define how its provisions should be enforced. This indirectly poses a broader problem of governance and essentially

154 Id. Article 91.
155 Id. Article 31.
156 Id. Articles 98–100.

does not provide a comprehensive framework for an effective permitting system. The Law's emphasis on the enforcement aspect is indeed too weak. In this respect, numerous Articles include general, and sometimes vague, formulas such as "The State Council shall determine the application process and concrete implementation procedures", "the state shall conduct total emission control of key air pollutants", and "local governments at various levels shall be responsible for … They shall formulate plans and take actions …".[157] As a result, many provisions appear more as expressions of intent rather than clear indications of the government's powers and legislative means under which the Law should ultimately be implemented. Hence, the concrete outcomes of, for instance, the above-mentioned Article 99 of the Law on Air Pollution Prevention and Control on penalties (like Articles 59 and 63 of the EPL, again on penalties), will depend on how local BEEs or the MEE itself will apply and enforce such provisions.[158] The same argument can also be made with regard to the issue of public participation. Despite, as argued above, an entire Chapter of the Law being devoted to this critical realm, the text of the legislation fails to provide the solid framework needed to allow, regulate and put in place an effective and pro-active public participation.

Much like the 2014 EPL, the 2015 Air Law still exhibits serious deficiencies in regulatory and enforcement capacity. The introduction of the above-mentioned modern regulatory principles, in line with the actual environmental challenges China is facing, is a necessary but not sufficient condition to secure the implementation of permits, which strongly relies on the capacity of the institutions to put them into practice. Only with a tailored and more robust legislation, which includes the coordination of policy tools, the setting of clear liabilities and encourages citizen participation, can the permitting system achieve the ultimate effectiveness needed.

4.3.3 China's new laws for water and soil pollution prevention and control

A new revised version of China's Water Pollution Prevention and Control Law was approved by the National People's Congress in late 2016, and entered into force on 1 January 2018. The amended Law is the legislative backbone of the 2016 Water Pollution Prevention and Control Action Plan (also known as "Water Ten Plan"), which in its aim to protect China's waters in a comprehensive way marked a definitive break with the past.

Resulting from a coordinated effort carried out by 12 different ministries, including the MEE, the plan set out numerous measures identifying the government authorities responsible for carrying out four main broad actions and establishing clear deadlines for compliance. The plan, as well as the subsequent law, focus in particular on the need to control the discharge of pollutants, for promoting economic and industrial transformation and saving or recycling natural or

157 See, for instance, Articles 3, 4, 19 and 21 of Air Pollution Prevention and Control Law 2015.

158 Jinnan Wang, "中国排污许可制度改革框架研究": 11.

production resources; to stimulate scientific and technological development, for facilitating the use of market mechanisms and implementing both laws and regulations; to reinforce management and guarantee water environment safety; and to assign clear responsibilities and favour public participation.[159]

Besides stipulating that the discharge quota mechanism must be applied to key water pollutants and that EIAs for new pollutant discharging projects will be deferred for regions which do not meet the discharge quota or water quality improvement targets, the newly revised Law reinforces the accountability and supervision of government authorities. Specifically, it does so by focusing and providing legislative support in four key areas: the inclusion of the river chief system,[160] drinking water safety protection, agricultural water pollution control and stronger enforcement.[161]

For the first time, the river chief system has been integrated into the new law. In this respect, both party and government leaders are accountable for tackling water pollution, with direct responsibility on water protection, waterline management, pollution prevention and control, and ecological remediation. Officials who are able to accomplish their goals are rewarded, whereas those who fail to meet their responsibilities are penalized through fines and loss of promotion opportunities.

The revised water Law, as is the case of the new soil law analysed in the following pages, particularly targets pollution deriving from agricultural sources, so that quality and utilization standards for fertilisers comply with the need to preserve water environmental protection.[162]

The new Law also regulates the management and protection of drinking water sources and quality. It stipulates that emergency and reserve water resources should be set up in cities. Drinking water suppliers who fail to meet standards are subject to fines or their operations are stopped until they are able to re-achieve the targets.[163]

Chapter VII of the new water Law also sets out more severe penalties for environmental violators. The fines for illegal pollutant discharge by enterprises have been increased and may reach up to 1 million RMB, an increase of 2 to 5 times compared with previous pollutant discharge fees. The environmental protection authorities can impose ***administrative penalties*** for unauthorised water pollution. These include forcing a polluter to make adjustments, making a polluter

159 China Water Risk, "New 'Water Ten Plan' to Safeguard China's Waters"; available at www.chinawaterrisk.org/notices/new-water-ten-plan-to-safeguard-Chinas-waters.

160 The river chief system was originally established in 2007 in order to better regulate the responsibilities of governmental departments in charge of water-related issues. It assigns a given section of a river or lake to a selected official, whose performance as river chief directly affects his/her overall assessment. https://www.chinawaterrisk.org/resources/analysis-reviews/chinas-river-chiefs-who-are-they/.

161 Ibid.

162 Water Pollution Prevention and Control Law of the People's Republic of China (2017 Revision), *PkuLaw English Translation* (2017): Chapter IV, Section 4.

163 Id. Chapter V.

reduce production, temporarily or permanently stopping the business in question and issuing fines. *Administrative detention* is contemplated in several cases: when the violator refuses to stop building a construction project for which an EIA has not been approved, as laid out by the law; in cases in which the enterprise without a pollutant discharge permit refuses to comply with the mandate to stop the illegal discharge of pollutants; and when a company illegally discharges pollutants by installing underground pipelines, or by modifying monitoring data, or by other tools in order to avoid being caught. Shut downs and *criminal liabilities* are established by the Law for severe violations (i.e. violation of the state provisions for discharges causing serious environmental pollution) such as the discharge of radioactive waste, waste containing pathogens of any infectious disease and poisonous substances or any other hazardous waste.[164]

As well as ordering the violators to stop the illegal act and imposing fines against polluters, the new Law stipulates the need to implement remediation measures for the treatment of polluted waters within certain time limits. When companies or other operators carry out illegal actions in violation of the law, thus causing water pollution, the environmental protection authorities may impose the implementation of pollution treatment measures. If the violators do not take (adequate) measures for water pollution treatment within the set deadline, the environmental protection authorities can engage a third party to carry out the treatment at the expense of the violators. Moreover, a party suffering loss or damage due to the water pollution can submit a claim against the violator, obliging them to remediate the damage and pay compensation. Finally, certain civil society organizations, such as some Chinese NGOs active in the environmental field,[165] can file environmental public interest proceedings against actions polluting the environment, causing ecological damage and harming the public interest; if successful, these can require the polluters to terminate the violating act, remove obstacles, eliminate dangers, restore the site to its original state prior to the violation and compensate for losses.

Also, the revised Law sets out the liability of enterprises for the monitoring of water pollutants. Companies without monitoring equipment or with inefficient/ defective monitoring equipment can face fines up to 200,000 RMB. Environmental authorities expect that the river chief system, combined with the increased heavy penalties, will successfully improve China's water environmental management system and national water security.[166]

The new water Law puts pollution discharged by industry in the spotlight, thus prohibiting numerous activities, such as: "discharging waste water into water bodies without a pollutant discharge permit; setting up outfall in drinking water source reserves";

164 Id. Chapter VII.
165 For instance, see China Biodiversity Conservation and Green Development Foundation (see www.cbcgdf.org), All-China Environment Federation (see www.acef.com.cn) and China Environmental Protection Foundation (see www.cepf.org.cn).
166 Water Pollution Prevention and Control Law: Chapter VII, Article 75.

> building, renovating or enlarging any construction projects irrelevant to water supply facilities or to water source protection in a Grade I drinking water source reserve; building, reconstructing or enlarging any construction projects discharging pollutants into a Grade II drinking water source reserve; discharging oil, acid, alkaline or highly toxic waste liquids into waters; discharging or dumping soluble highly toxic waste residues containing mercury, cadmium, arsenic, chromium, lead, cyanide or yellow phosphorus into waters, or directly burying them underground; discharging or dumping radioactive solid waste or waste water containing highly and medium radioactive substances into waters; discharging or dumping industrial solid waste, urban refuse and other castoffs into waters; stockpiling or storing solid wastes and other pollutants at bench land and bank slopes below the highest water level of rivers, lakes, canals, channels and reservoirs; using any seepage well, sink, fissure or dissolved cavern to discharge or dump waste water containing pathogenic pollutants, sewage containing pathogen and other castoffs.[167]

As part of its "war on pollution", and following the entry into force of the above-analysed laws on the prevention and control of *air* and *water* pollution, in mid-2018 the National People's Congress (NPC) approved China's first dedicated law addressing soil pollution and protection, namely the Law on the Prevention and Control of Soil Pollution, which took effect on 1 January 2019.[168] Together with the pollution prevention and control laws on air (amended in 2015) and water (amended in 2017), the entry into force of the soil Law shows once again China's strong willingness to intensify its fight against pollution through legislation. In other words, the issuance of this new Law is another step in China's creation of a comprehensive legal regime for preventing and remediating the country's pollution.[169]

This Law represents a stronger version (and a step further) of the soil pollution action plan ("Soil Ten Plan") of May 2016. For instance, the new Law strengthens the method of soil categorization already present in the action plan by classifying both agricultural and building land into several categories, each managed in a way according to the level of pollution and type of land use.

Hitherto, soil pollution was tackled only through a scattering of provisions across different laws and regulations, causing a legal vacuum and much uncertainty for companies dealing with possible soil contamination issues and compliances. Instead, the new soil Law addresses some of the main challenges of soil pollution

167 China Law Insight, "Q&A: Water Pollution," King & Wood Mallesons, March 26, 2018.

168 The Law on the Prevention and Control of Soil Pollution was passed on August 31, 2018 by the Standing Committee of the National People's Congress (NPC). Adopted after its third reading, the Law took effect on January 1, 2019.

169 Alexandra Farmer and Michael Mahoney, "China's New Soil Pollution Prevention Law Creates Obligations and Liabilities for Companies with Industrial Sites in China," *Kirkland & Ellis*, January 23, 2019: 1.

by putting forward measures and provisions, particularly with regard to four main realms.[170]

First, and similar to the revised water and air legislations, the Law sets out various new obligations and potential responsibilities for enterprises and it strengthens the liabilities for government authorities. The Law stipulates that the polluter is mainly responsible for managing and controlling soil pollution risks and restoring polluted soil. In this respect, China's soil pollution Law puts forward new obligations and liabilities for enterprises and land-use rights holders in the country. The legislation advocates the "polluter-pays" principle and enlarges the use of incentives to give compensation, on one hand, and punish polluters on the other. Land-use rights holders must investigate and evaluate the soil conditions upon the transfer of property or in the occurrence of a pollution event. If the investigation shows pollution levels above the established thresholds, claims against the responsible parties for fees deriving from the investigation and remediation may be pursued. Fines for polluters have also been drastically augmented, so much so that violators may face penalties up to 2 million RMB (approx. 260,000 Euros). Moreover, the managers deemed to be responsible for severe violations can even face administrative detention or arrest without trial. However, those enterprises "engaged in soil pollution risk management, control, and restoration" may benefit from tax exemptions.[171]

In this light, manufacturing and operating companies and land use rights holders are pushed to implement operational measures for preventing and reducing soil pollution knowing they might be liable for any soil pollution they cause. In cases where survey, monitoring or inspection reveal the potential pollution of construction land, the land use rights holder will be requested to investigate the conditions and parameters related to the soil pollution. From this stage onwards, the party responsible for the pollution and the land use rights holder must fill in and submit a risk assessment report on the status of soil pollution. It is on the basis of the review of the risk assessment report that the competent authorities may consider to include the plot in a list of construction land subject to soil pollution risk management and control and restoration, in which case the party responsible for the soil pollution must implement adequate measures for managing and controlling soil pollution risks. If restoration is deemed necessary, the polluter must draft a restoration plan, which also covers prevention and remediation of contaminated groundwater. Once finalized, the polluter must appoint a certified independent entity to assess the results of its risk management and control and restoration measures. Hence, polluters are requested to draft soil restoration plans, register them before local authorities and accomplish such plans. Once completed, polluters have to mandate professional impartial bodies to assess the effects of the plan and report its outcomes to local governments. Furthermore, companies belonging to certain high polluting sectors will be listed by government authorities as entities

170 Id. 2–3.
171 Soil Pollution Prevention and Control Law of the People's Republic of China (2018 Revision), *PkuLaw English Translation* (2018): Articles 1–6.

subject to extensive evaluation and this implies that they will have to perform advanced investigations of soil pollution whenever there is a change in the use of, or transfer of, land used for production.[172]

That said, in those cases where it is not possible to ascertain the party responsible for the soil pollution, it is the land use rights holder who has to undertake the risk management and control and soil remediation. The Law stipulates that the MEE, in coordination with the relevant departments, will develop measures for determining the party responsible for soil pollution in cases where it is unclear or questionable.

Moreover, the Law defines the tasks and responsibilities of government authorities in administering and regulating soil pollution. Namely, the MEE is mainly responsible for overseeing and managing soil pollution, and in doing so it is assisted by the Ministry of Natural Resources and the Ministry of Agriculture and Rural Affairs. The Law assigns to these two ministries the task of setting up an environmental information platform on soil, and requests them to include soil pollution prevention and control in their economic development and environmental protection plans, as well as to create a soil environmental monitoring system. However, in parallel to this, and similar to the legislation on water and air, government officials will also be assessed and held accountable for the prevention and remediation of soil pollution.[173]

Second, the Law lays out a broad monitoring activity to be put in place through a network of monitoring stations distributed all over the country, with data and other information collected and distributed among authorities in the agricultural, environmental, natural and water resources, housing, health and forestry sectors. The main goal of this monitoring activity is to detect those contaminated sites (which soil contains harmful and toxic substances) within China's territory. Nevertheless, this monitoring activity does not exempt or relieve companies from their duty to carry out their own monitoring activity of soil pollution. As mentioned above, China's new Law on Soil Pollution Prevention and Control intensifies the monitoring activity of soil pollution and polluters, giving different roles to the MEE and the Ministries of Natural Resources, and Agriculture and Rural Affairs. Also, a national census on the status of soil is to be conducted – according to the new Law – at least once every 10 years. Finally, the central government is encouraging provincial and local governments to set up and dedicate a part of their own financial resources to the monitoring and prevention of soil pollution.[174]

Third, the Law promotes public participation in soil pollution management and inaugurates a framework for wider transparency and enhanced disclosure of information with regard to soil pollution. According to the new Law, the list of construction land subject to soil pollution risk management and control and

172 Alexandra Farmer and Michael Mahoney, "China's New Soil Pollution Prevention Law": 3–5.

173 Ibid.

174 Soil Pollution Prevention and Control Law: Chapter IV.

restoration needs to be regularly updated and made available to the public. Also, the competent authorities must fill in the data and information related to soil pollution activities in the social credit scores of entities and make such information accessible to the public through the National Credit Information Sharing Platform and the National Enterprise Credit Information Publicity System. In this way, such system will be able to provide the public with information about known polluters. Thus, soil monitoring data and analysis, risk assessment and remediation reports must be uploaded to the national soil environment information platform. Put another way, the new soil law aims to increase public participation and involvement in soil pollution management through a greater transparency and disclosure of pollution data and incidents.[175]

Indeed, in the past, a lack of transparency meant that the Chinese public was unaware of severe and long-lasting soil pollution cases. Though it is true, unlike water and air pollution, that soil pollution is often invisible and years can go by between the time when the pollutants are actually discharged and the time when the problem becomes evident, still, in 2005, the Ministry of Environmental Protection and the Ministry of Land and Resources had jointly launched a survey of soil at the national level for the following 8 years. The survey cost 1 billion RMB, and it showed evidence of severe soil pollution particularly in the proximity of mining and industrial sites with worrying consequences for arable land and the dangers of growing crops in vast (contaminated) areas of the country. However, the results were not made publicly available which triggered harsh disapproval and criticism. Thus, the creation of a system of information sharing on soil pollution set out in new soil Law may eventually tackle this issue by allowing the public access to environmental data and information on soil.

In this respect, the new soil Law stipulates that nationwide surveys focused on soil pollution must be carried out on a regular basis, with at least one survey per decade. Even though the testing sites will not be disclosed, so to avoid interference with the survey through site-specific remediation, the outcomes of the surveys will be made public.

Finally, the Law stipulates and requires the development of a system of comprehensive standards in order to foster soil pollution control and prevention. The MEE is required to define the national standards for soil pollution risk control according to soil contamination conditions, public health risks as well as ecological risks. Starting from this basis, local governments may then establish their own additional and more stringent standards that will be mandatory.

Thus, the issuing of the first Law on the prevention and control of soil pollution is in itself a breakthrough and is indeed a brand new starting point in the prevention, control and remediation of soil pollution in China. That said, the country's efforts to tackle the soil pollution problem still face very complex challenges, and a careful analysis of the Law can highlight some of its deficiencies and possible constraints.

175 Id. Chapter VII.

Indeed, the increase of obligations and broader liabilities stipulated by the new Law focuses exclusively on the land used for construction projects and rural or agricultural activities, thus missing the opportunity to improve the regulation over the environmental behaviour of enterprises. Moreover, similarly to the other pieces of legislation on water and air, local government officials will be also evaluated and held accountable for prevention and remediation of soil pollution. As in the case of other laws previously analysed, this Law is also mistaken in its choice of who should be responsible or made liable. To better regulate the environmental conduct of companies, the latter should become, as observed in the case of the EU and Italy, fully responsible for their polluting behaviour – knowing the law that applies to their activities and accepting legal enforcement actions in case of non-compliance with relevant permits.[176]

Furthermore, additional rules for implementation will be needed if the Law aims to be effective. For instance, with regard to the funds set up to tackle pollution of agricultural land and sites, even though a fund mechanism is contained within the Law, a deeper level of detail is needed to determine how such a mechanism should work in practice. As it stands, the State Council will draft the rules for the management of the funds in cooperation with the ministries and authorities governing environmental protection, agriculture, natural resources, housing and construction, and forestry. However, the presence of so many counterparts may act as an obstruction to the ultimate effectiveness of the process. In the same way, detailed implementing measures and tools still need to be developed by competent authorities and government bureaus.

Moreover, the new soil Law does not clarify where the financial resources for the fund will come from. In fact, the funding for soil remediation of polluted sites is currently not in place, and the actual expenditure for cleaning up polluted sites in China accounts for less than 1 per cent of the environmental protection sector as a whole. So, even though the fund tool is certainly a potentially efficient way for ensuring soil remediation, clear modalities of government funding, for example through a tax on potentially polluting firms and harsher fines imposed on companies or individuals found to have harmed the environment, could be the way forward.

Lastly, although the new soil Law makes steps forward in determining who will be responsible for paying for future soil pollution remediation, there are still numerous existing sites where responsibility still cannot be ascertained.[177]

4.4 The latest legislative steps and future challenges

In addition to these key recent laws and regulations,[178] and issued at China's national level with direct or indirect implications towards an improved permitting

176 Chen Wang, "Can China's New Soil Pollution Law Reverse Decades of Harm," *China Dialogue*, November 28, 2018: 2–3.

177 Ibid.

178 In addition to Sections 4.3.1, 4.3.2 and 4.3.3, see also Sections 4.1.2 and 4.1.3.

system, in 2018 the MEE launched a consultation specifically focused on the administration of pollutant emission permit regulations. This procedure led to the publication of two crucial and tailored draft documents – the "Measures for Pollutant Discharge Permitting Administration (for trial implementation)"[179] and the "Regulations on the Administration of Discharge Permits (draft for Comments)".[180]

Both documents consist of seven Chapters focusing on the general provisions, rules for application and issuance of permits; implementation and supervision of the latter; procedures for revising, renewing and revoking a permit; and legal liabilities. These new drafts are aimed at strengthening the existing legislation regulating the pollutant emissions permit. They are formulated in accordance with the 2014 EPL and the relevant laws and regulations analysed above with implications on the permitting system.

Therefore, the main objective is to put forward – within dedicated documents – the norms to regulate the discharge of pollutants by enterprises, so as to control pollutant emissions and improve the quality of the ecological environment. In this respect, Article 3 of the Measures stipulates that the MEE

> shall develop and issue according to law a classification administration list of pollutant discharge permitting for fixed pollution sources and specify the scope under pollutant discharge permitting administration and the application time limit. The enterprises, public institutions and other producers and businesses (hereinafter referred to as the 'pollutant discharging entities') on the list shall apply for and obtain a pollutant discharge permit according to the prescribed application time limit; and those not on the list are required to do so for the time being.[181]

As regards the application and issuance of permits, both the draft Measures and Regulations provide indications regarding the completion and submission of permit applications, listing the "package" of information that needs to be submitted to the National Pollution Discharge Permits Administration Information Platform. Indeed, Article 26 of the draft Measures lists nine elements to be presented:

> 1) The basic information of the pollutant discharging entity; main production facilities, main products and capacity, and main and accessory raw materials; exhaust gas, waste water, and other pollutant generating and discharging links

179 Ministry of Ecology and Environment, "Measures for Pollutant Discharge Permitting Administration (For Trial Implementation) 排污许可管理办法（试行）," January 10, 2018.

180 Ministry of Ecology and Environment, "Regulations on the Administration of Discharge Permits (draft for Comments) 排污许可管理条例（草案征求意见稿）," December 6, 2018.

181 Ministry of Ecology and Environment, "Measures for Pollutant Discharge Permitting": Article 3.

> and pollution prevention and control facilities; locations and number of the outlets under the application, discharging manner, and discharging destination; the types of pollutants discharged under the application by outlets, production facilities or workshops, pollutant concentrations, and quantity of pollutant discharged; and governing discharging standards; 2) The self-monitoring plan; 3) The undertaking signed or sealed by the legal representative or principal person in charge of the pollutant discharging entity. 4) Statements regarding the standardization of outlets made by the pollutant discharging entity. 5) The approval document number for the construction project environmental impact assessment document, or the supporting documents relating to the disposition, rectification or regulation conducted by the local people's government according to the relevant provisions to the extent of meeting the requirements. 6) The form of statements of the information disclosure before the application for a pollutant discharge permit. 7) An operating and managing entity of centralized sewage treatment facilities shall also provide the scope of sewage received, the list of sewage receiving or discharging entities, pipe networks, final destination of discharge, and other materials. 8) For a construction, reconstruction or expansion project of a pollutant discharging entity, upon the implementation of these Measures the total quantity control indicators of the discharge of priority pollutants is obtained through substitution or reduction by maintaining or cutting the quantity of pollutants discharged, and the pollutant discharging entity alienating the total quantity control indicators of the discharge of priority pollutants has already obtained a pollutant discharge permit, providing the materials relating to the completion of the modification of the pollutant discharge permit by the pollutant discharging entity alienating the total quantity control indicators of the discharge of priority pollutants. 9) Other materials as required by any law, regulation or rules.[182]

Furthermore, both the draft Measures and Regulations dedicate one of their seven Chapters to determining the procedures for revising, renewing and revoking permits. In particular, Articles 43 to 51 of the Measures and Articles 51 to 60 of the Regulations provide the circumstances, material to be submitted and rules characterizing the possible editing, revision, renewal and cancellation of a permit.

Also, three Articles of the draft Regulations touch upon the need to disclose permit related information to the public, in an attempt to promote public participation. Indeed, Article 14 refers to the disclosure of information before application by stipulating that the pollutant discharging entity implementing the key management of the discharge permit shall, prior to submitting the application materials for the discharge permit, select the national platform and other means that are easy accessible by the public. Article 32 regulates the *self-monitoring* activity by requiring the polluting plant to install or use instruments and equipment that comply with the relevant provisions of the State on ecological environment

182 Id. Article 26.

monitoring, measurement and certification, in order to perform self-monitoring and allow for prompt public monitoring. Finally, Article 47 instructs law enforcement personnel to adhere to the combination of punishment and education, inform the polluting plant about its problems and relevant requirements, and require the pollutant discharging entity to abide by the law. In accordance with the Regulations, punishments handed out to the polluters shall be disclosed to the public via the department responsible for ecology and environment.[183]

Moreover, a substantial part of the draft Regulations is devoted to further defining legal liabilities. Indeed, 22 of the 87 Articles of the draft Regulations define the fines and punishments for undocumented sewage discharge, violation of pollutant discharge (concentration and amount) requirements, violation of monitoring and pre-treatment requirements and lack of cooperation with inspectors. In this respect, according to Article 61, if the polluting plant fails to obtain a permit to discharge pollutants, the competent authority of ecology and environment, at or above the municipal level, shall order the cessation of sewage discharge or stop production. Polluting plants will be issued with a fine of between 5,000 and 50,000 RMB per day.[184] However, if the situation is serious and pollution discharge cannot be remediated, the case shall be reported to the people's government through the approval authority, so that the possible order of dismantling or closing the plant may be executed. To the same extent, if the location and quantity of the discharge, the way in which the pollutants are discharged and the whereabouts of the discharge as well as the specific measures for controlling pollutants do not meet the requirements laid out in the permit, the environmental authorities shall order the correction or restriction of production, or the stop of production and shall impose a fine of between 20,000 and 200,000 RMB.[185] Even though pollution discharge is not officially recognized as a crime by Chinese penal law, under these draft Regulations illegal discharge of pollutants may lead to detention (of between 10 and 15 days) and other criminal punishments.[186] As mentioned above, if the administrator of the polluting plant refuses to cooperate with the competent local bureau of ecology and environment, or if they exhibit fraudulent conduct during the inspection, the environmental authority at or above the municipal level shall issue a fine between 20,000 and 200,000 RMB. Again, in cases where the circumstances are deemed to be serious, the discharge permit can be revoked. Finally, Article 79 lays down "heavy punishment" if the polluting operator refuses or obstructs the inspection carried out by the competent local environmental authorities or commits fraud during the inspection, or if they falsify automatic monitoring data or interfere with automatic monitoring facilities.[187]

In the light of the critical features put forward by these two latest documents on permits, it is possible to argue that both the Measures and Regulations mark an

183 Ministry of Ecology and Environment, "Regulations on the Administration of Discharge Permits": Articles 14, 32, 47.
184 Id. Article 61.
185 Id. Article 62.
186 Id. Articles 76 and 77.
187 Id. Article 79.

important step towards the realization of an integrated permitting system. When I started to conceive the present study in early 2016, my analysis of the Chinese laws, regulations and policies available at that time did not provide a guarantee that China would aim to build an integrated permitting system. Yet now, the contents of these draft regulations clarify this willingness, which, as a matter of fact, is perfectly in line with the thesis I have espoused since the very beginning. Most of the fundamental elements for eventually building a solid permitting system are now present in such drafts, so much so that the final objective of thoroughly regulating pollution permits in China is no longer a mirage, but instead a feasible goal. Put another way, these two drafts address – more or less in depth – the application and issuance of permits; their supervision and management; public participation, monitoring activity and legal liabilities; enhanced accountability and remediation measures; and higher standards for polluting plants.

Still, there is a long way to go.

As observed through the analysis of other pieces of legislation, though providing a substantial step forward towards a solid permitting system, these draft Regulations and Measures also contain deficiencies which mostly involve the vagueness of their provisions. True, both documents tackle the key aspects which should always characterise an effective permitting system. Nevertheless, the rules for application and issuance of permits; implementation, supervision and management of permits; procedures for revising, renewing and revoking a permit; monitoring activity; and legal liabilities are still often too broad. In this respect, responsibilities of polluters are still weak and urgently need to be further strengthened, public participation is addressed in a too general and passive way, the identification of the authorities responsible for supervising and managing permits is ambiguous, and it is not clear, for example, either what the formula "heavy punishment" stands for,[188] or the timescale and methods to be used. For instance, in the 87 Articles of the Regulations the word "shall" appears 199 times; such a term, however, is not always followed by the specification of which subjects should carry out the identified actions and which methodologies and concrete actions should be implemented throughout the whole permitting process. In other words, the basics of a possibly efficient permitting system at the national level have now been set; yet, the path towards an integrated permitting system is still an arduous one and it is therefore crucial for China to take the appropriate next legislative steps, particularly in the light – I argue – of the lessons learnt from the EU and Italian integrated approach and legislation on environmental permits.

188 See Ministry of Ecology and Environment, "Regulations on the Administration of Discharge Permits": Article 79.

5 Proposals to enhance effectiveness and ensure integration in the development of China's legislation on environmental permits

5.1 Contextual and conceptual background of the proposals

In Chapter 1, the analysis of the traditional regulatory approach showed that the complexity of the *environment* and its many interrelations naturally led policy-makers to respond to pollution problems by adopting specific regulations focused on single environmental media; the need to tackle certain pollutants; and the need to regulate the subjects or activities affected by polluting substances. Thus, by embracing external integration and an incremental logic, single-medium permitting was able to improve environmental protection, eventually putting in place tailored and – to a certain extent – effective abatement and control measures against pollution. Nevertheless, it also highlighted some worrying limits of the traditional approach, which does not take into consideration either the *inputs* or the *outputs* of the polluting process, applies mere end-of-line pollution control methods and, even worse, ignores the media-shifting phenomenon.

A new awareness on such limits and, more broadly, on the human interaction with the environment as a whole, emerged from the increased scientific knowledge of environmental processes as well as from the 1972 Declaration of the UN Stockholm conference. The Declaration defined the first steps towards a holistic approach to the environment, understanding it as an eco-system and ultimately paving the way to the so-called integrated approach, namely integrated pollution control.

In order to tackle media-shifting pollution, this approach espoused not only external but also internal integration. Also, it prioritized *prevention* both as a key measure and an objective to reduce the (cross-media) discharge of hazardous substances, and it focused on both inputs and outputs, devoting more attention to polluting sources. Moreover, this holistic and ecological perspective triggered a transition from the aforementioned incrementalism to comprehensive rationality, hence dealing with the entire life cycle of polluting substances, demanding new tools of data collection and analysis and enhancing the integration of pollution control measures. In sum, by considering the environment as a whole, the integrated approach started to aim for the optimal solutions to environmental problems.

Since mid-1970s, a few EU countries began to introduce in their national legislation tailored instruments and mechanisms related to integrated pollution control. However, though an excellent starting point, these pioneering integration initiatives did not succeed in building organic systems able to put in place all the key elements of the integrated approach, which was eventually launched only in 1996 through the IPPC Directive.

At the beginning of the first chapter, I argued about the difficulty – if not the impossibility – of providing a unanimously accepted legal definition of environment. In light of this, it is possible to state that this difficulty is still present. However, the analysis has showed that rather than considering the environment in a compartmentalized way, all environmental elements should be considered as closely interlinked with each other. In this respect, I espouse an ecological definition of *environment*, understanding it as the ecological balance of the biosphere or of the single eco-systems of reference; and therefore I understand *environmental protection* as the protection of the biosphere or eco-system's ecological balance.[1]

This was the basis to further define those characteristics that an effective environmental regulation should have, in order to guarantee environmental protection and efficiently tackle pollution.

At this point, a key question arose as a result of the debate on the fundamentals of environmental permitting, i.e. what are the characteristics an effective environmental regulation should have in order to guarantee environmental protection and efficiently tackle pollution?

Starting from its very scope and going through its application, the analysis of the IPPC Directive (later the IED), carried out in Chapter 2 helped to address – inter alia – such a question.

Indeed, the IPPC Directive aimed to avoid and, where this is not possible, reduce emissions deriving from polluting activities, with the goal of achieving a high level of protection of the *environment as a whole*. It did so by introducing for the first time the definition – and hence the identification and application – of Best Available Techniques (BATs); (intrinsically) linking the latter, as well as the permit issuing, to set Emission Limit Values (ELVs); paving the way to BATs reference documents (BREFs) for the competent authorities; and taking into consideration both the technical characteristics of each plant and the environmental context in which it is located.

Nevertheless, if considered singly, the above-mentioned factors are not a novel in the realm of environmental regulation. Rather, it is in the specific *integration* of such tools that the EU regulation proved to be revolutionary. In other words, as it has been shown in the analysis of the second chapter, the regulation mechanism adopted by the IPPC Directive was unique in the landscape of environmental regulation known up until then. It established a close relationship between setting ELVs and the need to apply the best available technology, and, with reference to BAT, it also proposed a new yet revisited concept of best available technology in the light of the integrated approach.

1 In the very same week I was writing about the need to understand *environment* by espousing the ecological perspective, the Ministry of Environmental Protection of the P.R.C. (MEP) was turned into the Ministry of Ecology and Environment (MEE), as an outcome of China's "Two Sessions" (两会) held in Beijing in March 2018.

Consequently, the phenomenon of pollution is not only tackled "ex-post" and with the aim of eliminating harmful emissions, but also "ex-ante", intervening upstream during the single phases of the emission of pollutants, so as to trigger prevention as well as the abatement of emissions. Moreover, the use of the BATs is not aimed exclusively at obtaining lower levels of emissions, but rather it aspires to make the industrial process concerned more efficient – giving importance to other factors such as energy consumption, the exploitation of raw materials and the production and management of waste.

From the analysis of the EU legislation on integrated environmental permits, it also emerged that the features of *renewal, revision, substantial modification*, and more generally all those modifications that allow the updating of the permit conditions, work as instruments through which the legislator may ensure the objective of a progressively higher level of environmental protection. This objective is pursued through the constant reduction of polluting emissions produced by plants as subject to the IPPC regulations.

It is thanks to these measures that the competent administration is able to carry out a prevention activity that does not end with the issue of the permit. On a more specific and operational level, these measures confirm and further reinforce the regulatory mechanism based on the variable parameter of the BAT, which in this way amplifies its stimulating effects on the market of clean technologies and acts as a dynamic reference to achieve always current and more efficient environmental performance. Ultimately, BATs play a key role in the review and update of the environmental permits, confirming – under this particular aspect – that the integrated permit does not operate on a merely *procedural* level and with a simplifying function, but it rather constitutes a *substantial* innovation that can constantly increase the efficiency (and effectiveness) of the environmental protection system.

The analysis of the application of the IPPC Directive and IED in Italy, in Chapter 3, allowed for progress to be made in the identification of both the fundamental characteristics and the concrete (positive and negative) implications of the IPPC legislative model, particularly towards the achievement of sustainable development.

As a matter of fact, the IPPC Directive gave Member States a considerable margin of freedom in its implementation, so much so that it was up to each State to determine the actual emission limit values to be imposed by every single permit.[2]

On the basis of what has been discussed with regard to the concept of "integration", Chapter 3 investigated whether, through the implementation of the IPPC Directive, Italy had been able to implement "substantive integration", in line with the spirit of the Directive, or whether it merely achieved a "procedural simplification". Indeed, there are two possible approaches to integration: one entrusts the task of

2 Such a freedom will be reduced through the implementation of the IED which, in return, will facilitate the task of the competent administrations in determining in practice the ELVs on a case-by-case basis.

issuing the permit to a given subject while subdividing the substantial competences among several administrations; the other assigns to a single authority the individual environmental competences previously exercised by separate entities, thereby putting in place a full organizational concentration of tasks. The text of the Italian law does not operate this second type of integration, and therefore it is impossible to acknowledge that in creating the collegial body "Conferenza di Servizi", the legislator hoped to achieve comprehensive organizational integration. However, this integration is to be found once again in the parameter of the BATs, to which Italy refers to when setting ELVs for an authorized installation. More than anything else, the application of BATs allows an effective substantial integration to be made in the environmental assessments underlying the issuing of environmental permits.

Hence, the preliminary problem faced by the Italian competent authority was that of identifying what was *in practice* BAT from which to start the assessment leading to the establishment of the emission limits that must be respected by the plant operator. This step was however made more difficult by the further pointer that the BATs refer not only to the specific technological solutions that are applicable but also to the organizational and procedural measures that the plant operator can adopt to achieve the appropriate levels of environmental performance, which considerably widens the number of elements to be taken into consideration.

As part of the whole process of identification of the applicable BAT on a case-by-case basis, a critical and almost decisive aspect is the assessment of the *technical feasibility* and (especially) the *economic sustainability* of a given solution. Italy carried out such a task by making reference to the so-called Vito methodology and, more importantly, to the *General* and *Sectorial Guidelines* (see Legislative Decree n. 372/99). In particular, the latter provide benchmarks for each specific existing solution, so as to effectively put the operators and competent administrations in a position to grasp the pros and cons of one or the other technique, i.e. "BAT candidate". In this respect, "sustainability" must always be assessed on a case-by-case basis, in relation to the characteristics of the single plant subject to the evaluation. Therefore, there is no possible automaticity in considering how economically sustainable a given technique is, and hence the application of a "best technique" following the mere fact that it may be technically feasible. Once sustainability has been verified, the other parameter that comes into play is the "cost–benefit ratio". In line with EU legislation, the Italian competent administration identifies, among the BAT candidates that are economically sustainable, the one that, with the same achievable environmental performance, imposes lower costs on the concerned plant.

The introduction by the IED of the "BAT conclusions" was in direct response – inter alia – to the administrations' need to straightforwardly determine in practice the ELVs. As a result, the latter were now associated with the individual BAT, leaving to the competent administrations the task of verifying whether the technical and environmental conditions of the plant require setting different and less stringent ELVs than those established in the "BAT conclusions". In this way, the overall regulation system for polluting emissions seems to have become more rigid and has moved away from its fundamental characteristic of *flexibility* – understood not only as the ability to adapt to the single local environmental contexts (a possibility that is still allowed), but also in its capacity to stimulate the spontaneous development of environmental technologies by operators (namely, one of the implicit goals of the IPPC Directive). On the other hand, the role played by the IED is no less incisive, particularly taking into account its greater concern for the periodic updating of permits and the effective observance of their conditions, whose non-compliance is now regulated.

In order to demonstrate further, in practice, how Italy implemented the provisions of the IPPC and IED, and consequently the national legislation deriving from the latter, in Chapter 3 I then focused on the case study of the Ilva Company. Indeed, Ilva – the largest steel plant in Europe located in the South of Italy – caused one of the most serious health and environmental disasters in Italian and European history. The study scrutinised how the special administrative measures[3] applied following the (serious) non-compliance of the permit's provisions, and aimed at preserving the continuity of the business while ensuring the observance of the requirements of the integrated permit, proved to be effective only to a certain extent.[4] As showed by the legislation under examination, the special administrative measures ended up introducing a special treatment, which entailed a considerable expansion of the power to disapply (in essence) the contents of the integrated environmental permit (ordinarily foreseen by the Italian Law 152/2006, in implementation of the European legislation). Put another way, though the extraordinary commissioner was and still is a special solution to be used in case of serious non-compliance with the provisions of the integrated environmental permit, such a measure turns out to be a legislative tool that enables the application of the most incisive measure of the legislation to be avoided, namely the revocation of the permit with the consequent cessation of the productive activity.

In this respect, the analysis of the problems deriving from the plant's malfunctioning and the consequent violations of EU and Italian environmental law by one of the biggest steelworks in the world, as well as the problematic issues in the revision procedure of its integrated environmental permit, was also useful for the analysis on the permitting system in China and, more broadly, for the final objective of the present study – to provide China and its policy-makers with recommendations for ensuring the effectiveness of its permitting system and environmental regulation in the coming years.

That said, the implementation of the IPPC Directive and IED in Italy also demonstrates the innovative nature of such legislation, especially if compared with the traditional top-down, command-and-control and market-based regulations. The analysis proved the validity of the mechanisms put in place for the periodic review and updating of the permit conditions, and the intervention measures in

3 Namely, the *extraordinary commissioner, external administration* and *committee of experts.*

4 See, for instance, the setting up of an external administration as well as the allocation of the company's resources to cover the costs for carrying out the health and environmental remediation measures *versus* the ultimate derogation from the environmental compatibility requirements.

case of non-compliance with the limits set by the permit. Moreover, the set of "reflexive" norms ascribing an active role to operators in the process of elaboration of the technical rules (under the so-called Sevilla Process) and the "reflexive" provisions concerning the acknowledgement, management and use of information (including the key role of *public participation, disclosure* and *awareness*), proved to be crucial tools for the ultimate effective functioning of this substantially unprecedented environmental regulation.

Therefore, the IPPC Directive model results from the combination of many different legislative tools and it aims to build a system to tackle pollution and foster environmental protection; one able to bring the most effective aspects of its predecessors without re-proposing the limits of the past.

Also, by associating the integrated approach with the principles of reflexive law, the IPPC and IED legislation provide a regulatory model (reconciling environmental protection, production efficiency, innovation and economic growth) able to give practical substance to the concept of sustainable development, which is often perceived in the literature as a merely abstract and rhetorical notion.

In another way, the analysis of the implementation of the IPPC and IED in Italy revealed how "sustainable development" is also pursued through the weighting of the different needs. This means that a perfect balance between them may not be achieved, but ends, in many instances, with a *de facto* pre-eminence being attributed to the economic interest at the expense of environmental protection. In spite of what is provided by Article 1 of the IED, the Directive itself indeed presents some provisions that clearly show there is an often a greater focus on the economic side of the authorized activities instead of on environmental protection.

5.2 Recommendations to further develop China's legislation on environmental permits

In Chapter 1, I showed why and how one of the cardinal principles of European policy is sustainable development, and how, starting from 1987, this concept evolved, first at the international level and then within multinational and national contexts.

In the chapters that followed, the possible achievement of sustainable development was examined more deeply, in particular by analysing the key characteristics, applications and implications of the IPPC Directive and IED. As a result, it was possible to argue that, on one hand, sustainable development is not just a theoretical notion, as it is often perceived in literature but that, on the other hand, such a concept is pursued through the weighting of socio-economic and environmental needs, and this does not necessarily lead to a result of perfect balance between them.

The aim of Chapter 4 was to analyse the current status of Chinese legislation related to environmental permits and ascertain what needs to be further developed or modified, and why. To do so, rather than arguing about the paradigm of *sustainable development* and its implications, it was necessary to analyse and discuss the origins and development of the paradigm of *ecological civilization* – which culminated with President Xi's Thought on Ecological Civilization. Though different, the two concepts ultimately have the same objectives; hence, they do not and should not imply different implementation tools or different laws governing the impact of human activities towards nature.

Also, given the very balanced definition of the concept of sustainable development provided in Italian environmental law, and analysed in Chapter 3, it is possible to argue that the definition provided by the Italian legislation of "sustainable development" is much closer to the present Chinese conceptualization of ecological civilization compared with the more vague one present in the EU legislation. Indeed, in line with the concept of ecological civilization, Italian law introduces the duty of public authorities to "primarily take into consideration" the environmental protection issues when public and private interests are at stake, consequently establishing a hierarchy among the involved interests and providing a practical action rule which makes the set-out principle ready to be implemented.

In this light, the focus and objective of the present study acquired even more importance. Indeed, the ecological perspective shared by the Italian and Chinese approaches to environmental protection and sustainable development is fully in line with the ecological definition of environment given at the end of Chapter 1, eventually proving its consistency and coherence.

The theoretical foundations towards an effective environmental regulation are solid both in Italy and China. Consequently, the challenge is to understand which permitting legislative structure and means should China embrace in practice in order to strengthen environmental protection and efficiently tackle pollution.

In this context, the "war on pollution", launched in 2014 by Chinese Prime Minister Mr. Li Keqiang, became not only one of the instruments for supporting the achievement of ecological civilization but also a key step in focusing – in an unprecedented manner – on the need to protect the environment and prioritize this need over that of economic growth. This had direct and positive repercussions on the development of environmental permit regulation.

Since 2014 and even more intensely since 2018, the Chinese government and the Ministry of Ecology and Environment have made increasingly effective efforts in order to prevent, control and tackle exacerbated pollution levels in *air, water* and *soil.* As discussed, in these three realms, additional implementation and action plans have been released to further strengthen China's initiatives in the years to come. Specifically, the plan of inspections carried out by MEE starting from 2018 and the critical amendments to the Environmental Protection Law (in 2014) and the laws on air, water and soil pollution prevention and control (in 2015, 2018 and 2019, respectively) demonstrate the immense remedial efforts and key institutional solutions that China has put in place in recent years for protecting the environment as a whole, not least by focusing on environmental permitting.

This is the reason why it has been worth making a step backward in order to analyse Chinese environmental permits from their very first steps and then focus on the laws and regulations related to them. The objective was twofold. First, to identify the strengths and, above all, the weaknesses present in the Chinese laws and policy tools regulating permits; second, with reference to the EU and Italy, to draw recommendations for effectively developing the legislation regulating Chinese permitting so as to allow its full and successful implementation. If the latter does occur, the Chinese government will ultimately be able to strengthen ecological environmental protection and hence achieve the objectives set out in the Action Plans on air, water and soil pollution control; push forward high-quality development and provide qualitatively ecological goods to satisfy people's ever-growing demands for a beautiful life; make a breakthrough in the war of pollution prevention and control, and advance the building of a Beautiful China; foster green development and intensify the protection of ecosystems, so much so that (modern) ecological civilization will be finally built.

In addition to the scrutiny of the regulations and action plans put forward in recent years by the competent authorities, in Chapter 4 I analysed both the Chinese major policy tools gravitating around environmental permits and the country's most recently amended laws related to permits.

In examining China's policy tools on permits, I argued that Emission Standards, Total Emission Control, Environmental Impact Assessment and the New Environmental Protection Tax, provide valuable information and mechanisms for regulating the permitting system in China, giving support to the institutions responsible for the enforcement of the national legislations related to permits. Indeed, each tool stipulates often indispensable patterns as well as temporal and spatial criteria towards a more comprehensive pollution management system and, more generally, towards the accomplishment of ecological civilization. That said, the analysis allowed me to look also at the other side of the coin. Indeed, these environmental regulation solutions are characterized by the rigidity and immutability of their own prescriptions, which are typical of the classic command-and-control intervention model, incapable of effectively dealing with the complexities put forward by (dynamic and changeable) environmental matters and ecosystems. Moreover, such tools often suffered from the lack of continuity needed to eventually achieve consistent results, the scarcity of accurate and reliable data on pollution, the difficulty in establishing the exact outcomes of their implementation, the incapacity of preventing violations, and, above all, the absence of any form of integration among them – which undermined, from the start, their ultimate effectiveness. Such key deficiencies eventually accounted for increased levels of pollution, so much so that China's pollution has not registered a meaningful improvement since the implementation of these four environmental regulation solutions.

Also, the analysis of the 2014 EPL as well as the most recent laws on air, water and soil pollution prevention and control gives only half positive picture. Despite the undeniable progresses in terms of legal liabilities and penalties, civil society participation and awareness, regulatory specificity as well as environmental regulation enforcement (at least in contrast with the more generic predecessors), the new legislations do not provide a comprehensive framework for an effective and integrated permitting system. In addition, the newly amended laws often do not define how their provisions should be enforced, indirectly posing a broader problem of governance. Thus, the introduction of modern regulatory principles, in line with the actual environmental challenges China is facing, is a necessary but not entirely sufficient condition to secure the implementation of permits, which strongly relies on the capacity of the institutions to put them into practice.

Finally, Chapter 4 focused on the very latest efforts put in place by China specifically tailored to the administration of permit regulation for pollutant emission. The consultations, launched by the MEE during 2018, led to the publication of two crucial draft documents – the "Measures for Pollutant Discharge Permitting Administration (for trial implementation)" and the "Regulations on the Administration of Discharge Permits (draft for Comments)". As discussed, these mark an important – though still very preliminary – step towards the realization of an integrated permitting system.

When I started to conceive the present study in early 2016, the analysis of the Chinese laws, regulations and policies available at that time did not guarantee that China would have aimed for an *integrated* permitting system. To date instead, the contents of these draft regulations clarify this willingness, which, in fact, is perfectly in line with the thesis I have espoused since the very beginning. Most of the fundamental elements for eventually building a solid permitting system are now present in such drafts, so much so that the final objective of thoroughly regulating pollution permits in China is not a mirage anymore, but instead a feasible goal.

Yet, there is still margin for a decisive improvement.

As observed during the analysis of the laws and regulations scrutinised above, though providing a substantial step forward in the way towards a robust permitting system, these draft Regulations and Measures also exhibit deficiencies of which the major common denominator is the vagueness of their provisions. True, both documents tackle the key aspects, which should always characterise an effective permitting system. Nevertheless, the mentioned Articles focusing on the rules for application and issuance of permits; implementation, supervision and management of permits; procedures for revising, renewing and revoking a permit; monitoring activity; and legal liabilities are still often too broad. In this respect, the responsibilities of polluters are still weak and urgently need to be strengthened, public participation is addressed in a too general and passive way, the identification of the authorities responsible for supervising and managing permits is ambiguous.

In other words, the basics of a possibly efficient permitting system at the national level have now been set; yet, the way towards an integrated permitting system is still an arduous one and it is therefore crucial for China to take the right next legislative steps, particularly in the light – I argue – of the lessons learnt from the EU and Italian integrated approach and legislation on environmental permits.

Therefore, first of all, China's legislator needs to aim at an *improved environmental governance*. From the study of Chinese environmental legislation it can be seen that the emphasis on the enforcement aspect is still too weak and, as a result, provisions often appear as expressions of intent rather than clear indications of the government powers and legislative means under which the law should ultimately be enforced. The analysis carried out in previous chapters showed a deficiency common to most pieces of legislation studied, namely the lack of detail on how the provisions contained in the latest environmental laws and regulations should be enforced – indirectly posing a broader problem of governance and subsequently not providing a comprehensive framework for an effective permitting system. Hence, a greater level of detail is needed to tackle the vagueness of provisions and determine how their implementation needs to be carried out.

Besides, in order to foster environmental governance, a set of measures promoting functional simplification – understood as the application of suitable measures to achieve the legal results prescribed by regulation – should be implemented, starting from the *integration of the existing policy tools into a single piece of legislation*. The scrutiny carried out in this study of the numerous pieces of legislation and policy tools, as well as of the guidelines, action plans, regulations and opinions that China has issued under its war on pollution, highlights the persistence of fragmentation and overlaps. As well as reducing administrative costs, merging existing regulations on environmental permitting into a single document, following the Italian example under the EU Directive model, would inherently overcome the aforementioned deficiencies and clarify the role played by each legislative measure and policy tool related to permits. Thus, emulating the Italian "TUA" law of 2010 (Testo Unico dell'Ambiente), China could merge into a single piece of legislation an integrated and coordinated version of the various environmental regulations in force related to permits.

Moreover, *administrative layers should be appointed with clear and specific tasks*. Indeed, one of the aspects that emerged throughout the analysis of current Chinese environmental legislation is that its fragmentation and overlaps inevitably weaken the enforcement and impact of the (amended) laws and, at the very least, favour ambiguity and conflicts of interest among government authorities, eventually resulting in a lack of capacity to handle the implementation of environmental permits. Also, the introduction of modern regulatory principles, in line with the actual environmental challenges China is facing, proved to be a necessary but insufficient condition to secure the implementation of permits, the enforcement of which strongly depends on the capacity of the institutions to put the permitting regulations into practice. Hence, a rationalized division of roles is urgently needed. Following the "bottom-up approach" analysed in the case of Italy, in China: *cities* should be given the (broader) authority to decide – within given thresholds – the quantity of pollutants that enterprises may emit or discharge, ultimately empowering local BEEs to issue and enforce permits as well as supervise their implementation and possible non-compliance; *provinces*, under common national procedures, should relay to cities, with a certain degree of flexibility, the guiding principles to follow in granting, updating and revising permits; the *MEE*, following the example of the Italian Ministry for the Environment which structure it now mirrors, should regulate and supervise the entire process. By defining the respective tasks of each administrative layer and empowering local BEEs to implement permits as well as their consequent penalties, this measure may help to get rid of the conflicts among the different departments and institutions, contributing to solve the governance problem highlighted in the previous chapter. Finally, the creation of a coordination mechanism able to foster the compliance with the legislation as well as the performance of the administrative action – similar to the Italian "Conferenza di Servizi" – could strengthen China's decisional process on permits and give to the country an additional weapon in the war on pollution.

As a result, *accountability of enterprises should be enhanced.* If institutions should be responsible for enforcing, regulating and supervising permits then enterprises should be fully accountable for their own environmental behaviour. As argued above, the 2014 amended Environmental Protection Law introduced, among other significant elements, liability of governmental bodies and their officials. Following this, the newly revised Laws on Air and Water and the new Law on Soil Pollution Prevention and Control also reinforced the accountability of government authorities. Though making a step forward in terms of the attribution of legal liabilities, the Laws are mistaken in their choice of who should be (more) accountable. To better regulate the environmental behaviour of enterprises, the enterprises themselves should become, as observed in the case of EU and Italy, fully responsible for their polluting conduct – knowing the law that applies to their activities and accepting legal enforcement actions in case of non-compliance with relevant permits. In this respect, for instance, *ad hoc* amendments to the examined Articles 59 and 68 of Environmental Protection Law and Articles 99 and 123 of Law on Air Pollution Prevention and Control, which already deal with legal liabilities of polluters, may allow this transfer of civil and penal liabilities from institutions to enterprises, leaving to the former the sole tasks of verification, approval, monitoring and supervision. At the very least this will facilitate the creation of a genuine and continuous collaboration between plant operators and the competent administrations, positively acknowledged under the IED thanks to the so-called Sevilla Process. Only by becoming fully accountable for their polluting behaviour will operators recognise the laws that apply to their activities and accept legal enforcement actions in case of non-compliance with permits. From the other side, in order to make institutions more accountable, the competent administrations should be obliged – as happens under the IPPC Directive – to issue periodic reports on the implementation of permit legislation. In this way they may learn the possible limits of the regulation and be able to adapt their internal rules and provisions accordingly.

If applied, these two last recommendations – the attribution of specific tasks to administrative layers and the enhancement of accountability for enterprises – will in turn be crucial to advance and unmistakeably delineate the responsibilities and liabilities for pollutant control between public authorities and industrial facilities.

Additionally, China's legislator should *issue greater punishments for polluters.* It is true that the Chinese environmental legislation scrutinized in this study has showed some positive steps in this direction. The 2014 EPL, amendments to the Laws on EIA, Air, Water and Soil Pollution Prevention and Control, as well as the 2018 draft Regulations and Measures on permitting, all demonstrate clear and tangible efforts for increasing pecuniary fines and legal liabilities that need to be faced by violators. However, as demonstrated, too often the fines represent an irrelevant penalty, particularly for medium and large plants. Thus, following the example of the IED, in China violators should also face progressively harsher penalties, able – if necessary – to jeopardise, even in the case of medium and large enterprises, the existence of an entire business. Finally, the creation of a public environmental litigation system needs to be considered so as to provide a cost-effective remedy for the affected parties and for which, in the light of what has been argued in the previous chapters, the Italian legislation can be considered a model of reference.

Moreover, *environmental information disclosure and (consequent) higher public participation should be further promoted and ensured.* Although the latest Chinese environmental laws, regulations and measures undoubtedly provide the public and civil society organizations with the right to access environmental information and to participate in environmental governance, such a scheme is far from satisfactory, particularly compared with the level of involvement guaranteed by the EU and Italian legislation. Public participation is often addressed in a too general and passive way, so much so that an unfruitful top-down approach is taking place. Instead, its bottom-up potential is critical: public access to information leads to the promotion of public awareness of environmental problems and an increase in public environmental education as well as acceptance of the adopted decisions. Further to this, greater environmental transparency towards the public, with disclosure of pollution data and incidents, indirectly benefits the accuracy of remediation reports and eventually gives rise to more severe remediation measures. And, it goes without saying that a high level of information may inevitably facilitate the technical evaluations that competent authorities at the local level (i.e. BEEs) will have to carry out in order to set the conditions for the issuing of environmental permits and supervise their implementation.

Finally, China should *strengthen pollution monitoring for accurate data collection.* Obtaining reliable data on given pollutants is one of the biggest challenges of pollution management and control, whatever approach one decides to take. As aforementioned, recently such a deficiency has been tackled through the involvement of MEE teams in the thorough and intense activity of inspections for air and water pollution in specific areas of the country; however, a comprehensive coverage at the national level is still far from being accomplished. Similarly, with regard to the newly regulated and often "invisible" soil pollution, a national census on the status of soil needs to be urgently and accurately conducted. Therefore, improving the quality of technological equipment and its interconnection (including self-monitoring by the plants involved), levelling out the heterogeneity of polluting indicators as well as enhancing the (historically scarce) quantity of human resources at the MEE/BEEs' disposal is the way to tackle such weakness. As argued, collecting reliable and accountable pollution and emissions' data is of crucial importance for the ultimate success of the integrated approach. Lastly, a reliable monitoring system is also fundamental for establishing the exact outcomes resulting from the implementation of the laws and to amend these laws and adjust their measures if needed.

And yet, all these useful legislative measures, policies and tools stated in the above recommendations cannot be considered, if taken singularly, to be a game changer. As a matter of fact, one may claim that they are all present and reiterated – to different extents – in all the most recent pieces of regulation that China has issued, particularly from 2014 onwards. Nevertheless, as argued in this book, the novelty lies in their (substantial) *integration*, and it is this key element that China's environmental regulation is lacking. Without being integrated with one another under a comprehensive and holistic *integrated approach*, the aforementioned tools end up being inefficient – as shown by the lack of meaningful improvements of China's pollution levels over the last few decades.

Therefore, to overcome such a major deficiency, the implementation of permits as well as the definition of their conditions should be based on thoroughly defined *Best Available Techniques* (BATs). As broadly discussed in this book, such an instrument paves the way not only to the identification of the applicable technological solutions for specific polluting facilities (i.e. formulation of BREFs/BAT conclusions and consequent determination of the associated ELVs), but also to the organizational and procedural solutions to be followed both by the plant operators and competent administrations for eventually achieving appropriate levels of environmental performance (i.e. operators' participation in the elaboration of the technical rules, updating and revision of permits, public access to information and public participation) – ultimately benefitting the environment as a whole. As an evolving parameter, BATs allow for the periodic updating of environmental protection measures too, thus combining a rigorous approach with the flexibility provided by the possibility to revise the conditions of the issued permit over time. This enables a dynamic adjustment to exogeneous changes, thus reaching ever lower emission/pollution levels and making plant production processes more efficient, consequently ensuring increasingly greater levels of environmental protection overall. Put another way, such a combination of rigour in approach yet flexibility of revision allows: 1) achievement of the best possible level of environmental protection without compromising production; 2) better adaptation of the permit conditions to the local environmental context[5]; and 3) stimulation of the spontaneous development of environmental technologies by operators. This expansive capacity is extremely useful given the diversity and complexity of environmental issues, and it is even more valuable with regard to China, which is rich in different eco-systems and where it needs to ensure continuity in the achievement of consistent environmental targets and results.

Following this rigorous path provided by the binding BAT conclusions and their associated ELVs, and the flexibility granted by the dynamism and adaptability of BATs, the Chinese legislator may put forward a prevention activity which goes beyond the issuing of permits, thus combining an *ex-ante* approach to pollution to the *ex-post* one, and – through the integrated approach – trigger a substantial (and not merely procedural) innovation able to constantly enhance the efficiency and effectiveness of its environmental protection system.

5 i.e. The geographic location of the plant and its local environmental conditions (including the technical characteristics of the plant and its possible structural changes).

By following this path, the achievement of an effective emission permitting system "with Chinese characteristics" – characterized, inter alia, by clearly defined and mandatory standards of polluting plants; enhanced environmental governance, accountability and monitoring; strengthened punishments for polluters and public participation; all under the guidance of an integrated approach – will be possible. This will allow the spirit of the 19th National Congress of the CPC to be realised, improving the efficiency of environmental management and environmental quality and paving the way to success in the war on pollution and the ultimate attainment of building ecological civilization.

Conclusion

Concluding remarks

Enhancing effectiveness in the development of China's legislation on environmental permits is possible and the way to follow is the integrated approach.

This study aimed at identifying those permitting legislative structures and tools that China should embrace in practice so as to decisively strengthen environmental protection and effectively tackle pollution.

The scrutiny of the country's latest environmental laws and regulations allowed for an in-depth understanding of the very significant steps forward recently taken by the Chinese government in regulating pollution prevention and control. Nevertheless, the study also proved that, to achieve an effective legislation on environmental permits, there is still a long way to go and the lessons learnt at the international level may be a critical reference. When one tries to improve one's own legal system, be it as a legislator or as a scholar, it has become obvious to look at the other side of the borders. However, importing rules and solutions from abroad may not work because of a difference in context. Hence, a thorough contextual approach was required and, therefore, it was taken into account by this research.

By analysing the deficiencies and weaknesses of current Chinese regulations on permitting vis-à-vis EU legislation – and its Italian application – it was possible to draw a set of recommendations that, if applied by Chinese policy-makers, will pave the way to comprehensive legislation for ensuring an effective emission permitting system as well as efficient environmental regulation.

As a result, it is argued, that China's legislator should primarily foster environmental governance so as to tackle a deficiency common to most pieces of legislation taken into account; namely, the lack of definition on how the provisions contained in the latest Chinese environmental laws and regulations should be enforced. In order to do so, a set of measures ultimately promoting a functional simplification should be implemented, such as: the integration of the existing policy tools into a single piece of legislation; the clear definition of tasks for each administrative layer; and making enterprises more accountable.

With regard to administrative organization, this book highlighted how the introduction of modern regulatory principles, in line with the actual environmental challenges China is facing, is a necessary but not sufficient condition to secure the implementation of permits, the enforcement of which strongly depends on the capacity of the institutions to put them into practice. Hence, I argue, that Chinese cities should be given the broader authority to issue and enforce permits as well as to supervise their implementation and possible non-compliance; provinces should communicate to cities the guiding principles to follow in granting, updating and revising permits; the MEE, following the example of the Italian Ministry for the Environment, which structure it now mirrors, should regulate and supervise the entire process. By defining the respective tasks of each administrative layer and empowering local BEEs to implement permits as well as their consequent penalties, this measure may help to get rid of the conflicts among different departments and institutions, thus contributing to solve the governance problem highlighted above.

As a consequence, the accountability of enterprises should be enhanced. If, on one hand, institutions are responsible for enforcing, regulating and supervising permits, on the other hand, enterprises should be fully accountable for their environmental behaviour. Though making a step forward in terms of the attribution of legal liabilities, the most recent Chinese environmental laws and regulations are mistaken in their choice of who should be (more) accountable. To better regulate the environmental behaviour of enterprises, the enterprises themselves should become, as observed in the case of the EU and Italy, fully responsible for their polluting conduct – knowing the law that applies to their activities and accepting legal enforcement actions in case of non-compliance with relevant permits.

If applied, these recommendations will crucially reduce administrative costs and unmistakeably delineate the responsibilities and liabilities for the control of pollutants between public authorities and industrial facilities.

In addition to this, China's legislator should further strengthen punishments for polluters so much so that violators may eventually face progressively harsher penalties, able – if necessary – to jeopardise the existence of their entire business, even in the case of medium and large enterprises. Also the creation of a public environmental litigation system needs to be considered so as to provide a cost-effective remedy for the affected parties and, in the light of what argued in the present study, the Italian legislation could be considered a model from which to take inspiration.

Furthermore, environmental information disclosure and consequent higher public participation should be additionally promoted and ensured. Wider environmental transparency towards the public, with the disclosure of pollution data and incidents, indirectly benefits the accuracy of remediation reports and eventually gives rise to more severe remediation measures. Moreover, it goes without saying that a high level of information may inevitably facilitate the technical evaluations that competent authorities must carry out in order to set the conditions for the issuing of environmental permits and supervise their implementation.

Finally, China should strengthen its pollution monitoring for accurate data collection by improving the quality of technological equipment and its interconnection, levelling out the heterogeneity of polluting indicators as well as enhancing the historically scarce quantity of human resources at the MEE/BEEs' disposal.

And yet, if taken singularly, all these useful legislative measures, policies and tools cannot be considered as a game changer. Indeed, without being combined with one another under a comprehensive and holistic *integrated approach* these tools end up being inefficient, as shown by the lack of meaningful improvements to China's pollution levels over the last few decades.

Therefore, in order to overcome such a major deficiency, the implementation of permits as well as the definition of their conditions should be based on thoroughly defined Best Available Techniques (BATs). As widely discussed in the present work, such an instrument allows for the identification of the applicable technological solutions for specific polluting facilities, namely the formulation of BREFs/ BAT conclusions and consequent determination of the associated ELVs. But there is more. BATs also pave the way to the organizational and procedural solutions to be followed both by the plant operators and competent administrations for eventually achieving appropriate levels of environmental performance (i.e. operators' participation in the elaboration of the technical rules, updating and revision of permits, public access to information and public participation) – ultimately benefitting the environment as a whole. Moreover, being an evolving parameter, BATs allow for the periodic updating of environmental protection measures, thus combining a rigorous approach with the flexibility provided by the possibility to revise the conditions of the issued permit over time. This leads to the dynamic adjustment of exogenous changes, reaching ever lower emission/pollution levels and making the plant production process more efficient, eventually ensuring an increasingly greater level of environmental protection overall.

Put another way, such a combination allows the achievement of the best possible level of environmental protection without compromising production; better adaptation of the permit conditions to the local environmental context; and stimulation of the spontaneous development of environmental technologies by operators. This expansive capacity is extremely useful given the diversity and complexity of environmental issues, and it is even more valuable with regard to China, which is rich in different eco-systems and where there needs to be continuity in the achievement of consistent environmental targets and results.

Following this rigorous path provided by the binding BAT conclusions and their associated ELVs, and the flexibility granted by the dynamism and adaptability of BATs, the Chinese legislator may put forward a prevention activity which goes beyond the issuing of permits, thus combining an *ex-ante* approach to pollution to the *ex-post* one, and – through the integrated approach – trigger a substantial innovation able to constantly enhance the efficiency and effectiveness of its environmental protection system.

By doing this, the realization of an effective emission permitting system – characterized, inter alia, by clearly defined and mandatory standards of polluting plants; enhanced environmental governance, accountability and monitoring; strengthened punishments for polluters and public participation; all under the guidance of an integrated approach – will be possible.

As discussed, the environmental permitting system is at the frontier of China's environmental law and, while this study is being finalized, it is under the focus of the Chinese government, which is currently aiming to entirely reform and re-shape it. In this respect, the present study seizes the moment and, in this light, its focus and objective acquire even more importance not only under the academic perspective but also from a more practical point of view – aiming at becoming a valuable reference for Chinese policy-makers.

When I started to conceive the present study at the beginning of 2016, the change of pace in China's environmental efforts had already been triggered; however, it was hard to expect that Chinese government would have raised the bar even further during these last few years. As discussed, while this research was being conducted, profound reform has been carried out to enlarge the responsibilities and relevance of the Ministry of Environmental Protection (MEP), now Ministry of Ecology and Environment (MEE); several fundamental environmental laws and regulations have been amended and newly issued; and numerous action plans, guidelines, opinions, campaigns and inspection activities have set new targets and deadlines. In other words, given the extremely short time frame in which they have occurred, the efforts and legislative progress implemented by Chinese authorities towards a more comprehensive environmental regulation system have been both tremendous and somehow unexpected. Such a background is definitely an encouraging premise for the further legislative improvements to come.

Bibliography

Books

Amirante, Domenico. *Diritto ambientale italiano e comparato*. Napoli: Jovene, 2003.

Avanzini, Giulia. *Il commissario straordinario*. Torino: Giappichelli, 2013.

Bohne, Eberhard. *The Quest for Environmental Regulatory Integration in the European Union: Integrated Pollution Prevention and Control, Environment Impact Assessment and Major Accident Prevention*. Amsterdam: Kluwer Law International, 2006.

Bonelli, Angelo. *Good Morning diossina*. Brussels: Green European Foundation, 2014.

Cafagno, Maurizio. *Principi e Strumenti di Tutela dell'Ambiente*. Torino: Giappichelli, 2007.

Carter, Neil and Arthur P.J. Mol. *Environmental Governance in China*. New York, NY: Routledge, 2007.

Davies Clarence and Jan Mazurek, *Pollution Control in United States: Evaluating the System (Resources for the Future)*. Washington, D.C.: Routledge, 1998.

De Sadeleer, Nicolas. *Essential Concepts of Global Environmental Governance*. New York, NY: Routledge, 2015.

Di Mento, Joseph. *The Global Environment and International Law*. Austin, TX: University of Texas Press, 2003.

Freeman, Cristopher and Luc Soete. *The Economics of Industrial Innovation*. Cambridge, MA: MIT Press, 1997.

Gabolde, Christian. *Les Installations Classées pour la Protection de l'Environnement*. Paris: Sirey, 1978.

Giannini, Massimo. *Istituzioni di diritto amministrativo*. Milano: Giuffre, 2000.

Gouldson, Andrew and Joseph Murphy. *Regulatory Realities*. London: Routledge, 1998.

Holm, Jesper. *Modernisation and Flexible Environmental Regulation*. Bielefeld: Zentrum für Interdisziplinäre, 1999.

Knill, Cristoph. *Implementing EU Environmental Policy*. Manchester: Manchester University Press, 2000.

Lange, Bettina. *Implementing EU Pollution Control. Law and Integration*. Cambridge: Cambridge University Press, 2008.

Lee, Maria. *EU Environmental Law, Governance and Decision-Making*. Portland, OR: Hart Publishing, 2014.

Lugaresi, Nicola. *Diritto dell'Ambiente*. Vicenza: Wolters Kluwer, 2015.

Pan, Jiahua. *China's Environmental Governing and Ecological Civilization*. Beijing: China Social Sciences Press, 2014.

Rodgers, William. *Environmental Law*. Eagan, MN: West Publishing Company, 1994.

Sands, Philippe. *Principles of International Environmental Law*. Manchester: Manchester University Press, 1995.

Selznick, Philip. *The Moral Commonwealth: Social Theory and the Promise of Community*. Berkeley, CA: University of California Press, 1992.

Scarcella, Alessio. *L'Autorizzazione Integrata Ambientale*. Milano: Giuffrè, 2005.

Tonoletti, Bruno. *L'accertamento amministrativo*. Padua: Cedam, 2001.

United Nations, *Report of the World Commission on Environment and Development: Our Common Future*. Oxford: Oxford University Press, 1987.

UNDP, *China Human Development Report 2013. Sustainable and Liveable Cities: Toward Ecological Urbanisation*. Beijing: China Translation and Publishing Corporation, 2013.

Wathern, Peter. *Environmental Impact Assessment: Theory and Practice*. London: Routledge, 2013.

Zhao, Zhikui. *Socialism with Distinct Chinese Characteristics*. Beijing: Beijing Times Chinese Press, 2014.

Chapter or other part of a book

Faure, Michael. "Optimal Specificity in Environmental Standard-Setting," in *Critical Issues in Environmental Taxation, International and Comparative Perspectives*, Vol. VIII, edited by C. Dias Soares, J.E. Milne, H. Aschiabor, L. Kreiser, and K. Deketelaere, Oxford: Oxford University Press, 2010.

Heinelt, Hubert, Tanja Malek, Nicola Staeck and Annette E. Töller. "Environmental Policy: The European Union and a Paradigm Shift," in *European Union Environmental Policy and New Forms of Governance*, edited by H. Heinelt, T. Malek, R. Smith and A.E. Töller. Ashgate: Aldershot, 2001.

Jaffe, Adam, Richard G. Newell and Robert N. Stavins. "Technological Change and the Environment," in *Handbook of Environmental Economics*, Vol. 1, edited by K.G. Maler and J.R. Vincent. Amsterdam and Boston, MA: Elsevier Science, 2003.

Journal articles

Ackerman, Bruce. "Beyond the New Deal: Coal and the Clean Air Act." *Faculty Scholarship Series* 155 (1980): 1466–1572.

Applegate, John. "The Taming of the Precautionary Principle." *William and Mary Environmental Law and Policy Review* 13 (2002): 13–78.

Aviles, Luis. "Sustainable Development and the Legal Protection of the Environment in Europe." *Sustainable Development Law & Policy* 12 (3) (2012): 29–34.

Barnhizer, David. "Waking from Sustainability's 'Impossible Dream': The Decision-Making Realities of Business and Government." *Georgetown International Environmental Law Review* 18 (2006): 1–90.

Barone, Antonio. "Le fonti di energia tra gestione precauzionale e diritto giurisprudenziale." *Federalismi* 16 (2013): 1–14.

Beijen, Barbara. "The Implementation of European Environmental Directives: Are Problems Caused by the Quality of the Directives?" *European Energy and Environmental Law Review* 20 (4) (2011): 150–163.

Bell, Stuart. "Statutory Pollution Prevention Objectives: Are They Rules or Aims?" *Journal of Environmental Law* 15 (1) (2003): 59–85.

Biondini, Paola. "Evoluzione, consistenza e prospettive di 'norme' e 'regole' tecniche nell'ordinamento europeo." *Studi parlamentari e di politica costituzionale*151–152 (2006): 77–135.

Brink, Patrickten and Andrew Farmer. "Implementation of the IPPC Direttive (96/61): Analysis and Progress of Issues." *Institute for European Environmental Policy (IEEP)*. (October 2003): 1–10.

Buonfrate, Angelo. "A.I.A. e impianti di rilevante impatto e preminente interesse nazionale: l'accordo dell' 'area industriale di Taranto' (parte seconda)." *Ambiente e Sviluppo* 7 (2009): 733–736.

Caggiano, Giandonato. "Il consolidamento della disciplina delle misure di esecuzione e della comitologia a trattato invariato." *Studi sull'integrazione europea*3 (2006): 505–525.

Cavanna, Valentina. "Caso ILVA e conflitto di attribuzione tra poteri dello Stato." Ambiente e Sviluppo 4 (2013): 326–329.

Cikankowitz, Anne and Valerie Laforest. "La directive IPPC: où en est-on et où va-t-on?" *La Revue Electronique en Sciences de l'Environnement* 10 (1) (2010): 2–21.

Currie, David. "Air Pollution Control in West Germany." *University of Chicago Law Review* 49 (1982): 355–393.

D'Angiulli, Stefano. "Caso Ilva di Taranto: adesso o mai più." *Ambiente e Sviluppo* 217 (2) (2013): 117–123.

Davies, Clarence. "Some Thoughts on Implementing Integration." *Environmental Law* 22 (1), in *Special Issue: Integrated Pollution Control: A Symposium* (1992): 139–147.

Deng, Xiangzheng, Jikun Huang, Scott Rozelle and Emi Uchida. "Growth, Population and Industrialization, and Urban Land Expansion of China." *Journal of Urban Economics* 63 (1): 96–115.

Di Cristina, Fabio. "Il decreto salva ILVA." *Giornale di Diritto Amministrativo* 4 (2013): 369–378.

Dijkmans, Roger. "Methodology for Selection of Best Available Techniques (BAT) at the Sector Level." *Journal of Cleaner Production* 8 (1) (2000): 11–21.

Diver, Colin. "Policymaking Paradigms in Administrative Law." *Harvard Law Review* 95 (2) (1981): 393–434.

Emmott Neil and Nigel Haigh. "Integrated Pollution Prevention and Control: UK and EC Approaches and Possible Next Steps." *Journal of Environmental Law* 8 (2) (1996): 301–311.

Erling, Uwe. "Approaches to Integrated Pollution Control in the United States and the European Union." *Tulane Environmental Law Journal* 15 (1) (2001): 1–42.

Farber, Daniel. "Environmental Protection as a Learning Experience." *Loyola of Los Angeles Law Review* 27 (1994): 791–807.

Farmer, Andrew. "Revising IPPC: Incremental Change Rather Than a Radical Overhaul of EU Industrial Emissions Policy." *Environmental Law Review* 10 (4) (2008): 258–282.

Faure, Michael. "The Harmonization, Codification and Integration of Environmental Law: A Search for Definitions." *European Environmental Law Review* 9 (2000): 174–182.

Faure Michael and Jurgen Lefevere. "The Draft Directive on Integrated Pollution Prevention and Control: An Economic Perspective." *European Environmental Law Review* 4 (1996): 112–122.

Ferrara, Rosario. "La protezione dell'ambiente e il procedimento ambientale nella società del rischio." *Diritto e Società* 4 (2006): 507–512.

Ferrara, Rosario. "La valutazione di impatto ambientale fra discrezionalità dell'amministrazione e sindacato del giudice amministrativo." *Foro Amministrativo II T.A.R* (2010): 3179–3184.

Fiorino, Daniel. "Rethinking Environmental Regulation: Perspectives on Law and Governance." *Harvard Environmental Law Review* 23 (1999): 441–469.

Follieri, Enrico. "L'ingegneria processuale del Consiglio di Stato." *Giurisprudenza Italiana 2* (2012): 439–442.

Fonderico, Francesco. "Valutazione d'impatto ambientale e amministrazione precauzionale." *Giornale di Diritto Amministrativo 1* (2012): 70–77.

Franke, Juergen. "Political Evolution of EMAS: Perspectives from the EU, National Governments and Industrial Groups." *European Environment* 5 (6) (1995): 155–159.

Fuzio, Riccardo. "Il bilanciamento di interessi costituzionalmente protetti nella nuova normativa sull'inquinamento atmosferico." *Foro italiano* 11 (1991): 39–43.

Gaines, Sanford. "Reflexive Law as a Legal Paradigm for Sustainable Development." *Buffalo Environmental Law Journal* 10 (1) (2002): 1–9.

Gare, Arran. "From 'Sustainable Development' to 'Ecological Civilization': Winning the War for Survival." *The Journal of Natural and Social Philosophy* 13 (3) (2017): 130–149.

Ge, Chazhong, Ji Chen, Jinnan Wang and Feng Long. "China's Total Emission Control Policy: A Critical Review." *Chinese Journal of Population Resources and Environment* 7 (2009): 50–58.

Geng, Yong and Joseph Sarkis. "Achieving National Emission Reduction Target – China's New Challenge and Opportunity." *Environmental Science and Technology* 46 (1) (2012): 107–108.

Gori, Massimo. "Attuata la direttiva sulla prevenzione e riduzione integrate dell'inquinamento." *Rivista Giuridica dell'Ambiente* (1999): 1126–1139.

Gray, John, Tim James and John Dickson. "Integrated Regulation. Experiences of IPPC in England and Wales." *Water and Environment Journal* 21 (1) (2007): 69–73.

Greenstone, Michael and Patrick Schwarz. "Is China Winning its War on Pollution?" *Air Quality Life Index Report*, March(2018): 1–8.

Guruswamy, Lakshman. "Integrating Thoughtways: Re-opening of the Environmental Mind?" *Wisconsin Law Review* 463 (1989): 463–537.

Hannett, Sarah. "Significant United Kingdom Environmental Cases January–December 2006." *Journal of Environmental Law* 19 (2) (2007): 267–276.

Hansen, Mette Halskov, Hongtao Li and Rune Svarverud. "Ecological Civilization: Interpreting the Chinese Past, Projecting the Global Future." *Global Environmental Change* 53 (2018): 195–203.

He, Guizhen, Lei Zhang, Arthur P.J.Mol, YonglongLu, JianguoLiu. "Revising China's Environmental Law," *Science and Law* 341 (2013): 133.

Heritier, Adrienne. "New Modes of Governance in Europe: Policy Making without Legislating?" *Political Science Series*, Institute for Advanced Studies, Vienna (2002): 1–33.

Hodas, David. "The Role of Law in Defining Sustainable Development: NEPA Reconsidered." *Widener Law Symposium Journal* 3 (1998): 1–58.

Hu, Qing, Xiaoliang Li, AijunLin, WeikangQi, XiujunLi and Xiao Ji Yang. "Total Emission Control Policy in China." *Environmental Development* 25 (2018): 126–129.

Irwin, Frances. "An Integrated Framework for Preventing Pollution and Protecting the Environment," *Environmental Law* 22 (1), in *Special Issue: Integrated Pollution Control: A Symposium* (1992): 1–76.

Jin, Yana, Henrik Andersson and Shiqiu Zhang. "Air Pollution Control Policies in China: A Retrospective and Prospects." *International Journal of Environmental Research and Public Health* 13 (12) (2016): 1–22.

Jin, Zining. "Environmental Impact Assessment Law in China's Courts: A Study of 107 Judicial Decisions." *Environmental Impact Assessment Review* 55 (2015): 35–44.

Jordan, Andrew. "Integrated Pollution Control and the Evolving Style and Structure of Environmental Regulation in the UK." *Environmental Politics* 2 (3) (1993): 405–427.

Keller, Werner Hans, Xia Zhang and Yong Liu. "Functions of Law in the Sustainable Development of China and a Model for Environmental Legislation." *European Business Review* 29 (4) (2017): 1–16.

Koutalakis, Charalampos, Aaron Buzogany and Tanja A. Börzel. "When Soft Regulation Is Not Enough: The Integrated Pollution Prevention and Control Directive of the European Union." *Regulation and Governance* 4 (3) (2010): 329–344.

Krier, James and Mark Brownstein. "On Integrated Pollution Control." *Environmental Law* 22 (1) (1992): 119–138.

Larssen, Thorjørnet al. "Acid Deposition and its Effects in China: An Overview." *Environmental Science & Policy* 2 (1) (1999): 9–24.

Lee, Maria. "The Industrial Emissions Directive." *Journal of London University College* (2012): 1–24.

Li, Zhiping. "The Challenges of China's Discharge Permit System and Effective Solutions." *Temple Journal of Science Technology and Environmental Law* 24 (2005): 375–384.

Lindblom, Charles E. "The Science of 'Muddling Through'." *Public Administration Review* 19 (2) (1959): 79–88.

Listokin, Yair. "Learning Through Policy Variation." *The Yale Law Journal* 118 (2008): 483–542.

Lubbe Wolff, Gertrude. "Efficient Environmental Legislation. Different Philosophies of Pollution Control in Europe." *Journal of Environmental Law* 13 (1) (2001): 79–87.

Ma, Yun. "Dynamics in Central-Local Division of the Authority of EIA Approval in China." *Journal of Environmental Law* 31 (2019): 29–57.

Macchia, Marco. "L'efficacia temporale delle sentenze del giudice amministrativo, prove di imitazione." *Giornale di Diritto Amminsitrativo* 12 (2011): 1313–1319.

Maglieri, Alessandra. "L'emersione dell'interesse ambientale nel procedimento amministrativo: prospettive e limiti della semplificazione." *Diritto Amministrativo* 14 (4) (2006): 847–902.

Marinelli, Maurizio. "How to Build a 'Beautiful China' in the Anthropocene. The Political Discourse and the Intellectual Debate on Ecological Civilization." *Journal of Chinese Political Science* 23 (2018): 365–386.

Marocco, Teodora. "La Direttiva IPPC e il suo Recepimento in Italia." *Rivista Giuridica dell'Ambiente 1* (2004): 35–46.

Massa, Michele. "Il commissariamento dell'ILVA e il diritto delle crisi industriali." *Quaderni Costituzionali* 3 (2013): 617–621.

Medugno, Mario. "Il recepimento da parte dell'Italia della direttiva 96/61 (c.d. IPPC)." *Rivista Giuridica dell'Ambiente* (2001): 1100–1107.

Milone, Alberta. "Il procedimento autorizzatorio degli impianti di produzione di energia rinnovabile: rapporti con VIA e AIA." *Ambiente e Sviluppo 12* (2009): 1123–1128.

Moorman, Jesse and Zhang Ge. "Promoting and Strengthening Public Participation in China's Environmental Impact Assessment Process: Comparing China's EIA and US NEPA." *Vermont Journal of Environmental Law* 8 (2006): 282–308.

Mu, Zhilin, Shuchun Bu and Bing Xue. "Environmental Legislation in China: Achievements, Challenges and Trends." *Sustainability* 6 (2014): 8967–8979.

Muratori, Alberto. "Decreto salva ILVA: scelte difficili." *Ambiente e Sviluppo* 1 (2013): 8–12.

Muratori, Alberto. "L'autorizzazione (quasi) unica per PMI e stabilimenti non-AIA: il regolamento definitivo." *Ambiente e Sviluppo* (2013): 305–308.

Muratori, Alberto. "La 'modifica sostanziale' di impianti e progetti tra definizioni normative, giurisprudenza e ricadute pratiche." *Ambiente e Sviluppo 2* (2012): 147–150.

Orts, Eric. "A Reflexive Model of Environmental Regulation." *Business Ethics Quarterly* 5 (1995): 779–794.

Orts, Eric. "Reflexive Environmental Law." *Northwestern University Law Review* 89 (1995): 1229 and 1312.

Owens, Susan. "Integrated Pollution-Control in the United Kingdom: Prospects and Problems." *Environment and Planning C: Government and Policy* 7 (1) (1989): 81–91.

Pallemaerts, Marc. "International Environmental Law from Stockholm to Río: Back to the Future?" *Review of European Community & International Environmental Law* 1 (1992): 254–266.

Pallemaerts, Marc. "The Proposed IPPC Directive: Re-Regulation or De-Regulation?" *European Environmental Law Review* 5 (6) (1996): 174–179.

Pan, Xiang-chao. "Research on Xi Jinping's Thought of Ecological Civilization and Environment Sustainable Development." *Earth and Environmental Science* 153 (2018): 1–6.

Peck, Alison. "Sustainable Development and the Reconciliation of Opposites." *St. Louis University Law Journal* 57 (2012): 151–183.

Postiglione, Amedeo. "Migliore tecnologia disponibile e costi eccessivi in materia di inquinamento atmosferico." *Rivista Giuridica dell'Ambiente 5* (1990): 303–310.

Qi, Gao. "Mainstreaming Climate Change into the EIA Procedures: A Perspective from China." *International Journal of Climate Change Strategies and Management* 10 (3) (2018): 342–358.

Rabe, Barry and Janet Zimmerman. "Cross-Media Environmental Integration in the Great Lakes Basin." *Environmental Law* 22 (1) (1992): 253–279.

Sandulli, Maria Alessandra. "Tutela dell'ambiente e sviluppo economico e infrastrutturale: un difficile ma necessario contemperamento." *Rivista Giuridica dell'Edilizia* 1 (2000): 1–15.

Scarone, Valerio. "La specialità del diritto all'informazione ambientale." *Foro Amministrativo 1* (2004): 75–82.

Scialò, Alfredo. "L'integrazione dell'AIA nel procedimento di VIA nel secondo decreto correttivo del TUA." *Ambiente e Sviluppo* 6 (2008): 524–529.

Scoca, Franco Gaetano. "Analisi giuridica della conferenza di servizi." *Diritto Amministrativo* 2 (1999): 255–297.

Schoenberger, Harald. "Integrated Pollution Prevention and Control in Large Industrial Installations on the basis of Best Available Techniques – The Sevilla Process." *Journal of Cleaner Production* 17 (2009): 1526–1529.

Smith, Susan. "Ecologically Sustainable Development: Integrating Economics, Ecology, and Law." *Willamette Law Review* 31 (2) (1995): 251–305.

Sorrell, Steven. "The meaning of BATNEEC: interpreting excessive costs in UK industrial pollution regulation." *Journal of Environmental Policy and Planning* 4 (1) (2002): 23–40.

Spina, Giulio. "Strumenti di tutela dell'ambiente. Dal diritto penale ai sistemi (volontari) di gestione ambientale." *Ambiente e Sviluppo 7* (2012): 639–649.

Stewart, Richard. "A New Generation of Environmental Regulation?" *Capital University Law Review 1* (2001): 21–37.

Travi, Aldo. "Accoglimento dell'impugnazione di un provvedimento e 'non annullamento' dell'atto illegittimo." *Urbanistica e Appalti 15 (8)* (2011): 936–939.

Vardi, Noah and Vincenzo Zeno-Zencovich, "From Rome to Nice: A Historical Profile of the Evolution of European Environmental Law." *Environmental Law Review* 1 (4) (2004): 219–240.

Videtta, Cristina. "Le valutazioni tecniche ambientali tra riserva procedimentale e self-restraint del giudice amministrativo." *Foro Amministrativo 4 (1)* (2005): 1359–1365.

Wang, Alex. "The Role of Law in Environmental Protection in China: Recent Developments." *Vermont Journal of Environmental Law* 8 (2006–2007):195–223.

Wang, Alex. "The Search for Sustainable Legitimacy: Environmental Law and Bureaucracy in China." *Harvard Environmental Law Review* 37 (2013): 365–440.
Wang, Jinnan. "中国排污许可制度改革框架研究". 环境保护 (*Environment Protection*) 44 (2016): 10–16.
Xu, Yuan. "Improvements in the Operation of SO_2 Scrubbers in China's Coal Power Plants." *Environmental Science and Technology* 45 (2) (2011): 380–385.
Xue, Wenbo, Jinnan Wang, Hao Niu, Jintian Yang, Baoping Han, Lei Yu, Hanli Chen and Chunlai Jiang. "Assessment of Air Quality Improvement Effect under the National Total Emission Control Program during the Twelfth National Five-Year Plan in China." *Atmospheric Environment* 68 (2013): 74–81.
Zhang, Lei, Guizhen He, Arthur P.J. Mol and Xiao Zhu. "Power Politics in the Revision of China's Environmental Protection Law," *Environmental Politics* 22 (6) (2013): 1029–1035.
Zhang, Kunmin and Zongguo Wen. "Review and Challenges of Policies of Environmental Protection and Sustainable Development in China." *Journal of Environmental Management* 88 (2008): 1249–1261.
Zhang, Zhen, Joshua Hinger, David Audretsch and Guojun Song. "Environmental Technology Transfer and Emission Standards for Industry in China." *The Journal of Technology Transfer* 40 (2015): 743–759.
Zhao, Ruonan, Yan Pingli, Xue Wen Hu and Lu Bai. "The New Orientation of Discharge Permit System in the Environmental Management System." *Applied Mechanics and Materials* 737 (2015): 984–988.
Zhu, Guangyao. "Ecological Civilization," *OurPlanet*, United Nations Environment Programme, Nairobi, Kenya, March 2016, 26–29.

Papers presented at a conference

Andrews, Richard. "The EPA at 40: An Historical Perspective." Paper presented at the Duke Environmental Law and Policy Forum Symposium, January 24, 2011.
Brechet, Thierry and Henry Tulkens. "From BAT (best available technique) to BCAT (best combination of available techniques)." Discussion Papers 2006105, Université Catholique de Louvain, Center for Operations Research and Econometrics (CORE), 2006.
China Council for International Cooperation on Environment and Development. "Progress in Environment and Development Policies in China and Policy Recommendations Impact." CCICED 2014 Annual General Meeting, December 1–3, 2014.
China Council for International Cooperation on Environment and Development. "Progress on Environment and Development Policies in China and Impact of CCICED's Policy Recommendations." 2017–2018.
China Council for International Cooperation on Environment and Development. "*Roundtable on Global Governance and Ecological Civilization.*" Roundtable Proceedings, Brussels, Belgium, June 2018.
China Council for International Cooperation on Environment and Development. "*Shocks, Innovation and Ecological Civilization. A 'New Green Era' for China and for the World.*" CCICED Issues Paper 2018.
Gislev, Magnus. "European Innovation and Exchange of Information about BAT." Paper presented at The Sevilla Process: A Driver for Environmental Performance in Industry, Stuttgart, Germany, April 6–7, 2000.

Hagstrom, Petra. "*BAT Process Selection and Split Views.*" Paper presented at The Sevilla Process: A Driver for Environmental Performance in Industry, Stuttgart, Germany, April 6–7, 2000.

Jones, Gregory. "Remedies in Judicial Review Proceedings for Breaches of EU Law." Paper presented at the ALBA Annual Summer Conference, July 16–18, 2010; available at www.adminlaw.org.uk (accessed on September 13, 2020).

Lanzi, Eugenio and Alfredo Pini. "I principi generali del controllo ambientale nella normativa europea IPPC." Paper presented at the conference "L'evoluzione dei controlli ambientali, in Italia ed in Europa," Bologna, Italy,February 2004.

Litten, Don. "BAT Reference Documents: What Are They and What Are They Not." Paper presented at The Sevilla Process: A Driver for Environmental Performance in Industry, Stuttgart, Germany, April 6–7, 2000.

Pini, Alfredo. "L'attuazione della direttiva IPPC in Italia ed il ruolo delle agenzie ambientali." Paper presented at the International Conference "Autorizzazione IPPC e mercato delle emissioni i gas serra", Turin, Italy,December 16, 2003.

Reichel, Almut. "Introduction and Summary of Discussion." Paper presented at The Sevilla Process: A Driver for Environmental Performance in Industry, Stuttgart, Germany, April 6–7, 2000.

Sanchez, Carolina. "From Local to Global: China's Role in Global Poverty Reduction and the Future of Development". Speech given by the Senior Director for Poverty and Equity of the World Bank at Taobao Village Summit, Heze – Shandong, China, December 7, 2017.

Schmidt Etkin, Dagmar. "Historical Overview of Oil Spills from All Sources (1960–1998)." (International Oil Spill Conference Proceedings, March 1999, Vol. 1999, No. 1): 1097–1102.

Sørup, Per. "The European IPPC Bureau; What Is It, Where Is It and What Does It Do." Paper presented at The Sevilla Process: A Driver for Environmental Performance in Industry, Stuttgart, Germany, April 6–7, 2000.

Tan, Weiping. "Chinese Approach to the Eradication of Poverty: Taking Targeted Measures to Lift People out of Poverty." Speech given at the Expert Panel on the Implementation of the Third UN Decade for the Eradication of Poverty (2018–2027), Addis Ababa, Ethiopia, April 18, 2018.

Tromans, Stephen. "Environmental Judicial Review." Paper presented at Judicial Review Seminar, March 6, 2006; available at www.39essex.com/doci/articles/STR_Judicial_Review_seminar _paper_060.306.pdf (accessed on September 13, 2020).

UN Environment Programme, "A Review of 20 Years' Air Pollution Control in Beijing," United Nations Environment Programme, Nairobi, Kenya, 2019.

Xu, Chun. "The Position of Ecological Civilization in the Human Civilization." Conference Proceedings of Ecological Civilization, Globalization and Human Development, Sanya, China, June 2009.

Yohannes, Mariam. "Environmental Sustainability and Regulation: To-Down Versus Bottom-Up Regulation." Munich Personal RePEc Archive Paper, 2001.

Thesis or dissertations

Ganzleben, C. *Integrated Pollution Prevention and Control: A Driver for Innovation in the European Community.* PhD diss., Oxford University, 2003.

Newspaper articles

Barone, Nicola and Andrea Gagliardi. "Ilva, siglato accordo al Mise. Da Arcelor ok a 10.700 assunti ." *Il Sole 24 Ore*, September 5, 2018.

Cicenia, Ana. "Environmental Protection Tax in China." *China Briefing*, January 18, 2018.

Hou, Liqiang. "Ecology Should Not be 'Sacrificed'." *China Daily*, March 12, 2019.

Lau Mimi and Frank Tang. "China's Environmental Clean-up Campaign Hasn't Cost Jobs or Hit Economy." *South China Morning Post*, October 23, 2017.

Loh, Christine. "China's Poverty Relief Approach is Exemplary." *China Daily*, April 4, 2019.

Wang, Zhihe, Huili He and Meijun Fan. "The Ecological Civilization Debate in China." *Monthly Review*, November 1, 2014.

Xinhua, "China Sees Fast PM2.5 Reduction in 2017." *China Daily*, January 18, 2018.

Zhang, Laney. "China: New Law Replacing Pollution Discharge Fee with Environmental Protection Tax." *Law Library of Congress*, February 8, 2017.

Electronic journals and websites

China Water Risk, "New 'Water Ten Plan' to Safeguard China's Waters," available at www.chinawaterrisk.org/notices/new-water-ten-plan-to-safeguard-Chinas-waters (accessed on September 13, 2020).

China Law Insight, "Q&A: Water Pollution," King & Wood Mallesons, March 26, 2018; available at https://www.chinalawinsight.com/2018/03/articles/environment-2/qa-water-pollution/

Di Rosa, Silvano. "A.I.A. Modifiche non sostanziali, ricevibilità o irrecivibilità?" (2012), available at www.ambientediritto.it (accessed on September 12, 2020).

Dong, Ruiqiang. "The General Plan for Pollution Prevention and Control for Three Years: The Problem of Environmental Protection First Accountable Provincial, Municipal, County Party Secretary?," *The Economic Observer*, June 30, 2018; available at http://westdollar.com/sbdm/guba/news,cjpl,769797788.html (accessed on September 12, 2020).

Farmer, Alexandra and Michael Mahoney. "China's New Soil Pollution Prevention Law Creates Obligations and Liabilities for Companies with Industrial Sites in China." *Kirkland & Ellis*, January 23, 2019.

Féderation Européenne des Activités de la Dépollution et de l'Environnement (FEAD). "The European Commission's Proposal for the Industrial Emission Directive." April 2008; available at www.fead.be (accessed on September 13, 2020).

Geninatti Satè, Luca. "Caso Ilva: la tutela dell'ambiente attraverso la rivalutazione del carattere formale del diritto." 16 May 2013; available at www.forumcostituzionale.it (accessed on September 13, 2020).

INES Database (i.e. National Register of Polluting Emissions); available at http://www.isprambiente.gov.it/files/aria/ines-eper-prtr.pdf (accessed on September 13, 2020).

International Institute for Sustainable Development (IISD). "*Financing Models for Soil Remediation in China.*" July 2018; available at https://www.iisd.org/sites/default/files/publications/financing-models-soil-remediation-china.pdf (accessed on September 12, 2020).

Lafergola, Margherita. "Procedimenti IPPC nell'Unione Europea: assetto organizzativo e normativo, approccio e valutazione integrate," edited by the Environmental Protection Agency for the Technical Services (APAT), now replaced by the Institute for Environmental Protection and Research (ISPRA), available at www.isprambiente.gov.it (accessed on September 12, 2020).

Laforest, Valerie and Remi Bertheas. “Ambiguité entre Technologies Propres et Meilleures Techniques Disponibles.” *La Revue Electronique en Sciences de l'Environnement* 6 (2) (2005); available at https://journals.openedition.org/vertigo/9657 (accessed on September 13, 2020).

Low, Chien Tat. “Key Water Policies 2018–2019.” March 18, 2019; available at http://www.chinawaterrisk.org/resources/analysis-reviews/key-water-policies-2018-2019/ (accessed on September 13, 2020).

Ma Tianjie and Qin Liu. “China Reshapes Ministries to Better Protect Environment.” *China Dialogue*, March 14, 2018; available at https://www.chinadialogue.net/article/show/single/en/10502-China-reshapes-ministries-to-better-protect-environment (accessed on September 13, 2020).

SINOPEC Beijing Yanshan Company website; available at www.sinopec.com/listco/en/about_sinopec/subsidiaries/refinery_petrochemical/20161109/news_20161109_378768480886.shtml (accessed on September 13, 2020).

Wang, Chen. “Can China's New Soil Pollution Law Reverse Decades of Harm.” *China Dialogue*, November 28, 2018. https://chinadialogue.net/en/pollution/10949-can-china-s-new-soil-pollution-law-reverse-decades-of-harm/

Wubbeke, Jost. “The Three-Year Battle for China's New Environmental Law,” *China Dialogue*, April 25, 2014. https://chinadialogue.net/en/pollution/6938-the-three-year-battle-for-china-s-new-environmental-law/

Xu, Wenhong and Hui Yang. “New Measures Further Reform Pollutants Discharge Permit System.” *International Law Office Broad and Bright*, 9 April 2018; available at https://www.lexology.com/library/detail.aspx?g=fd441021-26b9-49ef-85f7-bef9450ac40a (accessed on September 12, 2020).

Xu, Yuanchao, Debra Tan and Woody Chan. “Two Sessions, Five Highlights for Water.” China Water Risk, March 2018; available at http://chinawaterrisk.org/resources/analysis-reviews/two-sessions-five-highlights-for-water (accessed on September 12, 2020).

Yu, Liang. “Xi Vows Tough Battle against Pollution to Boost Ecological Advancement.” XinhuaNet, 20 May 2018; available at http://www.xinhuanet.com/english/2018-05/20/c_137191762.htm (accessed on September 12, 2020).

Pieces of legislation, recommendations and guidelines

13th 5-Year Plan for Environmental Protection (published in2016).

Clean Air Act section 169(3), 42 U.S.C. §7479(3).

Council Directive 70/157/EEC on the Approximation of the Laws of the Member States Relating to the Permissible Sound Level and the Exhaust System of Motor Vehicles, Official Journal L 42.

Council Directive 76/464/EEC on Pollution Caused by Certain Dangerous Substances Discharged into the Aquatic Environment of the Community, Official Journal L 129.

Council Directive 80/779/EEC on Air Quality Limit Values and Guide Values for Sulphur Dioxide and Suspended Particulates, Official Journal L 229.

Council Directive 84/360/EEC on the Combating of Air Pollution from Industrial Plants, Official Journal L 188.

Council Directive 84/491/EEC on Limit Values and Quality Objectives for Discharges of Hexachlorocyclohexane, Official Journal L 274.

Council Directive 85/337/EEC on the Assessment of the Effects of Certain Public and Private Projects on the Environment, Official Journal L 175.

Council Directive 87/217/EEC of 19 March1987*on the Prevention and Reduction of Environmental Pollution by Asbestos*, Official Journal L 085.
Council Directive 88/609/EEC on the Limitation of Emissions of Certain Pollutants into the Air from Large Combustion Plants, Official Journal L 336.
Council Directive 89/369/EEC on the prevention of air pollution from new municipal waste incineration plants, Official Journal L 163.
Council Directive 89/429/EEC of 21 June1989*on the Prevention on Air Pollution from New Municipal Waste Inceneration Plants*, Official Journal L 203.
Council Directive 91/692/EEC of 23 December1991*on Standardizing and Rationalizing Reports on the Implementation of certain Directives Relating to the Environment*, Official Journal L 377.
Council Directive 96/61/EC Concerning Integrated Pollution Prevention and Control (IPPC), Official Journal L 257.
Council Directive 96/82/EC on the Control of Major Accident Hazards Involving Dangerous Substances (Seveso II), Official Journal L 10.
Council Directive 2003/35/EC providing for Public Participation in respect of the Drawing Up of Certain Plans and Programmes relating to the Environment and Amending with regard to Public Participation and Access to Justice Council Directives 85/337/EEC and 96/61/EC, Official Journal L 156.
Council Directive2008/1/EC of 15 January 2008 concerning Integrated Pollution Prevention and Control, Official Journal L 24.
Council Directive2010/75/EU on Industrial Emissions (Integrated Pollution Prevention and Control), Official Journal L 334.
Council Regulation EEC n. 1836/93 of 29 June 1993 allowing Voluntary Participation by Companies in the Industrial Sector in a Community Eco-Management and Audit Scheme, Official Journal L 168.
Environmental ImpactAssessment Law of the People's Republic of China 2003 and 2018.
Environmental Protection Law of the People's Republic of China, 1989.
Environmental Protection Law of the People's Republic of China 2014, EU – China Environmental Governance Programme English Translation, 24 April 2014.
EPA, "An In-depth Look at the United Kingdom Integrated Permitting System," US Environmental Protection Agency, National Center for Environmental Innovation (NCEI), 2008.
European Court of Justice, section II of July 7, 2005, proceeding C-364/03 with reference to a case of non-compliance by the Hellenic Republic.
Eurostat, Statistical Classification of Economic Activities in the European Community – NACE Rev. 2 – Manufacturing Statistics, March 2020, 5–6; available at https://ec.europa.eu/eurostat/statistics-explained/pdfscache/10086.pdf
Eurostat, Industrial Production Statistics, December 2020; available at https://ec.europa.eu/eurostat/statistics-explained/index.php/Industrial_production_statistics#Industrial_production_by_country
Final, "Communication from the Commission on the Road to Sustainable Production." COM (2003) 354.
Final, "Report from the Commission on the Implementation of Directive 96/61/EC concerning Integrated Pollution Prevention and Control." COM (2005) 540.
Final, "Towards a More Effective Policy on Industrial Emissions." COM (2007) 843.
Final, "Report from the Commission on the Implementation of Directive 2008/1/EC concerning Integrated Pollution Prevention and Control and Directive 1999/13/EC on

the Limitation of Emissions of Volatile Organic Compounds due to the use of Organic Solvents in certain Activities and Installations." COM (2010) 593.

General Provisions of the Civil Law of the People's Republic of China, 2018.

Italian Constitutional Court sentences n. 127 of 1990*and n.* 250 of 24 July 2009.

Italian Council of State, Section IV, 9 April 1999 (2001), n. 601; Section VI, 6 June 2000, n. 3212; Section IV, 6 October 2001, n. 5287; Section IV, 17 July 2002, n. 4000; Section IV, 30 July 2002, n. 4071; Section IV, 29 November 2002, n. 6575; Section IV, 1 March 2002, n. 1259; Section VI, 23 May 2011, n. 3107; Section VI, 10 May 2011, n. 2755. All available at www.giustizia-amministrativa.it (accessed on September 12, 2020).

Italian Law 152 of 3rd April 2006 (known as TUA, Testo Unico dell'Ambiente).

Italian Legislative Decree of May 24, n. 203, on "Air Quality in Relation to Specific Pollutants and on Pollution Produced by Industrial Plants", 1988.

Italian Regional Administrative Court of the Abruzzo Region, Pescara, Section I, 28 November 2012, n. 507.

Italian Regional Administrative Court of the Lazio Region, Section III, 5 March 2008, n. 2121 and Section H, 14 October 2010, n. 32824.

Italian Regional Administrative Court of the Lombardy Region, Brescia, Section I, 22 January 2010, n. 211.

Italian Regional Administrative Court of the Piedmont Region, Turin, 26 July 2007, n. 2866 and15 January 2010, n. 214.

Italian Regional Administrative Court of the Puglia Region, Lecce, 9 March 2012, n. 201; 11 July 2012, n. 1187 and 19 September 2012, n. 1550.

Italian Regional Administrative Court of the Umbria Region, Perugia, 10 January 2003, n. 10.

Law on Air Pollution Prevention and Control of the People's Republic of China 2015, Clean Air Alliance of China English Translation, 2015.

Law on the Prevention and Control of Atmospheric Pollution of the People's Republic of China (2000 amendment).

Law on Prevention and Control of Water Pollution of the People's Republic of China (1996 amendment).

Law on Soil Pollution Prevention and Control Law of the People's Republic of China (2018 Revision), PkuLaw English Translation, 2018.

Law on Water Pollution Prevention and Control of the People's Republic of China (2017 Revision), PkuLaw English Translation, 2017.

Lisbon Treaty, Title I, VII, XIX and XX.

Ministry of Ecology and Environment, "Measures for Pollutant Discharge Permitting Administration (For Trial Implementation) 排污许可管理办法（试行）," January 10, 2018.

Ministry of Ecology and Environment, "Regulations on the Administration of Discharge Permits (draft for Comments) 排污许可管理条例（草案征求意见稿）," December 6, 2018.

Ministry of Ecology and Environment, *Three-Year Action Plan for Winning the Blue Sky Defense Battle*, Ministry of Ecology and Environment, July 13, 2018.

Ministry of Environmental Protection of China, *2016 State of Environment Report*; available at China Water Risk website http://www.chinawaterrisk.org/resources/analysis-reviews/2016-state-of-environment-report-review (accessed on September 12, 2020).

Ministry of Environmental Protection of China, *China's Environmental Status Report, 2006–2012*; available at http://jcs.mep.gov.cn/hjzl/zkgb (accessed on September 12, 2020).
OECD, "Council Recommendation on Integrated Pollution Prevention and Control." 1991.
OECD, "Guiding Principles of Effective Environmental Permitting Systems." 2007.
OECD, "Integrated Environmental Permitting Guidelines for EECCA Countries." 2005.
OECD, "Recommendation of the Council on Guiding Principles Concerning International Economic Aspects of Environmental Policies." 1972.
Presidency Conclusions of Goteborg European Council, June 15–16, 2001.
Resolution of the Council of the European Communities and of the Representatives of the Governments of the Member States, Meeting within the Council of 19 October 1987 on the Continuation and Implementation of a European Community Policy and Action Programme on the Environment (1987–1992).
Resolution of the Council of the European Communities and of the Representatives of the Governments of the Member States, Meeting within the Council of 7 February 1983 on the Continuation and Implementation of a European Community Policy and Action Programme on the Environment (1982–1986), Treaty on European Union, Official Journal C 326, 2012.
UN Documents, "*Gathering a Body of Global Agreements: Johannesburg Declaration on Sustainable Development.*" 2002.
UN Economic Commission for Europe, Convention on Access to Information, Public Participation in Decision-Making and Access to Justice in Environmental Matters, Aarhus, Denmark, June 25, 1998.
UN General Assembly, United Nations Conference on the Human Environment, December 15, 1972.
UN General Assembly, United Nations Conference on Sustainable Development, June 20–22, 2012.
UN General Assembly, United Nations Conference on Environment and Development, June 14, 1992.
UNEP, "Integrating Environment and Development 1972–2002." 2002.
Xi Jinping. "Thought on Ecological Civilization." 2018.

Index

For Product Safety Concerns and Information please contact our EU representative GPSR@taylorandfrancis.com
Taylor & Francis Verlag GmbH, Kaufingerstraße 24, 80331 München, Germany

www.ingramcontent.com/pod-product-compliance
Ingram Content Group UK Ltd.
Pitfield, Milton Keynes, MK11 3LW, UK
UKHW020012200926
475702UK00014B/1837
* 9 7 8 0 3 6 7 6 5 5 5 3 2 *